OSF/Motif™ Programmer's Reference

Revision 1.0

Open Software Foundation

Prentice Hall, Englewood Cliffs, New Jersey 07632

Cover design
and cover illustration: BETH FAGAN

This book was formatted with troff

Published by Prentice-Hall, Inc.
A Division of Simon & Schuster
Englewood Cliffs, New Jersey 07632

Printed in the United States of America
10 9 8 7 6 5 4 3 2 1

ISBN 0-13-640517-7

Prentice-Hall International (UK) Limited, *London*
Prentice-Hall of Australia PTY. Limited, *Sydney*
Prentice-Hall Canada Inc., *Toronto*
Prentice-Hall Hispanoamericana, S.A., *Mexico*
Prentice-Hall of India Private Limited, *New Delhi*
Prentice-Hall of Japan, Inc., *Tokyo*
Simon & Schuster Asia Pte. Ltd., *Singapore*
Editora Prentice-Hall do Brasil, Ltda., *Rio de Janeiro*

Contents

Preface

This is the reference manual for OSF/Motif ™ commands and functions. It contains toolkit, window manager, and user interface language commands and functions.

Audience

This document is written for programmers who want to write applications using Motif ™ interfaces to use as a reference.

Typographical Conventions

This volume uses the following typographical conventions:

- **Boldfaced** strings represent literals; type them exactly as they appear.
- *Italicized* strings represent variables (for example, function or macro arguments).
- Ellipses (...) indicate that additional arguments are optional.

Manual Page Format

The manual pages in this volume use the following format:

Purpose
: This section gives a short description of the interface.

Synopsis
: This section describes the appropriate syntax for using the interface.

Description
: This section describes the behavior of the interface. On widget man pages there are tables of resource values in the descriptions. Those tables have the following headers:

Name	Contains the name of the resource. Each new resource is described following the new resources table.
Class	Contains the class of the resource.
Type	Contains the type of the resource.
Default	Contains the default value of the resource.
Access	Contains the access permissions for the resource. A **C** in this column means the resource can be set at widget creation time. An **S** means the resource can be set anytime. A **G** means the resource's value can retrieved.

Examples
: This sections gives practical examples for using the interface.

Return Value
: This lists the values returned by function interfaces.

Errors
: This section describes the error conditions associated with using this interface.

Related Information
: This section provides cross references to related interfaces and header files described within this document.

mwm

Purpose

A Window Manager

Synopsis

mwm [*options*]

Description

mwm is an X Window System client that provides window management functionality and some session management functionality. It provides functions that facilitate control (by the user and the programmer) of elements of window states such as placement, size, icon/normal display, and input-focus ownership. It also provides session management functions such as stopping a client.

Options

-display *display*
This option specifies the display to use; see *X(1)*.

-xrm *resourcestring*
This option specifies a resource string to use.

Appearance

The following sections describe the basic default behaviors of windows, icons, the icon box, input focus, and window stacking. The appearance and behavior of the window manager can be altered by changing the configuration of specific resources. Resources are defined under the heading "X DEFAULTS."

Windows

Default MWM window frames have distinct components with associated functions:

Title Area
: In addition to displaying the client's title, the title area is used to move the window. To move the window, place the pointer over the title area, press button 1 and drag the window to a new location. A wire frame is moved during the drag to indicate the new location. When the button is released, the window is moved to the new location.

Title Bar
: The title bar includes the title area, the minimize button, the maximize button and the window menu button.

Minimize Button
: To turn the window back into its icon, click button 1 on the minimize button (the frame box with a *small* square in it).

Maximize Button
: To make the window fill the screen (or enlarge to the largest size allowed by the configuration files), click button 1 on the maximize button (the frame box with a *large* square in it).

Window Menu Button
: The window menu button is the frame box with a horizontal bar in it. To pop up the window menu, press button 1. While pressing, drag the pointer on the menu to your selection, then release the button when your selection is highlighted. Alternately, you can click button 1 to pop up the menu and keep it posted; then position the pointer and select.

Default Window Menu		
Selection	**Accelerator**	**Description**
Restore	Alt+F5	Inactive (not an option for windows)
Move	Alt+F7	Allows the window to be moved with keys or mouse
Size	Alt+F8	Allows the window to be resized
Minimize	Alt+F9	Turns the window into an icon
Maximize	Alt+F10	Makes the window fill the screen
Lower	Alt+F11	Moves window to bottom of window stack
Close	Alt+F4	Removes client from MWM management

Resize Border Handles
: To change the size of a window, move the pointer over a resize border handle (the cursor changes), press button 1, and drag the window to a new size. When the button is released, the window is resized. While dragging is being done, a rubber-band outline is displayed to indicate the new window size.

Matte
: An optional matte decoration can be added between the client area and the window frame. A matte is not actually part of the window frame. There is no functionality associated with a matte.

Icons

Icons are small graphic representations of windows. A window can be minimized (iconified) using the minimize button on the window frame. Icons provide a way to reduce clutter on the screen.

Pressing mouse button 1 when the pointer is over an icon causes the icon's window menu to pop up. Releasing the button (press + release without moving mouse = click) causes the menu to stay posted. The menu contains the following selections:

Icon Window Menu		
Selection	**Accelerator**	**Description**
Restore	Alt+F5	Opens the associated window
Move	Alt+F7	Allows the icon to be moved with keys
Size	Alt+F8	Inactive (not an option for icons)
Minimize	Alt+F9	Inactive (not an option for icons)
Maximize	Alt+F10	Opens the associated window and makes it fill the screen
Lower	Alt+F11	Moves icon to bottom of icon stack
Close	Alt+F4	Removes client from MWM management

Double-clicking button 1 on an icon normalizes the icon into its associated window. Double-clicking button 1 on the icon box's icon opens the icon box and allow access to the contained icons. (In general, double-clicking a mouse button is a quick way to perform a function.) Double-clicking button 1 with the pointer on the window menu button closes the window.

Icon Box

When icons begin to clutter the screen, they can be packed into an icon box. (To use an icon box, MWM must be started with the icon box configuration already set.) The icon box is an MWM window that holds client icons. Icons in the icon box can be manipulated with the mouse. The following table summarizes the behavior of this interface. Button actions apply whenever the pointer is on any part of the icon.

Button Action	Description
Button 1 click	Selects the icon
Button 1 double click	Normalizes (opens) the associated window.
Button 1 double click	Raises an already *open* window to the top of the stack
Button 1 drag	Moves the icon

The window menu of the icon box differs from the window menu of a client window: The Close selection is replaced with the PackIcons Alt+F12 selection. When selected, PackIcons packs the icons in the box to achieve neat rows with no empty slots.

Input Focus

MWM supports (by default) a keyboard input focus policy of explicit selection. This means when a window is selected to get keyboard input, it continues to get keyboard input until the window is withdrawn from window management, another window is explicitly selected to get keyboard input, or the window is iconified. Several resources control the input focus. The client window with the keyboard input focus has the active window appearance with a visually distinct window frame.

The following tables summarize the keyboard input focus selection behavior:

Button Action	Object	Function Description
Button 1 press	Window / window frame	Keyboard focus selection
Button 1 press	Icon	Keyboard focus selection

Key Action	Function Description
[Alt][Tab]	Move input focus to next window in window stack
[Alt][Shift][Tab]	Move input focus to previous window in window stack

Window stacking

The stacking order of windows may be changed as a result of setting the keyboard input focus, iconifying a window, or by doing a window manager window stacking function.

When a window is iconified, the window's icon is placed on the bottom of the stack.

The following table summarizes the default window stacking behavior of MWM.

Key Action	Function Description
[Alt][ESC]	Put bottom window on top of stack
[Alt][Shift][ESC]	Put top window on bottom of stack

A window can also be raised to the top when it gets the keyboard input focus (for example, by pressing button 1 on the window or by using [Alt][Tab]) if this auto-raise feature is enabled with the **focusAutoRaise** resource.

X Defaults

MWM is configured from its resource database. This database is built from the following sources. They are listed in order of precedence, low to high:

app-defaults/Mwm
RESOURCE_MANAGER root window property or $HOME/.Xdefaults
XENVIRONMENT variable or $HOME/.Xdefaults-host
mwm command line options

Entries in the resource database may refer to other resource files for specific types of resources. These include files that contain bitmaps, fonts, and MWM specific resources such as menus and behavior specifications (for example, button and key bindings).

Mwm is the resource class name of MWM and mwm is the resource name used by MWM to look up resources. In the following discussion of resource specification, "Mwm" and "mwm" can be used interchangeably.

MWM uses the following types of resources:

Component Appearance Resources:

These resources specify appearance attributes of window manager user interface components. They can be applied to the appearance of window manager menus, feedback windows (for example, the window reconfiguration feedback window), client window frames, and icons.

Specific Appearance and Behavior Resources:

These resources specify MWM appearance and behavior (for example, window management policies). They are not set separately for different MWM user interface components.

Client Specific Resources:

These MWM resources can be set for a particular client window or class of client windows. They specify client-specific icon and client window frame appearance and behavior.

Resource identifiers can be either a resource name (for example, foreground) or a resource class (for example, Foreground). If the value of a resource is a filename and if the filename is prefixed by "~/", then it is relative to the path contained in the *$HOME* environment variable (generally the user's home directory). This is the only environment variable that MWM uses directly ($XENVIRONMENT is used by the resource manager).

Component Appearance Resources

The syntax for specifying component appearance resources that apply to window manager icons, menus, and client window frames is

Mwm*resource_id*

For example, **Mwm*foreground** is used to specify the foreground color for MWM menus, icons, and client window frames.

The syntax for specifying component appearance resources that apply to a particular MWM component is

Mwm*[**menu|icon|client|feedback**]**resource_id*

If *menu* is specified, the resource is applied only to MWM menus; if *icon* is specified, the resource is applied to icons; and if *client* is specified, the resource is applied to client window frames. For example, **Mwm*icon*foreground** is used to specify the foreground color for MWM icons, **Mwm*menu*foreground** specifies the foreground color for MWM menus, and **Mwm*client*foreground** is used to specify the foreground color for MWM client window frames.

The appearance of the title area of a client window frame (including window management buttons) can be separately configured. The syntax for configuring the title area of a client window frame is:

Mwm*client*title*resource_id*

For example, **Mwm*client*title*foreground** specifies the foreground color for the title area. Defaults for title area resources are based on the values of the corresponding client window frame resources.

The appearance of menus can be configured based on the name of the menu. The syntax for specifying menu appearance by name is:

Mwm*menu*menu_name*resource_id*

For example, **Mwm*menu*my_menu*foreground** specifies the foreground color for the menu named **my_menu**.

The following component appearance resources that apply to all window manager parts can be specified:

Component Appearance Resources - All Window Manager Parts			
Name	**Class**	**Value Type**	**Default**
background	Background	color	varies*
backgroundPixmap	BackgroundPixmap	string**	varies*
bottomShadowColor	Foreground	color	varies*
bottomShadowPixmap	BottomShadowPixmap	string**	varies*
fontList	FontList	string***	"fixed"
foreground	Foreground	color	varies*
saveUnder	SaveUnder	T/F	F
topShadowColor	Background	color	varies*
topShadowPixmap	TopShadowPixmap	string**	varies*

*The default is chosen based on the visual type of the screen. **Pixmap image name. See XmInstallImage(3X). ***X11 R3 Font description.

background (class **Background)**
: This resource specifies the background color. Any legal X color may be specified. The default value is chosen based on the visual type of the screen.

backgroundPixmap (class **BackgroundPixmap)**
: This resource specifies the background pixmap of the MWM decoration when the window is inactive (does not have the keyboard focus). The default value is chosen based on the visual type of the screen.

bottomShadowColor (class **Foreground)**
: This resource specifies the bottom shadow color. This color is used for the lower and right bevels of the window manager decoration. Any legal X color may be specified. The default value is chosen based on the visual type of the screen.

bottomShadowPixmap (class **BottomShadowPixmap**)
This resource specifies the bottom shadow pixmap. This pixmap is used for the lower and right bevels of the window manager decoration. The default is chosen based on the visual type of the screen.

fontList (class **Font**)
This resource specifies the font used in the window manager decoration. The character encoding of the font should match the character encoding of the strings that are used. The default is "fixed."

foreground (class **Foreground**)
This resource specifies the foreground color. The default is chosen based on the visual type of the screen.

saveUnder (class **SaveUnder**)
This is used to indicate whether "save unders" are used for MWM components. For this to have any effect, save unders must be implemented by the X server. If save unders are implemented, the X server saves the contents of windows obscured by windows that have the save under attribute set. If the saveUnder resource is True, MWM sets the save under attribute on the window manager frame of any client that has it set. If saveUnder is False, save unders are not on any window manager frames. The default value is False.

topShadowColor (class **Background**)
This resource specifies the top shadow color. This color is used for the upper and left bevels of the window manager decoration. The default is chosen based on the visual type of the screen.

topShadowPixmap (class **TopShadowPixmap**)
This resource specifies the top shadow pixmap. This pixmap is used for the upper and left bevels of the window manager decoration. The default is chosen based on the visual type of the screen.

The following component appearance resources that apply to frame and icons can be specified:

Frame and Icon Components			
Name	**Class**	**Value Type**	**Default**
activeBackground	Background	color	varies*
activeBackgroundPixmap	BackgroundPixmap	string**	varies*
activeBottomShadowColor	Foreground	color	varies*
activeBottomShadowPixmap	BottomShadowPixmap	string**	varies*
activeForeground	Foreground	color	varies*
activeTopShadowColor	Background	color	varies*
activeTopShadowPixmap	TopShadowPixmap	string**	varies*

*The default is chosen based on the visual type of the screen. **See XmInstallImage(3X).

activeBackground (class **Background**)
This resource specifies the background color of the MWM decoration when the window is active (has the keyboard focus). The default is chosen based on the visual type of the screen.

activeBackgroundPixmap (class **ActiveBackgroundPixmap**)
This resource specifies the background pixmap of the MWM decoration when the window is active (has the keyboard focus). The default is chosen based on the visual type of the screen.

activeBottomShadowColor (class **Foreground**)
This resource specifies the bottom shadow color of the MWM decoration when the window is active (has the keyboard focus). The default is chosen based on the visual type of the screen.

activeBottomShadowPixmap (class **BottomShadowPixmap**)
This resource specifies the bottom shadow pixmap of the mwm decoration when the window is active (has the keyboard focus). The default is chosen based on the visual type of the screen.

activeForeground (class **Foreground**)
This resource specifies the foreground color of the MWM decoration when the window is active (has the keyboard focus). The default is chosen based on the visual type of the screen.

activeTopShadowColor (class **Background**)
This resource specifies the top shadow color of the MWM decoration when the window is active (has the keyboard focus). The default is chosen based on the visual type of the screen.

activeTopShadowPixmap (class **TopShadowPixmap**)
This resource specifies the top shadow pixmap of the MWM decoration when the window is active (has the keyboard focus). The default is chosen based on the visual type of the screen.

Specific Appearance and Behavior Resources

The syntax for specifying specific appearance and behavior resources is

Mwm*resource_id*

For example, **Mwm*keyboardFocusPolicy** specifies the window manager policy for setting the keyboard focus to a particular client window.

The following specific appearance and behavior resources can be specified:

Specific Appearance and Behavior Resources			
Name	**Class**	**Value Type**	**Default**
autoKeyFocus	AutoKeyFocus	T/F	T
autoRaiseDelay	AutoRaiseDelay	millisec	500
bitmapDirectory	BitmapDirectory	directory	/usr/include/\ X11/bitmaps
buttonBindings	ButtonBindings	string	NULL
cleanText	CleanText	T/F	T
clientAutoPlace	ClientAutoPlace	T/F	T
colormapFocusPolicy	ColormapFocusPolicy	string	keyboard
configFile	ConfigFile	file	.mwmrc
deiconifyKeyFocus	DeiconifyKeyFocus	T/F	T
doubleClickTime	DoubleClickTime	millisec.	500
enforceKeyFocus	EnforceKeyFocus	T/F	T
fadeNormalIcon	FadeNormalIcon	T/F	F
frameBorderWidth	FrameBorderWidth	pixels	5
iconAutoPlace	IconAutoPlace	T/F	T
iconBoxGeometry	IconBoxGeometry	string	6x1+0-0
iconBoxName	IconBoxName	string	iconbox
iconBoxTitle	IconBoxTitle	string	Icons
iconClick	IconClick	T/F	T
iconDecoration	IconDecoration	string	varies
iconImageMaximum	IconImageMaximum	wxh	50x50
iconImageMinimum	IconImageMinimum	wxh	32x32
iconPlacement	IconPlacement	string	left bottom
iconPlacementMargin	IconPlacementMargin	pixels	varies
interactivePlacement	InteractivePlacement	T/F	F

Name	Class	Value Type	Default
keyBindings	KeyBindings	string	system
keyboardFocusPolicy	KeyboardFocusPolicy	string	explicit
limitResize	LimitResize	T/F	T
lowerOnIconify	LowerOnIconify	T/F	T
maximumMaximumSize	MaximumMaximumSize	wxh (pixels)	2X screen w&h
moveThreshold	MoveThreshold	pixels	4
passButtons	PassButtons	T/F	F
passSelectButton	PassSelectButton	T/F	T
positionIsFrame	PositionIsFrame	T/F	T
positionOnScreen	PositionOnScreen	T/F	T
quitTimeout	QuitTimeout	millisec.	1000
resizeBorderWidth	ResizeBorderWidth	pixels	10
resizeCursors	ResizeCursors	T/F	T
showFeedback	ShowFeedback	string	all
startupKeyFocus	StartupKeyFocus	T/F	T
transientDecoration	TransientDecoration	string	system title
transientFunctions	TransientFunctions	string	-minimize -maximize
useIconBox	UseIconBox	T/F	F
wMenuButtonClick	WMenuButtonClick	T/F	T
wMenuButtonClick2	WMenuButtonClick2	T/F	T

autoKeyFocus (class **AutoKeyFocus)**

This resource is available only when the keyboard input focus policy is explicit. If autoKeyFocus is given a value of True, then when a window with the keyboard input focus is withdrawn from window management or is iconified, the focus is set to the previous window that had the focus. If the value given is False, there is no automatic setting of the keyboard input focus. The default value is True.

autoRaiseDelay (class **AutoRaiseDelay)**

This resource is available only when the focusAutoRaise resource is True and the keyboard focus policy is pointer. The autoRaiseDelay resource specifies the amount of time (in milliseconds) that MWM waits before raising a window after it gets the keyboard focus. The default value of this resource is 500 (ms).

bitmapDirectory (class **BitmapDirectory)**

This resource identifies a directory to be searched for bitmaps referenced by MWM resources. This directory is searched if a bitmap is specified without an absolute pathname. The default value for this resource is /usr/include/X11/bitmaps.

buttonBindings (class **ButtonBindings)**

This resource identifies the set of button bindings for window management functions. The named set of button bindings is specified in the **mwm resource description file**. These button bindings are *merged* with the built-in default bindings. The default value for this resource is NULL (that is, no button bindings are added to the built-in button bindings).

cleanText (class**CleanText)**

This resource controls the display of window manager text in the client title and feedback windows. If the default value of True is used, the text is drawn with a clear (no stipple) background. This makes text easier to read on monochrome systems where a backgroundPixmap is specified. Only the stippling in the area immediately around the text is cleared. If False, the text is drawn directly on top of the existing background.

clientAutoPlace (class **ClientAutoPlace**)
This resource determines the position of a window when the window has not been given a user specified position. With a value of True, windows are positioned with the top left corners of the frames offset horizontally and vertically. A value of False causes the currently configured position of the window to be used. In either case, MWM attempts to place the windows totally on-screen. The default value is True.

colormapFocusPolicy (class **ColormapFocusPolicy**)
This resource indicates the colormap focus policy that is to be used. If the resource value is explicit, a colormap selection action is done on a client window to set the colormap focus to that window. If the value is pointer, the client window containing the pointer has the colormap focus. If the value is keyboard, the client window that has the keyboard input focus has the colormap focus. The default value for this resource is keyboard.

configFile (class **ConfigFile**)
The resource value is the pathname for an **mwm resource description file**. The default is **.mwmrc** in the user's home directory (based on the $HOME environment variable) if this file exists, otherwise **/usr/lib/X11/system.mwmrc**.

deiconifyKeyFocus (class **DeiconifyKeyFocus**)
This resource applies only when the keyboard input focus policy is explicit. If a value of True is used, a window receives the keyboard input focus when it is normalized (deiconified). True is the default value.

doubleClickTime (class **DoubleClickTime**)
This resource is used to set the maximum time (in ms) between the clicks (button presses) that make up a double-click. The default value of this resource is 500 (ms).

enforceKeyFocus (class **EnforceKeyFocus)**
If this resource is given a value of True, the keyboard input focus is always explicitly set to selected windows even if there is an indication that they are "globally active" input windows. (An example of a globally active window is a scroll bar that can be operated without setting the focus to that client.) If the resource is False, the keyboard input focus is not explicitly set to globally active windows. The default value is True.

fadeNormalIcon (class **FadeNormalIcon)**
If this resource is given a value of True, an icon is grayed out whenever it has been normalized (its window has been opened). The default value is False.

frameBorderWidth (class **FrameBorderWidth)**
This resource specifies the width (in pixels) of a client window frame border without resize handles. The border width includes the 3-D shadows. The default value is 5 pixels.

iconAutoPlace (class **IconAutoPlace)**
This resource indicates whether icons are automatically placed on the screen by MWM, or are placed by the user. Users may specify an initial icon position and may move icons after initial placement; however, MWM adjusts the user-specified position to fit into an invisible grid. When icons are automatically placed, MWM places them into the grid using a scheme set with the iconPlacement resource. If the iconAutoPlace resource has a value of True, MWM does automatic icon placement. A value of False allows user placement. The default value of this resource is True.

iconBoxGeometry (class **IconBoxGeometry)**
This resource indicates the initial position and size of the icon box. The value of the resource is a standard window geometry string with the following syntax:

[=][*width***x***height*][{+-}*xoffset*{+-}*yoffset*]

If the offsets are not provided, the iconPlacement policy is used to determine the initial placement. The units for width and height are columns and rows.

The actual screen size of the icon box window depends on the iconImageMaximum (size) and iconDecoration resources. The default value for size is (6 * iconWidth + padding) wide by (1 * iconHeight + padding) high. The default value of the location is +0 -0.

iconBoxName (class **IconBoxName**)
: This resource specifies the name that is used to look up icon box resources. The default name is iconbox.

iconBoxTitle (class **IconBoxTitle**)
: This resource specifies the name that is used in the title area of the icon box frame. The default value is Icons.

iconClick (class **IconClick**)
: When this resource is given the value of True, the system menu is posted and left posted when an icon is clicked. The default value is True.

iconDecoration (class **IconDecoration**)
: This resource specifies the general icon decoration. The resource value is label (only the label part is displayed) or image (only the image part is displayed) or label image (both the label and image parts are displayed). A value of activelabel can also be specified to get a label (not truncated to the width of the icon) when the icon is selected. The default icon decoration for icon box icons is that each icon has a label part and an image part (label image). The default icon decoration for stand-alone icons is that each icon has an active label part, a label part and an image part (activelabel label image).

iconImageMaximum (class **IconImageMaximum**)
: This resource specifies the maximum size of the icon *image*. The resource value is *width***x***height* (for example, 64x64). The maximum supported size is 128x128. The default value of this resource is 50x50.

iconImageMinimum (class **IconImageMinimum**)

This resource specifies the minimum size of the icon *image*. The resource value is *width*x*height* (for example, 32x50). The minimum supported size is 16x16. The default value of this resource is 32x32.

iconPlacement (class **IconPlacement**)

This resource specifies the icon placement scheme to be used. The resource value has the following syntax:

primary_layout secondary_layout

The layout value is one of the following:

top Lay the icons out top to bottom
bottom Lay the icons out bottom to top
left Lay the icons out left to right
right Lay the icons out right to left

A horizontal (vertical) layout value should not be used for both the *primary_layout* and the *secondary_layout* (for example, don't use top for the *primary_layout* and bottom for the *secondary_layout*). The *primary_layout* indicates whether, when an icon placement is done, the icon is placed in a row or a column and the direction of placement. The *secondary_layout* indicates where to place new rows or columns. For example, top right indicates that icons should be placed top to bottom on the screen and that columns should be added from right to left on the screen. The default placement is left bottom (icons are placed left to right on the screen, with the first row on the bottom of the screen, and new rows added from the bottom of the screen to the top of the screen).

iconPlacementMargin (class **IconPlacementMargin**)

This resource sets the distance between the edge of the screen and the icons that are placed along the edge of the screen. The value should be greater than or equal to 0. A default value (see below) is used if the value specified is invalid. The default value for this resource is equal to the space between icons as they are placed on the screen (this space is based on maximizing the number of icons in each row and column).

interactivePlacement (class **InteractivePlacement**)
This resource controls the initial placement of new windows on the screen. If the value is True, the pointer shape changes before a new window is placed on the screen to indicate to the user that a position should be selected for the upper-left hand corner of the window. If the value is False, windows are placed according to the initial window configuration attributes. The default value of this resource is False.

keyBindings (class **KeyBindings**)
This resource identifies the set of key bindings for window management functions. If specified these key bindings *replace* the built-in default bindings. The named set of key bindings is specified in **mwm resource description file**. The default value for this resource is the set of system-compatible key bindings.

keyboardFocusPolicy (class **KeyboardFocusPolicy**)
If set to pointer, the keyboard focus policy is to have the keyboard focus set to the client window that contains the pointer (the pointer could also be in the client window decoration that MWM adds). If set to explicit, the policy is to have the keyboard focus set to a client window when the user presses button 1 with the pointer on the client window or any part of the associated MWM decoration. The default value for this resource is explicit.

limitResize (class **LimitResize**)
If this resource is True, the user is not allowed to resize a window to greater than the maximum size. The default value for this resource is True.

lowerOnIconify (class **LowerOnIconify**)
If this resource is given the default value of True, a window's icon appears on the bottom of the window stack when the window is minimized (iconified). A value of False places the icon in the stacking order at the same place as its associated window.

maximumMaximumSize (class **MaximumMaximumSize**)
This resource is used to limit the maximum size of a client window as set by the user or client. The resource value is *width*x*height* (for example, 1024x1024) where the width and height are in pixels. The default value of this resource is twice the screen width and height.

moveThreshold (class **MoveThreshold**)
This resource is used to control the sensitivity of dragging operations that move windows and icons. The value of this resource is the number of pixels that the locator is moved with a button down before the move operation is initiated. This is used to prevent window/icon movement when you click or double-click and there is unintentional pointer movement with the button down. The default value of this resource is 4 (pixels).

passButtons (class **PassButtons**)
This resource indicates whether or not button press events are passed to clients after they are used to do a window manager function in the client context. If the resource value is False, the button press is not passed to the client. If the value is True, the button press is passed to the client window. The window manager function is done in either case. The default value for this resource is False.

passSelectButton (class **PassSelectButton**)
This resource indicates whether or not the keyboard input focus selection button press (if keyboardFocusPolicy is explicit) is passed on to the client window or used to do a window management action associated with the window decorations. If the resource value is False, the button press is not used for any operation other than selecting the window to be the keyboard input focus; if the value is True, the button press is passed to the client window or used to do a window management operation, if appropriate. The keyboard input focus selection is done in either case. The default value for this resource is True.

positionIsFrame (class **PositionIsFrame**)
This resource indicates how client window position information (from the WM_NORMAL_HINTS property and from

configuration requests) is to be interpreted. If the resource value is True, the information is interpreted as the position of the MWM client window frame. If the value is False, it is interpreted as being the position of the client area of the window. The default value of this resource is True.

positionOnScreen (class **PositionOnScreen**)
This resource is used to indicate that windows should initially be placed (if possible) so that they are not clipped by the edge of the screen (if the resource value is True). If a window is larger than the size of the screen, at least the upper left corner of the window is on-screen. If the resource value is False, windows are placed in the requested position even if totally off-screen. The default value of this resource is True.

quitTimeout (class **QuitTimeout**)
This resource specifies the amount of time (in milliseconds) that MWM waits for a client to update the WM_COMMAND property after MWM has sent the WM_SAVE_YOURSELF message. This protocol is used only for those clients that have a WM_SAVE_YOURSELF atom and no WM_DELETE_WINDOW atom in the WM_PROTOCOLS client window property. The default value of this resource is 1000 (ms). (Refer to the f.kill function for additional information.)

resizeBorderWidth (class **ResizeBorderWidth**)
This resource specifies the width (in pixels) of a client window frame border with resize handles. The specified border width includes the 3-D shadows. The default is 10 (pixels).

resizeCursors (class **ResizeCursors**)
This is used to indicate whether the resize cursors are always displayed when the pointer is in the window size border. If True, the cursors are shown, otherwise the window manager cursor is shown. The default value is True.

showFeedback (class **ShowFeedback**)
This resource controls when feedback information is displayed. It controls both window position and size feedback during move or resize operations and initial client placement. It also controls window manager message and dialog boxes. The value for this

resource is a list of names of the feedback options to be enabled; the names must be separated by a space. The names of the feedback options are shown below:

Name	Description
all	Show all feedback (Default value)
behavior	Confirm behavior switch
move	Show position during move
none	Show no feedback
placement	Show position and size during initial placement
resize	Show size during resize
restart	Confirm MWM restart

The following command line illustrates the syntax for showFeedback:

Mwm*showFeedback: placement resize behavior restart

This resource specification provides feedback for initial client placement and resize, and enables the dialog boxes to confirm the restart and set behavior functions. It disables feedback for the move function.

startupKeyFocus (class **StartupKeyFocus**)
This resource is available only when the keyboard input focus policy is explicit. When given the default value of True, a window gets the keyboard input focus when the window is mapped (that is, initially managed by the window manager).

transientDecoration (class **TransientDecoration**)
This controls the amount of decoration that Mwm puts on transient windows. The decoration specification is exactly the same as for the **clientDecoration** (client specific) resource. Transient windows are identified by the WM_TRANSIENT_FOR property which is added by the client to indicate a relatively temporary window. The default value for this resource is menu title (that is, transient windows have resize borders and a titlebar with a window menu button).

transientFunctions (class **TransientFunctions)**
This resource is used to indicate which window management functions are applicable (or not applicable) to transient windows. The function specification is exactly the same as for the **clientFunctions** (client specific) resource. The default value for this resource is -minimize -maximize.

useIconBox (class **UseIconBox)**
If this resource is given a value of True, icons are placed in an icon box. When an icon box is not used, the icons are placed on the root window (default value).

wMenuButtonClick (class **WMenuButtonClick)**
This resource indicates whether a click of the mouse when the pointer is over the window menu button posts and leaves posted the system menu. If the value given this resource is True, the menu remains posted. True is the default value for this resource.

wMenuButtonClick2 (class **WMenuButtonClick2)**
When this resource is given the default value of True, a double-click action on the window menu button does an f.kill function.

Client Specific Resources

The syntax for specifying client specific resources is

Mwm*client_name_or_class***resource_id*

For example, **Mwm*mterm*windowMenu** is used to specify the window menu to be used with mterm clients.

The syntax for specifying client specific resources for all classes of clients is

Mwm*resource_id*

Specific client specifications take precedence over the specifications for all clients. For example, **Mwm*windowMenu** is used to specify the window menu to be used for all classes of clients that don't have a window menu specified.

The syntax for specifying resource values for windows that have an unknown name and class (that is, windows that do not have a WM_CLASS property associated with them) is

Mwm*defaults*_resource_id_

For example, **Mwm*defaults*iconImage** is used to specify the icon image to be used for windows that have an unknown name and class.

The following client specific resources can be specified:

Client Specific Resources			
Name	**Class**	**Value Type**	**Default**
clientDecoration	ClientDecoration	string	all
clientFunctions	ClientFunctions	string	all
focusAutoRaise	FocusAutoRaise	T/F	T
iconImage	IconImage	pathname	(image)
iconImageBackground	Background	color	icon background
iconImageBottomShadowColor	Foreground	color	icon bottom shadow
iconImageBottomShadowPixmap	BottomShadow-Pixmap	color	icon bottom shadow pixmap
iconImageForeground	Foreground	color	icon foreground
iconImageTopShadowColor	Background	color	icon top shadow color
iconImageTopShadowPixmap	TopShadow-Pixmap	color	icon top shadow pixmap
matteBackground	Background	color	background
matteBottomShadowColor	Foreground	color	bottom shadow color

Name	Class	Value Type	Default
matteBottomShadowPixmap	BottomShadow-Pixmap	color	bottom shadow pixmap
matteForeground	Foreground	color	foreground
matteTopShadowColor	Background	color	top shadow color
matteTopShadowPixmap	TopShadow-Pixmap	color	top shadow pixmap
matteWidth	MatteWidth	pixels	0
maximumClientSize	MaximumClientSize	wxh	fill the screen
useClientIcon	UseClientIcon	T/F	F
windowMenu	WindowMenu	string	string

clientDecoration (class **ClientDecoration**)

This resource controls the amount of window frame decoration. The resource is specified as a list of decorations to specify their inclusion in the frame. If a decoration is preceded by a minus sign, that decoration is excluded from the frame. The *sign* of the first item in the list determines the initial amount of decoration. If the sign of the first decoration is minus, MWM assumes all decorations are present and starts subtracting from that set. If the sign of the first decoration is plus (or not specified), MWM starts with no decoration and builds up a list from the resource.

Name	Description
all	Include all decorations (default value)
border	Window border
maximize	Maximize button (includes title bar)
minimize	Minimize button (includes title bar)
none	No decorations
resizeh	Border resize handles (includes border)
menu	Window menu button (includes title bar)
title	Title bar (includes border)

Examples:

Mwm*XClock.clientDecoration: -resizeh -maximize

This removes the resize handles and maximize button from XClock windows.

Mwm*XClock.clientDecoration: menu minimize border

This does the same thing as above. Note that either **menu** or **minimize** implies **title**.

clientFunctions (class **ClientFunctions**)
This resource is used to indicate which MWM functions are applicable (or not applicable) to the client window. The value for the resource is a list of functions. If the first function in the list has a minus sign in front of it, MWM starts with all functions and subtracts from that set. If the first function in the list has a plus sign in front of it, MWM starts with no functions and builds up a list. Each function in the list must be preceded by the appropriate plus or minus sign and separated from the next function by a space.

The table below lists the functions available for this resource:

Name	Description
all	Include all functions (default value)
none	No functions
resize	f.resize
move	f.move
minimize	f.minimize
maximize	f.maximize
close	f.kill

focusAutoRaise (class **FocusAutoRaise**)
When the value of this resource is True, clients are raised when they get the keyboard input focus. If the value is False, the stacking of windows on the display is not changed when a window gets the keyboard input focus. The default value is True.

iconImage (class **IconImage**)
This resource can be used to specify an icon image for a client (for example, "Mwm*myclock*iconImage"). The resource value is a pathname for a bitmap file. The value of the (client specific) useClientIcon resource is used to determine whether or not user supplied icon images are used instead of client supplied icon images. The default value is to display a built-in window manager icon image.

iconImageBackground (class **Background**)
This resource specifies the background color of the icon image that is displayed in the image part of an icon. The default value of this resource is the icon background color (that is, specified by "Mwm*background or Mwm*icon*background).

iconImageBottomShadowColor (class **Foreground**)
This resource specifies the bottom shadow color of the icon image that is displayed in the image part of an icon. The default value of this resource is the icon bottom shadow color (that is, specified by Mwm*icon*bottomShadowColor).

iconImageBottomShadowPixmap (class **BottomShadowPixmap)**
This resource specifies the bottom shadow pixmap of the icon image that is displayed in the image part of an icon. The default value of this resource is the icon bottom shadow pixmap (that is, specified by Mwm*icon*bottomShadowPixmap).

iconImageForeground (class **Foreground)**
This resource specifies the foreground color of the icon image that is displayed in the image part of an icon. The default value of this resource is the icon foreground color (that is, specified by "Mwm*foreground or Mwm*icon*foreground).

iconImageTopShadowColor (class **Background)**
This resource specifies the top shadow color of the icon image that is displayed in the image part of an icon. The default value of this resource is the icon top shadow color (that is, specified by Mwm*icon*topShadowColor).

iconImageTopShadowPixmap (class **TopShadowPixmap)**
This resource specifies the top shadow pixmap of the icon image that is displayed in the image part of an icon. The default value of this resource is the icon top shadow pixmap (that is, specified by Mwm*icon*topShadowPixmap).

matteBackground (class **Background)**
This resource specifies the background color of the matte, when **matteWidth** is positive. The default value of this resource is the client background color (that is, specified by "Mwm*background or Mwm*client*background).

matteBottomShadowColor (class **Foreground)**
This resource specifies the bottom shadow color of the matte, when **matteWidth** is positive. The default value of this resource is the client bottom shadow color (that is, specified by "Mwm*bottomShadowColor or Mwm*client*bottomShadowColor).

matteBottomShadowPixmap (class **BottomShadowPixmap**)
This resource specifies the bottom shadow pixmap of the matte, when **matteWidth** is positive. The default value of this resource is the client bottom shadow pixmap (that is, specified by "Mwm*bottomShadowPixmap or Mwm*client*bottomShadowPixmap).

matteForeground (class **Foreground**)
This resource specifies the foreground color of the matte, when **matteWidth** is positive. The default value of this resource is the client foreground color (that is, specified by "Mwm*foreground or Mwm*client*foreground).

matteTopShadowColor (class **Background**)
This resource specifies the top shadow color of the matte, when **matteWidth** is positive. The default value of this resource is the client top shadow color (that is, specified by "Mwm*topShadowColor or Mwm*client*topShadowColor).

matteTopShadowPixmap (class **TopShadowPixmap**)
This resource specifies the top shadow pixmap of the matte, when **matteWidth** is positive. The default value of this resource is the client top shadow pixmap (that is, specified by "Mwm*topShadowPixmap or Mwm*client*topShadowPixmap).

matteWidth (class **MatteWidth**)
This resource specifies the width of the optional matte. The default value is 0, which effectively disables the matte.

maximumClientSize (class **MaximumClientSize**)
This is a size specification that indicates the client size to be used when an application is maximized. The resource value is specified as *width***x***height*. The width and height are interpreted in the units that the client uses (for example, for terminal emulators this is generally characters). If this resource is not specified, the maximum size from the WM_NORMAL_HINTS property is used if set. Otherwise the default value is the size where the client window with window management borders fills the screen. When the maximum client size is not determined by the maximumClientSize resource, the maximumMaximumSize resource value is used as a constraint on the maximum size.

useClientIcon (class **UseClientIcon)**

If the value given for this resource is True, a client supplied icon image takes precedence over a user supplied icon image. The default value is False, giving the user supplied icon image higher precedence than the client supplied icon image.

windowMenu (class **WindowMenu)**

This resource indicates the name of the menu pane that is posted when the window menu is popped up (usually by pressing button 1 on the window menu button on the client window frame). Menu panes are specified in the MWM resource description file. Window menus can be customized on a client class basis by specifying resources of the form **Mwm***_client_name_or_class_***windowMenu** (See "MWM Resource Description File Syntax"). The default value of this resource is the name of the built-in window menu specification.

Resource Description File

The MWM resource description file is a supplementary resource file that contains resource descriptions that are referred to by entries in the defaults files (.Xdefaults, app-defaults/Mwm). It contains descriptions of resources that are to be used by MWM, and that cannot be easily encoded in the defaults files (a bitmap file is an analogous type of resource description file). A particular MWM resource description file can be selected using the **configFile** resource. The following types of resources can be described in the MWM resource description file:

Buttons Window manager functions can be bound (associated) with button events.

Keys Window manager functions can be bound (associated) with key press events.

Menus Menu panes can be used for the window menu and other menus posted with key bindings and button bindings.

MWM Resource Description File Syntax

The MWM resource description file is a standard text file that contains items of information separated by blanks, tabs, and new-line characters. Blank lines are ignored. Items or characters can be quoted to avoid special interpretation (for example, the comment character can be quoted to prevent it from being interpreted as the comment character). A quoted item can be contained in double quotes ("). Single characters can be quoted by preceding them by the back-slash character (\). All text from an unquoted **#** to the end of the line is regarded as a comment and is not interpreted as part of a resource description. If **!** is the first character in a line, the line is regarded as a comment. Window manager functions can be accessed with button and key bindings, and with window manager menus. Functions are indicated as part of the specifications for button and key binding sets, and menu panes. The function specification has the following syntax:

function =	*function_name* [*function_args*]
function_name =	*window manager function*
function_args =	{*quoted_item* | *unquoted_item*}

The following functions are supported. If a function is specified that isn't supported, it is interpreted by MWM as *f.nop*.

f.beep This function causes a beep.

f.circle_down [**icon** | **window**]
This function causes the window or icon that is on the top of the window stack to be put on the bottom of the window stack (so that it no longer obscures any other window or icon). This function affects only those windows and icons that obscure other windows and icons, or that are obscured by other windows and icons. Secondary windows (that is, transient windows) are restacked with their associated primary window. Secondary windows always stay on top of the associated primary window and there can be no other primary windows between the secondary windows and their primary window. If an **icon** function argument is specified, the function applies only to icons. If a **window** function argument is specified, the function applies only to windows.

f.circle_up [**icon** | **window**]
This function raises the window or icon on the bottom of the window stack (so that it is not obscured by any other windows). This function affects only those windows and icons that obscure other windows and icons, or that are obscured by other windows and icons. Secondary windows (that is, transient windows) are restacked with their associated primary window.
If an *icon* function argument is specified, the function applies only to icons. If an *window* function argument is specified, the function applies only to windows.

f.exec or **!** This function causes *command* to be executed (using the value of the *$SHELL* environment variable if it is set, otherwise */bin/sh*). The **!** notation can be used in place of the **f.exec** function name.

f.focus_color
This function sets the colormap focus to a client window. If this function is done in a root context, the default colormap (setup by the *X Window System* for the screen where MWM is running) is installed and there is no specific client window colormap focus. This function is treated as *f.nop* if *colormapFocusPolicy* is not explicit.

f.focus_key This function sets the keyboard input focus to a client window or icon. This function is treated as *f.nop* if *keyboardFocusPolicy* is not explicit or the function is executed in a root context.

f.kill If the WM_DELETE_WINDOW protocol is set up, the client is sent a client message event indicating that the client window should be deleted. If the WM_SAVE_YOURSELF protocol is set up and the WM_DELETE_WINDOW protocol is not set up, the client is sent a client message event indicating that the client needs to prepare to be terminated. If the client does not have the WM_DELETE_WINDOW or WM_SAVE_YOURSELF protocol set up, this function causes a client's X connection to be terminated (usually resulting in termination of the client). Refer to the description of the *quitTimeout* resource and the *WM_PROTOCOLS* property.

f.lower [*-client*]
This function lowers a client window to the bottom of the window stack (where it obscures no other window). Secondary windows (that is, transient windows) are restacked with their associated primary window. The *client* argument indicates the name or class of a client to lower. If the *client* argument is not specified, the context that the function was invoked in indicates the window or icon to lower.

f.maximize This function causes a client window to be displayed with its maximum size.

f.menu This function associates a cascading (pull-right) menu with a menu pane entry or a menu with a button or key binding. The *menu_name* function argument identifies the menu to be used.

f.minimize This function causes a client window to be minimized (iconified). When a window is minimized when no icon box is used, its icon is placed on the bottom of the window stack (so that it obscures no other window). If an icon box is used, the client's icon changes to its iconified form inside the icon box. Secondary windows (that is, transient windows) are minimized with their associated primary window. There is only one icon for a primary window and all its secondary windows.

f.move This function allows a client window to be interactively moved.

f.next_cmap This function installs the next colormap in the list of colormaps for the window with the colormap focus.

f.next_key [icon | window | transient]
This function sets the keyboard input focus to the next window/icon in the set of windows/icons managed by the window manager (the ordering of this set is based on the stacking of windows on the screen). This function is treated as *f.nop* if *keyboardFocusPolicy* is not explicit. The keyboard input focus is moved only to windows that do not have an associated secondary window that is application modal. If the **transient** argument is specified, transient (secondary) windows are traversed (otherwise, if only **window** is specified, traversal is done only to the last focused window in a transient group). If an **icon** function argument is specified, the function applies only to icons. If a **window** function argument is specified, the function applies only to windows.

f.nop This function does nothing.

f.normalize This function causes a client window to be displayed with its normal size. Secondary windows (that is, transient windows) are placed in their normal state along with their associated primary window.

f.pack_icons
This function is used to relayout icons (based on the layout policy being used) on the root window or in the icon box. In general this causes icons to be "packed" into the icon grid.

f.pass_keys This function is used to enable/disable (toggle) processing of key bindings for window manager functions. When it disables key-binding processing all keys are passed on to the window with the keyboard input focus and no window manager functions are invoked. If the *f.pass_keys* function is invoked with a key binding to disable key-binding processing, the same key binding can be used to enable key-binding processing.

f.post_wmenu
This function is used to post the window menu. If a key is used to post the window menu and a window menu button is present, the window menu is automatically placed with its top-left corner at the bottom-left corner of the window menu button for the client window. If no window menu button is present, the window menu is placed at the top-left corner of the client window.

f.prev_cmap
This function installs the previous colormap in the list of colormaps for the window with the colormap focus.

f.prev_key [**icon** | **window** | **transient**]
This function sets the keyboard input focus to the previous window/icon in the set of windows/icons managed by the window manager (the ordering of this set is based on the stacking of windows on the screen). This function is treated as *f.nop* if *keyboardFocusPolicy* is not explicit. The keyboard input focus is moved only to windows that do not have an associated secondary window that is application modal. If the *transient* argument is specified, transient (secondary) windows are traversed (otherwise, if only *window* is specified, traversal is done only to the last focused window in a transient group). If an *icon* function argument is specified, the function applies only to icons. If an *window* function argument is specified, the function applies only to windows.

f.quit_mwm This function terminates MWM (but not the X window system).

f.raise [-*client*]
This function raises a client window to the top of the window stack (where it is obscured by no other window). Secondary windows (that is, transient windows) are restacked with their associated primary window. The *client* argument indicates the name or class of a client to raise. If the *client* argument is not specified, the context that the function was invoked in indicates the window or icon to raise.

f.raise_lower
This function raises a client window to the top of the window stack if it is partially obscured by another window, otherwise it lowers the window to the bottom of the window stack. Secondary windows (that is, transient windows) are restacked with their associated primary window.

f.refresh This function causes all windows to be redrawn.

f.refresh_win
This function causes a client window to be redrawn.

f.resize This function allows a client window to be interactively resized.

f.restart This function causes MWM to be restarted (effectively terminated and re-executed).

f.send_msg *message_number*
This function sends a client message of the type _MOTIF_WM_MESSAGES with the *message_type* indicated by the *message_number* function argument. The client message is sent only if *message_number* is included in the client's _MOTIF_WM_MESSAGES property. A menu item label is grayed out if the menu item is used to do *f.send_msg* of a message that is not included in the client's _MOTIF_WM_MESSAGES property.

f.separator This function causes a menu separator to be put in the menu pane at the specified location (the label is ignored).

f.set_behavior
This function causes the window manager to restart with the default OSF(TM) behavior (if a custom behavior is configured) or a custom behavior (if an OSF default behavior is configured).

f.title This function inserts a title in the menu pane at the specified location.

Each function may be constrained as to which resource types can specify the function (for example, menu pane) and also what context the function can be used in (for example, the function is done to the selected client window). Function contexts are

root No client window or icon has been selected as an object for the function.

window A client window has been selected as an object for the function. This includes the window's title bar and frame. Some functions are applied only when the window is in its normalized state (for example, f.maximize) or its maximized state (for example, f.normalize).

icon An icon has been selected as an object for the function.

If a function is specified in a type of resource where it is not supported or is invoked in a context that does not apply, the function is treated as *f.nop*. The following table indicates the resource types and function contexts in which window manager functions apply.

Function	Contexts	Resources
f.beep	root,icon,window	button,key,menu
f.circle_down	root,icon,window	button,key,menu
f.circle_up	root,icon,window	button,key,menu
f.exec	root,icon,window	button,key,menu
f.focus_color	root,icon,window	button,key,menu
f.focus_key	root,icon,window	button,key,menu
f.kill	icon,window	button,key,menu
f.lower	root,icon,window	button,key,menu
f.maximize	icon,window(normal)	button,key,menu
f.menu	root,icon,window	button,key,menu
f.minimize	window	button,key,menu
f.move	icon,window	button,key,menu
f.next_cmap	root,icon,window	button,key,menu
f.next_key	root,icon,window	button,key,menu
f.nop	root,icon,window	button,key,menu
f.normalize	icon,window(maximized)	button,key,menu
f.pack_icons	root,icon,window	button,key,menu
f.pass_keys	root,icon,window	button,key,menu
f.post_wmenu	root,icon,window	button,key
f.prev_cmap	root,icon,window	button,key,menu
f.prev_key	root,icon,window	button,key,menu
f.quit_mwm	root	button,key,menu
f.raise	root,icon,window	button,key,menu
f.raise_lower	icon,window	button,key,menu
f.refresh	root,icon,window	button,key,menu
f.refresh_win	window	button,key,menu
f.resize	window	button,key,menu
f.restart	root	button,key,menu
f.send_msg	icon,window	button,key,menu
f.separator	root,icon,window	menu
f.set_behavior	root,icon,window	button,key,menu
f.title	root,icon,window	menu

Window Manager Event Specification

Events are indicated as part of the specifications for button and key- binding sets, and menu panes.

Button events have the following syntax:

button = [*modifier_list*]<*button_event_name*>
modifier_list = *modifier_name* {*modifier_name*}

All modifiers specified are interpreted as being exclusive (this means that only the specified modifiers can be present when the button event occurs). The following table indicates the values that can be used for *modifier_name*. The [Alt] key is frequently labeled [Extend] or [Meta]. Alt and Meta can be used interchangeably in event specification.

Modifier	Description
Ctrl	Control Key
Shift	Shift Key
Alt	Alt/Meta Key
Meta	Meta/Alt Key
Lock	Lock Key
Mod1	Modifier1
Mod2	Modifier2
Mod3	Modifier3
Mod4	Modifier4
Mod5	Modifier5

The following table indicates the values that can be used for *button_event_name*.

Button	Description
Btn1Down	Button 1 Press
Btn1Up	Button 1 Release
Btn1Click	Button 1 Press and Release
Btn1Click2	Button 1 Double Click
Btn2Down	Button 2 Press
Btn2Up	Button 2 Release
Btn2Click	Button 2 Press and Release
Btn2Click2	Button 2 Double Click
Btn3Down	Button 3 Press
Btn3Up	Button 3 Release
Btn3Click	Button 3 Press and Release
Btn3Click2	Button 3 Double Click
Btn4Down	Button 4 Press
Btn4Up	Button 4 Release
Btn4Click	Button 4 Press and Release
Btn4Click2	Button 4 Double Click
Btn5Down	Button 5 Press
Btn5Up	Button 5 Release
Btn5Click	Button 5 Press and Release
Btn5Click2	Button 5 Double Click

Key events that are used by the window manager for menu mnemonics and for binding to window manager functions are single key presses; key releases are ignored. Key events have the following syntax:

key = [*modifier_list*]**<Key>***key_name*
modifier_list = *modifier_name* {*modifier_name*}

All modifiers specified are interpreted as being exclusive (this means that only the specified modifiers can be present when the key event occurs). Modifiers for keys are the same as those that apply to buttons. The *key_name* is an X11 keysym name. Keysym names can be found in the keysymdef.h file (remove the *XK_* prefix).

Button Bindings

The **buttonBindings** resource value is the name of a set of button bindings that are used to configure window manager behavior. A window manager function can be done when a button press occurs with the pointer over a framed client window, an icon or the root window. The context for indicating where the button press applies is also the context for invoking the window manager function when the button press is done (significant for functions that are context sensitive).

The button binding syntax is

Buttons *bindings_set_name*
{
button context function
button context function
.
.
button context function
}

The syntax for the *context* specification is

context = *object*[|*context*]
object = **root** | **icon** | **window** | **title** | **frame** | **border** | **app**

The context specification indicates where the pointer must be for the button binding to be effective. For example, a context of **window** indicates that the pointer must be over a client window or window management frame for the button binding to be effective. The **frame** context is for the window management frame around a client window (including the border and titlebar), the **border** context is for the border part of the window management frame (not including the titlebar), the **title** context is for the title area of the window management frame, and the **app** context is for the application window (not including the window management frame).

If an *f.nop* function is specified for a button binding, the button binding is not done.

Key Bindings

The **keyBindings** resource value is the name of a set of key bindings that are used to configure window manager behavior. A window manager function can be done when a particular key is pressed. The context in which the key binding applies is indicated in the key binding specification. The valid contexts are the same as those that apply to button bindings.

The key binding syntax is

Keys *bindings_set_name*
{
  key context function
  key context function
  .
  .
  key context function
}

If an *f.nop* function is specified for a key binding, the key binding is not done. If an *f.post_wmenu* or *f.menu* function is bound to a key, MWM automatically uses the same key for removing the menu from the screen after it has been popped up.

The *context* specification syntax is the same as for button bindings. For key bindings, the **frame**, **title**, **border**, and **app** contexts are equivalent to the **window** context. The context for a key event is the window or icon that has the keyboard input focus (**root** if no window or icon has the keyboard input focus).

Menu Panes

Menus can be popped up using the *f.post_wmenu* and *f.menu* window manager functions. The context for window manager functions that are done from a menu is *root*, *icon* or *window* depending on how the menu was popped up. In the case of the *window* menu or menus popped up with a key binding, the location of the keyboard input focus indicates the context. For menus popped up using a button binding, the context of the button binding is the context of the menu.

The menu pane specification syntax is

Menu *menu_name*
{
label [*mnemonic*] [*accelerator*] *function*
label [*mnemonic*] [*accelerator*] *function*
.
.
label [*mnemonic*] [*accelerator*] *function*
}

Each line in the *Menu* specification identifies the label for a menu item and the function to be done if the menu item is selected. Optionally a menu button mnemonic and a menu button keyboard accelerator may be specified. Mnemonics are functional only when the menu is posted and keyboard traversal applies.

The *label* may be a string or a bitmap file. The label specification has the following syntax:

label =	*text* | *bitmap_file*
bitmap_file =	*@file_name*
text =	*quoted_item* | *unquoted_item*

The string encoding for labels must be compatible with the menu font that is used. Labels are greyed out for menu items that do the *f.nop* function or an invalid function or a function that doesn't apply in the current context.

A *mnemonic* specification has the following syntax

mnemonic = _*character*

The first matching *character* in the label is underlined. If there is no matching *character* in the label, no mnemonic is registered with the window manager for that label. Although the *character* must exactly match a character in the label, the mnemonic does not execute if any modifier (such as Shift) is pressed with the character key.

The *accelerator* specification is a key event specification with the same syntax as is used for key bindings to window manager functions.

Environment

MWM uses the environment variable **$HOME** specifying the user's home directory.

Files

/usr/lib/X11/system.mwmrc
/usr/lib/X11/app-defaults/Mwm
$HOME/.Xdefaults
$HOME/.mwmrc

Related Information

X(1)
VendorShell(3X)
XmInstallImage(3X)

uil

Purpose

The user interface language compiler for X window system

Synopsis

uil [*options*] *file*

Description

The **uil** command invokes the UIL compiler. The user interface language (UIL) is a specification language for describing the initial state of a user interface for a Motif(TM) application. The specification describes the objects (menus, dialog boxes, labels, push buttons, and so on) used in the interface and specifies the routines to be called when the interface changes state as a result of user interaction.

file Specifies the file to be compiled through the UIL compiler.

options Specifies one or more of the following options:

-I*pathname* This option causes the compiler to look for include files in the directory specified if the include files have not been found in the paths that already were searched. Specify this option followed by a pathname, with no intervening spaces.

-m — Machine code is listed. This directs the compiler to place in the listing file a description of the records that it added to the User Interface Database (UID). This helps you isolate errors. The default is no machine code.

-o *file* — Directs the compiler to produce a UID. By default, UIL creates a UID with the name **a.uid**. The file specifies the filename for the UID. No UID is produced if the compiler issues any diagnostics categorized as error or severe.

-v *file* — Directs the compiler to generate a listing. The file specifies the filename for the listing. If the **-v** option is not present, no listing is generated by the compiler. The default is no listing.

-w — Specifies that the compiler suppress all warning and informational messages. If this option is not present, all messages are generated, regardless of the severity.

For more information about UIL syntax, see the *OSF/Motif Programmer's Guide*.

Related Information

X(1X), **Uil(3X)**

ApplicationShell

Purpose

The ApplicationShell widget class

Synopsis

#include <Xm/Xm.h>
#include <X11/Shell.h>

Description

ApplicationShell is used as the main top-level window for an application. An application should have more than one ApplicationShell only if it implements multiple logical applications.

Classes

ApplicationShell inherits behavior and resources from **Core**, **Composite**, **Shell**, **WMShell**, **VendorShell**, and **TopLevelShell**.

The class pointer is **applicationShellWidgetClass**.

The class name is **ApplicationShell**.

New Resources

The following table defines a set of widget resources used by the programmer to specify data. The programmer can also set the resource values for the inherited classes to set attributes for this widget. To reference a resource by name or by class in a .Xdefaults file, remove the **XmN** or **XmC** prefix and use the remaining letters. To specify one of the defined values for a resource in a .Xdefaults file, remove the **Xm** prefix and use the remaining letters (in either lowercase or uppercase, but include any underscores between words). The codes in the access column indicate if the given resource can be set at creation time (**C**), set by using **XtSetValues** (**S**), retrieved by using **XtGetValues** (**G**), or is not applicable (**N/A**).

ApplicationShell Resource Set		
Name **Class**	**Default** **Type**	**Access**
XmNargc XmCNargc	NULL int	CSG
XmNargv XmCNargv	NULL String *	CSG

XmNargc Specifies the number of arguments given in the **XmNargv** resource. The function **XtInitialize** sets this resource on the shell widget instance it creates by using its parameters as the values.

XmNargv Specifies the argument list required by a session manager to restart the application, if it is killed. This list should be updated at appropriate points by the application if a new state has been reached which can be directly restarted. The function **XtInitialize** sets this resource on the shell widget instance it creates by using its parameters as the values.

Inherited Resources

ApplicationShell inherits behavior and resources from the following superclasses. For a complete description of each resource, refer to the man page for that superclass.

TopLevelShell Resource Set		
Name **Class**	**Default** **Type**	**Access**
XmNiconic XmCIconic	False Boolean	CSG
XmNiconName XmCIconName	NULL String	CSG

VendorShell Resource Set		
Name **Class**	**Default** **Type**	**Access**
XmNdeleteResponse XmCDeleteResponse	XmDESTROY unsigned char	CSG
XmNkeyboardFocusPolicy XmCKeyboardFocusPolicy	XmEXPLICIT unsigned char	CSG
XmNmwmDecorations XmCMwmDecorations	-1 int	CSG
XmNmwmFunctions XmCMwmFunctions	-1 int	CSG
XmNmwmInputMode XmCMwmInputMode	-1 int	CSG
XmNmwmMenu XmCMwmMenu	NULL String	CSG
XmNshellUnitType XmCShellUnitType	XmPIXELS unsigned char	CSG

WMShell Resource Set		
Name **Class**	**Default** **Type**	**Access**
XmNheightInc XmCHeightInc	-1 int	CSG
XmNiconMask XmCIconMask	NULL Pixmap	CSG
XmNiconPixmap XmCIconPixmap	NULL Pixmap	CSG
XmNiconWindow XmCIconWindow	NULL Window	CSG
XmNiconX XmCIconX	-1 int	CSG
XmNiconY XmCIconY	-1 int	CSG
XmNinitialState XmCInitialState	1 int	CSG
XmNinput XmCInput	True Boolean	CSG
XmNmaxAspectX XmCMaxAspectX	-1 int	CSG
XmNmaxAspectY XmCMaxAspectY	-1 int	CSG
XmNmaxHeight XmCMaxHeight	-1 int	CSG
XmNmaxWidth XmCMaxWidth	-1 int	CSG
XmNminAspectX XmCMinAspectX	-1 int	CSG
XmNminAspectY XmCMinAspectY	-1 int	CSG

Name Class	Default Type	Access
XmNminHeight XmCMinHeight	-1 int	CSG
XmNminWidth XmCMinWidth	-1 int	CSG
XmNtitle XmCTitle	NULL char *	CSG
XmNtransient XmCTransient	False Boolean	CSG
XmNwaitForWm XmCWaitForWm	True Boolean	CSG
XmNwidthInc XmCWidthInc	-1 int	CSG
XmNwindowGroup XmCWindowGroup	None XID	CSG
XmNwmTimeout XmCWmTimeout	fivesecond int	CSG

Shell Resource Set		
Name **Class**	**Default** **Type**	**Access**
XmNallowShellResize XmCAllowShellResize	False Boolean	CSG
XmNcreatePopupChildProc XmCCreatePopupChildProc	NULL XmCreatePopupChildProc	CSG
XmNgeometry XmCGeometry	NULL String	CSG
XmNoverrideRedirect XmCOverrideRedirect	False Boolean	CSG
XmNpopdownCallback XmCCallback	NULL XtCallbackList	C
XmNpopupCallback XmCCallback	NULL XtCallbackList	C
XmNsaveUnder XmCSaveUnder	False Boolean	CSG

Composite Resource Set		
Name **Class**	**Default** **Type**	**Access**
XmNinsertPosition XmCInsertPosition	NULL XmRFunction	CSG

Core Resource Set		
Name Class	Default Type	Access
XmNaccelerators XmCAccelerators	NULL XtTranslations	CSG
XmNancestorSensitive XmCSensitive	ShellAncestorSensitive Boolean	G
XmNbackground XmCBackground	White Pixel	CSG
XmNbackgroundPixmap XmCPixmap	XmUNSPECIFIED_PIXMAP Pixmap	CSG
XmNborderColor XmCBorderColor	Black Pixel	CSG
XmNborderPixmap XmCPixmap	XmUNSPECIFIED_PIXMAP Pixmap	CSG
XmNborderWidth XmCBorderWidth	1 Dimension	CSG
XmNcolormap XmCColormap	ShellColormap Colormap	CG
XmNdepth XmCDepth	ShellDepth int	CG
XmNdestroyCallback XmCCallback	NULL XtCallbackList	C
XmNheight XmCHeight	0 Dimension	CSG
XmNmappedWhenManaged XmCMappedWhenManaged	True Boolean	CSG
XmNscreen XmCScreen	XtCopyScreen Pointer	CG
XmNsensitive XmCSensitive	True Boolean	CSG

Name Class	Default Type	Access
XmNtranslations XmCTranslations	NULL XtTranslations	CSG
XmNwidth XmCWidth	0 Dimension	CSG
XmNx XmCPosition	0 Position	CSG
XmNy XmCPosition	0 Position	CSG

Related Information

Composite(3X), **Core(3X)**, **Shell(3X)**, **WMShell(3X)**, **VendorShell(3X)**, and **TopLevelShell(3X)**.

Composite

Purpose

The Composite widget class

Synopsis

#include <Xm/Xm.h>

Description

Composite widgets are intended to be containers for other widgets and can have an arbitrary number of children. Their responsibilities (implemented either directly by the widget class or indirectly by Intrinsics functions) include.

- Overall management of children from creation to destruction.
- Destruction of descendants when the composite widget is destroyed.
- Physical arrangement (geometry management) of a displayable subset of managed children.
- Mapping and unmapping of a subset of the managed children. Instances of composite widgets need to specify the order in which their children are kept. For example, an application may want a set of command buttons in some logical order grouped by function, and it may want buttons that represent filenames to be kept in alphabetical order.

Classes

Composite inherits behavior and resources from **Core**.

The class pointer is **compositeWidgetClass**.

The class name is **Composite**.

New Resources

The following table defines a set of widget resources used by the programmer to specify data. The programmer can also set the resource values for the inherited classes to set attributes for this widget. To reference a resource by name or by class in a .Xdefaults file, remove the **XmN** or **XmC** prefix and use the remaining letters. To specify one of the defined values for a resource in a .Xdefaults file, remove the **Xm** prefix and use the remaining letters (in either lowercase or uppercase, but include any underscores between words). The codes in the access column indicate if the given resource can be set at creation time (**C**), set by using **XtSetValues** (**S**), retrieved by using **XtGetValues** (**G**), or is not applicable (**N/A**).

Composite Resource Set		
Name **Class**	**Default** **Type**	**Access**
XmNinsertPosition XmCInsertPosition	NULL XmRFunction	CSG

XmNinsertPosition

Points to the **XtOrderProc** function described below.

The following procedure pointer in a composite widget instance is of type **XtOrderProc**:

Cardinal (* XtOrderProc) (*widget*)
    Widget   *w*;

w   Specifies the widget.

Composite widgets that allow clients to order their children (usually homogeneous boxes) can call their widget instance's insert_position procedure from the class's insert_child procedure to determine where a new child should go in its children array. Thus, a client of a composite class can apply different sorting criteria to widget instances of the class, passing in a different insert_position procedure when it creates each composite widget instance.

The return value of the insert_position procedure indicates how many children should go before the widget. Returning *zero* indicates that the widget should go before all other children; returning num_children indicates that it should go after all other children. The default insert_position function returns num_children and can be overridden by a specific composite widget's resource list or by the argument list provided when the composite widget is created.

Inherited Resources

Composite inherits behavior and resources from the following superclass. For a complete description of each resource, refer to the man page for that superclass.

Core Resource Set		
Name **Class**	**Default** **Type**	**Access**
XmNaccelerators XmCAccelerators	NULL XtTranslations	CSG
XmNancestorSensitive XmCSensitive	True Boolean	G
XmNbackground XmCBackground	White Pixel	CSG
XmNbackgroundPixmap XmCPixmap	XmUNSPECIFIED_PIXMAP Pixmap	CSG
XmNborderColor XmCBorderColor	Black Pixel	CSG
XmNborderPixmap XmCPixmap	XmUNSPECIFIED_PIXMAP Pixmap	CSG
XmNborderWidth XmCBorderWidth	1 Dimension	CSG
XmNcolormap XmCColormap	XtCopyFromParent Colormap	CG
XmNdepth XmCDepth	XtCopyFromParent int	CG
XmNdestroyCallback XmCCallback	NULL XtCallbackList	C
XmNheight XmCHeight	0 Dimension	CSG
XmNmappedWhenManaged XmCMappedWhenManaged	True Boolean	CSG
XmNscreen XmCScreen	XtCopyScreen Pointer	CG
XmNsensitive XmCSensitive	True Boolean	CSG

Name Class	Default Type	Access
XmNtranslations XmCTranslations	NULL XtTranslations	CSG
XmNwidth XmCWidth	0 Dimension	CSG
XmNx XmCPosition	0 Position	CSG
XmNy XmCPosition	0 Position	CSG

Related Information

Core(3X).

Constraint

Purpose

The Constraint widget class

Synopsis

#include <Xm/Xm.h>

Description

Constraint widgets maintain additional state data for each child. For example, client-defined constraints on the child's geometry may be specified.

When a constrained composite widget defines constraint resources, all of that widget's children inherit all of those resources as their own. These constraint resources are set and read just the same as any other resources defined for the child. This resource inheritance extends exactly one generation down, which means only the first-generation children of a constrained composite widget inherit the parent widget's constraint resources.

Because constraint resources are defined by the parent widgets and not the children, the child widgets never directly use the constraint resource data. Instead, the parents use constraint resource data to attach child-specific data to children.

Classes

Constraint inherits behavior and resources from **Composite** and **Core**.

The class pointer is **constraintWidgetClass**.

The class name is **Constraint**.

New Resources

Constraint defines no new resources.

Inherited Resources

Constraint inherits behavior and resources from **Composite** and **Core**. The following table defines a set of widget resources used by the programmer to specify data. The programmer can also set the resource values for the inherited classes to set attributes for this widget. To reference a resource by name or by class in a .Xdefaults file, remove the **XmN** or **XmC** prefix and use the remaining letters. To specify one of the defined values for a resource in a .Xdefaults file, remove the **Xm** prefix and use the remaining letters (in either lowercase or uppercase, but include any underscores between words). The codes in the access column indicate if the given resource can be set at creation time (**C**), set by using **XtSetValues** (**S**), retrieved by using **XtGetValues** (**G**), or is not applicable (**N/A**).

Core Resource Set		
Name **Class**	**Default** **Type**	**Access**
XmNaccelerators XmCAccelerators	NULL XtTranslations	CSG
XmNancestorSensitive XmCSensitive	True Boolean	G
XmNbackground XmCBackground	White Pixel	CSG
XmNbackgroundPixmap XmCPixmap	XmUNSPECIFIED_PIXMAP Pixmap	CSG
XmNborderColor XmCBorderColor	Black Pixel	CSG
XmNborderPixmap XmCPixmap	XmUNSPECIFIED_PIXMAP Pixmap	CSG
XmNborderWidth XmCBorderWidth	1 Dimension	CSG
XmNcolormap XmCColormap	XtCopyFromParent Colormap	CG
XmNdepth XmCDepth	XtCopyFromParent int	CG
XmNdestroyCallback XmCCallback	NULL XtCallbackList	C
XmNheight XmCHeight	0 Dimension	CSG
XmNmappedWhenManaged XmCMappedWhenManaged	True Boolean	CSG
XmNscreen XmCScreen	XtCopyScreen Pointer	CG
XmNsensitive XmCSensitive	True Boolean	CSG

Name Class	Default Type	Access
XmNtranslations XmCTranslations	NULL XtTranslations	CSG
XmNwidth XmCWidth	0 Dimension	CSG
XmNx XmCPosition	0 Position	CSG
XmNy XmCPosition	0 Position	CSG

Related Information

Composite(3X) and **Core(3X)**.

Core

Purpose

The Core widget class

Synopsis

#include <Xm/Xm.h>

Description

Core is the Xt Intrinsic base class for windowed widgets.

To add support for windowless widgets, three additional classes have been added above Core in the class hierarchy. They are **Object**, **RectObj**, and **WindowObj**. **WindowObj** is a synonym of Core that provides no added functionality but was necessary for implementation reasons.

Classes

All widgets are built from **Core**.

The class pointer is **widgetClass**.

The class name is **Core**.

New Resources

The following table defines a set of widget resources used by the programmer to specify data. The programmer can also set the resource values for the inherited classes to set attributes for this widget. To reference a resource by name or by class in a .Xdefaults file, remove the **XmN** or **XmC** prefix and use the remaining letters. To specify one of the defined values for a resource in a .Xdefaults file, remove the **Xm** prefix and use the remaining letters (in either lowercase or uppercase, but include any underscores between words). The codes in the access column indicate if the given resource can be set at creation time (**C**), set by using **XtSetValues** (**S**), retrieved by using **XtGetValues** (**G**), or is not applicable (**N/A**).

Core Resource Set		
Name **Class**	**Default** **Type**	**Access**
XmNaccelerators XmCAccelerators	NULL XtTranslations	CSG
XmNancestorSensitive XmCSensitive	True Boolean	G
XmNbackground XmCBackground	White Pixel	CSG
XmNbackgroundPixmap XmCPixmap	XmUNSPECIFIED_PIXMAP Pixmap	CSG
XmNborderColor XmCBorderColor	Black Pixel	CSG
XmNborderPixmap XmCPixmap	XmUNSPECIFIED_PIXMAP Pixmap	CSG
XmNborderWidth XmCBorderWidth	1 Dimension	CSG
XmNcolormap XmCColormap	XtCopyFromParent Colormap	CG
XmNdepth XmCDepth	XtCopyFromParent int	CG
XmNdestroyCallback XmCCallback	NULL XtCallbackList	C
XmNheight XmCHeight	0 Dimension	CSG
XmNmappedWhenManaged XmCMappedWhenManaged	True Boolean	CSG
XmNscreen XmCScreen	XtCopyScreen Pointer	CG
XmNsensitive XmCSensitive	True Boolean	CSG

Name Class	Default Type	Access
XmNtranslations XmCTranslations	NULL XtTranslations	CSG
XmNwidth XmCWidth	0 Dimension	CSG
XmNx XmCPosition	0 Position	CSG
XmNy XmCPosition	0 Position	CSG

XmNaccelerators
Specifies a translation table that is bound with its actions in the context of a particular widget. The accelerator table can then be installed on some destination widget.

XmNancestorSensitive
Specifies whether the immediate parent of the widget receives input events. Use the function **XtSetSensitive** to change the argument to preserve data integrity (see **XmNsensitive** below).

XmNbackground
Specifies the background color for the widget.

XmNbackgroundPixmap
Specifies a pixmap for tiling the background. The first tile is placed at the upper left-hand corner of the widget's window.

XmNborderColor
Specifies the color of the border in a pixel value.

XmNborderPixmap
Specifies a pixmap to be used for tiling the border. The first tile is placed at the upper left-hand corner of the border.

XmNborderWidth
Specifies the width of the border that surrounds the widget's window on all four sides. The width is specified in pixels. A width of zero means that no border shows.

XmNcolormap
Specifies the colormap that is used for conversions to the type **Pixel** for this widget instance. When changed, previously generated pixel values are not affected, but newly generated values are in the new colormap.

XmNdepth Specifies the number of bits that can be used for each pixel in the widget's window. Applications should not change or set the value of this resource as it is set by the Xt Intrinsics when the widget is created.

XmNdestroyCallback
Specifies a list of callbacks that is called when the widget is destroyed.

XmNheight Specifies the height of the widget's window in pixels, not including the border area.

XmNmappedWhenManaged
If set to True, it maps the widget (makes visible) as soon as it is both realized and managed. If set to False, the client is responsible for mapping and unmapping the widget. If the value is changed from True to False after the widget has been realized and managed, the widget is unmapped.

XmNscreen Specifies the screen on which a widget instance resides. It is read only, except for shells.

XmNsensitive
Determines whether a widget receives input events. If a widget is sensitive, the Xt Intrinsics's Event Manager dispatches to the widget all keyboard, mouse button, motion, window enter/leave, and focus events. Insensitive widgets do not receive these events. Use the function **XtSetSensitive** to change the sensitivity argument. Using **XtSetSensitive** ensures that if a parent widget has **XmNsensitive** set to False, the ancestor-sensitive flag of all its children is appropriately set.

XmNtranslations
Points to a translations list. A translations list is a list of events and actions that are to be performed when the events occur.

XmNwidth Specifies the width of the widget's window in pixels, not including the border area.

XmNx Specifies the x-coordinate of the widget's upper left-hand corner (excluding the border) in relation to its parent widget.

XmNy Specifies the y-coordinate of the widget's upper left-hand corner (excluding the border) in relation to its parent widget.

Related Information

WindowObj(3X).

MrmCloseHierarchy

Purpose

Closes a UID hierarchy

Synopsis

#include <Xm/Intrinsics>
#include <Mrm/MrmPublic.h>
Cardinal MrmCloseHierarchy(*hierarchy_id* **)**
    MrmHierarchy *hierarchy_id* **;**

Description

The **MrmCloseHierarchy** function closes a UID hierarchy previously opened by **MrmOpenHierarchy**. All files associated with the hierarchy are closed by the Motif Resource Manager (MRM) and all associated memory is returned.

hierarchy_id Specifies the ID of a previously opened UID hierarchy. The *hierarchy_id* was returned in a previous call to **MrmOpenHierarchy**.

Return Value

This function returns one of these status return constants:

MrmSUCCESS The function executed successfully.

MrmFAILURE The function failed.

Related Information

MrmOpenHierarchy(3X)

MrmFetchColorLiteral

Purpose

Fetches a named color literal from a UID file

Synopsis

#include <Xm/Intrinsics>
#include <Mrm/MrmPublic.h>
int MrmFetchColorLiteral(*hierarchy_id* , *index*, *display*, *colormap_id*, *pixel*)
    MrmHierarchy hierarchy_id;
    String *index*;
    Display **display*;
    Colormap *colormap_id*;
    Pixel **pixel*;

Description

The **MrmFetchColorLiteral** function fetches a named color literal from a UID file, and converts the color literal to a pixel color value.

hierarchy_id Specifies the ID of the UID hierarchy that contains the specified literal. The *hierarchy_id* was returned in a previous call to **MrmOpenHierarchy**.

index Specifies the UIL name of the color literal to fetch. You must define this name in UIL as an exported value.

display Specifies the display used for the pixmap. The *display* argument specifies the connection to the X server. For more information on the **Display** structure, see the Xlib function **XOpenDisplay**.

colormap_id Specifies the ID of the color map. If NULL, the default color map is used.

pixel Returns the ID of the color literal.

Return Value

This function returns one of these status return constants:

MrmSUCCESS The function executed successfully.

MrmNOT_FOUND The color literal was not found in the UIL file.

MrmFAILURE The function failed.

Related Information

MrmFetchIconLiteral(3X), **MrmFetchLiteral(3X)**, **XOpenDisplay(3X)**

MrmFetchIconLiteral

Purpose

Fetches an icon literal from a hierarchy

Synopsis

#include <Xm/Intrinsics>
#include <Mrm/MrmPublic.h>
int MrmFetchIconLiteral(*hierarchy_id* , *index*, *screen*, *display*, *fgpix*, *bgpix*, *pixmap*)
    MrmHierarchy *hierarchy_id*;
    String *index*;
    Screen **screen*;
    Display **display*;
    Pixel *fgpix*;
    Pixel *bgpix*;
    Pixmap *pixmap*;

Description

The **MrmFetchIconLiteral** function fetches an icon literal from an MRM hierarchy, and converts the icon literal to an X pixmap.

hierarchy_id Specifies the ID of the UID hierarchy that contains the specified icon literal. The *hierarchy_id* was returned in a previous call to **MrmOpenHierarchy**.

index Specifies the UIL name of the icon literal to fetch.

screen Specifies the screen used for the pixmap. The *screen* argument specifies a pointer to the Xlib structure **Screen** which contains the information about that screen and is linked to the **Display** structure. For more information on the **Display** and **Screen** structures, see the Xlib function **XOpenDisplay** and the associated screen information macros.

display Specifies the display used for the pixmap. The *display* argument specifies the connection to the X server. For more information on the **Display** structure, see the Xlib function **XOpenDisplay**.

fgpix Specifies the foreground color for the pixmap.

bgpix Specifies the background color for the pixmap.

pixmap Returns the resulting X pixmap value.

Return Value

This function returns one of these status return constants:

MrmSUCCESS The function executed successfully.

MrmNOT_FOUND The icon literal was not found in the hierarchy.

MrmFAILURE The function failed.

Related Information

MrmFetchLiteral(3X), **MrmFetchColorLiteral(3X)**, **XOpenDisplay(3X)**

MrmFetchInterfaceModule

Purpose

Fetches all the widgets defined in an interface module in the UID hierarchy.

Synopsis

#include <Xm/Intrinsics>
#include <Mrm/MrmPublic.h>
Cardinal MrmFetchInterfaceModule(*hierarchy_id* , *module_name*, *parent_widget*, *widget*)
  MrmHierarchy *hierarchy_id*;
  char **module_name*;
  Widget *parent_widget*;
  Widget **widget*;

Description

The **MrmFetchInterfaceModule** function fetches all the widgets defined in a UIL module in the UID hierarchy. Typically, each application has one or more modules that define its interface. Each must be fetched in order to initialize all the widgets the application requires. Applications do not need to define all their widgets in a single module.

If the module defines a main window widget, **MrmFetchInterfaceModule** returns its widget ID. If no main window widget is contained in the module, **MrmFetchInterfaceModule** returns NULL and no widgets are realized.

The application can obtain the IDs of widgets other than the main window widget by using creation callbacks.

hierarchy_id Specifies the ID of the UID hierarchy that contains the interface definition. The *hierarchy_id* was returned in a previous call to **MrmOpenHierarchy**.

module_name Specifies the name of the interface module, which you specified in the UIL module header. By convention, this is usually the generic name of the application.

parent_widget Specifies the parent widget ID for the topmost widgets being fetched from the module. The topmost widgets are those that have no parents specified in the UIL module. The parent widget is usually the top-level widget returned by **XtInitialize**.

widget Returns the widget ID for the last main window widget encountered in the UIL module, or NULL if no main window widget is found.

Return Value

This function returns one of these status return constants:

MrmSUCCESS The function executed successfully.

MrmFAILURE The function failed.

MrmNOT_FOUND The interface module or topmost widget not found.

MrmFetchLiteral

Purpose

Fetches a literal from a UID file

Synopsis

```
#include <Xm/Intrinsics>
#include <Mrm/MrmPublic.h>
int MrmFetchLiteral(hierarchy_id , index, display, value, type)
      MrmHierarchy hierarchy_id;
      String index;
      Display *display;
      caddr_t *value;
      MrmCode *type;
```

Description

The **MrmFetchLiteral** function reads and returns the value and type of a literal (named value) that is stored as a public resource in a single UID file. This function returns a pointer to the value of the literal. For example, an integer is always returned as a pointer to an integer, and a string is always returned as a pointer to a string.

Applications should not use **MrmmFetchLiteral** for fetching icon or color literals. If this is attempted, **MrmmFetchLiteral** returns an error.

hierarchy_id Specifies the ID of the UID hierarchy that contains the specified literal. The *hierarchy_id* was returned in a previous call to **MrmmOpenHierarchy**.

index Specifies the UIL name of the literal (pixmap) to fetch. You must define this name in UIL as an exported value.

display	Specifies the display used for the pixmap. The *display* argument specifies the connection to the X server. For more information on the **Display** structure see the Xlib function **XOpenDisplay**.
value	Returns the ID of the named literal's value.
type	Returns the named literal's data type.

Return Value

This function returns one of these status return constants:

MrmSUCCESS	The function executed successfully.
MrmWRONG_TYPE	The operation encountered an unsupported literal type.
MrmNOT_FOUND	The literal was not found in the UIL file.
MrmFAILURE	The function failed.

Related Information

MrmFetchIconLiteral(3X), **MrmFetchColorLiteral(3X)**, **XOpenDisplay(3X)**

MrmFetchSetValues

Purpose

Fetches the values to be set from literals stored in UID files.

Synopsis

#include <Xm/Intrinsics>
#include <Mrm/MrmPublic.h>
Cardinal MrmFetchSetValues(*hierarchy_id*, *widget*, *args*, *num_args*)
  MrmHierarchy *hierarchy_id*;
  Widget *widget*;
  ArgList *args*;
  Cardinal *num_args*;

Description

The **MrmFetchSetValues** function is similar to **XtSetValues**, except that the values to be set are defined by the UIL named values that are stored in the UID hierarchy. **MrmFetchSetValues** fetches the values to be set from literals stored in UID files.

hierarchy_id Specifies the ID of the UID hierarchy that contains the specified literal. The *hierarchy_id* was returned in a previous call to **MrmOpenHierarchy**.

widget Specifies the widget that is modified.

args Specifies an argument list that identifies the widget arguments to be modified as well as the index (UIL name) of the literal that defines the value for that argument. The name part of each argument (args[n].name) must begin with the string **XmN** followed by the name that uniquely identifies this attribute tag.

For example, **XmNwidth** is the attribute name associated with the core argument *width*. The value part (args[n].value) must be a string that gives the index (UIL name) of the literal. You must define all literals in UIL as exported values.

num_args Specifies the number of entries in *args*.

This function sets the values on a widget, evaluating the values as public literal resource references resolvable from a UID hierarchy. Each literal is fetched from the hierarchy, and its value is modified and converted as required. This value is then placed in the argument list and used as the actual value for an **XtSetValues** call. **MrmFetchSetValues** allows a widget to be modified after creation using UID file values exactly as is done for creation values in **MrmFetchWidget**.

As in **MrmFetchWidget**, each argument whose value can be evaluated from the UID hierarchy is set in the widget. Values that are not found or values in which conversion errors occur are not modified.

Each entry in the argument list identifies an argument to be modified in the widget. The name part identifies the tag, which begins with **XmN**. The value part must be a string whose value is the index of the literal. Thus, the following code would modify the label resource of the widget to have the value of the literal accessed by the index OK_button_label in the hierarchy: args[n].name = XmNlabel; args[n].value = "OK_button_label";

Return Value

This function returns one of these status return constants:

MrmSUCCESS The function executed successfully.

MrmFAILURE The function failed.

Related Information

XtSetValues(3X)

MrmFetchWidget

Purpose

Fetches and creates any indexed (UIL named) application widgets and its children.

Synopsis

#include <Xm/Intrinsics>
#include <Mrm/MrmPublic.h>
Cardinal MrmFetchWidget(*hierarchy_id*, *index*, *parent_widget*, *widget*, *class*)
    MrmHierarchy *hierarchy_id*;
    String *index*;
    Widget *parent_widget*;
    Widget **widget*;
    MrmType **class*;

Description

The **MrmFetchWidget** function fetches and creates an indexed application widget and its children. The indexed application widget is any widget that is named in UIL and that is not the child of any other widget in the **uid** hierarchy. In fetch operations, the fetched widget's subtree is also fetched and created. This widget must not appear as the child of a widget within its own subtree. **MrmFetchWidget** does not execute **XtManageChild** for the newly created widget.

hierarchy_id Specifies the ID of the **uid** hierarchy that contains the interface definition. The *hierarchy_id* was returned in a previous call to **MrmOpenHierarchy**.

index Specifies the UIL name of the widget to fetch.

parent_widget Specifies the parent widget ID.

widget Returns the widget ID of the created widget. If this is not NULL when you call **MrmFetchWidgetOverride**, MRM assumes that the widget has already been created and **MrmFetchWidgetOverride** returns **MrmFAILURE**.

class Returns the class code identifying MRM's widget class. The widget class code for the main window widget, for example, is **MRMwcMainWindow**. Literals identifying MRM widget class codes are defined in **Mrm.h**.

MrmFetchWidget fetches widgets where **MrmFetchInterfaceModule** is not used. **MrmFetchWidget** provides specific control over which widgets are fetched from a UIL file; **MrmFetchInterfaceModule**, on the other hand, fetches all widgets in a single call. An application can fetch any named widget in the **uid** hierarchy using **MrmFetchWidget**. **MrmFetchWidget** can be called at any time to fetch a widget that was not fetched at application startup. **MrmFetchWidget** determines if a widget has already been fetched by checking *widget* for a NULL value. Non-NULL values signify that the widget has already been fetched, and **MrmFetchWidget** fails. **MrmFetchWidget** can be used to defer fetching pop-up widgets until they are first referenced (presumably in a callback), and then used to fetch them once.

MrmFetchWidget can also create multiple instances of a widget (and its subtree). In this case, the **uid** definition functions as a template; a widget definition can be fetched any number of times. An application can use this to make multiple instances of a widget, for example, in a dialog box box or menu.

The index (UIL name) that identifies the widget must be known to the application.

Return Value

This function returns one of these status return constants:

MrmSUCCESS	The function executed successfully.
MrmNOT_FOUND	Widget not found in UID hierarchy.
MrmFAILURE	The function failed.

Related Information

MrmFetchWidgetOverride(3X)

MrmFetchWidgetOverride

Purpose

Fetches any indexed (UIL named) application widget. It overrides the arguments specified for this application widget in UIL.

Synopsis

#include <Xm/Intrinsics>
#include <Mrm/MrmPublic.h>
Cardinal MrmFetchWidgetOverride(*hierarchy_id* , *index*, *parent_widget*, *override_name*,
override_args, *override_num_args*, *widget*, *class*)
MrmHierarchy *hierarchy_id*;
String *index*;
Widget *parent_widget*;
String *override_name*;
ArgList *override_args*;
Cardinal *override_num_args*;
Widget ***widget*;
MrmType ***class*;

Description

The **MrmFetchWidgetOverride** function is the extended version of **MrmFetchWidget**. It is identical to **MrmFetchWidget**, except that it allows the caller to override the widget's name and any arguments that **MrmFetchWidget** would otherwise retrieve from the UID file or one of the defaulting mechanisms. That is, the override argument list is not limited to those arguments in the UID file.

The override arguments apply only to the widget fetched and returned by this function. Its children (subtree) do not receive any override parameters.

hierarchy_id Specifies the ID of the UID hierarchy that contains the interface definition. The *hierarchy_id* was returned in a previous call to **MrmOpenHierarchy**.

index Specifies the UIL name of the widget to fetch.

parent_widget Specifies the parent widget ID.

override_name Specifies the name to override the widget name. Use a NULL value if you do not want to override the widget name.

override_args Specifies the override argument list, exactly as given to **XtCreateWidget** (conversion complete and so forth). Use a NULL value if you do not want to override the argument list.

override_num_args Specifies the number of arguments in *override_args*.

widget Returns the widget ID of the created widget. If this is not NULL when you call **MrmFetchWidgetOverride**, MRM assumes that the widget has already been created and **MrmFetchWidgetOverride** returns **MrmFAILURE**.

class Returns the class code identifying MRM's widget class. The widget class code for the main window widget, for example, is **MRMwcMainWindow**. Literals identifying MRM widget class codes are defined in **Mrm.h**.

Return Value

This function returns one of these status return constants:

MrmSUCCESS	The function executed successfully.
MrmNOT_FOUND	Widget not found in UID hierarchy.
MrmFAILURE	The function failed.

Related Information

MrmFetchWidget(3X)

MrmInitialize

Purpose

Prepares an application to use MRM widget-fetching facilities.

Synopsis

void MrmInitialize()

Description

The **MrmInitialize** function must be called to prepare an application to use MRM widget-fetching facilities. You must call this function prior to fetching a widget. However, it is good programming practice to call **MrmInitialize** prior to performing any MRM operations.

MrmInitialize initializes the internal data structures that MRM needs to successfully perform type conversion on arguments and to successfully access widget creation facilities. An application must call **MrmInitialize** before it uses other MRM functions.

MrmOpenHierarchy

Purpose

Allocates a hierarchy ID and opens all the UID files in the hierarchy.

Synopsis

#include <Xm/Intrinsics>
#include <Mrm/MrmPublic.h>
Cardinal MrmOpenHierarchy(*num_files*, *file_names_list*,
ancillary_structures_list, *hierarchy_id*)
MrmCount *num_files*;
String *file_names_list* [];
MrmOsOpenParamPtr **ancillary_structures_list* ;
MrmHierarchy **hierarchy_id*;

Description

The **MrmOpenHierarchy** function allows the user to specify the list of UID files that MRM searches in subsequent fetch operations. All subsequent fetch operations return the first occurrence of the named item encountered while traversing the UID hierarchy from the first list element (UID file specification) to the last list element. This function also allocates a hierarchy ID and opens all the UID files in the hierarchy. It initializes the optimized search lists in the hierarchy. If **MrmOpenHierarchy** encounters any errors during its execution, any files that were opened are closed.

num_files Specifies the number of files in the name list.

file_names_list Specifies an array of pointers to character strings that identify the .UID files.

ancillary_structures_list
A list of operating-system-dependent ancillary structures corresponding to such things as filenames, clobber flag, and so forth. This argument should be NULL for most operations. If you need to reference this structure, see the definition of **MrmOsOpenParamPtr** in **MrmPublic.h** for more information.

hierarchy_id
Returns the search hierarchy ID. The search hierarchy ID identifies the list of .uid files that MRM searches (in order) when performing subsequent fetch calls.

Each UID file specified in *file_names_list* can specify either a full directory pathname or a filename. If a UID file does not specify the pathname, it does not contain any embedded slashes (/), and it is accessed through the UIDPATH environment variable.

The UIDPATH environment variable specifies search paths and naming conventions associated with UID files. It can contain the substitution fields %L and %N, where the current setting of the LANG environment variable is substituted for %L and the .uid name passed to **MrmOpenHierarchy** is substituted for %N. For example, the following UID path and **MrmOpenHierarchy** call causes MRM to open two separate .uid files:

```
UIDPATH=/uidlib/%L/%N.uid:/uidlib/%N/%L
static char *uid_files[] = {"/usr/users/me/test.uid", "test2"};
MrmHierarchy *Hierarchy_id;
MrmOpenHierarchy((MrmCount)2,uid_files, NULL, Hierarchy_id)
```

The first file, **/usr/users/me/test.uid**, is opened as specified, as this file specification includes a pathname. The second file, **test2**, is looked for first in **/uidlib/$LANG/test2.uid**, and second in **/uidlib/test2/$LANG**.

After **MrmOpenHierarchy** opens the UID hierarchy, you should not delete or modify the UID files until you close the UID hierarchy by calling **MrmCloseHierarchy**.

Return Value

This function returns one of these status return constants:

MrmSUCCESS	The function executed successfully.
MrmNOT_FOUND	File not found.
MrmFAILURE	The function failed.

Related Information

MrmCloseHierarchy(3X)

MrmRegisterClass

Purpose

Saves the information needed for MRM to access the widget creation function for user-defined widgets.

Synopsis

#include <Xm/Intrinsics>
#include <Mrm/MrmPublic.h>
Cardinal MrmRegisterClass(*class_code* , *class_name*, *create_name*, *create_proc*, *class_record*)
  MrmType *class_code*;
  String *class_name*;
  String *create_name*;
  Widget (* *create_proc*) ();
  WidgetClass *class_record*;

Description

The **MrmRegisterClass** function allows MRM to access user-defined widget classes. This function registers the necessary information for MRM to create widgets of this class. You must call **MrmRegisterClass** prior to fetching any user-defined class widget.

MrmRegisterClass saves the information needed to access the widget creation function and to do type conversion of argument lists by using the information in MRM databases.

class_code Specifies the code name of the class. For all application-defined widgets, this code name is **MRMwcUnknown**. For all Motif Toolkit widgets, each code name begins with the letters

MRMwc. The code names for all application widgets are defined in **Mrm.h**.

class_name Specifies the case-sensitive name of the class. The class names for all Motif Toolkit widgets are defined in **Mrm.h**. Each class name begins with the letters **MRMwcn**.

create_name Specifies the case-sensitive name of the low-level widget creation function for the class. An example from the Motif Toolkit is **XmCreateLabel**. Arguments are *parent_widget*, *name*, *override_arglist*, and *override_argcount*.

For user-defined widgets, *create_name* is the creation procedure in the UIL that defines this widget.

create_proc Specifies the address of the creation function that you named in *create_name*.

class_record Specifies a pointer to the class record.

Return Value

This function returns one of these status return constants:

MrmSUCCESS The function executed successfully.

MrmFAILURE The allocation of the class descriptor failed.

MrmRegisterNames

Purpose

Registers the values associated with the names referenced in UIL (for example, UIL callback function names or UIL identifier names).

Synopsis

#include <Xm/Intrinsics>
#include <Mrm/MrmPublic.h>
Cardinal MrmRegisterNames(*register_list* , *register_count*)
    MrmRegisterArglist *register_list* ;
    MrmCount *register_count* ;

Description

The **MrmRegisterNames** function registers a vector of names and associated values for access in MRM. The values can be callback functions, pointers to user-defined data, or any other values. The information provided is used to resolve symbolic references occurring in UID files to their run-time values. For callbacks, this information provides the procedure address required by the Motif Toolkit. For names used as identifiers in UIL, this information provides any run-time mapping the application needs.

register_list Specifies a list of name/value pairs for the names to be registered. Each name is a case-sensitive, NULL-terminated ASCII string. Each value is a 32-bit quantity, interpreted as a procedure address if the name is a callback function, and uninterpreted otherwise.

register_count Specifies the number of entries in *register_list*.

The names in the list are case-sensitive. The list can be either ordered or unordered.

Callback functions registered through **MrmRegisterNames** can be either regular or creation callbacks. Regular callbacks have declarations determined by Motif Toolkit and user requirements. Creation callbacks have the same format as any other callback:

void CallBackProc(*widget_id* **,** *tag* **,** *callback_data* **)**
  Widget **widget_id* **;**
  Opaque *tag* **;**
  XmAnyCallbackStruct **callback_data* **;**

widget_id Specifies the widget ID associated with the widget performing the callback (as in any callback function).

tag Specifies the tag value (as in any callback function).

callback_data Specifies a widget-specific data structure. This data structure has a minimum of two members: event and reason. The reason member is always set to **XmCRCreate**.

Note that the widget name and parent are available from the widget record accessible through *widget_id*.

Return Value

This function returns one of these status return constants:

MrmSUCCESS The function executed successfully.

MrmFAILURE Memory allocation failed.

Object

Purpose

The Object widget class

Synopsis

#include <Xm/Xm.h>

Description

Object is never instantiated. Its sole purpose is as a supporting superclass for other widget classes.

Classes

The class pointer is **objectClass**.

The class name is **Object**.

New Resources

The following table defines a set of widget resources used by the programmer to specify data. The programmer can also set the resource values for the inherited classes to set attributes for this widget. To reference a resource by name or by class in a .Xdefaults file, remove the **XmN** or

XmC prefix and use the remaining letters. To specify one of the defined values for a resource in a .Xdefaults file, remove the **Xm** prefix and use the remaining letters (in either lower case or upper case, but include any underscores between words). The codes in the access column indicate if the given resource can be set at creation time (**C**), set by using **XtSetValues** (**S**), retrieved by using **XtGetValues** (**G**), or is not applicable (**N/A**).

Object Resource Set		
Name **Class**	**Default** **Type**	**Access**
XmNdestroyCallback XmCCallback	NULL XtCallbackList	C

XmNdestroyCallback
Specifies a list of callbacks that is called when the gadget is destroyed.

OverrideShell

Purpose

The OverrideShell widget class

Synopsis

#include <Xm/Xm.h>
#include <X11/Shell.h>

Description

OverrideShell is used for shell windows that completely bypass the window manager, for example, PopupMenu shells.

Classes

OverrideShell inherits behavior and resources from **Core**, **Composite**, and **Shell**.

The class pointer is **overrideShellWidgetClass**.

The class name is **OverrideShell**.

New Resources

OverrideShell defines no new resources, but overrides the **XmNoverrideRedirect** and **XmNsaveUnder** resources in the **Shell** class.

Inherited Resources

OverrideShell inherits behavior and resources from the following superclasses. For a complete description of each resource, refer to the man page for that superclass.

The following table defines a set of widget resources used by the programmer to specify data. The programmer can also set the resource values for the inherited classes to set attributes for this widget. To reference a resource by name or by class in a .Xdefaults file, remove the **XmN** or **XmC** prefix and use the remaining letters. To specify one of the defined values for a resource in a .Xdefaults file, remove the **Xm** prefix and use the remaining letters (in either lowercase or uppercase, but include any underscores between words). The codes in the access column indicate if the given resource can be set at creation time (**C**), set by using **XtSetValues** (**S**), retrieved by using **XtGetValues** (**G**), or is not applicable (**N/A**).

Shell Resource Set		
Name **Class**	**Default** **Type**	**Access**
XmNallowShellResize XmCAllowShellResize	False Boolean	CSG
XmNancestorSensitive XmCSensitive	ShellAncestorSensitive Boolean	CSG
XmNcreatePopupChildProc XmCCreatePopupChildProc	NULL XmCreatePopupChildProc	CSG
XmNdepth XmCDepth	ShellDepth int	CSG
XmNgeometry XmCGeometry	NULL String	CSG
XmNoverrideRedirect XmCOverrideRedirect	True Boolean	CSG
XmNpopdownCallback XmCCallback	NULL XtCallbackList	C
XmNpopupCallback XmCCallback	NULL XtCallbackList	C
XmNsaveUnder XmCSaveUnder	True Boolean	CSG

Composite Resource Set		
Name **Class**	**Default** **Type**	**Access**
XmNinsertPosition XmCInsertPosition	NULL XmRFunction	CSG

Core Resource Set		
Name **Class**	**Default** **Type**	**Access**
XmNaccelerators XmCAccelerators	NULL XtTranslations	CSG
XmNancestorSensitive XmCSensitive	ShellAncestorSensitive Boolean	G
XmNbackground XmCBackground	White Pixel	CSG
XmNbackgroundPixmap XmCPixmap	XmUNSPECIFIED_PIXMAP Pixmap	CSG
XmNborderColor XmCBorderColor	Black Pixel	CSG
XmNborderPixmap XmCPixmap	XmUNSPECIFIED_PIXMAP Pixmap	CSG
XmNborderWidth XmCBorderWidth	1 Dimension	CSG
XmNcolormap XmCColormap	ShellColormap Colormap	CG
XmNdepth XmCDepth	ShellDepth int	CG
XmNdestroyCallback XmCCallback	NULL XtCallbackList	C
XmNheight XmCHeight	0 Dimension	CSG
XmNmappedWhenManaged XmCMappedWhenManaged	True Boolean	CSG
XmNscreen XmCScreen	XtCopyScreen Pointer	CG
XmNsensitive XmCSensitive	True Boolean	CSG

Name Class	Default Type	Access
XmNtranslations XmCTranslations	NULL XtTranslations	CSG
XmNwidth XmCWidth	0 Dimension	CSG
XmNx XmCPosition	0 Position	CSG
XmNy XmCPosition	0 Position	CSG

Related Information

Composite(3X), **Core(3X)**, and **Shell(3X)**.

RectObj

Purpose

The RectObj widget class

Synopsis

#include <Xm/Xm.h>

Description

RectObj is never instantiated. Its sole purpose is as a supporting superclass for other widget classes.

Classes

RectObj inherits behavior and a resource from **Object**.

The class pointer is **rectObjClass**.

The class name is **RectObj**.

New Resources

The following table defines a set of widget resources used by the programmer to specify data. The programmer can also set the resource values for the inherited classes to set attributes for this widget. To reference a resource by name or by class in a .Xdefaults file, remove the **XmN** or **XmC** prefix and use the remaining letters. To specify one of the defined values for a resource in a .Xdefaults file, remove the **Xm** prefix and use the remaining letters (in either lowercase or uppercase, but include any underscores between words). The codes in the access column indicate if the given resource can be set at creation time (**C**), set by using **XtSetValues** (**S**), retrieved by using **XtGetValues** (**G**), or is not applicable (**N/A**).

RectObj Resource Set		
Name **Class**	**Default** **Type**	**Access**
XmNancestorSensitive XmCSensitive	XtCopyFromParent Boolean	CSG
XmNborderWidth XmCBorderWidth	1 Dimension	CSG
XmNheight XmCHeight	0 Dimension	CSG
XmNsensitive XmCSensitive	True Boolean	CSG
XmNwidth XmCWidth	0 Dimension	CSG
XmNx XmCPosition	0 Position	CSG
XmNy XmCPosition	0 Position	CSG

XmNancestorSensitive
Specifies whether the immediate parent of the gadget receives input events. Use the function **XtSetSensitive** if you are changing the argument to preserve data integrity (see **XmNsensitive** below).

XmNborderWidth
Specifies the width of the border placed around the RectObj's rectangular display area.

XmNheight Specifies the height of the RectObj's rectangular display area.

XmNsensitive
Determines whether a RectObj receives input events. If a RectObj is sensitive, the parent dispatches to the gadget all keyboard, mouse button, motion, window enter/leave, and focus events. Insensitive gadgets do not receive these events. Use the function **XtSetSensitive** to change the sensitivity argument. If a parent widget has **XmNsensitive** set to False, the ancestor-sensitive flag of all its children is appropriately set.

XmNwidth Contains the width of the RectObj's rectangular display area.

XmNx
Contains the x-coordinate of the gadget's upper left-hand corner in relation to its parent's window.

XmNy
Contains the y-coordinate of the gadget's upper left-hand corner in relation to its parent's window.

Inherited Resources

RectObj inherits behavior and a resource from **Object**. For a description of this resource, refer to the **Object** man page.

Object Resource Set		
Name **Class**	**Default** **Type**	**Access**
XmNdestroyCallback XmCCallback	NULL XtCallbackList	C

Related Information

Object(3X).

Shell

Purpose

The Shell widget class

Synopsis

#include <Xm/Xm.h>
#include <X11/Shell.h>

Description

Shell is a top-level widget (with only one managed child) that encapsulates the interaction with the window manager.

Classes

Shell inherits behavior and resources from **Composite** and **Core**.

The class pointer is **shellWidgetClass**.

The class name is **Shell**.

New Resources

The following table defines a set of widget resources used by the programmer to specify data. The programmer can also set the resource values for the inherited classes to set attributes for this widget. To reference a resource by name or by class in a .Xdefaults file, remove the **XmN** or **XmC** prefix and use the remaining letters. To specify one of the defined values for a resource in a .Xdefaults file, remove the **Xm** prefix and use the remaining letters (in either lowercase or uppercase, but include any underscores between words). The codes in the access column indicate if the given resource can be set at creation time (**C**), set by using **XtSetValues** (**S**), retrieved by using **XtGetValues** (**G**), or is not applicable (**N/A**).

Shell Resource Set

Name Class	Default Type	Access
XmNallowShellResize XmCAllowShellResize	False Boolean	CSG
XmNcreatePopupChildProc XmCCreatePopupChildProc	NULL XmCreatePopupChildProc	CSG
XmNgeometry XmCGeometry	NULL String	CSG
XmNoverrideRedirect XmCOverrideRedirect	False Boolean	CSG
XmNpopdownCallback XmCCallback	NULL XtCallbackList	C
XmNpopupCallback XmCCallback	NULL XtCallbackList	C
XmNsaveUnder XmCSaveUnder	False Boolean	CSG

XmNallowShellResize

Specifies that if this resource is False, the Shell widget instance returns **XtGeometryNo** to all geometry requests from its children.

XmNcreatePopupChildProc

Specifies the pointer to a function which is called when the Shell widget instance is popped up by **XtPopup**.

XmNgeometry
Specifies the desired geometry for the widget instance. This resource is examined only when the widget instance is unrealized and the number of its managed children is changed. It is to change the values of the **XmNx**, **XmNy**, **XmNwidth**, and **XmNheight** resources.

XmNoverrideRedirect
Specifies this is True if the widget instance is a temporary window which should be ignored by the window manager. Applications and users should not normally alter this resource.

XmNpopdownCallback
Specifies a list of callbacks that is called when the widget instance is popped down by **XtPopdown**.

XmNpopupCallback
Specifies a list of callbacks that is called when the widget instance is popped up by **XtPopup**.

XmNsaveUnder
Specifies a True value if it is desirable to save the contents of the screen beneath this widget instance, avoiding expose events when the instance is unmapped. This is a hint, and an implementation may save contents whenever it desires, including always or never.

Inherited Resources

Shell inherits behavior and resources from the following superclass. For a complete description of each resource, refer to the man page for that superclass.

Composite Resource Set		
Name **Class**	**Default** **Type**	**Access**
XmNinsertPosition XmCInsertPosition	NULL XmRFunction	CSG

Core Resource Set		
Name **Class**	**Default** **Type**	**Access**
XmNaccelerators XmCAccelerators	NULL XtTranslations	CSG
XmNancestorSensitive XmCSensitive	ShellAncestorSensitive Boolean	G
XmNbackground XmCBackground	White Pixel	CSG
XmNbackgroundPixmap XmCPixmap	XmUNSPECIFIED_PIXMAP Pixmap	CSG
XmNborderColor XmCBorderColor	Black Pixel	CSG
XmNborderPixmap XmCPixmap	XmUNSPECIFIED_PIXMAP Pixmap	CSG
XmNborderWidth XmCBorderWidth	1 Dimension	CSG
XmNcolormap XmCColormap	ShellColormap Colormap	CG

Name Class	Default Type	Access
XmNdepth XmCDepth	ShellDepth int	CG
XmNdestroyCallback XmCCallback	NULL XtCallbackList	C
XmNheight XmCHeight	0 Dimension	CSG
XmNmappedWhenManaged XmCMappedWhenManaged	True Boolean	CSG
XmNscreen XmCScreen	XtCopyScreen Pointer	CG
XmNsensitive XmCSensitive	True Boolean	CSG
XmNtranslations XmCTranslations	NULL XtTranslations	CSG
XmNwidth XmCWidth	0 Dimension	CSG
XmNx XmCPosition	0 Position	CSG
XmNy XmCPosition	0 Position	CSG

Related Information

Composite(3X) and **Core(3X)**.

TopLevelShell

Purpose

The TopLevelShell widget class

Synopsis

#include <Xm/Xm.h>
#include <X11/Shell.h>

Description

TopLevelShell is used for normal top-level windows such as any additional top-level widgets an application needs.

Classes

TopLevelShell inherits behavior and resources from **Core**, **Composite**, **Shell**, **WMShell**, and **VendorShell**.

The class pointer is **topLevelShellWidgetClass**.

The class name is **TopLevelShell**.

New Resources

The following table defines a set of widget resources used by the programmer to specify data. The programmer can also set the resource values for the inherited classes to set attributes for this widget. To reference a resource by name or by class in a .Xdefaults file, remove the **XmN** or **XmC** prefix and use the remaining letters. To specify one of the defined values for a resource in a .Xdefaults file, remove the **Xm** prefix and use the remaining letters (in either lowercase or uppercase, but include any underscores between words). The codes in the access column indicate if the given resource can be set at creation time (**C**), set by using **XtSetValues** (**S**), retrieved by using **XtGetValues** (**G**), or is not applicable (**N/A**).

TopLevelShell Resource Set		
Name **Class**	**Default** **Type**	**Access**
XmNiconic XmCIconic	False Boolean	CSG
XmNiconName XmCIconName	NULL String	CSG

XmNiconic Specifies that if this is True when the widget instance is realized, the widget instance indicates to the window manager that the application wishes to start as an icon, irrespective of the **XtNinitialState** resource. This resource is examined by the Intrinsics only during a call to **XtRealize**; it is ignored at all other times.

XmNiconName
Specifies the short form of the application name to be displayed by the window manager when the application is iconified.

Inherited Resources

TopLevelShell inherits behavior and resources from the following superclasses. For a complete description of each resource, refer to the man page for that superclass.

VendorShell Resource Set		
Name **Class**	**Default** **Type**	**Access**
XmNdeleteResponse XmCDeleteResponse	XmDESTROY unsigned char	CSG
XmNkeyboardFocusPolicy XmCKeyboardFocusPolicy	XmEXPLICIT unsigned char	CSG
XmNmwmDecorations XmCMwmDecorations	-1 int	CSG
XmNmwmFunctions XmCMwmFunctions	-1 int	CSG
XmNmwmInputMode XmCMwmInputMode	-1 int	CSG
XmNmwmMenu XmCMwmMenu	NULL String	CSG
XmNshellUnitType XmCShellUnitType	XmPIXELS unsigned char	CSG

WMShell Resource Set		
Name **Class**	**Default** **Type**	**Access**
XmNheightInc XmCHeightInc	-1 int	CSG
XmNiconMask XmCIconMask	NULL Pixmap	CSG
XmNiconPixmap XmCIconPixmap	NULL Pixmap	CSG
XmNiconWindow XmCIconWindow	NULL Window	CSG
XmNiconX XmCIconX	-1 int	CSG
XmNiconY XmCIconY	-1 int	CSG
XmNinitialState XmCInitialState	1 int	CSG
XmNinput XmCInput	True Boolean	CSG
XmNmaxAspectX XmCMaxAspectX	-1 int	CSG
XmNmaxAspectY XmCMaxAspectY	-1 int	CSG
XmNmaxHeight XmCMaxHeight	-1 int	CSG
XmNmaxWidth XmCMaxWidth	-1 int	CSG
XmNminAspectX XmCMinAspectX	-1 int	CSG
XmNminAspectY XmCMinAspectY	-1 int	CSG

Name Class	Default Type	Access
XmNminHeight XmCMinHeight	-1 int	CSG
XmNminWidth XmCMinWidth	-1 int	CSG
XmNtitle XmCTitle	NULL char *	CSG
XmNtransient XmCTransient	False Boolean	CSG
XmNwaitForWm XmCWaitForWm	True Boolean	CSG
XmNwidthInc XmCWidthInc	-1 int	CSG
XmNwindowGroup XmCWindowGroup	None XID	CSG

Name Class	Default Type	Access
XmNwmTimeout XmCWmTimeout	fivesecond int	CSG

Shell Resource Set		
Name **Class**	**Default** **Type**	**Access**
XmNallowShellResize XmCAllowShellResize	False Boolean	CSG
XmNcreatePopupChildProc XmCCreatePopupChildProc	NULL XmCreatePopupChildProc	CSG
XmNgeometry XmCGeometry	NULL String	CSG
XmNoverrideRedirect XmCOverrideRedirect	False Boolean	CSG
XmNpopdownCallback XmCCallback	NULL XtCallbackList	C
XmNpopupCallback XmCCallback	NULL XtCallbackList	C
XmNsaveUnder XmCSaveUnder	False Boolean	CSG

Composite Resource Set		
Name **Class**	**Default** **Type**	**Access**
XmNinsertPosition XmCInsertPosition	NULL XmRFunction	CSG

Core Resource Set		
Name **Class**	**Default** **Type**	**Access**
XmNaccelerators XmCAccelerators	NULL XtTranslations	CSG
XmNancestorSensitive XmCSensitive	ShellAncestorSensitive Boolean	G
XmNbackground XmCBackground	White Pixel	CSG
XmNbackgroundPixmap XmCPixmap	XmUNSPECIFIED_PIXMAP Pixmap	CSG
XmNborderColor XmCBorderColor	Black Pixel	CSG
XmNborderPixmap XmCPixmap	XmUNSPECIFIED_PIXMAP Pixmap	CSG
XmNborderWidth XmCBorderWidth	1 Dimension	CSG
XmNcolormap XmCColormap	ShellColormap Colormap	CG
XmNdepth XmCDepth	ShellDepth int	CG
XmNdestroyCallback XmCCallback	NULL XtCallbackList	C
XmNheight XmCHeight	0 Dimension	CSG
XmNmappedWhenManaged XmCMappedWhenManaged	True Boolean	CSG
XmNscreen XmCScreen	XtCopyScreen Pointer	CG
XmNsensitive XmCSensitive	True Boolean	CSG

Name Class	Default Type	Access
XmNtranslations XmCTranslations	NULL XtTranslations	CSG
XmNwidth XmCWidth	0 Dimension	CSG
XmNx XmCPosition	0 Position	CSG
XmNy XmCPosition	0 Position	CSG

Related Information

Composite(3X), **Core(3X)**, **Shell(3X)**, **WMShell(3X)**, and **VendorShell(3X)**.

TransientShell

Purpose

The TransientShell widget class

Synopsis

#include <Xm/Xm.h>
#include <X11/Shell.h>

Description

TransientShell is used for shell windows that can be manipulated by the window manager but are not allowed to be iconified separately. For example, Dialog boxes make no sense without their associated application. They are iconified by the window manager only if the main application shell is iconified.

Classes

TransientShell inherits behavior and resources from **Core**, **Composite**, **Shell**, **WMShell**, and **VendorShell**.

The class pointer is **transientShellWidgetClass**.

The class name is **TransientShell**.

New Resources

TransientShell defines no new resources, but overrides the **XmNsaveUnder** resource in **Shell** and the **XmNtransient** resource in **WMShell**.

Inherited Resources

TransientShell inherits behavior and resources from the following superclasses. For a complete description of each resource, refer to the man page for that superclass.

The following table defines a set of widget resources used by the programmer to specify data. The programmer can also set the resource values for the inherited classes to set attributes for this widget. To reference a resource by name or by class in a .Xdefaults file, remove the **XmN** or **XmC** prefix and use the remaining letters. To specify one of the defined values for a resource in a .Xdefaults file, remove the **Xm** prefix and use the remaining letters (in either lowercase or uppercase, but include any underscores between words). The codes in the access column indicate if the given resource can be set at creation time (**C**), set by using **XtSetValues** (**S**), retrieved by using **XtGetValues** (**G**), or is not applicable (**N/A**).

VendorShell Resource Set		
Name **Class**	**Default** **Type**	**Access**
XmNdeleteResponse XmCDeleteResponse	XmDESTROY unsigned char	CSG
XmNkeyboardFocusPolicy XmCKeyboardFocusPolicy	XmEXPLICIT unsigned char	CSG
XmNmwmDecorations XmCMwmDecorations	-1 int	CSG
XmNmwmFunctions XmCMwmFunctions	-1 int	CSG
XmNmwmInputMode XmCMwmInputMode	-1 int	CSG
XmNmwmMenu XmCMwmMenu	NULL String	CSG
XmNshellUnitType XmCShellUnitType	XmPIXELS unsigned char	CSG

WMShell Resource Set		
Name **Class**	**Default** **Type**	**Access**
XmNheightInc XmCHeightInc	-1 int	CSG
XmNiconMask XmCIconMask	NULL Pixmap	CSG
XmNiconPixmap XmCIconPixmap	NULL Pixmap	CSG
XmNiconWindow XmCIconWindow	NULL Window	CSG
XmNiconX XmCIconX	-1 int	CSG
XmNiconY XmCIconY	-1 int	CSG
XmNinitialState XmCInitialState	1 int	CSG
XmNinput XmCInput	True Boolean	CSG
XmNmaxAspectX XmCMaxAspectX	-1 int	CSG
XmNmaxAspectY XmCMaxAspectY	-1 int	CSG
XmNmaxHeight XmCMaxHeight	-1 int	CSG
XmNmaxWidth XmCMaxWidth	-1 int	CSG
XmNminAspectX XmCMinAspectX	-1 int	CSG
XmNminAspectY XmCMinAspectY	-1 int	CSG

Name Class	Default Type	Access
XmNminHeight XmCMinHeight	-1 int	CSG
XmNminWidth XmCMinWidth	-1 int	CSG
XmNtitle XmCTitle	NULL char *	CSG
XmNtransient XmCTransient	False Boolean	CSG
XmNwaitForWm XmCWaitForWm	True Boolean	CSG
XmNwidthInc XmCWidthInc	-1 int	CSG
XmNwindowGroup XmCWindowGroup	None XID	CSG
XmNwmTimeout XmCWmTimeout	fivesecond int	CSG

Shell Resource Set		
Name **Class**	**Default** **Type**	**Access**
XmNallowShellResize XmCAllowShellResize	False Boolean	CSG
XmNcreatePopupChildProc XmCCreatePopupChildProc	NULL XmCreatePopupChildProc	CSG
XmNgeometry XmCGeometry	NULL String	CSG
XmNoverrideRedirect XmCOverrideRedirect	False Boolean	CSG
XmNpopdownCallback XmCCallback	NULL XtCallbackList	C
XmNpopupCallback XmCCallback	NULL XtCallbackList	C
XmNsaveUnder XmCSaveUnder	False Boolean	CSG

Composite Resource Set		
Name **Class**	**Default** **Type**	**Access**
XmNinsertPosition XmCInsertPosition	NULL XmRFunction	CSG

Core Resource Set		
Name **Class**	**Default** **Type**	**Access**
XmNaccelerators XmCAccelerators	NULL XtTranslations	CSG
XmNancestorSensitive XmCSensitive	ShellAncestorSensitive Boolean	G
XmNbackground XmCBackground	White Pixel	CSG
XmNbackgroundPixmap XmCPixmap	XmUNSPECIFIED_PIXMAP Pixmap	CSG
XmNborderColor XmCBorderColor	Black Pixel	CSG
XmNborderPixmap XmCPixmap	XmUNSPECIFIED_PIXMAP Pixmap	CSG
XmNborderWidth XmCBorderWidth	1 Dimension	CSG
XmNcolormap XmCColormap	ShellColormap Colormap	CG
XmNdepth XmCDepth	ShellDepth int	CG
XmNdestroyCallback XmCCallback	NULL XtCallbackList	C
XmNheight XmCHeight	0 Dimension	CSG
XmNmappedWhenManaged XmCMappedWhenManaged	True Boolean	CSG
XmNscreen XmCScreen	XtCopyScreen Pointer	CG
XmNsensitive XmCSensitive	True Boolean	CSG

Name Class	Default Type	Access
XmNtranslations XmCTranslations	NULL XtTranslations	CSG
XmNwidth XmCWidth	0 Dimension	CSG
XmNx XmCPosition	0 Position	CSG
XmNy XmCPosition	0 Position	CSG

Related Information

Composite(3X), **Core(3X)**, **Shell(3X)**, **VendorShell(3X)**, and **WMShell(3X)**.

Uil

Purpose

Invokes the UIL compiler from within an application

Synopsis

#include <uil/UilDef.h>
Uil_status_type Uil(*command_desc*, *compile_desc*, *message_cb*, *message_data*,
status_cb, *status_data*)
Uil_command_type **command_desc*;
Uil_compile_desc_type **compile_desc*;
Uil_continue_type (**message_cb*) ();
char **message_data*;
Uil_continue_type (**status_cb*) ();
char **status_data*;

Description

The **Uil** function provides a callable entry point for the UIL compiler. The **Uil** callable interface can be used to process a UIL source file and to generate UID files, as well as return a detailed description of the UIL source module in the form of a symbol table (parse tree).

command_desc	Specifies the **uil** command line.
compile_desc	Returns the results of the compilation.
message_cb	Specifies a callback function that is called when the compiler encounters errors in the UIL source.

message_data Specifies user data that is passed to the message callback function (message_cb). Note that this argument is not interpreted by UIL, and is used exclusively by the calling application.

status_cb Specifies a callback function that is called to allow X applications to service X events such as updating the screen. This function is called at various check points, which have been hard coded into the UIL compiler. The status_update_delay argument in command_desc specifies the number of check points to be passed before the status_cb function is invoked.

status_data Specifies user data that is passed to the status callback function (status_cb). Note that this argument is not interpreted by the UIL compiler, and is used exclusively by the calling application.

The data structures Uil_command_type and Uil_compile_desc_type are detailed below.

```
typedef struct Uil_command_type {
    char *source_file;
        /* single source to compile */
    char *resource_file; /* name of output file */
    char *listing_file; /* name of listing file */
    unsigned int *include_dir_count;
        /* number of dirs. in include_dir */
    char *((*include_dir) []);
        /* dir. to search for include files */
    unsigned listing_file_flag: 1;
        /* produce a listing */
    unsigned resource_file_flag: 1;
        /* generate UID output */
    unsigned machine_code_flag: 1;
        /* generate machine code */
    unsigned report_info_msg_flag: 1;
        /* report info messages */
    unsigned report_warn_msg_flag: 1;
```

```
        /* report warnings */
    unsigned parse_tree_flag: 1;
        /* generate parse tree */
    unsigned int status_update_delay;
        /* number of times a status point is */
        /* passed before calling status_cb */
        /* function 0 means called every time */
    };

    typedef struct Uil_compile_desc_type {
        unsigned int compiler_version;
            /* version number of compiler */
        unsigned int data_version;
            /* version number of structures */
        char *parse_tree_root; /* parse tree output */
        unsigned int message_count [Uil_k_max_status+1];
                /* array of severity counts /*
        };
```

Return Value

This function returns one of these status return constants:

Uil_k_success_status	The operation succeeded.
Uil_k_info_status	The operation succeeded, and an informational message is returned.
Uil_k_warning_status	The operation succeeded, and a warning message is returned.
Uil_k_error_status	The operation failed due to an error.
Uil_k_severe_status	The operation failed due to an error.

Related Information

UilDumpSymbolTable(3X), **uil(1X)**

UilDumpSymbolTable

Purpose

Dumps the contents of a named UIL symbol table to standard output.

Synopsis

#include <uil/UilDef.h>
void UilDumpSymbolTable (*root_ptr*)
    sym_root_entry_type **root_ptr*;

Description

The **UilDumpSymbolTable** function dumps the contents of a UIL symbol table pointer to standard output

root_ptr Specifies a pointer to the the symbol table root entry. This value can be taken from the **parse_tree_root** part the **Uil_compile_desc_type** data structure returned by **Uil**.

By following the link from the root entry, you can traverse the entire parse tree. Symbol table entries are in the following format:

hex.address
symbol.type
symbol.data
 prev.source.position
 source.position
 modification.record

Where:

hex.address — Specifies the hexadecimal address of this entry in the symbol table.

symbol.type — Specifies the type of this symbol table entry. Some possible types are **root**, **module**, **value**, **procedure**, and **widget**.

symbol.data — Specifies data for the symbol table entry. The data varies with the type of the entry. Often it contains pointers to other symbol table entries, or the actual data for the data type.

prev.source.position — Specifies the end point in the source code for the previous source item.

source.position — Specifies the range of positions in the source code for this symbol.

The exact data structures for each symbol type are defined in the include file **UilSymDef.h**. Note that this file is automatically included when an application includes the file **UilDef.h**.

Related Information

Uil(3X)

VendorShell

Purpose

The VendorShell widget class

Synopsis

#include <Xm/Xm.h>
#include <X11/Shell.h>

Description

VendorShell is a Motif widget class used as a supporting superclass for all shell classes that are visible to the window manager and that are not override redirect. It contains the resources that describe the MWM-specific look and feel. It also manages the MWM-specific communication needed by all VendorShell subclasses. See the **mwm** man page for more information.

Classes

VendorShell inherits behavior and resources from **Core**, **Composite**, **Shell**, and **WMShell** classes.

The class pointer is **vendorShellWidgetClass**.

The class name is **VendorShell**.

New Resources

The following table defines a set of widget resources used by the programmer to specify data. The programmer can also set the resource values for the inherited classes to set attributes for this widget. To reference a resource by name or by class in a .Xdefaults file, remove the **XmN** or **XmC** prefix and use the remaining letters. To specify one of the defined values for a resource in a .Xdefaults file, remove the **Xm** prefix and use the remaining letters (in either lowercase or uppercase, but include any underscores between words). The codes in the access column indicate if the given resource can be set at creation time (**C**), set by using **XtSetValues** (**S**), retrieved by using **XtGetValues** (**G**), or is not applicable (**N/A**).

VendorShell Resource Set		
Name **Class**	**Default** **Type**	**Access**
XmNdeleteResponse XmCDeleteResponse	XmDESTROY unsigned char	CSG
XmNkeyboardFocusPolicy XmCKeyboardFocusPolicy	XmEXPLICIT unsigned char	CSG
XmNmwmDecorations XmCMwmDecorations	-1 int	CSG
XmNmwmFunctions XmCMwmFunctions	-1 int	CSG
XmNmwmInputMode XmCMwmInputMode	-1 int	CSG
XmNmwmMenu XmCMwmMenu	NULL String	CSG
XmNshellUnitType XmCShellUnitType	XmPIXELS unsigned char	CSG

XmNkeyboardFocusPolicy

Determines allocation of keyboard focus within the widget hierarchy rooted at this shell. The X keyboard focus must be directed to somewhere in the hierarchy for this client-side focus management to take effect.

XmNdeleteResponse

Determines what action the shell takes in response to a **WM_DELETE_WINDOW** message. The setting can be one of three values: **XmDESTROY, XmUNMAP, and XmDO_NOTHING**. The resource is scanned, and the appropriate action is taken, after the **WM_DELETE_WINDOW** callback list (if any) that is registered with the Protocol manager has been called.

XmNmwmDecorations

Includes the decoration flags (specific decorations to add or remove from the window manager frame) for **MWM_HINTS**.

XmNmwmFunctions

Includes the function flags (specific window manager functions to include or exclude from the system menu) for **MWM_HINTS**.

XmNmwmInputMode

Includes the input mode flag (application modal or system modal input focus constraints) for **MWM_HINTS**.

XmNmwmMenu

Specifies the menu items that the Motif window manager should add to the end of the system menu. The string contains a list of items separated by **\n** with the following format:

label [mnemonic] [accelerator] function

If more than one item is specified, the items should be separated by a newline character.

XmNshellUnitType

Determines geometric resource interpretation. The following values are allowed:

- **XmPIXELS** — all values provided to the widget are treated as normal pixel values.
- **Xm100TH_MILLIMETERS** — all values provided to the widget are treated as 1/100 millimeter.
- **Xm1000TH_INCHES** — all values provided to the widget are treated as 1/1000 inch.
- **Xm100TH_POINTS** — all values provided to the widget are treated as 1/100 point. A point is a unit used in text processing applications and is defined as 1/72 inch.
- **Xm100TH_FONT_UNITS** — all values provided to the widget are treated as 1/100-font unit. The value used for the font unit is determined in one of two ways: The resource **XmNfont** can be used in a defaults file or on the command line; or, the standard command line options of **-fn** and **-font** can be used. The font unit value is taken as the **QUAD_WIDTH** property of the font. The function **XmSetFontUnits** allows applications to specify the font unit values.

Inherited Resources

VendorShell inherits behavior and resources from the following superclasses. For a complete description of each resource, refer to the man page for that superclass.

WMShell Resource Set		
Name **Class**	**Default** **Type**	**Access**
XmNheightInc XmCHeightInc	-1 int	CSG
XmNiconMask XmCIconMask	NULL Pixmap	CSG
XmNiconPixmap XmCIconPixmap	NULL Pixmap	CSG
XmNiconWindow XmCIconWindow	NULL Window	CSG
XmNiconX XmCIconX	-1 int	CSG
XmNiconY XmCIconY	-1 int	CSG
XmNinitialState XmCInitialState	1 int	CSG
XmNinput XmCInput	True Boolean	CSG
XmNmaxAspectX XmCMaxAspectX	-1 int	CSG
XmNmaxAspectY XmCMaxAspectY	-1 int	CSG
XmNmaxHeight XmCMaxHeight	-1 int	CSG
XmNmaxWidth XmCMaxWidth	-1 int	CSG
XmNminAspectX XmCMinAspectX	-1 int	CSG
XmNminAspectY XmCMinAspectY	-1 int	CSG

Name Class	Default Type	Access
XmNminHeight XmCMinHeight	-1 int	CSG
XmNminWidth XmCMinWidth	-1 int	CSG
XmNtitle XmCTitle	NULL char *	CSG
XmNtransient XmCTransient	False Boolean	CSG
XmNwaitForWm XmCWaitForWm	True Boolean	CSG
XmNwidthInc XmCWidthInc	-1 int	CSG
XmNwindowGroup XmCWindowGroup	None XID	CSG

VendorShell(3X)

Name Class	Default Type	Access
XmNwmTimeout XmCWmTimeout	fivesecond int	CSG

Shell Resource Set		
Name **Class**	**Default** **Type**	**Access**
XmNallowShellResize XmCAllowShellResize	False Boolean	CSG
XmNcreatePopupChildProc XmCCreatePopupChildProc	NULL XmCreatePopupChildProc	CSG
XmNgeometry XmCGeometry	NULL String	CSG
XmNoverrideRedirect XmCOverrideRedirect	False Boolean	CSG
XmNpopdownCallback XmCCallback	NULL XtCallbackList	C
XmNpopupCallback XmCCallback	NULL XtCallbackList	C
XmNsaveUnder XmCSaveUnder	False Boolean	CSG

Composite Resource Set		
Name **Class**	**Default** **Type**	**Access**
XmNinsertPosition XmCInsertPosition	NULL XmRFunction	CSG

Core Resource Set		
Name **Class**	**Default** **Type**	**Access**
XmNaccelerators XmCAccelerators	NULL XtTranslations	CSG
XmNancestorSensitive XmCSensitive	ShellAncestorSensitive Boolean	G
XmNbackground XmCBackground	White Pixel	CSG
XmNbackgroundPixmap XmCPixmap	XmUNSPECIFIED_PIXMAP Pixmap	CSG
XmNborderColor XmCBorderColor	Black Pixel	CSG
XmNborderPixmap XmCPixmap	XmUNSPECIFIED_PIXMAP Pixmap	CSG
XmNborderWidth XmCBorderWidth	1 Dimension	CSG
XmNcolormap XmCColormap	ShellColormap Colormap	CG
XmNdepth XmCDepth	ShellDepth int	CG
XmNdestroyCallback XmCCallback	NULL XtCallbackList	C
XmNheight XmCHeight	0 Dimension	CSG
XmNmappedWhenManaged XmCMappedWhenManaged	True Boolean	CSG
XmNscreen XmCScreen	XtCopyScreen Pointer	CG
XmNsensitive XmCSensitive	True Boolean	CSG

Name Class	Default Type	Access
XmNtranslations XmCTranslations	NULL XtTranslations	CSG
XmNwidth XmCWidth	0 Dimension	CSG
XmNx XmCPosition	0 Position	CSG
XmNy XmCPosition	0 Position	CSG

Related Information

Composite(3X), **Core(3X)**, **mwm(1X)**, **Shell(3X)**, **WMShell(3X)**, **XmActivateProtocol(3X)**, **XmActivateWMProtocol(3X)**, **XmAddProtocolCallback(3X)**, **XmAddWMProtocolCallback(3X)**, **XmAddProtocols(3X)**, **XmAddWMProtocols(3X)**, **XmDeactivateProtocol(3X)**, **XmDeactivateWMProtocol(3X)**, **XmGetAtomName(3X)**, **XmInternAtom(3X)**, **XmIsMotifWMRunning(3X)**, **XmRemoveProtocolCallback(3X)**, **XmRemoveWMProtocolCallback(3X)**, **XmRemoveProtocols(3X)**, **XmRemoveWMProtocols(3X)**, **XmSetProtocolHooks(3X)**, and **XmSetWMProtocolHooks(3X)**.

WMShell

Purpose

The WMShell widget class

Synopsis

#include <Xm/Xm.h>
#include <X11/Shell.h>

Description

WMShell is a top-level widget that encapsulates the interaction with the window manager.

Classes

WMShell inherits behavior and resources from **Core**, **Composite**, and **Shell** classes.

The class pointer is **wmShellWidgetClass**.

The class name is **WMShell**.

New Resources

The following table defines a set of widget resources used by the programmer to specify data. The programmer can also set the resource values for the inherited classes to set attributes for this widget. To reference a resource by name or by class in a .Xdefaults file, remove the **XmN** or **XmC** prefix and use the remaining letters. To specify one of the defined values for a resource in a .Xdefaults file, remove the **Xm** prefix and use the remaining letters (in either lowercase or uppercase, but include any underscores between words). The codes in the access column indicate if the given resource can be set at creation time (**C**), set by using **XtSetValues** (**S**), retrieved by using **XtGetValues** (**G**), or is not applicable (**N/A**).

WMShell Resource Set		
Name **Class**	**Default** **Type**	**Access**
XmNheightInc XmCHeightInc	-1 int	CSG
XmNiconMask XmCIconMask	NULL Pixmap	CSG
XmNiconPixmap XmCIconPixmap	NULL Pixmap	CSG
XmNiconWindow XmCIconWindow	NULL Window	CSG
XmNiconX XmCIconX	-1 int	CSG
XmNiconY XmCIconY	-1 int	CSG
XmNinitialState XmCInitialState	1 int	CSG
XmNinput XmCInput	True Boolean	CSG
XmNmaxAspectX XmCMaxAspectX	-1 int	CSG
XmNmaxAspectY XmCMaxAspectY	-1 int	CSG
XmNmaxHeight XmCMaxHeight	-1 int	CSG
XmNmaxWidth XmCMaxWidth	-1 int	CSG
XmNminAspectX XmCMinAspectX	-1 int	CSG
XmNminAspectY XmCMinAspectY	-1 int	CSG

Name Class	Default Type	Access
XmNminHeight XmCMinHeight	-1 int	CSG
XmNminWidth XmCMinWidth	-1 int	CSG
XmNtitle XmCTitle	NULL char *	CSG
XmNtransient XmCTransient	False Boolean	CSG
XmNwaitForWm XmCWaitForWm	True Boolean	CSG
XmNwidthInc XmCWidthInc	-1 int	CSG
XmNwindowGroup XmCWindowGroup	None XID	CSG
XmNwmTimeout XmCWmTimeout	fivesecond int	CSG

XmNheightInc
Specifies allowable height for the widget instance by the window manager if this resource is defined. The sizes are **XmNminimumHeight** plus an integral multiple of **XmNheightInc**, subject to the **XmNmaximumHeight** resource.

XmNiconMask
Specifies a bitmap that could be used by the window manager to clip the **XmNiconPixmap** bitmap to make the icon nonrectangular.

XmNiconPixmap
Specifies a bitmap that could be used by the window manager as the application's icon.

XmNiconWindow
Specifies the ID of a window that could be used by the window manager as the application's icon.

XmNiconX Specifies a suitable place to put the application's icon; this is a hint to the window manager in root window coordinates. Since the window manager controls icon placement policy, this may be ignored.

XmNiconY Specifies a suitable place to put the application's icon; this is a hint to the window manager in root window coordinates. Since the window manager controls icon placement policy, this may be ignored.

XmNinitialState
Specifies the state in which the application wishes the widget instance to start. It must be one of the constants **NormalState** or **IconicState**.

XmNinput Gives the application's input model for this widget and its descendants.

XmNmaxAspectX
Gives the maximum aspect ratio (X/Y) that the application wishes the widget instance to have.

XmNmaxAspectY
Gives the maximum aspect ratio (X/Y) that the application wishes the widget instance to have.

XmNmaxHeight
Gives the maximum height that the application wishes the widget instance to have.

XmNmaxWidth
Gives the maximum width that the application wishes the widget instance to have.

XmNminAspectX
Gives the minimum aspect ratio (X/Y) that the application wishes the widget instance to have.

XmNminAspectY
Gives the minimum aspect ratio (X/Y) that the application wishes the widget instance to have.

XmNminHeight
Specifies the minimum height that the application wishes the widget instance to have.

XmNminWidth
Specifies the minimum width that the application wishes the widget instance to have.

XmNtitle Specifies the application name to be displayed by the window manager.

XmNtransient
Specifies a Boolean value that is True if the widget instance is a transient window and should be treated more lightly by the window manager. Applications and users should not normally alter this resource.

XmNwaitForWm
Specifies that the Intrinsics waits the length of time given by the **XmNwmTimeout** resource for the window manager to respond to certain actions when True, before assuming that there is no window manager present. This resource is altered by the Intrinsics as it receives, or fails to receive, responses from the window manager.

XmNwidthInc
Specifies allowable width for the widget instance by the window manager if this resource is defined. The sizes are **XmNminimumWidth** plus an integral multiple of **XmNwidthInc**, subject to the **XmNmaximumWidth** resource.

XmNwindowGroup

Specifies the ID of a window for which this widget instance is associated; a window manager may treat all windows in a group in some way, for example, by always moving or iconifying them together.

If this is set on a Shell widget instance that has no parent but has pop-up children, this resource is set to the same value on all pop-up children of the widget instance, all pop-up children of these children, and so on. See also the **XmNtransient** resource.

XmNwmTimeout

Specifies the length of time that the Intrinsics waits for the window manager to respond to certain actions before assuming that there is no window manager present.

Inherited Resources

WMShell inherits behavior and resources from the following superclasses. For a complete description of each resource, refer to the man page for that superclass.

Shell Resource Set		
Name **Class**	**Default** **Type**	**Access**
XmNallowShellResize XmCAllowShellResize	False Boolean	CSG
XmNcreatePopupChildProc XmCCreatePopupChildProc	NULL XmCreatePopupChildProc	CSG
XmNgeometry XmCGeometry	NULL String	CSG
XmNoverrideRedirect XmCOverrideRedirect	False Boolean	CSG
XmNpopdownCallback XmCCallback	NULL XtCallbackList	C
XmNpopupCallback XmCCallback	NULL XtCallbackList	C
XmNsaveUnder XmCSaveUnder	False Boolean	CSG

Composite Resource Set		
Name **Class**	**Default** **Type**	**Access**
XmNinsertPosition XmCInsertPosition	NULL XmRFunction	CSG

Core Resource Set		
Name **Class**	**Default** **Type**	**Access**
XmNaccelerators XmCAccelerators	NULL XtTranslations	CSG
XmNancestorSensitive XmCSensitive	ShellAncestorSensitive Boolean	G
XmNbackground XmCBackground	White Pixel	CSG
XmNbackgroundPixmap XmCPixmap	XmUNSPECIFIED_PIXMAP Pixmap	CSG
XmNborderColor XmCBorderColor	Black Pixel	CSG
XmNborderPixmap XmCPixmap	XmUNSPECIFIED_PIXMAP Pixmap	CSG
XmNborderWidth XmCBorderWidth	1 Dimension	CSG
XmNcolormap XmCColormap	ShellColormap Colormap	CG
XmNdepth XmCDepth	ShellDepth int	CG
XmNdestroyCallback XmCCallback	NULL XtCallbackList	C
XmNheight XmCHeight	0 Dimension	CSG
XmNmappedWhenManaged XmCMappedWhenManaged	True Boolean	CSG
XmNscreen XmCScreen	XtCopyScreen Pointer	CG
XmNsensitive XmCSensitive	True Boolean	CSG

Name Class	Default Type	Access
XmNtranslations XmCTranslations	NULL XtTranslations	CSG
XmNwidth XmCWidth	0 Dimension	CSG
XmNx XmCPosition	0 Position	CSG
XmNy XmCPosition	0 Position	CSG

Related Information

Composite(3X), **Core(3X)**, and **Shell(3X)**.

WindowObj

Purpose

The WindowObj widget class

Synopsis

#include <Xm/Xm.h>

Description

WindowObj is an internal Xt Intrinsic widget class. It is a synonym of Core class that provides no added functionality but was necessary for implementation reasons.

Classes

WindowObj inherits behavior and resources from **Object** and **RectObj** classes.

The class pointer is **windowObjClass**.

The class name is **WindowObj**.

Related Information

Core(3X), **Object(3X)**, **RectObj(3X)**.

XmActivateProtocol

Purpose

A VendorShell function that activates a protocol.

Synopsis

#include <Xm/Xm.h>
#include <X11/Protocols.h>

void XmActivateProtocol (*shell, property, protocol*)
    Widget *shell*;
    Atom *property*;
    Atom *protocol*;

void XmActivateWMProtocol (*shell, protocol*)
    Widget *shell*;
    Atom *protocol*;

Description

XmActivateProtocol activates a protocol. It updates the handlers and the *property* if the *shell* is realized. It is sometimes useful to allow a protocol's state information (callback lists, etc.) to persist, even though the client may choose to temporarily resign from the interaction. This is supported by allowing a *protocol* to be in one of two states: active or inactive. If the *protocol* is active and the *shell* is realized, the *property* contains the *protocol* **Atom**. If the *protocol* is inactive, the **Atom** is not present in the *property*.

XmActivateWMProtocol is a convenience interface. It calls **XmActivateProtocol** with the property value set to the atom returned by interning **WM_PROTOCOLS**.

shell Specifies the widget with which the protocol property is associated.

property Specifies the protocol property.

protocol Specifies the protocol **Atom** (or an **int** type cast to **Atom**).

For a complete definition of VendorShell and its associated resources, see **VendorShell(3X)**.

Related Information

VendorShell(3X), **XmActivateWMProtocol(3X)** and **XmInternAtom(3X)**.

XmActivateWMProtocol

Purpose

A VendorShell convenience interface that activates a protocol.

Synopsis

```
#include <Xm/Xm.h>
#include <X11/Protocols.h>

void XmActivateWMProtocol (shell, protocol)
        Widget      shell;
        Atom        protocol;
```

Description

XmActivateWMProtocol is a convenience interface. It calls **XmActivateProtocol** with the property value set to the atom returned by interning **WM_PROTOCOLS**.

shell Specifies the widget with which the protocol property is associated.

protocol Specifies the protocol **Atom** (or an **int** type cast to **Atom**).

For a complete definition of VendorShell and its associated resources, see **VendorShell(3X)**.

Related Information

VendorShell(3X), **XmActivateProtocol(3X)**, and **XmInternAtom(3X)**.

XmAddProtocolCallback

Purpose

A VendorShell function that adds client callbacks for a protocol.

Synopsis

```
#include <Xm/Xm.h>
#include <X11/Protocols.h>

void XmAddProtocolCallback (shell, property, protocol, callback, closure)
        Widget          shell;
        Atom            property;
        Atom            protocol;
        XtCallbackProc  callback;
        caddr_t         closure;

void XmAddWMProtocolCallback (shell, protocol, callback, closure)
        Widget          shell;
        Atom            protocol;
        XtCallbackProc  callback;
        caddr_t         closure;
```

Description

XmAddProtocolCallback adds client callbacks for a protocol. It checks if the protocol is registered, and if it is not, calls **XmAddProtocols**. It then adds the callback to the internal list. These callbacks are called when the corresponding client message is received.

XmAddWMProtocolCallback is a convenience interface. It calls **XmAddProtocolCallback** with the property value set to the atom returned by interning **WM_PROTOCOLS**.

shell Specifies the widget with which the protocol property is associated.

property Specifies the protocol property.

protocol Specifies the protocol **Atom** (or an **int** type cast to **Atom**).

callback Specifies the procedure to call when a protocol message is received.

closure Specifies the client data to be passed to the callback when it is invoked.

For a complete definition of VendorShell and its associated resources, see **VendorShell(3X)**.

Related Information

VendorShell(3X), **XmAddProtocols(3X)**, **XmAddWMProtocolCallback(3X)**, and **XmInternAtom(3X)**.

XmAddProtocols

Purpose

A VendorShell function that adds the protocols to the protocol manager and allocates the internal tables.

Synopsis

#include <Xm/Xm.h>
#include <X11/Protocols.h>

void XmAddProtocols (*shell, property, protocols, num_protocols*)

Widget	*shell*;
Atom	*property*;
Atom	* *protocols*;
Cardinal	*num_protocols*;

void XmAddWMProtocols (*shell, protocols, num_protocols*)

Widget	*shell*;
Atom	* *protocols*;
Cardinal	*num_protocols*;

Description

XmAddProtocols adds the protocols to the protocol manager and allocates the internal tables.

XmAddWMProtocols is a convenience interface. It calls **XmAddProtocols** with the property value set to the atom returned by interning **WM_PROTOCOLS**.

shell Specifies the widget with which the protocol property is associated.

property Specifies the protocol property.

protocols Specifies the protocol **Atoms** (or **int** types cast to **Atom**).

num_protocols Specifies the number of elements in *protocols*.

For a complete definition of VendorShell and its associated resources, see **VendorShell(3X)**.

Related Information

VendorShell(3X), **XmAddWMProtocols(3X)**, and **XmInternAtom(3X)**.

XmAddTabGroup

Purpose

A function that adds a manager or a primitive widget to the list of tab groups.

Synopsis

```
#include <Xm/Xm.h>

void XmAddTabGroup (tab_group)
        Widget        tab_group;
```

Description

AddTabGroup adds a manager or primitive widget to the list of tab groups associated with a particular widget hierarchy. Each instance of the List widget, each multiline Text edit widget, each OptionMenu widget, and each ScrollBar widget must be placed within its own tab group; do not place other widgets in these groups. This allows the arrow keys to function in their normal fashion within these widgets.

When using the keyboard to traverse through a widget hierarchy, primitive or manager widgets are grouped together into what are known as **tab groups**. Any manager or primitive widget can be a tab group. Within a tab group, move the focus to the next widget within the tab group by using the arrow keys. To move to another tab group, enter the Tab, or <Shift>Tab.

tab_group Specifies the manager or primitive widget ID.

Related Information

XmManager(3X), **XmPrimitive(3X)** and **XmRemoveTabGroup(3X)**.

XmAddWMProtocolCallback

Purpose

A VendorShell convenience interface that adds client callbacks for a protocol.

Synopsis

```
#include <Xm/Xm.h>
#include <X11/Protocols.h>

void XmAddWMProtocolCallback (shell, protocol, callback, closure)
        Widget          shell;
        Atom            protocol;
        XtCallbackProccallback;
        caddr_t         closure;
```

Description

XmAddWMProtocolCallback is a convenience interface. It calls **XmAddProtocolCallback** with the property value set to the atom returned by interning **WM_PROTOCOLS**.

shell Specifies the widget with which the protocol property is associated.

protocol Specifies the protocol **Atom** (or an **int** type cast to **Atom**).

callback Specifies the procedure to call when a protocol message is received.

closure Specifies the client data to be passed to the callback when it is invoked.

For a complete definition of VendorShell and its associated resources, see **VendorShell(3X)**.

Related Information

VendorShell(3X), **XmAddProtocolCallback(3X)**, **XmInternAtom(3X)**.

XmAddWMProtocols

Purpose

A VendorShell convenience interface that adds the protocols to the protocol manager and allocates the internal tables.

Synopsis

```
#include <Xm/Xm.h>
#include <X11/Protocols.h>

void XmAddWMProtocols (shell, protocols, num_protocols)
        Widget      shell;
        Atom        * protocols;
        Cardinal    num_protocols;
```

Description

XmAddWMProtocols is a convenience interface. It calls **XmAddProtocols** with the property value set to the atom returned by interning **WM_PROTOCOLS**.

shell — Specifies the widget with which the protocol property is associated.

protocols — Specifies the protocol **Atoms** (or **int** types cast to **Atom**).

num_protocols — Specifies the number of elements in *protocols*.

For a complete definition of VendorShell and its associated resources, see **VendorShell(3X)**.

Related Information

VendorShell(3X), **XmAddProtocols(3X)**, and **XmInternAtom(3X)**.

XmArrowButton

Purpose

The ArrowButton widget class

Synopsis

#include <Xm/ArrowB.h>

Description

ArrowButton consists of a directional arrow surrounded by a border shadow. When it is selected, the shadow moves to give the appearance that the ArrowButton has been pressed in. When the ArrowButton is unselected, the shadow moves to give the appearance that the ArrowButton is released, or out.

Classes

ArrowButton inherits behavior and resources from **Core** and **XmPrimitive** classes.

The class pointer is **xmArrowButtonWidgetClass**.

The class name is **XmArrowButton**.

New Resources

The following table defines a set of widget resources used by the programmer to specify data. The programmer can also set the resource values for the inherited classes to set attributes for this widget. To reference a resource by name or by class in a .Xdefaults file, remove the **XmN** or **XmC** prefix and use the remaining letters. To specify one of the defined values for a resource in a .Xdefaults file, remove the **Xm** prefix and use the remaining letters (in either lowercase or uppercase, but include any underscores between words). The codes in the access column indicate if the given resource can be set at creation time (**C**), set by using **XtSetValues** (**S**), retrieved by using **XtGetValues** (**G**), or is not applicable (**N/A**).

XmArrowButton Resource Set		
Name **Class**	**Default** **Type**	**Access**
XmNactivateCallback XmCCallback	NULL XtCallbackList	C
XmNarmCallback XmCCallback	NULL XtCallbackList	C
XmNarrowDirection XmCArrowDirection	XmARROW_UP unsigned char	CSG
XmNdisarmCallback XmCCallback	NULL XtCallbackList	C

XmNactivateCallback

Specifies a list of callbacks that is called when the ArrowButton is activated. To activate the button, press and release mouse button 1 while the pointer is inside the ArrowButton widget. Activating the ArrowButton also disarms it. The reason sent by this callback is **XmCR_ACTIVATE**.

XmNarmCallback

Specifies a list of callbacks that is called when the ArrowButton is armed. To arm this widget, press mouse button 1 while the pointer is inside the ArrowButton. The reason sent by this callback is **XmCR_ARM**.

XmNarrowDirection

Sets the arrow direction. The following are values for this resource:

- **XmARROW_UP**.
- **XmARROW_DOWN**.
- **XmARROW_LEFT**.
- **XmARROW_RIGHT**.

XmNdisarmCallback

Specifies a list of callbacks that is called when the ArrowButton is disarmed. To disarm this widget, press and release mouse button 1 while the pointer is inside the ArrowButton. The reason sent by this callback is **XmCR_DISARM**.

Inherited Resources

ArrowButton inherits behavior and resources from the following superclasses. For a complete description of each resource, refer to the man page for that superclass.

XmPrimitive Resource Set		
Name **Class**	**Default** **Type**	**Access**
XmNbottomShadowColor XmCForeground	dynamic Pixel	CSG
XmNbottomShadowPixmap XmCBottomShadowPixmap	XmUNSPECIFIED_PIXMAP Pixmap	CSG
XmNforeground XmCForeground	dynamic Pixel	CSG
XmNhelpCallback XmCCallback	NULL XtCallbackList	C
XmNhighlightColor XmCForeground	Black Pixel	CSG
XmNhighlightOnEnter XmCHighlightOnEnter	False Boolean	CSG
XmNhighlightPixmap XmCHighlightPixmap	dynamic Pixmap	CSG
XmNhighlightThickness XmCHighlightThickness	0 short	CSG
XmNshadowThickness XmCShadowThickness	2 short	CSG
XmNtopShadowColor XmCBackground	dynamic Pixel	CSG
XmNtopShadowPixmap XmCTopShadowPixmap	XmUNSPECIFIED_PIXMAP Pixmap	CSG
XmNtraversalOn XmCTraversalOn	False Boolean	CSG
XmNunitType XmCUnitType	XmPIXELS unsigned char	CSG
XmNuserData XmCUserData	NULL caddr_t	CSG

Core Resource Set		
Name **Class**	**Default** **Type**	**Access**
XmNaccelerators XmCAccelerators	NULL XtTranslations	CSG
XmNancestorSensitive XmCSensitive	True Boolean	G
XmNbackground XmCBackground	dynamic Pixel	CSG
XmNbackgroundPixmap XmCPixmap	XmUNSPECIFIED_PIXMAP Pixmap	CSG
XmNborderColor XmCBorderColor	Black Pixel	CSG
XmNborderPixmap XmCPixmap	XmUNSPECIFIED_PIXMAP Pixmap	CSG
XmNborderWidth XmCBorderWidth	0 Dimension	CSG
XmNcolormap XmCColormap	XtCopyFromParent Colormap	CG
XmNdepth XmCDepth	XtCopyFromParent int	CG
XmNdestroyCallback XmCCallback	NULL XtCallbackList	C
XmNheight XmCHeight	0 Dimension	CSG
XmNmappedWhenManaged XmCMappedWhenManaged	True Boolean	CSG
XmNscreen XmCScreen	XtCopyScreen Pointer	CG
XmNsensitive XmCSensitive	True Boolean	CSG

Name Class	Default Type	Access
XmNtranslations XmCTranslations	NULL XtTranslations	CSG
XmNwidth XmCWidth	0 Dimension	CSG
XmNx XmCPosition	0 Position	CSG
XmNy XmCPosition	0 Position	CSG

Callback Information

The following structure is returned with each callback:

```
typedef struct
{
    int         reason;
    XEvent      * event;
} XmAnyCallbackStruct;
```

reason Indicates why the callback was invoked.

event Points to the **XEvent** that triggered the callback. This event is NULL for the **XmNactivateCallback** if the callback was triggered when Primitive's resource **XmNtraversalOn** was True or if the callback was accessed through the **ArmAndActivate** action routine.

Behavior

<Btn1Down>:
This action causes the arrow to be armed, and the shadow to be drawn in the selected state. The callbacks for **XmNarmCallback** are called.

<Btn1Up>:
If the mouse button release occurs when the pointer is within the ArrowButton, the arrow shadows are redrawn in the unselected state. The callbacks for **XmNactivateCallback** are called, followed by callbacks for **XmNdisarmCallback**.

If the mouse button release occurs when the pointer is outside the ArrowButton, the callbacks for **XmNdisarmCallback** are called.

<Leave Window>:
If the mouse button is pressed and the cursor leaves the widget's window, the arrow shadow is redrawn in its unselected state.

<Enter Window>:
If the mouse button is pressed and the cursor leaves and re-enters the widget's window, the arrow shadow is drawn in the same manner as when the button was first armed.

Default Translations

<Btn1Down>:	**Arm()**
<Btn1Up>:	**Activate()**
	Disarm()
<Key>Return:	**ArmAndActivate()**
<Key>Space:	**ArmAndActivate()**
<EnterWindow>:	**Enter()**
<LeaveWindow>:	**Leave()**

Keyboard Traversal

For information on keyboard traversal, see the man page for **XmPrimitive(3X)** and its sections on behavior and default translations.

Related Information

Core(3X), **XmCreateArrowButton(3X)**, and **XmPrimitive(3X)**.

XmArrowButtonGadget

Purpose

The ArrowButtonGadget widget class

Synopsis

#include <Xm/ArrowBG.h>

Description

ArrowButtonGadget consists of a directional arrow surrounded by a border shadow. When it is selected, the shadow moves to give the appearance that the ArrowButtonGadget has been pressed in. When it is unselected, the shadow moves to give the appearance that the button is released, or out.

Classes

ArrowButtonGadget inherits behavior and resources from **Object**, **RectObj**, and **XmGadget** classes.

The class pointer is **xmArrowButtonGadgetClass**.

The class name is **XmArrowButtonGadget**.

New Resources

The following table defines a set of widget resources used by the programmer to specify data. The programmer can also set the resource values for the inherited classes to set attributes for this widget. To reference a resource by name or by class in a .Xdefaults file, remove the **XmN** or **XmC** prefix and use the remaining letters. To specify one of the defined values for a resource in a .Xdefaults file, remove the **Xm** prefix and use the remaining letters (in either lowercase or uppercase, but include any underscores between words). The codes in the access column indicate if the given resource can be set at creation time (**C**), set by using **XtSetValues** (**S**), retrieved by using **XtGetValues** (**G**), or is not applicable (**N/A**).

ArrowButtonGadget Resource Set		
Name **Class**	**Default** **Type**	**Access**
XmNactivateCallback XmCCallback	NULL XtCallbackList	C
XmNarmCallback XmCCallback	NULL XtCallbackList	C
XmNarrowDirection XmCArrowDirection	XmARROW_UP int	CSG
XmNdisarmCallback XmCCallback	NULL XtCallbackList	C

XmNactivateCallback

Specifies a list of callbacks that is called when the ArrowButtonGadget is activated. To activate the button, press and release mouse button 1 while the pointer is inside the ArrowButtonGadget. Activating the ArrowButtonGadget also disarms it. The reason sent by this callback is **XmCR_ACTIVATE**.

XmNarmCallback

Specifies a list of callbacks that is called when the ArrowButtonGadget is armed. To arm this widget, press mouse button 1 while the pointer is inside the ArrowButtonGadget. The reason sent by this callback is **XmCR_ARM**.

XmNarrowDirection
Sets the arrow direction. The values for this resource are:

- **XmARROW_UP**.
- **XmARROW_DOWN**.
- **XmARROW_LEFT**.
- **XmARROW_RIGHT**.

XmNdisarmCallback
Specifies a list of callbacks that is called when the ArrowButtonGadget is disarmed. To disarm this widget, press and release mouse button one while the pointer is inside the ArrowButtonGadget. The reason sent by this callback is **XmCR_DISARM**.

Inherited Resources

ArrowButtonGadget inherits behavior and resources from the following superclasses. For a complete description of each resource, refer to the man page for that superclass.

XmGadget Resource Set		
Name **Class**	**Default** **Type**	**Access**
XmNhelpCallback XmCCallback	NULL XtCallbackList	C
XmNhighlightOnEnter XmCHighlightOnEnter	False Boolean	CSG
XmNhighlightThickness XmCHighlightThickness	0 short	CSG
XmNshadowThickness XmCShadowThickness	2 short	CSG
XmNtraversalOn XmCTraversalOn	False Boolean	CSG
XmNunitType XmCUnitType	XmPIXELS unsigned char	CSG
XmNuserData XmCUserData	NULL caddr_t	CSG

RectObj Resource Set		
Name **Class**	**Default** **Type**	**Access**
XmNancestorSensitive XmCSensitive	XtCopyFromParent Boolean	CSG
XmNborderWidth XmCBorderWidth	0 Dimension	CSG
XmNheight XmCHeight	0 Dimension	CSG
XmNsensitive XmCSensitive	True Boolean	CSG
XmNwidth XmCWidth	0 Dimension	CSG
XmNx XmCPosition	0 Position	CSG
XmNy XmCPosition	0 Position	CSG

Object Resource Set		
Name **Class**	**Default** **Type**	**Access**
XmNdestroyCallback XmCCallback	NULL XtCallbackList	C

Callback Information

The following structure is returned with each callback:

```
typedef struct
{
    int         reason;
    XEvent      * event;
} XmAnyCallbackStruct;
```

reason Indicates why the callback was invoked.

event Points to the **XEvent** that triggered the callback. This event is NULL for the **XmNactivateCallback** if the callback was triggered when Primitive's resource **XmNtraversalOn** was True or if the callback was accessed through the **ArmAndActivate** action routine.

Behavior

<Btn1Down>:
This action causes the arrow to be armed, and the shadow to be drawn in the selected state. The callbacks for **XmNarmCallback** are called.

<Btn1Up> :
If the mouse-button release occurs when the pointer is within the ArrowButtonGadget, the arrow shadows are redrawn in the unselected state. The callbacks for **XmNactivateCallback** are called, followed by callbacks for **XmNdisarmCallback**.

If the mouse-button release occurs when the pointer is outside the ArrowButtonGadget, the callbacks for **XmNdisarmCallback** are called.

<Leave Window>:
If the mouse button is pressed and the cursor leaves the widget's window, the arrow shadow is redrawn in its unselected state.

<Enter Window>:
If the mouse button is pressed and the cursor leaves and re-enters the widget's window, the arrow shadow is drawn in the same manner as when the button was first armed.

Keyboard Traversal

For information on keyboard traversal, see the man page for **XmGadget(3X)** and its sections on behavior and default translations.

Related Information

Object(3X), **RectObj(3X)**, **XmCreateArrowButtonGadget(3X)**, and **XmGadget(3X)**.

XmBulletinBoard

Purpose

The BulletinBoard widget class

Synopsis

#include <Xm/BulletinB.h>

Description

BulletinBoard is a composite widget that provides simple geometry management for children widgets. It does not force positioning on its children, but can be set to reject geometry requests that result in overlapping children. BulletinBoard is the base widget for most dialog widgets and is also used as a general container widget.

Modal and modeless dialogs are implemented as collections of widgets that include a DialogShell, a BulletinBoard (or subclass) child of the shell, and various dialog components (buttons, labels, etc.) that are children of BulletinBoard. BulletinBoard defines callbacks useful for dialogs (focus, map, unmap), which are available for application use. If its parent is a DialogShell, BulletinBoard passes title and input mode (based on dialog style) information to the parent, which is responsible for appropriate communication with the window manager.

Classes

BulletinBoard inherits behavior and resources from **Core**, **Composite**, **Constraint**, and **XmManager** classes.

The class pointer is **xmBulletinBoardWidgetClass**.

The class name is **XmBulletinBoard**.

New Resources

The following table defines a set of widget resources used by the programmer to specify data. The programmer can also set the resource values for the inherited classes to set attributes for this widget. To reference a resource by name or by class in a .Xdefaults file, remove the **XmN** or **XmC** prefix and use the remaining letters. To specify one of the defined values for a resource in a .Xdefaults file, remove the **Xm** prefix and use the remaining letters (in either lowercase or uppercase, but include any underscores between words). The codes in the access column indicate if the given resource can be set at creation time (**C**), set by using **XtSetValues** (**S**), retrieved by using **XtGetValues** (**G**), or is not applicable (**N/A**).

XmBulletinBoard Resource Set		
Name **Class**	**Default** **Type**	**Access**
XmNallowOverlap XmCAllowOverlap	True Boolean	CSG
XmNautoUnmanage XmCAutoUnmanage	True Boolean	CSG
XmNbuttonFontList XmCButtonFontList	NULL XmFontList	CSG
XmNcancelButton XmCWidget	NULL Widget	SG
XmNdefaultButton XmCWidget	NULL Widget	SG
XmNdefaultPosition XmCDefaultPosition	True Boolean	CSG
XmNdialogStyle XmCDialogStyle	dynamic unsigned char	CSG
XmNdialogTitle XmCXmString	NULL XmString	CSG
XmNfocusCallback XmCCallback	NULL XtCallbackList	C
XmNlabelFontList XmCLabelFontList	NULL XmFontList	CSG
XmNmapCallback XmCCallback	NULL XtCallbackList	C
XmNmarginHeight XmCMarginHeight	10 short	CSG
XmNmarginWidth XmCMarginWidth	10 short	CSG
XmNnoResize XmCNoResize	False Boolean	CSG

Name Class	Default Type	Access
XmNresizePolicy XmCResizePolicy	XmRESIZE_ANY unsigned char	CSG
XmNshadowType XmCShadowType	XmSHADOW_OUT unsigned char	CSG
XmNstringDirection XmCStringDirection	XmSTRING_DIRECTION_L_TO_R XmStringDirection	CSG
XmNtextFontList XmCTextFontList	NULL XmFontList	CSG
XmNtextTranslations XmCTranslations	NULL XtTranslations	C
XmNunmapCallback XmCCallback	NULL XtCallbackList	C

XmNallowOverlap

Controls the policy for overlapping children widgets. If True, BulletinBoard allows geometry requests that result in overlapping children.

XmNautoUnmanage

Controls whether or not BulletinBoard is automatically unmanaged after a button is activated. If True, BulletinBoard adds a callback to button children (PushButtons, PushButtonGadgets, and DrawnButtons) that unmanages the BulletinBoard when a button is activated; and, the unmap callbacks are called if the parent of the BulletinBoard is a DialogShell. If False, the BulletinBoard is not automatically unmanaged.

XmNbuttonFontList

Specifies the font list used for BulletinBoard's button children (PushButtons, PushButtonGadgets, ToggleButtons, and ToggleButtonGadgets). If NULL, the **XmNtextFontList** is used for buttons.

XmNcancelButton

Specifies the widget ID of the **Cancel** button. BulletinBoard's subclasses, which define a **Cancel** button, set this resource. BulletinBoard does not directly provide any behavior for that button.

XmNdefaultButton

Specifies the widget ID of the default button. BulletinBoard's subclasses, which define a default button, set this resource. BulletinBoard defines translations and installs accelerators that activate that button when the Return key is pressed.

XmNdefaultPosition

Controls whether or not the BulletinBoard is automatically positioned by its parent. If True, and the parent of the BulletinBoard is a DialogShell, the BulletinBoard is centered within or around the parent of the DialogShell when the BulletinBoard is mapped and managed. If False, the BulletinBoard is not automatically positioned.

XmNdialogStyle

Indicates the dialog style associated with BulletinBoard. If the parent of BulletinBoard is a DialogShell, the parent is configured according to this resource and DialogShell sets the **XmNinputMode** of VendorShell accordingly. Possible values for this resource include the following:

- **XmDIALOG_SYSTEM_MODAL** — used for dialogs that must be responded to before any other interaction in any application
- **XmDIALOG_APPLICATION_MODAL** — used for dialogs that must be responded to before some other interactions in the same application
- **XmDIALOG_MODELESS** — used for dialogs that do not interrupt interaction of any application
- **XmDIALOG_WORK_AREA** — used for non-dialog BulletinBoard widgets (parent is not a subclass of DialogShell)

XmNdialogTitle
Specifies the dialog title. If this resource is not NULL, and the parent of the BulletinBoard is a subclass of WMShell, BulletinBoard sets the **XmNtitle** of its parent to the value of this resource.

XmNfocusCallback
Specifies the list of callbacks that is called when the BulletinBoard widget or one of its descendants accepts the input focus. The callback reason is **XmCR_FOCUS**.

XmNlabelFontList
Specifies the font list used for BulletinBoard's Label children (Labels and LabelGadgets). If NULL, **XmNtextFontList** is used for labels also.

XmNmapCallback
Specifies the list of callbacks that is called only when the parent of the BulletinBoard is a DialogShell; in which case, this callback list is invoked when the BulletinBoard widget is mapped. The callback reason is **XmCR_MAP**.

XmNmarginHeight
Specifies the minimum spacing in pixels between the top or bottom edge of BulletinBoard and any child widget.

XmNmarginWidth
Specifies the minimum spacing in pixels between the left or right edge of BulletinBoard and any child widget.

XmNnoResize
Controls whether or not resize controls are included in the window manager frame around the dialog. If set to True, MWM does not include resize controls in the window manager frame containing the DialogShell or TopLevelShell parent of the BulletinBoard. If set to False, the window manager frame does include resize controls. The preferred way to manipulate the set of controls provided by MWM is to specify values for the MWM resources provided by VendorShell.

XmNresizePolicy

Controls the policy for resizing BulletinBoard widgets. Possible values include the following:

- **XmRESIZE_NONE** — fixed size
- **XmRESIZE_ANY** — shrink or grow as needed
- **XmRESIZE_GROW** — grow only

XmNshadowType

Describes the shadow drawing style for BulletinBoard. This resource can have the following values:

- **XmSHADOW_IN** — draws the BulletinBoard shadow so that it appears inset. This means that the bottom shadow visuals and top shadow visuals are reversed.
- **XmSHADOW_OUT** — draws the BulletinBoard shadow so that it appears outset
- **XmSHADOW_ETCHED_IN** — draws the BulletinBoard shadow using a double line giving the effect of a line etched into the window, similar to the Separator widget
- **XmSHADOW_ETCHED_OUT** — draws the BulletinBoard shadow using a double line giving the effect of a line coming out of the window, similar to the Separator widget

BulletinBoard widgets draw shadows just within their borders if **XmNshadowThickness** is greater than zero. If the parent of a BulletinBoard widget is a DialogShell, BulletinBoard dynamically changes the default for **XmNshadowThickness** from 0 to 1.

XmNstringDirection

Specifies the initial rendering direction for text within a dialog. BulletinBoard's subclasses, such as MessageBox and SelectionBox, which create **XmString** components, such as LabelGadgets, PushButtonGadgets, and Lists, set **XmNstringDirection** of these components based on the value of this resource. BulletinBoard does not directly provide any behavior for this resource.

XmNtextFontList

Specifies the font list used for BulletinBoard's Text children. If there is no **XmNbuttonFontList**, this resource is used for buttons; and, if there is no **XmNlabelFontList**, this resource is used for labels also.

XmNtextTranslations

Adds translations to any Text widget or Text widget subclass that is added as a child of BulletinBoard.

XmNunmapCallback

Specifies the list of callbacks that is called only when the parent of the BulletinBoard is a DialogShell; in which case, this callback list is invoked when the BulletinBoard widget is unmapped. The callback reason is **XmCR_UNMAP**.

Inherited Resources

BulletinBoard inherits behavior and resources from the following superclasses. For a complete description of each resource, refer to the man page for that superclass.

XmManager Resource Set		
Name **Class**	**Default** **Type**	**Access**
XmNbottomShadowColor XmCForeground	dynamic Pixel	CSG
XmNbottomShadowPixmap XmCBottomShadowPixmap	XmUNSPECIFIED_PIXMAP Pixmap	CSG
XmNforeground XmCForeground	dynamic Pixel	CSG
XmNhelpCallback XmCCallback	NULL XtCallbackList	C
XmNhighlightColor XmCForeground	Black Pixel	CSG
XmNhighlightPixmap XmCHighlightPixmap	dynamic Pixmap	CSG
XmNshadowThickness XmCShadowThickness	dynamic short	CSG
XmNtopShadowColor XmCBackground	dynamic Pixel	CSG
XmNtopShadowPixmap XmCTopShadowPixmap	XmUNSPECIFIED_PIXMAP Pixmap	CSG
XmNunitType XmCUnitType	XmPIXELS unsigned char	CSG
XmNuserData XmCUserData	NULL caddr_t	CSG

Composite Resource Set		
Name **Class**	**Default** **Type**	**Access**
XmNinsertPosition XmCInsertPosition	NULL XmRFunction	CSG

Core Resource Set		
Name **Class**	**Default** **Type**	**Access**
XmNaccelerators XmCAccelerators	NULL XtTranslations	CSG
XmNancestorSensitive XmCSensitive	True Boolean	G
XmNbackground XmCBackground	dynamic Pixel	CSG
XmNbackgroundPixmap XmCPixmap	XmUNSPECIFIED_PIXMAP Pixmap	CSG
XmNborderColor XmCBorderColor	Black Pixel	CSG
XmNborderPixmap XmCPixmap	XmUNSPECIFIED_PIXMAP Pixmap	CSG
XmNborderWidth XmCBorderWidth	0 Dimension	CSG

Name **Class**	**Default** **Type**	**Access**
XmNcolormap XmCColormap	XtCopyFromParent Colormap	CG
XmNdepth XmCDepth	XtCopyFromParent int	CG
XmNdestroyCallback XmCCallback	NULL XtCallbackList	C
XmNheight XmCHeight	0 Dimension	CSG
XmNmappedWhenManaged XmCMappedWhenManaged	True Boolean	CSG
XmNscreen XmCScreen	XtCopyScreen Pointer	CG
XmNsensitive XmCSensitive	True Boolean	CSG
XmNtranslations XmCTranslations	NULL XtTranslations	CSG
XmNwidth XmCWidth	0 Dimension	CSG
XmNx XmCPosition	0 Position	CSG
XmNy XmCPosition	0 Position	CSG

Callback Information

The following structure is returned with each callback.

typedef struct
{
  int *reason*;
  XEvent * *event*;
} **XmAnyCallbackStruct;**

reason Indicates why the callback was invoked.

event Points to the **XEvent** that triggered the callback.

Behavior

BulletinBoard behavior is summarized below.

<Cancel Button Activated>:
When the **Cancel** button is pressed, the activate callbacks of the **Cancel** button are called.

<Default Button Activated> or **<Key>Return**:
When the default button or Return key is pressed, the activate callbacks of the default button are called.

<Help Button Activated> or **<Key>F1**:
When the **Help** button or **Function key 1** is pressed, the callbacks for **XmNhelpCallback** are called.

<FocusIn>: When a **FocusIn** *event* is generated on the widget window, the callbacks for **XmNfocusCallback** are called.

<MapWindow>:
When a BulletinBoard, which is the child of a DialogShell, is mapped, the callbacks for **XmNmapCallback** are invoked. When a BulletinBoard that is not the child of a DialogShell is mapped, the callbacks are not invoked.

<UnmapWindow>:
When a BulletinBoard that is the child of a DialogShell is unmapped, the callbacks for **XmNunmapCallback** are invoked. When a BulletinBoard that is not the child of a DialogShell is unmapped, the callbacks are not invoked.

Default Translations

The following are the default translations defined for BulletinBoard widgets:

```
<EnterWindow>:  Enter()
<FocusIn>:      FocusIn()
<Btn1Down>:     Arm()
<Btn1Up>:       Activate()
<Key>F1:        Help()
<Key>Return:    Return()
<Key>KP_Enter:  Return()
```

Default Accelerators

The following are the default accelerator translations that are added to descendants of a BulletinBoard if the parent of the BulletinBoard is a DialogShell:

#override	
<Key>F1:	**Help()**
<Key>Return:	**Return()**
<Key>KP_Enter:	**Return()**

Keyboard Traversal

By default, if the parent of a BulletinBoard widget is a DialogShell, BulletinBoard uses the Return key for activating the default button and installs accelerators on all descendant widgets to make this possible. These accelerators disable the normal keyboard traversal behavior of the Return key. This traversal behavior may be restored (and the default button behavior disabled) by replacing BulletinBoard's default accelerators with an alternative set of translations that do not specify the Return action. For more information on keyboard traversal, see the man page for **XmManager(3X)** and its sections on behavior and default translations.

Related Information

Composite(3X), **Constraint(3X)**, **Core(3X)**, **XmCreateBulletinBoard(3X)**, **XmCreateBulletinBoardDialog(3X)**, **XmDialogShell(3X)**, **and XmManager(3X).**

XmCascadeButton

Purpose

The CascadeButton widget class

Synopsis

#include <Xm/CascadeB.h>

Description

CascadeButton links two MenuPanes or a MenuBar to a MenuPane.

It is used in menu systems and must have a RowColumn parent with its **XmNrowColumnType** resource set to **XmMENU_BAR**, **XmMENU_POPUP** or **XmMENU_PULLDOWN**.

It is the only widget that can have a Pulldown MenuPane attached to it as a submenu. The submenu is displayed when this widget is activated within a MenuBar, a PopupMenu, or a PulldownMenu. Its visuals can include a label or pixmap and a cascading indicator when it is in a Popup or Pulldown MenuPane; or, it can include only a label or a pixmap when it is in a MenuBar.

The default behavior associated with a CascadeButton depends on the type of menu system in which it resides. By default, mouse button 1 controls the behavior of the CascadeButton if it resides in a PulldownMenu or a MenuBar; and, mouse button 3 controls the behavior of the CascadeButton if it resides in a PopupMenu. The actual mouse button used is determined by its RowColumn parent.

A CascadeButton's visuals differ from most other button gadgets. When the button becomes armed, its visuals change from a 2-D to a 3-D look, and it displays the submenu that has been attached to it. If no submenu is attached, it simply changes its visuals.

When a CascadeButton within a Pulldown or Popup MenuPane is armed as the result of the user moving the mouse pointer into the widget, it does not immediately display its submenu. Instead, it waits a short amount of time to see if the arming was temporary (that is, the user was simply passing through the widget), or whether the user really wanted the submenu posted. This time delay is configurable via **XmNmappingDelay**.

CascadeButton provides a single mechanism for activating the widget from the keyboard. This mechanism is referred to as a keyboard mnemonic. If a mnemonic has been specified for the widget, the user may activate the CascadeButton by simply typing the mnemonic while the CascadeButton is visible. If the CascadeButton is in a MenuBar, the **meta** key must be pressed with the mnemonic. Mnemonics are typically used to interact with a menu via the keyboard interface.

If in a Pulldown or Popup MenuPane and there is a submenu attached, the **XmNmarginBottom**, **XmNmarginRight**, and **XmNmarginTop** resources enlarge to accommodate **XmNcascaadePixmap**. **XmNmarginWidth** defaults to 6 if this resource is in a MenuBar; otherwise, it takes Label's default, which is 2.

Classes

CascadeButton inherits behavior and resources from **Core**, **XmPrimitive**, and **XmLabel** classes.

The class pointer is **xmCascadeButtonWidgetClass**.

The class name is **XmCascadeButton**.

New Resources

The following table defines a set of widget resources used by the programmer to specify data. The programmer can also set the resource values for the inherited classes to set attributes for this widget. To reference a resource by name or by class in a .Xdefaults file, remove the **XmN** or **XmC** prefix and use the remaining letters. To specify one of the defined values for a resource in a .Xdefaults file, remove the **Xm** prefix and use the remaining letters (in either lowercase or uppercase, but include any underscores between words). The codes in the access column indicate if the given resource can be set at creation time (**C**), set by using **XtSetValues** (**S**), retrieved by using **XtGetValues** (**G**), or is not applicable (**N/A**).

XmCascadeButton Resource Set		
Name **Class**	**Default** **Type**	**Access**
XmNactivateCallback XmCCallback	NULL XtCallbackList	C
XmNcascadePixmap XmCPixmap	"menu-cascade" Pixmap	CSG
XmNcascadingCallback XmCCallback	NULL XtCallbackList	C
XmNmappingDelay XmCMappingDelay	100 int	CSG
XmNsubMenuId XmCMenuWidget	0 Widget	CSG

XmNactivateCallback

Specifies the list of callbacks that is called when the user activates the CascadeButton widget, and there is no submenu attached to pop up. The activation occurs by releasing a mouse button or by typing the mnemonic associated with the widget. The specific mouse button depends on information in the RowColumn parent. The reason sent by the callback is **XmCR_ACTIVATE**.

XmNcascadePixmap
Specifies the cascade pixmap displayed on the right end of the widget when a CascadeButton is used within a Popup or Pulldown MenuPane and a submenu is attached. The Label class resources **XmNmarginRight**, **XmNmarginTop**, and **XmNmarginBottom** may be modified to ensure that room is left for the cascade pixmap. The default cascade pixmap is an arrow pointing to the right.

XmNcascadingCallback
Specifies the list of callbacks that is called just prior to the mapping of the submenu associated with CascadeButton. The reason sent by the callback is **XmCR_CASCADING**.

XmNmappingDelay
Specifies the amount of time, in milliseconds, between when a CascadeButton becomes armed and when it maps its submenu. This delay is used only when the widget is within a Popup or Pulldown MenuPane.

XmNsubMenuId
Specifies the widget ID for the Pulldown MenuPane to be associated with this CascadeButton. The specified MenuPane is displayed when the CascadeButton becomes armed. The MenuPane must have been created with the appropriate parentage depending on the type of menu used. See **XmCreateMenuBar(3X)**, **XmCreatePulldownMenu(3X)**, and **XmCreatePopupMenu(3X)** for more information on the menu systems.

Inherited Resources

CascadeButton inherits behavior and resources from the following superclasses. For a complete description of each resource, refer to the man page for that superclass.

XmLabel Resource Set		
Name **Class**	**Default** **Type**	**Access**
XmNaccelerator XmCAccelerator	NULL String	CSG
XmNacceleratorText XmCAcceleratorText	NULL XmString	CSG
XmNalignment XmCAlignment	XmALIGNMENT_CENTER unsigned char	CSG
XmNfontList XmCFontList	"Fixed" XmFontList	CSG
XmNlabelInsensitivePixmap XmCLabelInsensitivePixmap	XmUNSPECIFIED_PIXMAP Pixmap	CSG
XmNlabelPixmap XmCPixmap	XmUNSPECIFIED_PIXMAP Pixmap	CSG
XmNlabelString XmCXmString	NULL XmString	CSG
XmNlabelType XmCLabelType	XmSTRING unsigned char	CSG
XmNmarginBottom XmCMarginBottom	dynamic short	CSG
XmNmarginHeight XmCMarginHeight	2 short	CSG
XmNmarginLeft XmCMarginLeft	0 short	CSG
XmNmarginRight XmCMarginRight	dynamic short	CSG
XmNmarginTop XmCMarginTop	dynamic short	CSG
XmNmarginWidth XmCMarginWidth	dynamic short	CSG

Name Class	Default Type	Access
XmNmnemonic XmCMnemonic	'\0' char	CSG
XmNrecomputeSize XmCRecomputeSize	True Boolean	CSG
XmNstringDirection XmCStringDirection	XmSTRING_DIRECTION_L_TO_R XmStringDirection	CSG

XmPrimitive Resource Set		
Name **Class**	**Default** **Type**	**Access**
XmNbottomShadowColor XmCForeground	dynamic Pixel	CSG
XmNbottomShadowPixmap XmCBottomShadowPixmap	XmUNSPECIFIED_PIXMAP Pixmap	CSG
XmNforeground XmCForeground	dynamic Pixel	CSG
XmNhelpCallback XmCCallback	NULL XtCallbackList	C
XmNhighlightColor XmCForeground	Black Pixel	CSG
XmNhighlightOnEnter XmCHighlightOnEnter	False Boolean	CSG
XmNhighlightPixmap XmCHighlightPixmap	dynamic Pixmap	CSG
XmNhighlightThickness XmCHighlightThickness	0 short	CSG
XmNshadowThickness XmCShadowThickness	2 short	CSG
XmNtopShadowColor XmCBackground	dynamic Pixel	CSG
XmNtopShadowPixmap XmCTopShadowPixmap	XmUNSPECIFIED_PIXMAP Pixmap	CSG
XmNtraversalOn XmCTraversalOn	False Boolean	CSG
XmNunitType XmCUnitType	XmPIXELS unsigned char	CSG
XmNuserData XmCUserData	NULL caddr_t	CSG

Core Resource Set		
Name **Class**	**Default** **Type**	**Access**
XmNaccelerators XmCAccelerators	NULL XtTranslations	CSG
XmNancestorSensitive XmCSensitive	True Boolean	G
XmNbackground XmCBackground	dynamic Pixel	CSG
XmNbackgroundPixmap XmCPixmap	XmUNSPECIFIED_PIXMAP Pixmap	CSG
XmNborderColor XmCBorderColor	Black Pixel	CSG
XmNborderPixmap XmCPixmap	XmUNSPECIFIED_PIXMAP Pixmap	CSG
XmNborderWidth XmCBorderWidth	0 Dimension	CSG
XmNcolormap XmCColormap	XtCopyFromParent Colormap	CG
XmNdepth XmCDepth	XtCopyFromParent int	CG
XmNdestroyCallback XmCCallback	NULL XtCallbackList	C
XmNheight XmCHeight	0 Dimension	CSG
XmNmappedWhenManaged XmCMappedWhenManaged	True Boolean	CSG
XmNscreen XmCScreen	XtCopyScreen Pointer	CG
XmNsensitive XmCSensitive	True Boolean	CSG

Name Class	Default Type	Access
XmNtranslations XmCTranslations	NULL XtTranslations	CSG
XmNwidth XmCWidth	0 Dimension	CSG
XmNx XmCPosition	0 Position	CSG
XmNy XmCPosition	0 Position	CSG

Callback Information

The following structure is returned with each callback:

```
typedef struct
{
    int         reason;
    XEvent      * event;
} XmAnyCallbackStruct;
```

reason Indicates why the callback was invoked.

event Points to the **XEvent** that triggered the callback or is NULL if this callback was not triggered due to an **XEvent**.

Behavior

The default behavior associated with a CascadeButton widget depends on whether the button is part of a PopupMenu system or a PulldownMenu system. The RowColumn parent determines the mouse button that is used through its **XmNrowColumnType** and **XmNwhichButton** resources.

Default PopupMenu System

Btn3Down<EnterWindow>:
This action arms the CascadeButton and posts the associated submenu after a short delay.

Btn3Down<LeaveWindow>:
The action that takes place depends on whether the mouse pointer has moved into the submenu associated with this CascadeButton. If it has, this event is ignored; if not, the CascadeButton is disarmed and its submenu unposted.

<Btn3Up>:
This action posts the submenu attached to the CascadeButton and enables keyboard traversal within the menu. If the CascadeButton does not have a submenu attached, this event activates the CascadeButton and unposts the menu.

<Btn3Down>:
This action disables traversal for the menu and returns the user to drag mode in which the menu is manipulated using the mouse. The submenu associated with this CascadeButton is posted.

<Key>Return:
This event posts the submenu attached to the CascadeButton if keyboard traversal is enabled in the menu. If the CascadeButton does not have a submenu attached, this event activates the CascadeButton and unposts the menu.

Default MenuBar

<Btn1Down>:
This event arms both the CascadeButton and the MenuBar and posts the associated submenu. If the menu is already active, this event disables traversal for the menu and returns the user to the mode where the menu is manipulated using the mouse.

Btn1Down<EnterWindow>:
This event unposts any visible MenuPanes if they are associated with a different MenuBar entry, arms the CascadeButton, and posts the associated submenu.

Btn1Down<LeaveWindow>:
This event disarms the CascadeButton if the submenu associated with it is not currently posted or if there is no submenu associated with this CascadeButton. Otherwise, this event is ignored.

<Btn1Up>:
This event posts the submenu attached to the CascadeButton and enables keyboard traversal within the menu. If the CascadeButton does not have a submenu attached, this event activates the CascadeButton and unposts the menu.

<Key>Return:
This event posts the submenu attached to the CascadeButton if keyboard traversal is enabled in the menu. If the CascadeButton does not have a submenu attached, the CascadeButton is activated, and unposts the menu.

Default PulldownMenu System from a MenuBar

Btn1Down<EnterWindow>:
This event arms the CascadeButton widget, and after a short delay, posts the associated submenu.

Btn1Down<LeaveWindow>:
The event is ignored if the mouse pointer has moved into the submenu. In all other cases, the CascadeButton is disarmed and its submenu unposted.

<Btn1Up>:
This event posts the submenu attached to the CascadeButton and enables keyboard traversal within the menu. If the CascadeButton does not have a submenu attached, this event selects the CascadeButton and unposts the menu.

<Btn1Down>:
This event disables traversal for the menu and returns the user to the drag mode. The submenu associated with this CascadeButton is posted.

<Key>Return:
This event posts the submenu attached to the CascadeButton if keyboard traversal is enabled in the menu. If the CascadeButton does not have a submenu attached, this event activates the CascadeButton and unposts the menu.

Default Translations

The following are default translations for CascadeButton in a MenuBar:

```
<BtnDown>:         MenuBarSelect()
<EnterWindow>:     MenuBarEnter()
<LeaveWindow>:     MenuBarLeave()
<BtnUp>:           DoSelect()
<Key>Return:       KeySelect()
<Key>Escape:       CleanupMenuBar()
```

Default translations for CascadeButton in a Popup or Pulldown MenuPane are:

<BtnDown>:	**StartDrag()**
<EnterWindow>:	**DelayedArm()**
<LeaveWindow>:	**CheckDisarm()**
<BtnUp>:	**DoSelect()**
<Key>Return:	**KeySelect()**
<Key>Escape:	**MenuShellPopdownDone()**

Keyboard Traversal

The keyboard traversal translations are listed below:

<Unmap>:	**Unmap()**
<FocusOut>:	**FocusOut()**
<FocusIn>:	**FocusIn()**
<Key>space:	**Noop()**
<Key>Left:	**MenuTraverseLeft()**
<Key>Right:	**MenuTraverseRight()**
<Key>Up:	**MenuTraverseUp()**
<Key>Down:	**MenuTraverseDown()**
<Key>Home:	**Noop()**

Related Information

Core(3X), XmCascadeButtonHighlight(3X), XmCreateCascadeButton(3X), XmCreateMenuBar(3X), XmCreatePulldownMenu(3X), XmCreatePopupMenu(3X), XmLabel(3X), XmPrimitive(3X), and XmRowColumn(3X).

XmCascadeButtonGadget

Purpose

The CascadeButtonGadget widget class

Synopsis

#include <Xm/CascadeBG.h>

Description

CascadeButtonGadget links two MenuPanes or an OptionMenu to a MenuPane.

It is used in menu systems and must have a RowColumn parent with its **XmNrowColumnType** resource set to **XmMENU_POPUP**, **XmMENU_PULLDOWN**, or **XmMENU_OPTION**.

It is the only gadget that can have a Pulldown MenuPane attached to it as a submenu. The submenu is displayed when this gadget is activated within a PopupMenu, a PulldownMenu, or an OptionMenu. Its visuals can include a label or pixmap and a cascading indicator when it is in a Popup or Pulldown MenuPane; or it can include only a label or a pixmap when it is in an OptionMenu.

The default behavior associated with a CascadeButtonGadget depends on the type of menu system in which it resides. By default, mouse button 1 controls the behavior of the CascadeButtonGadget if it resides in a PulldownMenu or an OptionMenu; and, mouse button 3 controls the behavior of the CascadeButtonGadget if it resides in a PopupMenu. The actual mouse button used is determined by its RowColumn parent.

A CascadeButtonGadget's visuals differ from most other button gadgets. When the button becomes armed, its visuals change from a 2-D to a 3-D look, and it displays the submenu that has been attached to it. If no submenu is attached, it simply changes its visuals.

When a CascadeButtonGadget within a Pulldown or Popup MenuPane is armed as the result of the user moving the mouse pointer into the gadget, it does not immediately display its submenu. Instead, it waits a short time to see if the arming was temporary (that is, the user was simply passing through the gadget), or the user really wanted the submenu posted. This delay is configurable via **XmNmappingDelay**.

CascadeButtonGadget provides a single mechanism for activating the gadget from the keyboard. This mechanism is referred to as a keyboard mnemonic. If a mnemonic has been specified for the gadget, the user may activate it by simply typing the mnemonic while the CascadeButtonGadget is visible. Mnemonics are typically used to interact with a menu via the keyboard.

If a CascadeButtonGadget is in a Pulldown or Popup MenuPane and there is a submenu attached, the **XmNmarginBottom**, **XmNmarginRight**, and **XmNmarginTop** resources enlarge to accommodate **XmNcascadePixmap**.

Classes

CascadeButtonGadget inherits behavior and resources from **Object**, **RectObj**, **XmGadget**, and **XmLabelGadget** classes.

The class pointer is **xmCascadeButtonGadgetClass**.

The class name is **XmCascadeButtonGadget**.

New Resources

The following table defines a set of widget resources used by the programmer to specify data. The programmer can also set the resource values for the inherited classes to set attributes for this widget. To reference a resource by name or by class in a .Xdefaults file, remove the **XmN** or

XmC prefix and use the remaining letters. To specify one of the defined values for a resource in a .Xdefaults file, remove the **Xm** prefix and use the remaining letters (in either lowercase or uppercase, but include any underscores between words). The codes in the access column indicate if the given resource can be set at creation time (**C**), set by using **XtSetValues** (**S**), retrieved by using **XtGetValues** (**G**), or is not applicable (**N/A**).

XmCascadeButtonGadget		
Name **Class**	**Default** **Type**	**Access**
XmNactivateCallback XmCCallback	NULL XtCallbackList	C
XmNcascadePixmap XmCPixmap	"menu_cascade" Pixmap	CSG
XmNcascadingCallback XmCCallback	NULL XtCallbackList	C
XmNmappingDelay XmCMappingDelay	100 int	CSG
XmNsubMenuId XmCMenuWidget	0 Widget	CSG

XmNactivateCallback

Specifies the list of callbacks that is called when the user activates the CascadeButtonGadget, and there is no submenu attached to pop up. The activation occurs by releasing a mouse button or by typing the mnemonic associated with the gadget. The specific mouse button depends on information in the RowColumn parent. The reason sent by the callback is **XmCR_ACTIVATE**.

XmNcascadePixmap

Specifies the cascade pixmap displayed on the right end of the gadget when a CascadeButtonGadget is used within a Popup or Pulldown MenuPane and a submenu is attached. The LabelGadget class resources **XmNmarginRight**, **XmNmarginTop**, and **XmNmarginBottom** may be modified to ensure that room is left for the cascade pixmap. The default cascade pixmap is an arrow pointing to the right.

XmNcascadingCallback
Specifies the list of callbacks that is called just prior to the mapping of the submenu associated with the CascadeButtonGadget. The reason sent by the callback is **XmCR_CASCADING**.

XmNmappingDelay
Specifies the amount of time, in milliseconds, between when a CascadeButtonGadget becomes armed and when it maps its submenu. This delay is used only when the gadget is within a Popup or Pulldown MenuPane.

XmNsubMenuId
Specifies the widget ID for the Pulldown MenuPane to be associated with this CascadeButtonGadget. The specified MenuPane is displayed when the CascadeButtonGadget becomes armed. The MenuPane must have been created with the appropriate parentage depending on the type of menu used. See **XmCreatePulldownMenu(3X)**, **XmCreatePopupMenu(3X)**, and **XmCreateOptionMenu(3X)** for more information on the menu systems.

Inherited Resources

CascadeButtonGadget inherits behavior and resources from the following superclasses. For a complete description of each resource, refer to the man page for that superclass.

XmLabelGadget Resource Set

Name Class	Default Type	Access
XmNalignment XmCAlignment	XmALIGNMENT_CENTER unsigned char	CSG
XmNfontList XmCFontList	"Fixed" XmFontList	CSG
XmNlabelInsensitivePixmap XmCLabelInsensitivePixmap	XmUNSPECIFIED_PIXMAP Pixmap	CSG
XmNlabelPixmap XmCPixmap	XmUNSPECIFIED_PIXMAP Pixmap	CSG
XmNlabelString XmCXmString	NULL XmString	CSG
XmNlabelType XmCLabelType	XmSTRING unsigned char	CSG
XmNmarginBottom XmCMarginBottom	dynamic short	CSG
XmNmarginHeight XmCMarginHeight	2 short	CSG
XmNmarginLeft XmCMarginLeft	0 short	CSG
XmNmarginRight XmCMarginRight	dynamic short	CSG
XmNmarginTop XmCMarginTop	dynamic short	CSG
XmNmarginWidth XmCMarginWidth	2 short	CSG
XmNmnemonic XmCMnemonic	'\0' char	CSG
XmNrecomputeSize XmCRecomputeSize	True Boolean	CSG

Name Class	Default Type	Access
XmNstringDirection XmCStringDirection	XmSTRING_DIRECTION_L_TO_R XmStringDirection	CSG

XmGadget Resource Set		
Name **Class**	**Default** **Type**	**Access**
XmNhelpCallback XmCCallback	NULL XtCallbackList	C
XmNhighlightOnEnter XmCHighlightOnEnter	False Boolean	CSG
XmNhighlightThickness XmCHighlightThickness	0 short	CSG
XmNshadowThickness XmCShadowThickness	2 short	CSG
XmNtraversalOn XmCTraversalOn	False Boolean	CSG
XmNunitType XmCUnitType	XmPIXELS unsigned char	CSG
XmNuserData XmCUserData	NULL caddr_t	CSG

RectObj Resource Set		
Name **Class**	**Default** **Type**	**Access**
XmNancestorSensitive XmCSensitive	XtCopyFromParent Boolean	CSG
XmNborderWidth XmCBorderWidth	1 Dimension	CSG
XmNheight XmCHeight	0 Dimension	CSG
XmNsensitive XmCSensitive	True Boolean	CSG
XmNwidth XmCWidth	0 Dimension	CSG
XmNx XmCPosition	0 Position	CSG
XmNy XmCPosition	0 Position	CSG

Object Resource Set		
Name **Class**	**Default** **Type**	**Access**
XmNdestroyCallback XmCCallback	NULL XtCallbackList	C

Callback Information

The following structure is returned with each callback:

```
typedef struct
{
    int         reason;
    XEvent      * event;
} XmAnyCallbackStruct;
```

reason Indicates why the callback was invoked.

event Points to the **XEvent** that triggered the callback or is NULL if this callback was not triggered by an **XEvent**.

Behavior

The default behavior associated with a CascadeButtonGadget depends on whether the button is part of a PopupMenu system, a Pulldown MenuPane in a MenuBar, or an OptionMenu system. The RowColumn parent determines the mouse button which is used through its **XmNrowColumnType** and **XmNwhichButton** resources.

Default PopupMenu System

Btn3Down<EnterWindow>:
This action arms the CascadeButtonGadget and posts the associated submenu after a short delay.

Btn3Down<LeaveWindow>:
The action that takes place depends on whether the mouse pointer has moved into the submenu associated with this CascadeButtonGadget. If it has, this event is ignored; if not, the CascadeButtonGadget is disarmed and its submenu unposted.

<Btn3Up>: This action posts the submenu attached to the CascadeButtonGadget and enables keyboard traversal within the menu. If the CascadeButtonGadget does not have a submenu attached, this event activates the CascadeButtonGadget and unposts the menu.

<Btn3Down>:
This action disables traversal for the menu and returns the user to drag mode, in which the menu is manipulated using the mouse. The submenu associated with this CascadeButtonGadget is posted.

<Key>Return:
This event posts the submenu attached to the CascadeButtonGadget if keyboard traversal is enabled in the menu. If the CascadeButtonGadget does not have a submenu attached, this event activates the CascadeButtonGadget and unposts the menu.

Default Pulldown MenuPane from a MenuBar or from an OptionMenu

Btn1Down<EnterWindow>:
This event arms the CascadeButtonGadget, and after a short delay, posts the associated submenu.

Btn1Down<LeaveWindow>:
The event is ignored if the mouse pointer has moved into the submenu. In all other cases, the CascadeButtonGadget is disarmed and its submenu unposted.

<Btn1Up>:
This event posts the submenu attached to the CascadeButtonGadget and enables keyboard traversal within the menu. If the CascadeButtonGadget does not have a submenu attached, this event activates the CascadeButtonGadget and unposts the menu.

<Btn1Down>:
This event disables traversal for the menu and returns the user to the drag mode. The submenu associated with this CascadeButtonGadget is posted.

<Key>Return:
This event posts the submenu attached to the CascadeButtonGadget if keyboard traversal is enabled in the menu. If the CascadeButtonGadget does not have a submenu attached, this event activates the CascadeButtonGadget and unposts the menu.

Default OptionMenu

<Btn1Down>:
This event arms the CascadeButtonGadget and posts the associated submenu.

<Key>Return:
This event posts the associated submenu and enables traversal within the menu.

Keyboard Traversal

For information on keyboard traversal, see the man page for **XmRowColumn(3X)** and its sections on behavior and default translations.

Related Information

Object(3X), **RectObj(3X)**, **XmCascadeButtonHighlight(3)**, **XmCreateCascadeButtonGadget(3X)**, **XmCreatePulldownMenu(3X)**, **XmCreatePopupMenu(3X)**, **XmCreateOptionMenu(3X)**, **XmGadget(3X)**, **XmLabelGadget(3X)**, **and XmRowColumn(3X).**

XmCascadeButtonHighlight

Purpose

A CascadeButton and CascadeButtonGadget function that sets the highlight state.

Synopsis

#include <Xm/CascadeB.h>
#include <Xm/CascadeBG.h>

void XmCascadeButtonHighlight (*cascadeButton, highlight*)
  Widget *cascadeButton*;
  Boolean *highlight*;

Description

XmCascadeButtonHighlight either draws or erases the shadow highlight around the CascadeButton or the CascadeButtonGadget.

cascadeButton Specifies the CascadeButton or CascadeButtonGadget to be highlighted or unhighlighted.

highlight Specifies whether to highlight (True) or to unhighlight (False).

For a complete definition of CascadeButton or CascadeButtonGadget and their associated resources, see **XmCascadeButton(3X)** or **XmCascadeButtonGadget(3X)**.

Related Information

XmCascadeButton(3X) and **XmCascadeButtonGadget(3X)**.

XmClipboardCancelCopy

Purpose

A clipboard function that cancels a copy to the clipboard.

Synopsis

#include <Xm/Xm.h>
#include <Xm/CutPaste.h>

void XmClipboardCancelCopy (*display, window, item_id*)
  Display * *display*;
  Window *window*;
  long *item_id*;

Description

XmClipboardCancelCopy cancels the copy to clipboard that is in progress and frees up temporary storage. When a copy is to be performed, **XmClipboardStartCopy** allocates temporary storage for the clipboard data. **XmClipboardCopy** copies the appropriate data into the the temporary storage. **XmClipboardEndCopy** copies the data to the clipboard structure and frees up the temporary storage structures. If **XmClipboardCancelCopy** is called, the **XmClipboardEndCopy** function does not have to be called. A call to **XmClipboardCancelCopy** is valid only after a call to **XmClipboardStartCopy** and before a call to **XmClipboardEndCopy**.

display Specifies a pointer to the **Display** structure that was returned in a previous call to **XOpenDisplay** or **XtDisplay**.

window Specifies a widget's window ID that relates the application window to the clipboard. The widget's window ID can be obtained by using **XtWindow**. The same application instance should pass the same window ID to each of the clipboard functions that it calls.

item_id Specifies the number assigned to this data item. This number was returned by a previous call to **XmClipboardStartCopy**.

Related Information

XmClipboardCopy(3X), **XmClipboardEndCopy(3X)**, and **XmClipboardStartCopy(3X)**.

XmClipboardCopy

Purpose

A clipboard function that copies a data item to temporary storage for later copying to clipboard.

Synopsis

#include <Xm/Xm.h>
#include <Xm/CutPaste.h>

int XmClipboardCopy (*display, window, item_id, format_name, buffer, length, private_id, data_id*)

Display	* *display*;
Window	*window*;
long	*item_id*;
char	* *format_name*;
char	* *buffer*;
unsigned long	*length*;
int	*private_id*;
int	* *data_id*;

Description

XmClipboardCopy copies a data item to temporary storage. The data item is moved from temporary storage to the clipboard data structure when a call to **XmClipboardEndCopy** is made. Additional calls to **XmClipboardCopy** before a call to **XmClipboardEndCopy** adds additional data item formats to the same data item or append data to an existing format. Formats are described in the *Inter-Client Communications Conventions Manual* (ICCCM) as targets.

NOTE: Do not call **XmClipboardCopy** before a call to **XmClipboardStartCopy** has been made. The latter function allocates temporary storage required by **XmClipboardCopy**.

If the *buffer* argument is NULL, the data is considered to be passed by name. When data that has been passed by name is later requested by another application, the application that owns the data receives a callback with a request for the data. The application that owns the data must then transfer the data to the clipboard with the **XmClipboardCopyByName** function. When a data item that was passed by name is deleted from the clipboard, the application that owns the data receives a callback stating that the data is no longer needed.

For information on the callback function, see the callback argument description for **XmClipboardStartCopy**.

display Specifies a pointer to the **Display** structure that was returned in a previous call to **XOpenDisplay** or **XtDisplay**.

window Specifies a widget's window ID that relates the application window to the clipboard. The widget's window ID can be obtained by using **XtWindow**. The same application instance should pass the same window ID to each of the clipboard functions that it calls.

item_id Specifies the number assigned to this data item. This number was returned by a previous call to **XmClipboardStartCopy**.

format_name Specifies the name of the format in which the data item is stored on the clipboard. Format is known as target in the ICCC manual.

buffer Specifies the buffer from which the clipboard copies the data.

length Specifies the length of the data being copied to the clipboard.

private_id Specifies the private data that the application wants to store with the data item.

data_id Specifies an identifying number assigned to the data item that uniquely identifies the data item and the format. This argument is required only for data that is passed by name.

Return Value

ClipboardSuccess
The function is successful.

ClipboardLocked
The function failed because the clipboard was locked by another application. The application can continue to call the function again with the same parameters until the lock goes away. This gives the application the opportunity to ask if the user wants to keep trying or to give up on the operation.

Related Information

XmClipboardCopyByName(3X), **XmClipboardEndCopy(3X)**, and **XmClipboardStartCopy(3X)**.

XmClipboardCopyByName

Purpose

A clipboard function that copies a data item passed by name.

Synopsis

#include <Xm/Xm.h>
#include <Xm/CutPaste.h>

int XmClipboardCopyByName (*display, window, data_id, buffer, length, private_id*)
  Display * *display*;
  Window *window*;
  int *data_id*;
  char * *buffer*;
  unsigned long*length*;
  int *private_id*;

Description

XmClipboardCopyByName copies the actual data for a data item that was previously passed by name to the clipboard. Data is considered to be passed by name when a call to **XmClipboardCopy** is made with a NULL buffer parameter. Additional calls to this function append new data to the existing data. When making additional calls to this function, the clipboard should be locked to ensure the integrity of the clipboard data. To lock the clipboard, use **XmClipboardLock**. Unlock the clipboard when copying is completed; to unlock the clipboard, use **XmClipboardUnlock**.

display Specifies a pointer to the **Display** structure that was returned in a previous call to **XOpenDisplay** or **XtDisplay**.

window Specifies a widget's window ID that relates the application window to the clipboard. The widget's window ID can be obtained by using **XtWindow**. The same application instance should pass the same window ID to each clipboard function it calls.

data_id Specifies an identifying number assigned to the data item that uniquely identifies the data item and the format. This number was assigned by **XmClipboardCopy** to the data item.

buffer Specifies the buffer from which the clipboard copies the data.

length Specifies the number of bytes in the data item.

private_id Specifies the private data that the application wants to store with the data item.

Return Value

ClipboardSuccess
The function is successful.

ClipboardLocked
The function failed because the clipboard was locked by another application. The application can continue to call the function again with the same parameters until the lock goes away. This gives the application the opportunity to ask if the user wants to keep trying or to give up on the operation.

Related Information

XmClipboardCopy(3X), **XmClipboardLock(3X)**, **XmClipboardStartCopy(3X)**, and **XmClipboardUnlock(3X)**.

XmClipboardEndCopy

Purpose

A clipboard function that ends a copy to the clipboard.

Synopsis

#include <Xm/Xm.h>
#include <Xm/CutPaste.h>

int XmClipboardEndCopy (*display, window, item_id*)
  Display * *display*;
  Window *window*;
  long *item_id*;

Description

XmClipboardEndCopy locks the clipboard from access by other applications, places data in the clipboard data structure, and unlocks the clipboard. Data items copied to the clipboard by **XmClipboardCopy** are not actually entered in the clipboard data structure until the call to **XmClipboardEndCopy**.

This function also frees up temporary storage that was allocated by **XmClipboardStartCopy**, which must be called before **XmClipboardEndCopy**. The latter function should not be called if **XmClipboardCancelCopy** has been called.

display Specifies a pointer to the **Display** structure that was returned in a previous call to **XOpenDisplay** or **XtDisplay**.

window Specifies a widget's window ID that relates the application window to the clipboard. The widget's window ID can be obtained by using **XtWindow**. The same application instance should pass the same window ID to each clipboard function it calls.

item_id Specifies the number assigned to this data item. This number was returned by a previous call to **XmClipboardStartCopy**.

Return Value

ClipboardSuccess
The function is successful.

ClipboardLocked
The function failed because the clipboard was locked by another application. The application can continue to call the function again with the same parameters until the lock goes away. This gives the application the opportunity to ask if the user wants to keep trying or to give up on the operation.

Related Information

XmClipboardCancelCopy(3X), **XmClipboardCopy(3X)** and **XmClipboardStartCopy(3X)**.

XmClipboardEndRetrieve

Purpose

A clipboard function that ends a copy from the clipboard.

Synopsis

#include <Xm/Xm.h>
#include <Xm/CutPaste.h>

int XmClipboardEndRetrieve (*display, window*)
    Display * *display*;
    Window *window*;

Description

XmClipboardEndRetrieve suspends copying data incrementally from the clipboard. It tells the clipboard routines that the application is through copying an item from the clipboard. Until this function is called, data items can be retrieved incrementally from the clipboard by calling **XmClipboardRetrieve**. If the application calls **XmClipboardStartRetrieve**, it must call **XmClipboardEndRetrieve**. If data is not being copied incrementally, **XmClipboardStartRetrieve** and **XmClipboardEndRetrieve** do not need to be called.

display Specifies a pointer to the **Display** structure that was returned in a previous call to **XOpenDisplay** or **XtDisplay**.

window Specifies a widget's window ID that relates the application window to the clipboard. The widget's window ID can be obtained by using **XtWindow**. The same application instance should pass the same window ID to each of the clipboard functions that it calls.

Return Value

ClipboardSuccess
The function is successful.

ClipboardLocked
The function failed because the clipboard was locked by another application. The application can continue to call the function again with the same parameters until the lock goes away. This gives the application the opportunity to ask if the user wants to keep trying or to give up on the operation.

Related Information

XmClipboardRetrieve(3X), **XmClipboardStartCopy(3X)**, and **XmClipboardStartRetrieve(3X)**.

XmClipboardInquireCount

Purpose

A clipboard function that returns the number of data item formats.

Synopsis

#include <Xm/Xm.h>
#include <Xm/CutPaste.h>

int XmClipboardInquireCount (*display, window, count, max_format_name_length*)
  Display * *display*;
  Window *window*;
  int * *count*;
  int * *max_format_name_length*;

Description

XmClipboardInquireCount returns the number of data item formats available for the data item in the clipboard. This function also returns the maximum name-length for all formats in which the data item is stored.

display Specifies a pointer to the **Display** structure that was returned in a previous call to **XOpenDisplay** or **XtDisplay**.

window — Specifies a widget's window ID that relates the application window to the clipboard. The widget's window ID can be obtained by using **XtWindow**. The same application instance should pass the same window ID to each of the clipboard functions that it calls.

count — Returns the number of data item formats available for the data item in the clipboard. If no formats are available, this argument equals zero. The count includes the formats that were passed by name.

max_format_name_length — Specifies the maximum length of all format names for the data item in the clipboard.

Return Value

ClipboardSuccess — The function is successful.

ClipboardLocked — The function failed because the clipboard was locked by another application. The application can continue to call the function again with the same parameters until the lock goes away. This gives the application the opportunity to ask if the user wants to keep trying or to give up on the operation.

ClipboardNoData — The function could not find data on the clipboard corresponding to the format requested. This could occur because the clipboard is empty; there is data on the clipboard but not in the requested format; or the data in the requested format was passed by name and is no longer available.

Related Information

XmClipboardStartCopy(3X).

XmClipboardInquireFormat

Purpose

A clipboard function that returns a specified format name.

Synopsis

#include <Xm/Xm.h>
#include <Xm/CutPaste.h>

int XmClipboardInquireFormat (*display, window, index, format_name_buf, buffer_len, copied_len*)
 Display * *display*;
 Window *window*;
 int *index*;
 char * *format_name_buf*;
 unsigned long *buffer_len*;
 unsigned long * *copied_len*;

Description

XmClipboardInquireFormat returns a specified format name for the data item in the clipboard. If the name must be truncated, the function returns a warning status.

display Specifies a pointer to the **Display** structure that was returned in a previous call to **XOpenDisplay** or **XtDisplay**.

window Specifies a widget's window ID that relates the application window to the clipboard. The widget's window ID can be obtained by using **XtWindow**. The same application instance should pass the same window ID to each of the clipboard functions that it calls.

index Specifies which of the ordered format names to obtain. If this index is greater than the number of formats for the data item, this function returns a zero in the *copied_len* argument.

format_name_buf Specifies the buffer that receives the format name.

buffer_len Specifies the number of bytes in the format name buffer.

copied_len Specifies the number of bytes in the string copied to the buffer. If this argument equals zero, there is no *nth* format for the data item.

Return Value

ClipboardSuccess
The function is successful.

ClipboardLocked
The function failed because the clipboard was locked by another application. The application can continue to call the function again with the same parameters until the lock goes away. This gives the application the opportunity to ask if the user wants to keep trying or to give up on the operation.

ClipboardTruncate
The data returned is truncated because the user did not provide a buffer large enough to hold the data.

ClipboardNoData
The function could not find data on the clipboard corresponding to the format requested. This could occur because the clipboard is empty; there is data on the clipboard but not in the requested format; or the data in the requested format was passed by name and is no longer available.

Related Information

XmClipboardStartCopy(3X).

XmClipboardInquireLength

Purpose

A clipboard function that returns the length of the stored data.

Synopsis

#include <Xm/Xm.h>
#include <Xm/CutPaste.h>

int XmClipboardInquireLength (*display, window, format_name, length*)
  Display * *display*;
  Window *window*;
  char * *format_name*;
  unsigned long* *length*;

Description

XmClipboardInquireLength returns the length of the data stored under a specified format name for the clipboard data item. If no data is found for the specified format, or if there is no item on the clipboard, this function returns a value of zero.

Any format passed by name is assumed to have the *length* passed in a call to **XmClipboardCopy**, even though the data has not yet been transferred to the clipboard in that format.

display — Specifies a pointer to the **Display** structure that was returned in a previous call to **XOpenDisplay** or **XtDisplay**.

window — Specifies a widget's window ID that relates the application window to the clipboard. The widget's window ID can be obtained by using **XtWindow**. The same application instance should pass the same window ID to each of the clipboard functions that it calls.

format_name — Specifies the name of the format for the data item.

length — Specifies the length of the next data item in the specified format. This argument equals zero if no data is found for the specified format, or if there is no item on the clipboard.

Return Value

ClipboardSuccess
The function is successful.

ClipboardLocked
The function failed because the clipboard was locked by another application. The application can continue to call the function again with the same parameters until the lock goes away. This gives the application the opportunity to ask if the user wants to keep trying or to give up on the operation.

ClipboardNoData
The function could not find data on the clipboard corresponding to the format requested. This could occur because the clipboard is empty; there is data on the clipboard but not in the requested format; or the data in the requested format was passed by name and is no longer available.

Related Information

XmClipboardCopy(3X) and **XmClipboardStartCopy(3X)**.

XmClipboardInquirePendingItems

Purpose

A clipboard function that returns a list of *data_id/private_id* pairs.

Synopsis

```
#include <Xm/Xm.h>
#include <Xm/CutPaste.h>

int XmClipboardInquirePendingItems (display, window, format_name,
item_list, count)
      Display                   * display;
      Window                    window;
      char                      * format_name;
      XmClipboardPendingList*   item_list;
      unsigned long             * count;
```

Description

XmClipboardInquirePendingItems returns a list of *data_id/private_id* pairs for the specified format name. A data item is considered pending if the application originally passed it by name, the application has not yet copied the data, and the item has not been deleted from the clipboard. The application is responsible for freeing the memory provided by this function to store the list.

This function is used by an application when exiting, to determine if the data that is passed by name should be sent to the clipboard.

display Specifies a pointer to the **Display** structure that was returned in a previous call to **XOpenDisplay** or **XtDisplay**.

window Specifies a widget's window ID that relates the application window to the clipboard. The widget's window ID can be obtained by using **XtWindow**. The same application instance should pass the same window ID to each of the clipboard functions that it calls.

format_name Specifies a string that contains the name of the format for which the list of data ID/private ID pairs is to be obtained.

item_list Specifies the address of the array of data ID/private ID pairs for the specified format name. This argument is a type **XmClipboardPendingList**. The application is responsible for freeing the memory provided by this function for storing the list.

item_count Specifies the number of items returned in the list. If there is no data for the specified format name, or if there is no item on the clipboard, this argument equals zero.

Return Value

ClipboardSuccess
The function is successful.

ClipboardLocked
The function failed because the clipboard was locked by another application. The application can continue to call the function again with the same parameters until the lock goes away. This gives the application the opportunity to ask if the user wants to keep trying or to give up on the operation.

Related Information

XmClipboardStartCopy(3X).

XmClipboardLock

Purpose

A clipboard function that locks the clipboard

Synopsis

#include <Xm/Xm.h>
#include <Xm/CutPaste.h>

int XmClipboardLock (*display, window*)
    Display * *display*;
    Window *window*;

Description

XmClipboardLock locks the clipboard from access by another application until **XmClipboardUnlock** is called. All clipboard functions lock and unlock the clipboard to prevent simultaneous access. This function allows the application to keep the clipboard data from changing between calls to **Inquire** and other clipboard functions. The application does not need to lock the clipboard between calls to **XmClipboardStartCopy** and **XmClipboardEndCopy** or to **XmClipboardStartRetrieve** and **XmClipboardEndRetrieve**.

The application should lock the clipboard before multiple calls to **XmClipboardCopyByName** and should unlock the clipboard after completion.

If the clipboard is already locked by another application, **XmClipboardLock** returns an error status. Multiple calls to this function by the same application increases the lock level.

display Specifies a pointer to the **Display** structure that was returned in a previous call to **XOpenDisplay** or **XtDisplay**.

window Specifies a widget's window ID that relates the application window to the clipboard. The widget's window ID can be obtained by using **XtWindow**. The same application instance should pass the same window ID to each of the clipboard functions that it calls.

Return Value

ClipboardSuccess
The function is successful.

ClipboardLocked
The function failed because the clipboard was locked by another application. The application can continue to call the function again with the same parameters until the lock goes away. This gives the application the opportunity to ask if the user wants to keep trying or to give up on the operation.

Related Information

XmClipboardCopyByName(3X), **XmClipboardEndCopy(3X)**, **XmClipboardEndRetrieve(3X)**, **XmClipboardStartCopy(3X)**, **XmClipboardStartRetrieve(3X)**, and **XmClipboardUnlock(3X)**.

XmClipboardRegisterFormat

Purpose

A clipboard function that registers a new format.

Synopsis

```
#include <Xm/Xm.h>
#include <Xm/CutPaste.h>

int XmClipboardRegisterFormat (display, format_name, format_length)
        Display          * display;
        char             * format_name;
        unsigned long    format_length;
```

Description

XmClipboardRegisterFormat registers a new format. Each format stored on the clipboard should have a length associated with it; this length must be known to the clipboard routines. Formats are known as targets in the *Inter-Client Communications Conventions Manual* (ICCCM). All of the formats specified by the ICCCM conventions are preregistered. Any other format that the application wants to use must either be 8-bit data or be registered via this routine. Failure to register the length of the data results in incompatible applications across platforms having different byte-swapping orders.

display	Specifies a pointer to the **Display** structure that was returned in a previous call to **XOpenDisplay** or **XtDisplay**.
format_name	Specifies the string name for the new format (target).
format_length	Specifies the format length in bits (8, 16, or 32).

Return Value

ClipboardBadFormat
The *format_name* must not be NULL, and the *format_length* must be 8, 16, or 32.

ClipboardSuccess The function is successful.

ClipboardLocked The function failed because the clipboard was locked by another application. The application can continue to call the function again with the same parameters until the lock goes away. This gives the application the opportunity to ask if the user wants to keep trying or to give up on the operation.

Related Information

XmClipboardStartCopy(3X).

XmClipboardRetrieve

Purpose

A clipboard function that retrieves a data item from the clipboard.

Synopsis

```
#include <Xm/Xm.h>
#include <Xm/CutPaste.h>

int XmClipboardRetrieve (display, window, format_name, buffer, length,
num_bytes, private_id)
        Display        * display;
        Window         window;
        char           * format_name;
        char           * buffer;
        unsigned long  length;
        unsigned long  * num_bytes;
        int            * private_id;
```

Description

XmClipboardRetrieve retrieves the current data item from clipboard storage. It returns a warning if the clipboard is locked; if there is no data on the clipboard; or if the data needs to be truncated because the buffer length is too short.

Between a call to **XmClipboardStartRetrieve** and a call to **XmClipboardEndRetrieve**, multiple calls to **XmClipboardRetrieve** with the same format name results in data being incrementally copied from the clipboard until the data in that format has all been copied.

The return value **ClipboardTruncate** from calls to **XmClipboardRetrieve** indicates that more data remains to be copied in the given format. It is recommended that any calls to the **Inquire** functions that the application needs to make to effect the copy from the clipboard be made between the call to ClipboardStartRetrieve and the first call to **XmClipboardRetrieve**. That way, the application does not need to call **XmClipboardLock** and **XmClipboardUnlock**. Applications do not need to use **XmClipboardStartRetrieve** and **XmClipboardEndRetrieve**, in which case **XmClipboardRetrieve** works as it did before.

display Specifies a pointer to the **Display** structure that was returned in a previous call to **XOpenDisplay** or **XtDisplay**.

window Specifies a widget's window ID that relates the application window to the clipboard. The widget's window ID can be obtained by using **XtWindow**. The same application instance should pass the same window ID to each of the clipboard functions that it calls.

format_name Specifies the name of a format in which the data is stored on the clipboard.

buffer Specifies the buffer to which the application wants the clipboard to copy the data.

length Specifies the length of the application buffer.

num_bytes Specifies the number of bytes of data copied into the application buffer.

private_id Specifies the private data stored with the data item by the application that placed the data item on the clipboard. If the application did not store private data with the data item, this argument returns zero.

Return Value

ClipboardSuccess
The function is successful.

ClipboardLocked
The function failed because the clipboard was locked by another application. The application can continue to call the function again with the same parameters until the lock goes away. This gives the application the opportunity to ask if the user wants to keep trying or to give up on the operation.

ClipboardTruncate
The data returned is truncated because the user did not provide a buffer large enough to hold the data.

ClipboardNoData
The function could not find data on the clipboard corresponding to the format requested. This could occur because the clipboard is empty; there is data on the clipboard but not in the requested format; or the data in the requested format was passed by name and is no longer available.

Related Information

XmClipboardEndRetrieve(3X), **XmClipboardLock(3X)**, **XmClipboardStartCopy(3X)**, **XmClipboardStartRetrieve(3X)**, and **XmClipboardUnlock(3X)**.

XmClipboardStartCopy

Purpose

A clipboard function that sets up a storage and data structure.

Synopsis

#include <Xm/Xm.h>
#include <Xm/CutPaste.h>

int XmClipboardStartCopy (*display, window, clip_label, timestamp, widget, callback, item_id*)

Display	* *display*;
Window	*window*;
XmString	*clip_label*;
Time	*timestamp*;
Widget	*widget*;
VoidProc	*callback*;
long	* *item_id*;

Description

XmClipboardStartCopy sets up storage and data structures to receive clipboard data. An application calls this function during a cut or copy operation. The data item that these structures receive then becomes the next data item in the clipboard.

Copying a large piece of data to the clipboard can take a long time. It is possible that, once copied, no application will ever request that data. The Motif Toolkit provides a mechanism so that an application does not need to actually pass data to the clipboard until the data has been requested by some application.

Instead, the application passes format and length information in **XmClipboardCopy** to the clipboard functions, along with a widget ID and a callback function address that is passed in **XmClipboardStartCopy**. The widget ID is needed for communications between the clipboard functions in the application that owns the data and the clipboard functions in the application that requests the data.

The callback functions are responsible for copying the actual data to the clipboard via **XmClipboardCopyByName**. The callback function is also called if the data item is removed from the clipboard, and the actual data is therefore no longer needed.

display — Specifies a pointer to the **Display** structure that was returned in a previous call to **XOpenDisplay** or **XtDisplay**.

window — Specifies a widget's window ID that relates the application window to the clipboard. The widget's window ID can be obtained by using **XtWindow**. The same application instance should pass the same window ID to each of the clipboard functions that it calls.

clip_label — Specifies the label to be associated with the data item. This argument is used to identify the data item, for example, in a clipboard viewer. An example of a label is the name of the application that places the data in the clipboard.

timestamp — Specifies the time of the event that triggered the copy.

widget — Specifies the ID of the widget that receives messages requesting data previously passed by name. This argument must be present in order to pass data by name. Any valid widget ID in your application can be used for this purpose and all the message handling is taken care of by the cut and paste functions.

callback Specifies the address of the callback function that is called when the clipboard needs data that was originally passed by name. This is also the callback to receive the **delete** message for items that were originally passed by name. This argument must be present in order to pass data by name.

item_id Specifies the number assigned to this data item. The application uses this number in calls to **XmClipboardCopy**, **XmClipboardEndCopy**, and **XmClipboardCancelCopy**.

For more information on passing data by name, see **XmClipboardCopy(3X)** and **XmClipboardCopyByName(3X)**.

The *widget* and *callback* arguments must be present in order to pass data by name. The callback format is as follows:

function name
  Widget *widget*;
  int * *data_id*;
  int * *private*;
  int * *reason*;

widget Specifies the ID of the widget passed to this function.

data_id Specifies the identifying number returned by **XmClipboardCopy**, which identifies the pass-by-name data.

private Specifies the private information passed to **XmClipboardCopy**.

reason Specifies the reason, which is either **XmCR_CLIPBOARD_DATA_DELETE** or **XmCR_CLIPBOARD_DATA_REQUEST**.

Return Value

ClipboardSuccess
The function is successful.

ClipboardLocked
The function failed because the clipboard was locked by another application. The application can continue to call the function again with the same parameters until the lock goes away. This gives the application the opportunity to ask if the user wants to keep trying or to give up on the operation.

Related Information

XmClipboardCancelCopy(3X), **XmClipboardCopy(3X)**, **XmClipboardCopyByName(3X)**, **XmClipboardEndCopy(3X)**, **XmClipboardEndRetrieve(3X)**, **XmClipboardInquireCount(3X)**, **XmClipboardInquireFormat(3X)**, **XmClipboardInquireLength(3X)**, **XmClipboardInquirePendingItems(3X)**, **XmClipboardLock(3X)**, **XmClipboardRegisterFormat(3X)**, **XmClipboardRetrieve(3X)**, **XmClipboardStartRetrieve(3X)**, **XmClipboardUndoCopy(3X)**, **XmClipboardUnlock(3X)**, and **XmClipboardWithdrawFormat(3X)**.

XmClipboardStartRetrieve

Purpose

A function that starts a copy from the clipboard.

Synopsis

#include <Xm/Xm.h>
#include <Xm/CutPaste.h>

int XmClipboardStartRetrieve (*display, window, timestamp*)
    Display * *display*;
    Window *window*;
    Time *timestamp*;

Description

XmClipboardStartRetrieve tells the clipboard routines that the application is ready to start copying an item from the clipboard. The clipboard will be locked by this routine, and will stay locked until **XmClipboardEndRetrieve** is called. Between a call to **XmClipboardStartRetrieve** and **XmClipboardEndRetrieve**, multiple calls to **XmClipboardRetrieve** with the same format name will result in data being incrementally copied from the clipboard until the data in that format has all been copied.

The return value **ClipboardTruncate** from calls to **XmClipboardRetrieve** indicates that more data remains to be copied in the given format. It is recommended that any calls to the **Inquire** functions that the application needs to make to effect the copy from the clipboard be made between the call to **XmClipboardStartRetrieve** and the first call to **XmClipboardRetrieve**. That way, the application does not need to call **XmClipboardLock** and **XmClipboardUnlock**. Applications do not need to use **XmClipboardStartRetrieve** and **XmClipboardEndRetrieve**, in which case **XmClipboardRetrieve** works as it did before.

display Specifies a pointer to the **Display** structure that was returned in a previous call to **XOpenDisplay** or **XtDisplay**.

window Specifies a widget's window ID that relates the application window to the clipboard. The widget's window ID can be obtained by using **XtWindow**. The same application instance should pass the same window ID to each of the clipboard functions that it calls.

timestamp Specifies the time of the event that triggered the copy.

Return Value

ClipboardSuccess
The function is successful.

ClipboardLocked
The function failed because the clipboard was locked by another application. The application can continue to call the function again with the same parameters until the lock goes away. This gives the application the opportunity to ask if the user wants to keep trying or to give up on the operation.

Related Information

XmClipboardEndRetrieve(3X), **XmClipboardInquireCount(3X)**, **XmClipboardInquireFormat(3X)**, **XmClipboardInquireLength(3X)**, **XmClipboardInquirePendingItems(3X)**, **XmClipboardLock(3X)**, **XmClipboardRetrieve(3X)**, **XmClipboardStartCopy(3X)**, and **XmClipboardUnlock(3X)**.

XmClipboardUndoCopy

Purpose

A clipboard function that deletes the last item placed on the clipboard.

Synopsis

```
#include <Xm/Xm.h>
#include <Xm/CutPaste.h>

int XmClipboardUndoCopy (display, window)
        Display      * display;
        Window       window;
```

Description

XmClipboardUndoCopy deletes the last item placed on the clipboard if the item was placed there by an application with the passed *display* and *window* arguments. Any data item deleted from the clipboard by the original call to **XmClipboardCopy** is restored. If the *display* or *window* IDs do not match the last copied item, no action is taken, and this function has no effect.

display Specifies a pointer to the **Display** structure that was returned in a previous call to **XOpenDisplay** or **XtDisplay**.

window Specifies a widget's window ID that relates the application window to the clipboard. The widget's window ID can be obtained by using **XtWindow**. The same application instance should pass the same window ID to each of the clipboard functions that it calls.

Return Value

ClipboardSuccess
The function is successful.

ClipboardLocked
The function failed because the clipboard was locked by another application. The application can continue to call the function again with the same parameters until the lock goes away. This gives the application the opportunity to ask if the user wants to keep trying or to give up on the operation.

Related Information

XmClipboardLock(3X) and **XmClipboardStartCopy(3X)**.

XmClipboardUnlock

Purpose

A clipboard function that unlocks the clipboard

Synopsis

#include <Xm/Xm.h>
#include <Xm/CutPaste.h>

int XmClipboardUnlock (*display, window, remove_all_locks*)
    Display * *display*;
    Window *window*;
    Boolean *remove_all_locks*;

Description

XmClipboardUnlock unlocks the clipboard, enabling it to be accessed by other applications.

If multiple calls to **XmClipboardLock** have occurred, the same number of calls to **XmClipboardUnlock** is necessary to unlock the clipboard, unless *remove_all_locks* is set to True.

The application should lock the clipboard before multiple calls to **XmClipboardCopyByName** and should unlock the clipboard after completion.

display — Specifies a pointer to the **Display** structure that was returned in a previous call to **XOpenDisplay** or **XtDisplay**.

window — Specifies a widget's window ID that relates the application window to the clipboard. The widget's window ID can be obtained by using **XtWindow**. The same application instance should pass the same window ID to each of the clipboard functions that it calls.

remove_all_locks
When true, indicates that all nested locks should be removed. When False, indicates that only one level of lock should be removed.

Return Value

ClipboardSuccess
The function is successful.

ClipboardLocked
The function failed because the clipboard was locked by another application. The application can continue to call the function again with the same parameters until the lock goes away. This gives the application the opportunity to ask if the user wants to keep trying or to give up on the operation.

Related Information

XmClipboardCancelCopy(3X), **XmClipboardCopy(3X)**, **XmClipboardCopyByName(3X)**, **XmClipboardEndCopy(3X)**, **XmClipboardEndRetrieve(3X)**, **XmClipboardInquireCount(3X)**, **XmClipboardInquireFormat(3X)**, **XmClipboardInquireLength(3X)**, **XmClipboardInquirePendingItems(3X)**, **XmClipboardLock(3X)**, **XmClipboardRegisterFormat(3X)**, **XmClipboardRetrieve(3X)**, **XmClipboardStartCopy(3X)**, **XmClipboardStartRetrieve(3X)**, **XmClipboardUndoCopy(3X)**, and **XmClipboardWithdrawFormat(3X)**.

XmClipboardWithdrawFormat

Purpose

A clipboard function that indicates that the application no longer wants to supply a data item.

Synopsis

```
#include <Xm/Xm.h>
#include <Xm/CutPaste.h>

int XmClipboardWithdrawFormat (display, window, data_id)
        Display     * display;
        Window      window;
        int         data_id;
```

Description

XmClipboardWithdrawFormat indicates that the application no longer supplies a data item to the clipboard that the application had previously passed by name.

display Specifies a pointer to the **Display** structure that was returned in a previous call to **XOpenDisplay** or **XtDisplay**.

window Specifies a widget's window ID that relates the application window to the clipboard. The widget's window ID can be obtained by using **XtWindow**. The same application instance should pass the same window ID to each clipboard function it calls.

data_id Specifies an identifying number assigned to the data item that uniquely identifies the data item and the format. This was assigned to the item when it was originally passed by **XmClipboardCopy**.

Return Value

ClipboardSuccess
The function is successful.

ClipboardLocked
The function failed because the clipboard was locked by another application. The application can continue to call the function again with the same parameters until the lock goes away. This gives the application the opportunity to ask if the user wants to keep trying or to give up on the operation.

Related Information

XmClipboardCopy(3X) and **XmClipboardStartCopy(3X)**.

XmCommand

Purpose

The Command widget class

Synopsis

#include <Xm/Command.h>

Description

Command is a special-purpose composite widget for command entry that provides a built-in command-history mechanism. Command includes a command-line text-input field, a command-line prompt, and a command-history list region.

One additional **WorkArea** child may be added to the Command after creation.

Whenever a command is entered, it is automatically added to the end of the command-history list and made visible. This does not change the selected item in the list, if there is one.

Many of the new resources specified for Command are actually SelectionBox resources that have been renamed for clarity and ease of use.

Classes

Command inherits behavior and resources from **Core**, **Composite**, **Constraint**, **XmManager**, **XmBulletinBoard**, and **XmSelectionBox** classes.

The class pointer is **xmCommandWidgetClass**.

The class name is **XmCommand**.

New Resources

The following table defines a set of widget resources used by the programmer to specify data. The programmer can also set the resource values for the inherited classes to set attributes for this widget. To reference a resource by name or by class in a .Xdefaults file, remove the **XmN** or **XmC** prefix and use the remaining letters. To specify one of the defined values for a resource in a .Xdefaults file, remove the **Xm** prefix and use the remaining letters (in either lowercase or uppercase, but include any underscores between words). The codes in the access column indicate if the given resource can be set at creation time (**C**), set by using **XtSetValues** (**S**), retrieved by using **XtGetValues** (**G**), or is not applicable (**N/A**).

XmCommand Resource Set		
Name **Class**	**Default** **Type**	**Access**
XmNcommand XmCTextString	NULL XmString	CSG
XmNcommandChangedCallback XmCCallback	NULL XtCallbackList	C
XmNcommandEnteredCallback XmCCallback	NULL XtCallbackList	C
XmNhistoryItems XmCItems	NULL XmStringTable	CSG
XmNhistoryItemCount XmCItemCount	0 int	CSG
XmNhistoryMaxItems XmCMaxItems	100 int	CSG
XmNhistoryVisibleItemCount XmCVisibleItemCount	8 int	CSG
XmNpromptString XmCXmString	">" XmString	CSG

XmNcommand

Contains the current command-line text. This is the **XmNtextString** resource in SelectionBox, renamed for Command. This resource can also be modified via **XmCommandSetValue** and **XmCommandAppendValue** functions. The command area is a Text widget.

XmNcommandChangedCallback

Specifies the list of callbacks that is called when the value of the command changes. The callback reason is **XmCR_COMMAND_CHANGED**. This is equivalent to the **XmNvalueChangedCallback** of the Text widget, except that an **XmCommandCallbackStructure** is returned, loaded with the **XmString**.

XmNcommandEnteredCallback
Specifies the list of callbacks that is called when a command is entered in the Command. The callback reason is **XmCR_COMMAND_ENTERED**. An **XmCommandCallback** structure is returned.

XmNhistoryItems
Lists **XmString** items that make up the contents of the history list. This is the **XmNlistItems** resource in SelectionBox, renamed for Command.

XmNhistoryItemCount
Specifies the number of **XmStrings** in **XmNhistoryItems**. This is the **XmNlistItemCount** resource in SelectionBox, renamed for Command.

XmNhistoryMaxItems
Specifies the maximum number of items allowed in the history list. Once this number is reached, an existing list item must be removed before a new item can be added to the list. For each command entered, the first list item is removed from the list, so the new command can be added to the list.

XmNhistoryVisibleItemCount
Specifies the number of items in the history list that should be visible at one time. In effect, it sets the height (in lines) of the history list window. This is the **XmNvisibleItemCount** resource in SelectionBox, renamed for Command.

XmNpromptString
Prompts for the command line. This is the **XmNselectionLabelString** resource in SelectionBox, renamed for Command.

Inherited Resources

Command inherits behavior and resources from the following superclasses. For a complete description of each resource, refer to the man page for that superclass.

XmSelectionBox Resource Set		
Name **Class**	**Default** **Type**	**Access**
XmNapplyCallback XmCCallback	NULL XtCallbackList	N/A
XmNapplyLabelString XmCApplyLabelString	"Apply" XmString	N/A
XmNcancelCallback XmCCallback	NULL XtCallbackList	N/A
XmNcancelLabelString XmCXmString	"Cancel" XmString	N/A
XmNdialogType XmCDialogType	XmDIALOG_COMMAND unsigned char	G
XmNhelpLabelString XmCXmString	"Help" XmString	N/A
XmNlistItemCount XmCItemCount	0 int	N/A
XmNlistItems XmCItems	NULL XmStringList	N/A
XmNlistLabelString XmCXmString	NULL XmString	N/A
XmNlistVisibleItemCount XmCVisibleItemCount	8 int	N/A
XmNminimizeButtons XmCminimizeButtons	False Boolean	N/A
XmNmustMatch XmCMustMatch	False Boolean	N/A
XmNnoMatchCallback XmCCallback	NULL XtCallbackList	N/A
XmNokCallback XmCCallback	NULL XtCallbackList	N/A

Name Class	Default Type	Access
XmNokLabelString XmCXmString	"OK" XmString	N/A
XmNselectionLabelString XmCXmString	"Selection" XmString	CSG
XmNtextAccelerators XmCTextAccelerators	see description XtTranslations	C
XmNtextColumns XmCTextColumns	20 int	CSG
XmNtextValue XmCTextValue	NULL XmString	N/A

XmBulletinBoard Resource Set		
Name **Class**	**Default** **Type**	**Access**
XmNallowOverlap XmCAllowOverlap	True Boolean	N/A
XmNautoUnmanage XmCAutoUnmanage	False Boolean	CSG
XmNbuttonFontList XmCButtonFontList	NULL XmFontList	N/A
XmNcancelButton XmCWidget	NULL Widget	N/A
XmNdefaultButton XmCWidget	NULL Widget	N/A
XmNdefaultPosition XmCDefaultPosition	False Boolean	CSG
XmNdialogStyle XmCDialogStyle	dynamic unsigned char	CSG
XmNdialogTitle XmCXmString	NULL XmString	CSG
XmNfocusCallback XmCCallback	NULL XtCallbackList	C
XmNlabelFontList XmCLabelFontList	NULL XmFontList	CSG
XmNmapCallback XmCCallback	NULL XtCallbackList	C
XmNmarginHeight XmCMarginHeight	10 short	CSG
XmNmarginWidth XmCMarginWidth	10 short	CSG
XmNnoResize XmCNoResize	False Boolean	CSG

Name Class	Default Type	Access
XmNresizePolicy XmCResizePolicy	XmRESIZE_NONE unsigned char	CSG
XmNshadowType XmCShadowType	XmSHADOW_OUT unsigned char	CSG
XmNstringDirection XmCStringDirection	XmSTRING_DIRECTION_L_TO_R XmStringDirection	CSG
XmNtextFontList XmCTextFontList	NULL XmFontList	CSG
XmNtextTranslations XmCTranslations	NULL XtTranslations	C
XmNunmapCallback XmCCallback	NULL XtCallbackList	C

XmManager Resource Set		
Name **Class**	**Default** **Type**	**Access**
XmNbottomShadowColor XmCForeground	dynamic Pixel	CSG
XmNbottomShadowPixmap XmCBottomShadowPixmap	XmUNSPECIFIED_PIXMAP Pixmap	CSG
XmNforeground XmCForeground	dynamic Pixel	CSG
XmNhelpCallback XmCCallback	NULL XtCallbackList	C
XmNhighlightColor XmCForeground	Black Pixel	CSG
XmNhighlightPixmap XmCHighlightPixmap	dynamic Pixmap	CSG
XmNshadowThickness XmCShadowThickness	dynamic short	CSG
XmNtopShadowColor XmCBackground	dynamic Pixel	CSG
XmNtopShadowPixmap XmCTopShadowPixmap	XmUNSPECIFIED_PIXMAP Pixmap	CSG
XmNunitType XmCUnitType	XmPIXELS unsigned char	CSG
XmNuserData XmCUserData	NULL caddr_t	CSG

Composite Resource Set		
Name **Class**	**Default** **Type**	**Access**
XmNinsertPosition XmCInsertPosition	NULL XmRFunction	CSG

Core Resource Set		
Name **Class**	**Default** **Type**	**Access**
XmNaccelerators XmCAccelerators	NULL XtTranslations	CSG
XmNancestorSensitive XmCSensitive	True Boolean	G
XmNbackground XmCBackground	dynamic Pixel	CSG
XmNbackgroundPixmap XmCPixmap	XmUNSPECIFIED_PIXMAP Pixmap	CSG
XmNborderColor XmCBorderColor	Black Pixel	CSG
XmNborderPixmap XmCPixmap	XmUNSPECIFIED_PIXMAP Pixmap	CSG

Name Class	Default Type	Access
XmNborderWidth XmCBorderWidth	0 Dimension	CSG
XmNcolormap XmCColormap	XtCopyFromParent Colormap	CG
XmNdepth XmCDepth	XtCopyFromParent int	CG
XmNdestroyCallback XmCCallback	NULL XtCallbackList	C
XmNheight XmCHeight	0 Dimension	CSG
XmNmappedWhenManaged XmCMappedWhenManaged	True Boolean	CSG
XmNscreen XmCScreen	XtCopyScreen Pointer	CG
XmNsensitive XmCSensitive	True Boolean	CSG
XmNtranslations XmCTranslations	NULL XtTranslations	CSG
XmNwidth XmCWidth	0 Dimension	CSG
XmNx XmCPosition	0 Position	CSG
XmNy XmCPosition	0 Position	CSG

Callback Information

The following structure is returned with each callback.

typedef struct
{
  int *reason*;
  XEvent * *event*;
  XmString *value*;
  int *length*;
} **XmCommandCallbackStruct**;

reason Indicates why the callback was invoked

event Points to the **XEvent** that triggered the callback

value Specifies the **XmString** in the CommandArea

length Specifies the size of the command in **XmString**

Behavior

Command behavior is summarized below.

<Key>: When any change is made to the text edit widget, the callbacks for **XmNcommandChangedCallback** are called.

<Key>Return: When the Return key is pressed, the callbacks for **XmNcommandEnteredCallback** and **XmNcommandChangedCallback** are called.

<Key>Up or **<Key>Down**:
When the up-arrow or down-arrow key is pressed within the Text subwidget of Command, the text value is replaced with the previous or next item in the List subwidget. The selected item in the list is also changed to the previous or the next item. The callbacks for **XmNcommandChangedCallback** are called.

<DoubleClick>:
When an item in the List subwidget is double clicked, that item is selected and added to the end of the list in one action. The callbacks for **XmNcommandEnteredCallback** and **XmNcommandChangedCallback** are called.

<Key>F1: When the **Function Key 1** is pressed, the callbacks for **XmNhelpCallback** are called.

<FocusIn>: When a **FocusIn** *event* is generated on the widget window, the callbacks for **XmNfocusCallback** are called.

<MapWindow>:
When a Command that is the child of a DialogShell is mapped, the callbacks for **XmNmapCallback** are invoked. When a Command that is not the child of a DialogShell is mapped, the callbacks are not invoked.

<UnmapWindow>:
When a Command that is the child of a DialogShell is unmapped, the callbacks for **XmNunmapCallback** are invoked. When a Command that is not the child of a DialogShell is unmapped, the callbacks are not invoked.

Default Translations

Command inherits default translations from SelectionBox.

Default Accelerators

The default accelerator translations added to descendants of a BulletinBoard if the parent of the BulletinBoard is a DialogShell are:

```
#override
<Key>F1:          Help()
<Key>Return:      Return()
<Key>KP_Enter:    Return()
```

Default Text Accelerators

The default text accelerators inherited from SelectionBox are:

```
#override
<Key>Up:          UpOrDown(0)
<Key>Down:        UpOrDown(1)
<Key>F1:          Help()
<Key>Return:      Return()
<Key>KP_Enter:    Return()
```

Keyboard Traversal

For information on keyboard traversal, see the man page for **XmManager(3X)** and its sections on behavior and default translations.

Related Information

Composite(3X), **Constraint(3X)**, **Core(3X)**, **XmBulletinBoard(3X)**, **XmCommandAppendValue(3X)**, **XmCommandError(3X)**, **XmCommandGetChild(3X)**, **XmCommandSetValue(3X)**, **XmCreateCommand(3X)**, **XmManager(3X)**, and **XmSelectionBox(3X)**.

XmCommandAppendValue

Purpose

A Command function that appends the passed XmString to the end of the string displayed in the command area of the widget.

Synopsis

#include <Xm/Command.h>

void XmCommandAppendValue (*widget, command*)
 Widget *widget*;
 XmString *command*;

Description

XmCommandAppendValue appends the passed **XmString** to the end of the string displayed in the command area of the Command widget.

widget Specifies the Command widget ID

command Specifies the passed **XmString**

For a complete definition of Command and its associated resources, see **XmCommand(3X)**.

Related Information

XmCommand(3X).

XmCommandError

Purpose

A Command function that displays an error message

Synopsis

```
#include <Xm/Command.h>

void XmCommandError (widget, error)
 Widget          widget;
 XmString        error;
```

Description

XmCommandError displays an error message in the history area of the Command widget. The **XmString** error is displayed until the next command entered occurs.

widget Specifies the Command widget ID

error Specifies the passed **XmString**

For a complete definition of Command and its associated resources, see **XmCommand(3X)**.

Related Information

XmCommand(3X).

XmCommandGetChild

Purpose

A Command function that is used to access a component.

Synopsis

#include <Xm/Command.h>

Widget XmCommandGetChild (*widget, child*)
Widget *widget*;
unsigned char *child*;

Description

XmCommandGetChild is used to access a component within a Command. The parameters given to the function are the Command widget and a value indicating which child to access.

widget Specifies the Command widget ID

child Specifies a component within the Command. The following are legal values for this parameter:

- **XmDIALOG_COMMAND_TEXT**
- **XmDIALOG_PROMPT_LABEL**
- **XmDIALOG_HISTORY_LIST**

For a complete definition of Command and its associated resources, see **XmCommand(3X)**.

Return Value

Returns the widget ID of the specified Command child.

Related Information

XmCommand(3X).

XmCommandSetValue

Purpose

A Command function that replaces a displayed string

Synopsis

#include <Xm/Command.h>

void XmCommandSetValue (*widget, command*)
 Widget *widget*;
 XmString *command*;

Description

XmCommandSetValue replaces the string displayed in the command area of the Command widget with the passed **XmString**.

widget Specifies the Command widget ID

command Specifies the passed **XmString**

For a complete definition of Command and its associated resources, see **XmCommand(3X)**.

Related Information

XmCommand(3X).

XmConvertUnits

Purpose

A function that converts a value in one unit type to another unit type.

Synopsis

#include <Xm/Xm.h>

int XmConvertUnits (*widget, orientation, from_unit_type, from_value, to_unit_type*)

Widget	*widget*;
int	*orientation*;
int	*from_unit_type*;
int	*from_value*;
int	*to_unit_type*;

Description

XmConvertUnits converts the value and returns it as the return value from the function.

widget Specifies the widget for which the data is to be converted *orientation* Specifies whether the converter uses the horizontal or vertical screen resolution when performing the conversions. *orientation* can have values of **XmHORIZONTAL** or **XmVERTICAL**.

from_unit_type Specifies the current unit type of the supplied value

from_value Specifies the value to be converted

to_unit_type Converts the value to the unit type specified

The parameters *from_unit_type* and *to_unit_type* can have the following values:

- **XmPIXELS** — all values provided to the widget are treated as normal pixel values. This is the default for the resource.
- **Xm100TH_MILLIMETERS** — all values provided to the widget are treated as 1/100 millimeter.
- **Xm1000TH_INCHES** — all values provided to the widget are treated as 1/1000 inch.
- **Xm100TH_POINTS** — all values provided to the widget are treated as 1/100 point. A point is a unit typically used in text processing applications and is defined as 1/72 inch.
- **Xm100TH_FONT_UNITS** — all values provided to the widget are treated as 1/100-font unit. The value to be used for the font unit is determined in one of two ways. The resource **XmNfont** can be used in a defaults file or on the command line. The standard command-line options of **-fn** and **-font** can also be used. The font unit value is taken as the **QUAD_WIDTH** property of the font. The function **XmSetFontUnits** allows applications to specify the font unit values.

Return Value

Returns the converted value.

Errors

If a NULL widget, incorrect *orientation*, or incorrect *unit_type* is supplied as parameter data, 0 is returned.

Related Information

XmSetFontUnit(3X)

XmCreateArrowButton

Purpose

The ArrowButton widget creation function

Synopsis

#include <Xm/ArrowB.h>

Widget XmCreateArrowButton (*parent, name, arglist, argcount*)
    Widget *parent*;
    String *name*;
    ArgList *arglist*;
    Cardinal *argcount*;

Description

XmCreateArrowButton creates an instance of an ArrowButton widget and returns the associated widget ID.

parent Specifies the parent widget ID

name Specifies the name of the created widget

arglist Specifies the argument list

argcount Specifies the number of attribute/value pairs in the argument list (*arglist*)

For a complete definition of ArrowButton and its associated resources, see **XmArrowButton(3X)**.

Return Value

Returns the ArrowButton widget ID.

Related Information

XmArrowButton(3X).

XmCreateArrowButtonGadget

Purpose

The ArrowButtonGadget creation function.

Synopsis

```
#include <Xm/ArrowB.h>

Widget XmCreateArrowButtonGadget (parent, name, arglist, argcount)
        Widget      parent;
        String      name;
        ArgList     arglist;
        Cardinal    argcount;
```

Description

XmCreateArrowButtonGadget creates an instance of an ArrowButtonGadget widget and returns the associated widget ID.

parent Specifies the parent widget ID

name Specifies the name of the created widget

arglist Specifies the argument list

argcount Specifies the number of attribute/value pairs in the argument list (*arglist*)

For a complete definition of ArrowButtonGadget and its associated resources, see **XmArrowButtonGadget(3X)**.

Return Value

Returns the ArrowButtonGadget widget ID.

Related Information

XmArrowButtonGadget(3X).

XmCreateBulletinBoard

Purpose

The BulletinBoard widget creation function

Synopsis

#include <Xm/BulletinB.h>

Widget XmCreateBulletinBoard (*parent, name, arglist, argcount*)
Widget *parent*;
String *name*;
ArgList *arglist*;
Cardinal *argcount*;

Description

XmCreateBulletinBoard creates an instance of a BulletinBoard widget and returns the associated widget ID.

parent Specifies the parent widget ID

name Specifies the name of the created widget

arglist Specifies the argument list

argcount Specifies the number of attribute/value pairs in the argument list (*arglist*)

For a complete definition of BulletinBoard and its associated resources, see **XmBulletinBoard(3X)**.

Return Value

Returns the BulletinBoard widget ID.

Related Information

XmBulletinBoard(3X).

XmCreateBulletinBoardDialog

Purpose

The BulletinBoard BulletinBoardDialog convenience creation function.

Synopsis

#include <Xm/BulletinB.h>

Widget XmCreateBulletinBoardDialog (*parent, name, arglist, argcount*)
    Widget *parent*;
    String *name*;
    ArgList *arglist*;
    Cardinal *argcount*;

Description

XmCreateBulletinBoardDialog is a convenience creation function that creates a DialogShell and an unmanaged BulletinBoard child of the DialogShell. A BulletinBoardDialog is used for interactions not supported by the standard dialog set. This function does not automatically create any labels, buttons, or other dialog components. Such components should be added by the application after the BulletinBoardDialog is created.

Use **XtManageChild** to pop up the BulletinBoardDialog (passing the BulletinBoard as the widget parameter); use **XtUnmanageChild** to pop it down.

parent Specifies the parent widget ID

name Specifies the name of the created widget

arglist Specifies the argument list

argcount Specifies the number of attribute/value pairs in the argument list (*arglist*)

For a complete definition of BulletinBoard and its associated resources, see **XmBulletinBoard(3X)**.

Return Value

Returns the BulletinBoard widget ID.

Related Information

XmBulletinBoard(3X).

XmCreateCascadeButton

Purpose

The CascadeButton widget creation function

Synopsis

#include <Xm/CascadeB.h>

Widget XmCreateCascadeButton (*parent, name, arglist, argcount*)
Widget *parent*;
String *name*;
ArgList *arglist*;
Cardinal *argcount*;

Description

XmCreateCascadeButton creates an instance of a CascadeButton widget and returns the associated widget ID.

parent Specifies the parent widget ID. The parent must be a RowColumn widget.

name Specifies the name of the created widget

arglist Specifies the argument list

argcount Specifies the number of attribute/value pairs in the argument list (*arglist*)

For a complete definition of CascadeButton and its associated resources, see **XmCascadeButton(3X)**.

Return Value

Returns the CascadeButton widget ID.

Related Information

XmCascadeButton(3X).

XmCreateCascadeButtonGadget

Purpose

The CascadeButtonGadget creation function.

Synopsis

```
#include <Xm/CascadeBG.h>

Widget XmCreateCascadeButtonGadget (parent, name, arglist, argcount)
        Widget      parent;
        String      name;
        ArgList     arglist;
        Cardinal    argcount;
```

Description

XmCreateCascadeButtonGadget creates an instance of a CascadeButtonGadget and returns the associated widget ID.

parent Specifies the parent widget ID. The parent must be a RowColumn widget.

name Specifies the name of the created widget

arglist Specifies the argument list

argcount Specifies the number of attribute/value pairs in the argument list (*arglist*)

For a complete definition of CascadeButtonGadget and its associated resources, see **XmCascadeButtonGadget(3X)**.

Return Value

Returns the CascadeButtonGadget widget ID.

Related Information

XmCascadeButtonGadget(3X).

XmCreateCommand

Purpose

The Command widget creation function

Synopsis

```
#include <Xm/Command.h>

Widget XmCreateCommand (parent, name, arglist, argcount)
      Widget      parent;
      String      name;
      ArgList     arglist;
      Cardinal    argcount;
```

Description

XmCreateCommand creates an instance of a Command widget and returns the associated widget ID.

parent Specifies the parent widget ID

name Specifies the name of the created widget

arglist Specifies the argument list

argcount Specifies the number of attribute/value pairs in the argument list (*arglist*)

For a complete definition of Command and its associated resources, see **XmCommand(3X)**.

Return Value

Returns the Command widget ID.

Related Information

XmCommand(3X).

XmCreateDialogShell

Purpose

The DialogShell widget creation function

Synopsis

```
#include <Xm/DialogS.h>

Widget XmCreateDialogShell (parent, name, arglist, argcount)
        Widget      parent;
        String      name;
        ArgList     arglist;
        Cardinal    argcount;
```

Description

XmCreateDialogShell creates an instance of a DialogShell widget and returns the associated widget ID.

parent Specifies the parent widget ID

name Specifies the name of the created widget

arglist Specifies the argument list

argcount Specifies the number of attribute/value pairs in the argument list (*arglist*)

For a complete definition of DialogShell and its associated resources, see **XmDialogShell(3X)**.

Return Value

Returns the DialogShell widget ID.

Related Information

XmDialogShell(3X).

XmCreateDrawingArea

Purpose

The DrawingArea widget creation function

Synopsis

```
#include <Xm/DrawingA.h>

Widget XmCreateDrawingArea (parent, name, arglist, argcount)
        Widget      parent;
        String      name;
        ArgList     arglist;
        Cardinal    argcount;
```

Description

XmCreateDrawingArea creates an instance of a DrawingArea widget and returns the associated widget ID.

parent Specifies the parent widget ID

name Specifies the name of the created widget

arglist Specifies the argument list

argcount Specifies the number of attribute/value pairs in the argument list (*arglist*)

For a complete definition of DrawingArea and its associated resources, see **XmDrawingArea(3X)**.

Return Value

Returns the DrawingArea widget ID.

Related Information

XmDrawingArea(3X).

XmCreateDrawnButton

Purpose

The DrawnButton widget creation function

Synopsis

```
#include <Xm/DrawnB.h>

Widget XmCreateDrawnButton (parent, name, arglist, argcount)
      Widget      parent;
      String      name;
      ArgList     arglist;
      Cardinal    argcount;
```

Description

XmCreateDrawnButton creates an instance of a DrawnButton widget and returns the associated widget ID.

parent Specifies the parent widget ID

name Specifies the name of the created widget

arglist Specifies the argument list

argcount Specifies the number of attribute/value pairs in the argument list (*arglist*)

For a complete definition of DrawnButton and its associated resources, see **XmDrawnButton(3X)**.

Return Value

Returns the DrawnButton widget ID.

Related Information

XmDrawnButton(3X).

XmCreateErrorDialog

Purpose

The MessageBox ErrorDialog convenience creation function.

Synopsis

#include <Xm/MessageB.h>

Widget XmCreateErrorDialog (*parent, name, arglist, argcount*)
    Widget *parent*;
    String *name*;
    ArgList *arglist*;
    Cardinal *argcount*;

Description

XmCreateErrorDialog is a convenience creation function that creates a DialogShell and an unmanaged MessageBox child of the DialogShell. An ErrorDialog warns the user of an invalid or potentially dangerous condition. It includes a symbol, a message, and three buttons. The default symbol is an octagon with a diagonal slash. The default button labels are **OK**, **Cancel**, and **Help**.

Use **XtManageChild** to pop up the ErrorDialog (passing the MessageBox as the widget parameter); use **XtUnmanageChild** to pop it down.

parent Specifies the parent widget ID

name Specifies the name of the created widget

arglist Specifies the argument list

argcount Specifies the number of attribute/value pairs in the argument list (*arglist*)

For a complete definition of MessageBox and its associated resources, see **XmMessageBox(3X)**.

Return Value

Returns the MessageBox widget ID.

Related Information

XmMessageBox(3X).

XmCreateFileSelectionBox

Purpose

The FileSelectionBox widget creation function

Synopsis

```
#include <Xm/FileSB.h>

Widget XmCreateFileSelectionBox (parent, name, arglist, argcount)
      Widget      parent;
      String      name;
      ArgList     arglist;
      Cardinal    argcount;
```

Description

XmCreateFileSelectionBox creates an unmanaged FileSelectionBox. A FileSelectionBox is used to select a file and includes the following:

- An editable text field for the directory mask
- A scrolling list of file names
- An editable text field for the selected file
- Labels for the list and text fields
- Four buttons

The default button labels are **OK**, **Filter**, **Cancel**, and **Help**. One additional **WorkArea** child may be added to the FileSelectionBox after creation.

If the parent of the FileSelectionBox is a DialogShell, use **XtManageChild** to pop up the FileSelectionDialog (passing the FileSelectionBox as the widget parameter); use **XtUnmanageChild** to pop it down.

parent Specifies the parent widget ID

name Specifies the name of the created widget

arglist Specifies the argument list

argcount Specifies the number of attribute/value pairs in the argument list (*arglist*)

For a complete definition of FileSelectionBox and its associated resources, see **XmFileSelectionBox(3X)**.

Return Value

Returns the FileSelectionBox widget ID.

Related Information

XmFileSelectionBox(3X).

XmCreateFileSelectionDialog

Purpose

The FileSelectionBox FileSelectionDialog convenience creation function.

Synopsis

```
#include <Xm/FileSB.h>

Widget XmCreateFileSelectionDialog (parent, name, arglist, argcount)
      Widget      parent;
      String      name;
      ArgList     arglist;
      Cardinal    argcount;
```

Description

XmCreateFileSelectionDialog is a convenience creation function that creates a DialogShell and an unmanaged FileSelectionBox child of the DialogShell. A FileSelectionDialog selects a file. It includes the following:

- An editable text field for the directory mask
- A scrolling list of filenames
- An editable text field for the selected file
- Labels for the list and text fields
- Four buttons

The default button labels are: **OK**, **Filter**, **Cancel**, and **Help**. One additional **WorkArea** child may be added to the FileSelectionBox after creation.

Use **XtManageChild** to pop up the FileSelectionDialog (passing the FileSelectionBox as the widget parameter); use **XtUnmanageChild** to pop it down.

parent Specifies the parent widget ID

name Specifies the name of the created widget

arglist Specifies the argument list

argcount Specifies the number of attribute/value pairs in the argument list (*arglist*)

For a complete definition of FileSelectionBox and its associated resources, see **XmFileSelectionBox(3X)**.

Return Value

Returns the FileSelectionBox widget ID.

Related Information

XmFileSelectionBox(3X).

XmCreateForm

Purpose

The Form widget creation function

Synopsis

#include <Xm/Form.h>

Widget XmCreateForm (*parent, name, arglist, argcount*)
    Widget *parent*;
    String *name*;
    ArgList *arglist*;
    Cardinal *argcount*;

Description

XmCreateForm creates an instance of a Form widget and returns the associated widget ID.

parent Specifies the parent widget ID

name Specifies the name of the created widget

arglist Specifies the argument list

argcount Specifies the number of attribute/value pairs in the argument list (*arglist*)

For a complete definition of Form and its associated resources, see **XmForm(3X)**.

Return Value

Returns the Form widget ID.

Related Information

XmForm(3X).

XmCreateFormDialog

Purpose

A Form FormDialog convenience creation function

Synopsis

#include <Xm/Form.h>

Widget XmCreateFormDialog (*parent, name, arglist, argcount*)
  Widget *parent*;
  String *name*;
  ArgList *arglist*;
  Cardinal *argcount*;

Description

XmCreateFormDialog is a convenience creation function that creates a DialogShell and an unmanaged Form child of the DialogShell. A FormDialog is used for interactions not supported by the standard dialog set. This function does not automatically create any labels, buttons, or other dialog components. Such components should be added by the application after the FormDialog is created.

Use **XtManageChild** to pop up the FormDialog (passing the Form as the widget parameter); use **XtUnmanageChild** to pop it down.

parent Specifies the parent widget ID

name Specifies the name of the created widget

arglist Specifies the argument list

argcount Specifies the number of attribute/value pairs in the argument list (*arglist*)

For a complete definition of Form and its associated resources, see **XmForm(3X)**.

Return Value

Returns the Form widget ID.

Related Information

XmForm(3X).

XmCreateFrame

Purpose

The Frame widget creation function

Synopsis

```
#include <Xm/Frame.h>

Widget XmCreateFrame (parent, name, arglist, argcount)
        Widget      parent;
        String      name;
        ArgList     arglist;
        Cardinal    argcount;
```

Description

XmCreateFrame creates an instance of a Frame widget and returns the associated widget ID.

parent Specifies the parent widget ID

name Specifies the name of the created widget

arglist Specifies the argument list

argcount Specifies the number of attribute/value pairs in the argument list (*arglist*)

For a complete definition of Frame and its associated resources, see **XmFrame(3X)**.

Return Value

Returns the Frame widget ID.

Related Information

XmFrame(3X).

XmCreateInformationDialog

Purpose

The MessageBox InformationDialog convenience creation function.

Synopsis

```
#include <Xm/MessageB.h>

Widget XmCreateInformationDialog (parent, name, arglist, argcount)
        Widget      parent;
        String      name;
        ArgList     arglist;
        Cardinal    argcount;
```

Description

XmCreateInformationDialog is a convenience creation function that creates a DialogShell and an unmanaged MessageBox child of the DialogShell. An InformationDialog gives the user information, such as the status of an action. It includes a symbol, a message, and three buttons. The default symbol is a lower case **i**. The default button labels are **OK**, **Cancel**, and **Help**.

Use **XtManageChild** to pop up the InformationDialog (passing the MessageBox as the widget parameter); use **XtUnmanageChild** to pop it down.

parent Specifies the parent widget ID

name Specifies the name of the created widget

arglist Specifies the argument list

argcount Specifies the number of attribute/value pairs in the argument list (*arglist*)

For a complete definition of MessageBox and its associated resources, see **XmMessageBox(3X)**.

Return Value

Returns the MessageBox widget ID.

Related Information

XmMessageBox(3X).

XmCreateLabel

Purpose

The Label widget creation function

Synopsis

```
#include <Xm/Label.h>

Widget XmCreateLabel (parent, name, arglist, argcount)
        Widget      parent;
        String      name;
        ArgList     arglist;
        Cardinal    argcount;
```

Description

XmCreateLabel creates an instance of a Label widget and returns the associated widget ID.

parent Specifies the parent widget ID

name Specifies the name of the created widget

arglist Specifies the argument list

argcount Specifies the number of attribute/value pairs in the argument list (*arglist*)

For a complete definition of Label and its associated resources, see **XmLabel(3X)**.

Return Value

Returns the Label widget ID.

Related Information

XmLabel(3X).

XmCreateLabelGadget

Purpose

The LabelGadget creation function

Synopsis

```
#include <Xm/LabelG.h>

Widget XmCreateLabelGadget (parent, name, arglist, argcount)
        Widget      parent;
        String      name;
        ArgList     arglist;
        Cardinal    argcount;
```

Description

XmCreateLabelGadget creates an instance of a LabelGadget widget and returns the associated widget ID.

parent Specifies the parent widget ID

name Specifies the name of the created widget

arglist Specifies the argument list

argcount Specifies the number of attribute/value pairs in the argument list (*arglist*)

For a complete definition of LabelGadget and its associated resources, see **XmLabelGadget(3X)**.

Return Value

Returns the LabelGadget widget ID.

Related Information

XmLabelGadget(3X).

XmCreateList

Purpose

The List widget creation function

Synopsis

#include <Xm/List.h>

Widget XmCreateList (*parent, name, arglist, argcount*))
    Widget *parent*;
    String *name*;
    ArgList *arglist*;
    Cardinal *argcount*;

Description

XmCreateList creates an instance of a List widget and returns the associated widget ID.

parent Specifies the parent widget ID

name Specifies the name of the created widget

arglist Specifies the argument list

argcount Specifies the number of attribute/value pairs in the argument list (*arglist*)

For a complete definition of List and its associated resources, see **XmList(3X)**.

Return Value

Returns the List widget ID.

Related Information

XmList(3X).

XmCreateMainWindow

Purpose

The MainWindow widget creation function

Synopsis

#include <Xm/MainW.h>

Widget XmCreateMainWindow (*parent, name, arglist, argcount*)
    Widget *parent*;
    String *name*;
    ArgList *arglist*;
    Cardinal *argcount*;

Description

XmCreateMainWindow creates an instance of a MainWindow widget and returns the associated widget ID.

parent Specifies the parent widget ID

name Specifies the name of the created widget

arglist Specifies the argument list

argcount Specifies the number of attribute/value pairs in the argument list (*arglist*)

For a complete definition of MainWindow and its associated resources, see **XmMainWindow(3X)**.

Return Value

Returns the MainWindow widget ID.

Related Information

XmMainWindow(3X).

XmCreateMenuBar

Purpose

A RowColumn widget convenience creation function

Synopsis

```
#include <Xm/RowColumn.h>

Widget XmCreateMenuBar (parent, name, arglist, argcount)
      Widget      parent;
      String      name;
      ArgList     arglist;
      Cardinal    argcount;
```

Description

XmCreateMenuBar creates an instance of a RowColumn widget of type **XmMENU_BAR** and returns the associated widget ID.

It is provided as a convenience function for creating RowColumn widgets configured to operate as a MenuBar and is not implemented as a separate widget class.

The MenuBar widget is generally used for building a Pulldown menu system. Typically, a MenuBar is created and placed along the top of the application window, and several CascadeButtons are inserted as the children. Each of the CascadeButtons has a Pulldown MenuPane associated with it. These Pulldown MenuPanes must have been created as children of the MenuBar. The user interacts with the MenuBar by using either the mouse or the keyboard.

The MenuBar displays a 3-D shadow along its border. The application controls the shadow attributes using the visual-related resources supported by **XmManager**.

The MenuBar widget is homogeneous in that it accepts only children that are a subclass of **XmCascadeButton**. Attempting to insert a child of a different class results in a warning message.

If the MenuBar does not have enough room to fit all of its subwidgets on a single line, the MenuBar attempts to wrap the remaining entries onto additional lines if allowed by the geometry manager of the parent widget.

parent Specifies the parent widget ID

name Specifies the name of the created widget

arglist Specifies the argument list

argcount Specifies the number of attribute/value pairs in the argument list (*arglist*)

For a complete definition of RowColumn and its associated resources, see **XmRowColumn(3X)**.

Return Value

Returns the RowColumn widget ID.

Related Information

XmCascadeButton(3X), **XmCreatePulldownMenu(3X)**, **XmManager(3X)**, and **XmRowColumn(3X)**.

XmCreateMenuShell

Purpose

The MenuShell widget creation function

Synopsis

#include <Xm/MenuShell.h>

Widget XmCreateMenuShell (*parent, name, arglist, argcount*)
  Widget *parent*;
  String *name*;
  ArgList *arglist*;
  Cardinal *argcount*;

Description

XmCreateMenuShell creates an instance of a MenuShell widget and returns the associated widget ID.

parent Specifies the parent widget ID

name Specifies the name of the created widget

arglist Specifies the argument list

argcount Specifies the number of attribute/value pairs in the argument list (*arglist*)

For a complete definition of MenuShell and its associated resources, see **XmMenuShell(3X)**.

Return Value

Returns the MenuShell widget ID.

Related Information

XmMenuShell(3X).

XmCreateMessageBox

Purpose

The MessageBox widget creation function

Synopsis

#include <Xm/MessageB.h>

Widget XmCreateMessageBox (*parent, name, arglist, argcount*)
    Widget *parent*;
    String *name*;
    ArgList *arglist*;
    Cardinal *argcount*;

Description

XmCreateMessageBox creates an unmanaged MessageBox. A MessageBox is used for common interaction tasks, which include giving information, asking questions, and reporting errors. It includes n optional symbol, a message, and three buttons.

By default, there is no symbol. The default button labels are **OK**, **Cancel**, and **Help**.

If the parent of the MessageBox is a DialogShell, use **XtManageChild** to pop up the MessageBox (passing the MessageBox as the widget parameter); use **XtUnmanageChild** to pop it down.

parent Specifies the parent widget ID

name Specifies the name of the created widget

arglist Specifies the argument list

argcount Specifies the number of attribute/value pairs in the argument list (*arglist*)

For a complete definition of MessageBox and its associated resources, see **XmMessageBox(3X)**.

Return Value

Returns the MessageBox widget ID.

Related Information

XmMessageBox(3X).

XmCreateMessageDialog

Purpose

The MessageBox MessageDialog convenience creation function.

Synopsis

#include <Xm/MessageB.h>

Widget XmCreateMessageDialog (*parent, name, arglist, argcount*)
    Widget *parent*;
    String *name*;
    ArgList *arglist*;
    Cardinal *argcount*;

Description

XmCreateMessageDialog is a convenience creation function that creates a DialogShell and an unmanaged MessageBox child of the DialogShell. A MessageDialog is used for common interaction tasks, which include giving information, asking questions, and reporting errors. It includes a symbol, a message, and three buttons. By default, there is no symbol. The default button labels are **OK**, **Cancel**, and **Help**.

Use **XtManageChild** to pop up the MessageDialog (passing the MessageBox as the widget parameter); use **XtUnmanageChild** to pop it down.

parent Specifies the parent widget ID

name Specifies the name of the created widget

arglist Specifies the argument list

argcount Specifies the number of attribute/value pairs in the argument list (*arglist*)

For a complete definition of MessageBox and its associated resources, see **XmMessageBox(3X)**.

Return Value

Returns the MessageBox widget ID.

Related Information

XmMessageBox(3X).

XmCreateOptionMenu

Purpose

A RowColumn widget convenience creation function

Synopsis

#include <Xm/RowColumn.h>

Widget XmCreateOptionMenu (*parent, name, arglist, argcount*)
  Widget *parent*;
  String *name*;
  ArgList *arglist*;
  Cardinal *argcount*;

Description

XmCreateOptionMenu creates an instance of a RowColumn widget of type **XmMENU_OPTION** and returns the associated widget ID.

It is provided as a convenience function for creating a RowColumn widget configured to operate as an OptionMenu and is not implemented as a separate widget class.

The OptionMenu widget is a specialized RowColumn manager composed of a label, a selection area, and a single Pulldown MenuPane. When an application creates an OptionMenu widget, it supplies the label string and the Pulldown MenuPane. In order to succeed, there must be a valid **XmNsubMenuId** resource set when calling this function. When the

OptionMenu is created, the Pulldown MenuPane must have been created as a child of the OptionMenu's parent and must be specified. The LabelGadget and the selection area (a CascadeButtonGadget) are created by the OptionMenu.

An OptionMenu is laid out with the label displayed on the left side of the widget and the selection area on the right side. The selection area has a dual purpose; it displays the label of the last item selected from the associated Pulldown MenuPane, and it provides the means for posting the Pulldown MenuPane.

The OptionMenu typically does not display any 3-D visuals around itself or the internal LabelGadget. By default, the internal CascadeButtonGadget has a visible 3-D shadow. The application may change this by getting the CascadeButtonGadget ID using **XmOptionButtonGadget**, and then calling **XtSetValues** using the standard visual-related resources.

The Pulldown MenuPane is posted by moving the mouse pointer over the selection area and pressing the mouse button defined by OptionMenu's **XmNwhichButton** resource. The Pulldown MenuPane is posted and positioned so that the last selected item is directly over the selection area. The mouse is then used to arm the desired menu item. When the mouse button is released, the armed menu item is selected and the label within the selection area is changed to match that of the selected item. By default, mouse button 1 is used to interact with an OptionMenu. The default can be changed via the RowColumn resource **XmNwhichButton**.

The OptionMenu also operates by using the keyboard interface mechanism. If the application has established a mnemonic with the OptionMenu, typing the mnemonic causes the Pulldown MenuPane to be posted with traversal enabled. The standard traversal keys can then be used to move within the MenuPane. Selection can occur as the result of pressing the Return key or typing a mnemonic or accelerator for one of the menu items.

An application may use the **XmNmenuHistory** resource to indicate which item in the Pulldown MenuPane should be treated as the current choice and have its label displayed in the selection area. By default, the first item in the Pulldown MenuPane is used.

parent Specifies the parent widget ID

name Specifies the name of the created widget

arglist Specifies the argument list

argcount Specifies the number of attribute/value pairs in the argument list (*arglist*)

For a complete definition of RowColumn and its associated resources, see **XmRowColumn(3X)**.

Return Value

Returns the RowColumn widget ID.

Related Information

XmCascadeButtonGadget(3X), **XmCreatePulldownMenu(3X)**, **XmLabelGadget(3X)**, and **XmRowColumn(3X)**.

XmCreatePanedWindow

Purpose

The PanedWindow widget creation function.

Synopsis

#include <Xm/PanedW.h>

Widget XmCreatePanedWindow (*parent, name, arglist, argcount*)
  Widget *parent*;
  String *name*;
  ArgList *arglist*;
  Cardinal *argcount*;

Description

XmCreatePanedWindow creates an instance of a PanedWindow widget and returns the associated widget ID.

parent Specifies the parent widget ID

name Specifies the name of the created widget

arglist Specifies the argument list

argcount Specifies the number of attribute/value pairs in the argument list (*arglist*)

For a complete definition of PanedWindow and its associated resources, see **XmPanedWindow(3X)**.

Return Value

Returns the PanedWindow widget ID.

Related Information

XmPanedWindow(3X).

XmCreatePopupMenu

Purpose

A RowColumn widget convenience creation function

Synopsis

#include <Xm/RowColumn.h>

Widget XmCreatePopupMenu (*parent, name, arglist, argcount*)
    Widget *parent*;
    String *name*;
    ArgList *arglist*;
    Cardinal *argcount*;

Description

XmCreatePopupMenu creates an instance of a RowColumn widget of type **XmMENU_POPUP** and returns the associated widget ID. When using this function to create the Popup MenuPane, a MenuShell widget is automatically created as the parent of the MenuPane. The parent of the MenuShell widget is the widget indicated by the *parent* parameter.

XmCreatePopupMenu is provided as a convenience function for creating RowColumn widgets configured to operate as Popup MenuPanes and is not implemented as a separate widget class.

The PopupMenu is used as the first MenuPane within a PopupMenu system; all other MenuPanes are of the Pulldown type. A Popup MenuPane displays a 3-D shadow, unless the feature is disabled by the application. The shadow appears around the edge of the MenuPane.

The Popup MenuPane must be created as the child of a MenuShell widget in order to function properly when it is incorporated into a menu. If the application uses this convenience function for creating a Popup MenuPane, the MenuShell is automatically created as the real parent of the MenuPane. If the application does not use this convenience function to create the RowColumn to function as a Popup MenuPane, it is the application's responsibility to create the MenuShell widget.

To access the PopupMenu, the application must first position the widget using the **XmMenuPosition** function and then manage it using **XtManageChild**.

parent Specifies the parent widget ID

name Specifies the name of the created widget

arglist Specifies the argument list

argcount Specifies the number of attribute/value pairs in the argument list (*arglist*)

For a complete definition of RowColumn and its associated resources, see **XmRowColumn(3X)**.

Return Value

Returns the RowColumn widget ID.

Related Information

XmMenuPosition(3X), **XmMenuShell(3X)**, and **XmRowColumn(3X)**.

XmCreatePromptDialog

Purpose

The SelectionBox PromptDialog convenience creation function.

Synopsis

#include <Xm/SelectioB.h>

Widget XmCreatePromptDialog (*parent, name, arglist, argcount*)
    Widget *parent*;
    String *name*;
    ArgList *arglist*;
    Cardinal *argcount*;

Description

XmCreatePromptDialog is a convenience creation function that creates a DialogShell and an unmanaged SelectionBox child of the DialogShell. A PromptDialog prompts the user for text input. It includes a message, a text input region, and three managed buttons. The default button labels are **OK**, **Cancel**, and **Help**. An additional button, with **Apply** as the default label, is created unmanaged; it may be explicitly managed if needed. One additional **WorkArea** child may be added to the SelectionBox after creation.

Use **XtManageChild** to pop up the PromptDialog (passing the SelectionBox as the widget parameter); use **XtUnmanageChild** to pop it down.

parent Specifies the parent widget ID

name Specifies the name of the created widget

arglist Specifies the argument list

argcount Specifies the number of attribute/value pairs in the argument list (*arglist*)

For a complete definition of SelectionBox and its associated resources, see **XmSelectionBox(3X)**.

Return Value

Returns the SelectionBox widget ID.

Related Information

XmSelectionBox(3X).

XmCreatePulldownMenu

Purpose

A RowColumn widget convenience creation function

Synopsis

```
#include <Xm/RowColumn.h>

Widget XmCreatePulldownMenu (parent, name, arglist, argcount)
        Widget     parent;
        String     name;
        ArgList    arglist;
        Cardinal   argcount;
```

Description

XmCreatePulldownMenu creates an instance of a RowColumn widget of type **XmMENU_PULLDOWN** and returns the associated widget ID. When using this function to create the Pulldown MenuPane, a MenuShell widget is automatically created as the parent of the MenuPane. If the widget specified by the *parent* parameter is a Popup or a Pulldown MenuPane, the MenuShell widget is created as a child of the *parent*'s MenuShell; otherwise, it is created as a child of the specified *parent* widget.

XmCreatePulldownMenu is provided as a convenience function for creating RowColumn widgets configured to operate as Pulldown MenuPanes and is not implemented as a separate widget class.

A Pulldown MenuPane displays a 3-D shadow, unless the feature is disabled by the application. The shadow appears around the edge of the MenuPane.

A Pulldown MenuPane is used when creating submenus that are to be attached to a CascadeButton or a CascadeButtonGadget. This is the case for all MenuPanes that are part of a PulldownMenu system (a MenuBar), the MenuPane associated with an OptionMenu, and any MenuPanes that cascade from a Popup MenuPane. Pulldown MenuPanes that are to be associated with an OptionMenu must be created before the OptionMenu is created.

The Pulldown MenuPane must be attached to a CascadeButton or CascadeButtonGadget that resides in a MenuBar, a Popup MenuPane, a Pulldown MenuPane, or an OptionMenu. This is done by using the button resource **XmNsubMenuId**.

A MenuShell widget is required between the Pulldown MenuPane and its parent. If the application uses this convenience function for creating a Pulldown MenuPane, the MenuShell is automatically created as the real parent of the MenuPane; otherwise, it is the application's responsibility to create the MenuShell widget.

To function correctly when incorporated into a menu, the Pulldown MenuPane's hierarchy must be considered; this hierarchy depends on the type of menu system that is being built as follows:

- If the Pulldown MenuPane is to be pulled down from a MenuBar, its *parent* must be the MenuBar.
- If the Pulldown MenuPane is to be pulled down from a Popup or another Pulldown MenuPane, its *parent* must be that Popup or Pulldown MenuPane.
- If the Pulldown MenuPane is to be pulled down from an OptionMenu, its *parent* must be the same as the OptionMenu parent.

parent Specifies the parent widget ID

name Specifies the name of the created widget

arglist Specifies the argument list

argcount Specifies the number of attribute/value pairs in the argument list (*arglist*)

For a complete definition of RowColumn and its associated resources, see **XmRowColumn(3X)**.

Return Value

Returns the RowColumn widget ID.

Related Information

XmCascadeButton(3X), **XmCascadeButtonGadget(3X)**, **XmCreateOptionMenu(3X)**, **XmCreatePopupMenu(3X)**, **XmCreatePulldownMenu(3X)**, **XmMenuShell(3X)**, and **XmRowColumn(3X)**.

XmCreatePushButton

Purpose

The PushButton widget creation function

Synopsis

```
#include <Xm/PushB.h>

Widget XmCreatePushButton (parent, name, arglist, argcount)
        Widget      parent;
        String      name;
        ArgList     arglist;
        Cardinal    argcount;
```

Description

XmCreatePushButton creates an instance of a PushButton widget and returns the associated widget ID.

parent Specifies the parent widget ID

name Specifies the name of the created widget

arglist Specifies the argument list

argcount Specifies the number of attribute/value pairs in the argument list (*arglist*)

For a complete definition of PushButton and its associated resources, see **XmPushButton(3X)**.

Return Value

Returns the PushButton widget ID.

Related Information

XmPushButton(3X).

XmCreatePushButtonGadget

Purpose

The PushButtonGadget creation function

Synopsis

#include <Xm/PushBG.h>

Widget XmCreatePushButtonGadget (*parent, name, arglist, argcount*)
    Widget *parent*;
    String *name*;
    ArgList *arglist*;
    Cardinal *argcount*;

Description

XmCreatePushButtonGadget creates an instance of a PushButtonGadget widget and returns the associated widget ID.

parent Specifies the parent widget ID

name Specifies the name of the created widget

arglist Specifies the argument list

argcount Specifies the number of attribute/value pairs in the argument list (*arglist*)

For a complete definition of PushButtonGadget and its associated resources, see **XmPushButtonGadget(3X)**.

Return Value

Returns the PushButtonGadget widget ID.

Related Information

XmPushButtonGadget(3X).

XmCreateQuestionDialog

Purpose

The MessageBox QuestionDialog convenience creation function.

Synopsis

```
#include <Xm/MessageB.h>

Widget XmCreateQuestionDialog (parent, name, arglist, argcount)
      Widget      parent;
      String      name;
      ArgList     arglist;
      Cardinal    argcount;
```

Description

XmCreateQuestionDialog is a convenience creation function that creates a DialogShell and an unmanaged MessageBox child of the DialogShell. A QuestionDialog is used to get the answer to a question from the user. It includes a symbol, a message, and three buttons. The default symbol is a question mark. The default button labels are **OK**, **Cancel**, and **Help**.

Use **XtManageChild** to pop up the QuestionDialog (passing the MessageBox as the widget parameter); use **XtUnmanageChild** to pop it down.

parent Specifies the parent widget ID

name Specifies the name of the created widget

arglist Specifies the argument list

argcount Specifies the number of attribute/value pairs in the argument list (*arglist*)

For a complete definition of MessageBox and its associated resources, see **XmMessageBox(3X)**.

Return Value

Returns the MessageBox widget ID.

Related Information

XmMessageBox(3X).

XmCreateRadioBox

Purpose

A RowColumn widget convenience creation function

Synopsis

```
#include <Xm/RowColumn.h>

Widget XmCreateRadioBox (parent, name, arglist, argcount)
    Widget    parent;
    String    name;
    ArgList   arglist;
    Cardinal  argcount;
```

Description

XmCreateRadioBox creates an instance of a RowColumn widget of type **XmWORK_AREA** and returns the associated widget ID. Typically, this is a composite widget that contains multiple ToggleButtonGadgets. The RadioBox arbitrates and ensures that at most one ToggleButtonGadget is on at any time.

The ToggleButtons are forced to have the resources **XmNindicatorType** set to **XmONE_OF_MANY** and **XmNvisibleWhenOff** set to True.

It is provided as a convenience function for creating RowColumn widgets.

parent Specifies the parent widget ID

name Specifies the name of the created widget

arglist Specifies the argument list

argcount Specifies the number of attribute/value pairs in the argument list (*arglist*)

For a complete definition of RowColumn and its associated resources, see **XmRowColumn(3X)**.

Return Value

Returns the RowColumn widget ID.

Related Information

XmRowColumn(3X).

XmCreateRowColumn

Purpose

The RowColumn widget creation function

Synopsis

```
#include <Xm/RowColumn.h>

Widget XmCreateRowColumn (parent, name, arglist, argcount)
        Widget      parent;
        String      name;
        ArgList     arglist;
        Cardinal    argcount;
```

Description

XmCreateRowColumn creates an instance of a RowColumn widget and returns the associated widget ID. If **XmNrowColumnType** is not specified, then it is created with **XmWORK_AREA**, which is the default.

If this function is used to create a Popup Menu of type **XmMENU_POPUP** or a Pulldown Menu of type **XmMENU_PULLDOWN**, a MenuShell widget is not automatically created as the parent of the MenuPane. The application must first create the MenuShell by using either **XmCreateMenuShell** or the standard toolkit create function.

parent Specifies the parent widget ID

name Specifies the name of the created widget

arglist Specifies the argument list

argcount Specifies the number of attribute/value pairs in the argument list (*arglist*)

For a complete definition of RowColumn and its associated resources, see **XmRowColumn(3X)**.

Return Value

Returns the RowColumn widget ID.

Related Information

XmCreateMenuShell(3X), **XmCreatePopupMenu(3X)**, **XmCreatePulldownMenu(3X)**, and **XmRowColumn(3X)**.

XmCreateScale

Purpose

The Scale widget creation function

Synopsis

#include <Xm/Scale.h>

Widget XmCreateScale (*parent, name, arglist, argcount*)
  Widget *parent*;
  String *name*;
  ArgList *arglist*;
  Cardinal *argcount*;

Description

XmCreateScale creates an instance of a Scale widget and returns the associated widget ID.

parent Specifies the parent widget ID

name Specifies the name of the created widget

arglist Specifies the argument list

argcount Specifies the number of attribute/value pairs in the argument list (*arglist*)

For a complete definition of Scale and its associated resources, see **XmScale(3X)**.

Return Value

Returns the Scale widget ID.

Related Information

XmScale(3X).

XmCreateScrollBar

Purpose

The ScrollBar widget creation function

Synopsis

```
#include <Xm/ScrollBar.h>

Widget XmCreateScrollBar (parent, name, arglist, argcount)
        Widget      parent;
        String      name;
        ArgList     arglist;
        Cardinal    argcount;
```

Description

XmCreateScrollBar creates an instance of a ScrollBar widget and returns the associated widget ID.

parent Specifies the parent widget ID

name Specifies the name of the created widget

arglist Specifies the argument list

argcount Specifies the number of attribute/value pairs in the argument list (*arglist*)

For a complete definition of ScrollBar and its associated resources, see **XmScrollBar(3X)**.

Return Value

Returns the ScrollBar widget ID.

Related Information

XmScrollBar(3X).

XmCreateScrolledList

Purpose

The List ScrolledList convenience creation function.

Synopsis

#include <Xm/List.h>

Widget XmCreateScrolledList (*parent, name, arglist, argcount)*)
Widget *parent*;
String *name*;
ArgList *arglist*;
Cardinal *argcount*;

Description

XmCreateScrolledList creates an instance of a List widget that is contained within a ScrolledWindow. All ScrolledWindow subarea widgets are automatically created by this function. The ID returned by this function is that of the List widget. Use this ID for all normal List operations, as well as those that are relevant for the ScrolledList widget.

Other aspects of the appearance and behavior of the ScrolledList should be controlled by using the ScrolledWindow widget resources. For instance, an application writer who wishes to specify the *x,y* location of a ScrolledList within a larger manager should set the **XmNx** and **XmNy** resources of the ScrolledWindow rather than of the List widget.

To obtain the ID of the ScrolledWindow widget associated with the ScrolledList, use the Xt Intrinsics **XtParent** function. The name of the ScrolledWindow created by this function is formed by concatenating the letters **SW** onto the end of the *name* specified in the parameter list.

parent Specifies the parent widget ID

name Specifies the name of the created widget

arglist Specifies the argument list

argcount Specifies the number of attribute/value pairs in the argument list (*arglist*)

For a complete definition of List and its associated resources, see **XmList(3X)**.

Return Value

Returns the List widget ID.

Related Information

XmList(3X) and **XmScrolledWindow(3X)**.

XmCreateScrolledText

Purpose

The Text ScrolledText convenience creation function.

Synopsis

```
#include <Xm/Text.h>

Widget XmCreateScrolledText (parent, name, arglist, argcount)
        Widget      parent;
        String      name;
        ArgList     arglist;
        Cardinal    argcount;
```

Description

XmCreateScrolledText creates an instance of a Text widget that is contained within a ScrolledWindow. All ScrolledWindow subarea widgets are automatically created by this function. The ID returned by this function is that of the Text widget. Use this ID for all normal Text operations, as well as those that are relevant for the ScrolledText widget.

The Text widget defaults to single-line text edit; therefore, no ScrollBars are displayed. The Text resource **XmNeditMode** must be set to **XmMULTI-LINE-EDIT** to display the ScrollBars.

Other aspects of the appearance and behavior of the ScrolledText should be controlled by using the ScrolledWindow widget resources. For instance, an application writer who wishes to specify the *x,y* location of a ScrolledText within a larger manager should set the **XmNx** and **XmNy** resources of the ScrolledWindow rather than of the Text widget.

To obtain the ID of the ScrolledWindow widget associated with the ScrolledText, use the Xt Intrinsics **XtParent** function. The name of the ScrolledWindow created by this function is formed by concatenating the letters **SW** onto the end of the *name* specified in the parameter list.

parent Specifies the parent widget ID

name Specifies the name of the created widget

arglist Specifies the argument list

argcount Specifies the number of attribute/value pairs in the argument list (*arglist*)

For a complete definition of Text and its associated resources, see **XmText(3X)**.

Return Value

Returns the Text widget ID.

Related Information

XmScrolledWindow(3X) and **XmText(3X)**.

XmCreateScrolledWindow

Purpose

The ScrolledWindow widget creation function.

Synopsis

#include <Xm/ScrolledW.h>

Widget XmCreateScrolledWindow (*parent, name, arglist, argcount*)
Widget *parent*;
String *name*;
ArgList *arglist*;
Cardinal *argcount*;

Description

XmCreateScrolledWindow creates an instance of a ScrolledWindow widget and returns the associated widget ID.

parent Specifies the parent widget ID

name Specifies the name of the created widget

arglist Specifies the argument list

argcount Specifies the number of attribute/value pairs in the argument list (*arglist*)

For a complete definition of ScrolledWindow and its associated resources, see **XmScrolledWindow(3X)**.

Return Value

Returns the ScrolledWindow widget ID.

Related Information

XmScrolledWindow(3X).

XmCreateSelectionBox

Purpose

The SelectionBox widget creation function

Synopsis

#include <Xm/SelectioB.h>

Widget XmCreateSelectionBox (*parent, name, arglist, argcount*)
    Widget *parent*;
    String *name*;
    ArgList *arglist*;
    Cardinal *argcount*;

Description

XmCreateSelectionBox creates an unmanaged SelectionBox. A SelectionBox is used to get a selection from a list of alternatives from the user and includes the following:

- A scrolling list of alternatives
- An editable text field for the selected alternative
- Labels for the list and text field
- Three buttons

The default button labels are **OK**, **Cancel**, and **Help**. An **Apply** button is created unmanaged and may be explicitly managed as needed. One additional **WorkArea** child may be added to the SelectionBox after creation.

parent Specifies the parent widget ID

name Specifies the name of the created widget

arglist Specifies the argument list

argcount Specifies the number of attribute/value pairs in the argument list (*arglist*)

For a complete definition of SelectionBox and its associated resources, see **XmSelectionBox(3X)**.

Return Value

Returns the SelectionBox widget ID.

Related Information

XmSelectionBox(3X)

XmCreateSelectionDialog

Purpose

The SelectionBox SelectionDialog convenience creation function.

Synopsis

#include <Xm/SelectioB.h>

Widget XmCreateSelectionDialog (*parent, name, arglist, argcount*)
  Widget *parent*;
  String *name*;
  ArgList *arglist*;
  Cardinal *argcount*;

Description

XmCreateSelectionDialog is a convenience creation function that creates a DialogShell and an unmanaged SelectionBox child of the DialogShell. A SelectionDialog offers the user a choice from a list of alternatives and gets a selection. It includes the following:

- A scrolling list of alternatives
- An editable text field for the selected alternative
- Labels for the text field
- Three buttons

The default button labels are **OK**, **Cancel**, and **Help**. One additional **WorkArea** child may be added to the SelectionBox after creation.

Use **XtManageChild** to pop up the SelectionDialog (passing the SelectionBox as the widget parameter); use **XtUnmanageChild** to pop it down.

parent Specifies the parent widget ID

name Specifies the name of the created widget

arglist Specifies the argument list

argcount Specifies the number of attribute/value pairs in the argument list (*arglist*)

For a complete definition of SelectionBox and its associated resources, see **XmSelectionBox(3X)**.

Return Value

Returns the SelectionBox widget ID.

Related Information

XmSelectionBox(3X).

XmCreateSeparator

Purpose

The Separator widget creation function.

Synopsis

```
#include <Xm/Separator.h>

Widget XmCreateSeparator (parent, name, arglist, argcount)
        Widget      parent;
        String      name;
        ArgList     arglist;
        Cardinal    argcount;
```

Description

XmCreateSeparator creates an instance of a Separator widget and returns the associated widget ID.

parent Specifies the parent widget ID

name Specifies the name of the created widget

arglist Specifies the argument list

argcount Specifies the number of attribute/value pairs in the argument list (*arglist*)

For a complete definition of Separator and its associated resources, see **XmSeparator(3X)**.

Return Value

Returns the Separator widget ID.

Related Information

XmSeparator(3X).

XmCreateSeparatorGadget

Purpose

The SeparatorGadget creation function.

Synopsis

#include <Xm/SeparatoG.h>

Widget XmCreateSeparatorGadget (*parent, name, arglist, argcount*)
Widget *parent*;
String *name*;
ArgList *arglist*;
Cardinal *argcount*;

Description

XmCreateSeparatorGadget creates an instance of a SeparatorGadget widget and returns the associated widget ID.

parent Specifies the parent widget ID

name Specifies the name of the created widget

arglist Specifies the argument list

argcount Specifies the number of attribute/value pairs in the argument list (*arglist*)

For a complete definition of SeparatorGadget and its associated resources, see **XmSeparatorGadget(3X)**.

Return Value

Returns the SeparatorGadget widget ID.

Related Information

XmSeparatorGadget(3X).

XmCreateText

Purpose

The Text widget creation function

Synopsis

#include <Xm/Text.h>

Widget XmCreateText (*parent, name, arglist, argcount*)
    Widget *parent*;
    String *name*;
    ArgList *arglist*;
    Cardinal *argcount*;

Description

XmCreateText creates an instance of a Text widget and returns the associated widget ID.

parent Specifies the parent widget ID

name Specifies the name of the created widget

arglist Specifies the argument list

argcount Specifies the number of attribute/value pairs in the argument list (*arglist*)

For a complete definition of Text and its associated resources, see **XmText(3X)**.

Return Value

Returns the Text widget ID.

Related Information

XmText(3X).

XmCreateToggleButton

Purpose

The ToggleButton widget creation function

Synopsis

#include <Xm/ToggleB.h>

Widget XmCreateToggleButton (*parent, name, arglist, argcount*)
  Widget *parent*;
  String *name*;
  ArgList *arglist*;
  Cardinal *argcount*;

Description

XmCreateToggleButton creates an instance of a ToggleButton widget and returns the associated widget ID.

parent Specifies the parent widget ID

name Specifies the name of the created widget

arglist Specifies the argument list

argcount Specifies the number of attribute/value pairs in the argument list (*arglist*)

For a complete definition of ToggleButton and its associated resources, see **XmToggleButton(3X)**.

Return Value

Returns the ToggleButton widget ID.

Related Information

XmToggleButton(3X).

XmCreateToggleButtonGadget

Purpose

The ToggleButtonGadget creation function.

Synopsis

#include <Xm/ToggleBG.h>

Widget XmCreateToggleButtonGadget (*parent, name, arglist, argcount*)
    Widget *parent*;
    String *name*;
    ArgList *arglist*;
    Cardinal *argcount*;

Description

XmCreateToggleButtonGadget creates an instance of a ToggleButtonGadget and returns the associated widget ID.

parent Specifies the parent widget ID

name Specifies the name of the created widget

arglist Specifies the argument list

argcount Specifies the number of attribute/value pairs in the argument list (*arglist*)

For a complete definition of ToggleButtonGadget and its associated resources, see **XmToggleButtonGadget(3X)**.

Return Value

Returns the ToggleButtonGadget widget ID.

Related Information

XmToggleButtonGadget(3X).

XmCreateWarningDialog

Purpose

A MessageBox WarningDialog convenience creation function.

Synopsis

#include <Xm/MessageB.h>

Widget XmCreateWarningDialog (*parent, name, arglist, argcount*)
  Widget *parent*;
  String *name*;
  ArgList *arglist*;
  Cardinal *argcount*;

Description

XmCreateWarningDialog is a convenience creation function that creates a DialogShell and an unmanaged MessageBox child of the DialogShell. A WarningDialog warns users of action consequences and gives them a choice of resolutions. It includes a symbol, a message, and three buttons. The default symbol is an exclamation point. The default button labels are **OK**, **Cancel**, and **Help**.

Use **XtManageChild** to pop up the WarningDialog (passing the MessageBox as the widget parameter); use **XtUnmanageChild** to pop it down.

parent Specifies the parent widget ID

name Specifies the name of the created widget

arglist Specifies the argument list

argcount Specifies the number of attribute/value pairs in the argument list (*arglist*)

For a complete definition of MessageBox and its associated resources, see **XmMessageBox(3X)**.

Return Value

Returns the MessageBox widget ID.

Related Information

XmMessageBox(3X).

XmCreateWorkingDialog

Purpose

The MessageBox WorkingDialog convenience creation function.

Synopsis

```
#include <Xm/MessageB.h>

Widget XmCreateWorkingDialog (parent, name, arglist, argcount)
       Widget     parent;
       String     name;
       ArgList    arglist;
       Cardinal   argcount;
```

Description

XmCreateWorkingDialog is a convenience creation function that creates a DialogShell and an unmanaged MessageBox child of the DialogShell. A WorkingDialog informs users that there is a time-consuming operation in progress and allows them to cancel the operation. It includes a symbol, a message, and three buttons. The default symbol is an hourglass. The default button labels are **OK**, **Cancel**, and **Help**.

Use **XtManageChild** to pop up the WorkingDialog (passing the MessageBox as the widget parameter); use **XtUnmanageChild** to pop it down.

parent Specifies the parent widget ID

name Specifies the name of the created widget

arglist Specifies the argument list

argcount Specifies the number of attribute/value pairs in the argument list (*arglist*)

For a complete definition of MessageBox and its associated resources, see **XmMessageBox(3X)**.

Return Value

Returns the MessageBox widget ID.

Related Information

XmMessageBox(3X).

XmCvtStringToUnitType

Purpose

A function that converts a string to a unit-type value.

Synopsis

#include <Xm/Xm.h>

void XmCvtStringToUnitType (*args, num_args, from_val, to_val*)
    XrmValuePtr*args*;
    Cardinal * *num_args*;
    XrmValue * *from_val*;
    XrmValue * *to_val*;

Description

XmCvtStringToUnitType converts a string to a unit type. Refer to the man pages for **XmGadget**, **XmManager**, or **XmPrimitive** for a description of the valid unit types.

Install this function as a resource converter using the Xt Intrinsics function **XtAddConverter**, rather than calling it directly. The following code segment shows how to install the converter into the toolkit's converter cache that will allow the resource **XmNunitType** to be specified through a resource file.

XtAddConverter (XmRString, XmRUnitType, XmCvtStringToUnitType, NULL, 0);

This function should be installed only by applications that need to allow the unit type resource to be specified through a resource file. It must be installed before any widget that is to have its **XmNunitType** resource set by data in a resource file is created.

args Specifies a list of additional **XrmValue** arguments to the converter if additional context is needed to perform the conversion. For example, the string-to-font converter needs the widget's screen and the string-to-pixel converter needs the widget's screen and color map. This argument is often NULL.

num_args
Specifies the number of additional **XrmValue** arguments. This argument is often zero.

from_val Specifies the value to convert

to_val Specifies the descriptor to use to return the converted value

Related Information

XmGadget(3X), **XmManager(3X)**, and **XmPrimitive(3X)**.

XmDeactivateProtocol

Purpose

A VendorShell function that deactivates a protocol without removing it.

Synopsis

#include <Xm/Xm.h>
#include <X11/Protocols.h>

void XmDeactivateProtocol (*shell, property, protocol*)
    Widget *shell*;
    Atom *property*;
    Atom *protocol*;

void XmDeactivateWMProtocol (*shell, protocol*)
    Widget *shell*;
    Atom *protocol*;

Description

XmDeactivateProtocol deactivates a protocol without removing it. It updates the handlers and the *property*, if the *shell* is realized. It is sometimes useful to allow a protocol's state information (callback lists, etc.) to persist, even though the client may choose to temporarily resign from the interaction. The main use of this capability is to gray/ungray **f.send_msg** entries in the Mwm system menu. This is supported by allowing a *protocol* to be in one of two states: active or inactive. If the *protocol* is active and the *shell* is realized, the *property* contains the *protocol* **Atom**. If the *protocol* is inactive, the **Atom** is not present in the *property*.

XmDeactivateWMProtocol is a convenience interface. It calls **XmDeactivateProtocol** with the property value set to the atom returned by interning **WM_PROTOCOLS**.

shell Specifies the widget with which the protocol property is associated

property Specifies the protocol property

protocol Specifies the protocol atom (or an int type cast to Atom)

For a complete definition of VendorShell and its associated resources, see **VendorShell(3X)**.

Related Information

mwm(1X), **VendorShell(3X)**, **XmDeactivateWMProtocol(3X)**, and **XmInternAtom(3X)**.

XmDeactivateWMProtocol

Purpose

A VendorShell convenience interface that deactivates a protocol without removing it.

Synopsis

```
#include <Xm/Xm.h>
#include <X11/Protocols.h>

void XmDeactivateWMProtocol (shell, protocol)
        Widget     shell;
        Atom       protocol;
```

Description

XmDeactivateWMProtocol is a convenience interface. It calls **XmDeactivateProtocol** with the property value set to the atom returned by interning **WM_PROTOCOLS**.

shell Specifies the widget with which the protocol property is associated

protocol Specifies the protocol atom (or an int type cast to Atom)

For a complete definition of VendorShell and its associated resources, see **VendorShell(3X)**.

Related Information

VendorShell(3X), **XmDeactivateProtocol(3X)**, and **XmInternAtom(3X)**.

XmDestroyPixmap

Purpose

A pixmap caching function that removes a pixmap from the pixmap cache.

Synopsis

#include <Xm/Xm.h>

Boolean XmDestroyPixmap (*screen, pixmap*)
    Screen   * *screen*;
    Pixmap   *pixmap*;

Description

XmDestroyPixmap removes pixmaps that are no longer used. Pixmaps are completely freed only when there is no further reference to them.

screen Specifies the display screen for which the pixmap was requested

pixmap Specifies the pixmap to be destroyed

Return Value

Returns True when successful; returns False if there is no matching screen and pixmap in the pixmap cache.

Related Information

XmInstallImage(3X), **XmUninstallImage(3X)**, and **XmGetPixmap(3X)**.

XmDialogShell

Purpose

The DialogShell widget class

Synopsis

#include <Xm/DialogS.h>

Description

Modal and modeless dialogs use DialogShell as the Shell parent. DialogShell widgets cannot be iconified. Instead, all secondary DialogShell widgets associated with an ApplicationShell widget are iconified and de-iconified as a group with the primary widget.

The client indirectly manipulates DialogShell via the convenience interfaces during creation, and it can directly manipulate its BulletinBoard-derived child. Much of the functionality of DialogShell assumes that its child is a BulletinBoard subclass, although it can potentially stand alone.

Classes

DialogShell inherits behavior and resources from **Core**, **Composite**, **Shell**, **WMShell**, **VendorShell**, and **TransientShell** classes.

The class pointer is **xmDialogShellWidgetClass**.

The class name is **XmDialogShell**.

New Resources

DialogShell defines no new resources but overrides the **XmNdeleteResponse** resource in the **VendorShell** class.

Inherited Resources

DialogShell inherits behavior and resources from the following superclasses. For a complete description of each resource, refer to the man page for that superclass.

The following table defines a set of widget resources used by the programmer to specify data. The programmer can also set the resource values for the inherited classes to set attributes for this widget. To reference a resource by name or by class in a .Xdefaults file, remove the **XmN** or **XmC** prefix and use the remaining letters. To specify one of the defined values for a resource in a .Xdefaults file, remove the **Xm** prefix and use the remaining letters (in either lowercase or uppercase, but include any underscores between words). The codes in the access column indicate if the given resource can be set at creation time (**C**), set by using **XtSetValues** (**S**), retrieved by using **XtGetValues** (**G**), or is not applicable (**N/A**).

TransientShell Resource Set		
Name **Class**	**Default** **Type**	**Access**
XmNsaveUnder XmCSaveUnder	True Boolean	CSG
XmNtransient XmCTransient	True Boolean	CSG

VendorShell Resource Set		
Name **Class**	**Default** **Type**	**Access**
XmNdeleteResponse XmCDeleteResponse	XmUNMAP unsigned char	CSG
XmNkeyboardFocusPolicy XmCKeyboardFocusPolicy	XmEXPLICIT unsigned char	CSG
XmNmwmDecorations XmCMwmDecorations	-1 int	CSG
XmNmwmFunctions XmCMwmFunctions	-1 int	CSG
XmNmwmInputMode XmCMwmInputMode	-1 int	CSG
XmNmwmMenu XmCMwmMenu	NULL String	CSG
XmNshellUnitType XmCShellUnitType	XmPIXELS unsigned char	CSG

WMShell Resource Set		
Name **Class**	**Default** **Type**	**Access**
XmNheightInc XmCHeightInc	-1 int	CSG
XmNiconMask XmCIconMask	NULL Pixmap	CSG
XmNiconPixmap XmCIconPixmap	NULL Pixmap	CSG
XmNiconWindow XmCIconWindow	NULL Window	CSG
XmNiconX XmCIconX	-1 int	CSG
XmNiconY XmCIconY	-1 int	CSG
XmNinitialState XmCInitialState	1 int	CSG
XmNinput XmCInput	True Boolean	CSG
XmNmaxAspectX XmCMaxAspectX	-1 int	CSG
XmNmaxAspectY XmCMaxAspectY	-1 int	CSG
XmNmaxHeight XmCMaxHeight	-1 int	CSG
XmNmaxWidth XmCMaxWidth	-1 int	CSG
XmNminAspectX XmCMinAspectX	-1 int	CSG
XmNminAspectY XmCMinAspectY	-1 int	CSG

Name Class	Default Type	Access
XmNminHeight XmCMinHeight	-1 int	CSG
XmNminWidth XmCMinWidth	-1 int	CSG
XmNtitle XmCTitle	NULL char *	CSG
XmNtransient XmCTransient	False Boolean	CSG
XmNwaitForWm XmCWaitForWm	True Boolean	CSG
XmNwidthInc XmCWidthInc	-1 int	CSG
XmNwindowGroup XmCWindowGroup	None XID	CSG
XmNwmTimeout XmCWmTimeout	fivesecond int	CSG

Shell Resource Set		
Name **Class**	**Default** **Type**	**Access**
XmNallowShellResize XmCAllowShellResize	False Boolean	CSG
XmNcreatePopupChildProc XmCCreatePopupChildProc	NULL XmCreatePopupChildProc	CSG
XmNgeometry XmCGeometry	NULL String	CSG
XmNoverrideRedirect XmCOverrideRedirect	False Boolean	CSG
XmNpopdownCallback XmCCallback	NULL XtCallbackList	C
XmNpopupCallback XmCCallback	NULL XtCallbackList	C
XmNsaveUnder XmCSaveUnder	False Boolean	CSG

Composite Resource Set		
Name **Class**	**Default** **Type**	**Access**
XmNinsertPosition XmCInsertPosition	NULL XmRFunction	CSG

Core Resource Set		
Name **Class**	**Default** **Type**	**Access**
XmNaccelerators XmCAccelerators	NULL XtTranslations	CSG
XmNancestorSensitive XmCSensitive	ShellAncestorSensitive Boolean	G
XmNbackground XmCBackground	White Pixel	CSG
XmNbackgroundPixmap XmCPixmap	XmUNSPECIFIED_PIXMAP Pixmap	CSG
XmNborderColor XmCBorderColor	Black Pixel	CSG
XmNborderPixmap XmCPixmap	XmUNSPECIFIED_PIXMAP Pixmap	CSG
XmNborderWidth XmCBorderWidth	1 Dimension	CSG
XmNcolormap XmCColormap	ShellColormap Colormap	CG
XmNdepth XmCDepth	ShellDepth int	CG
XmNdestroyCallback XmCCallback	NULL XtCallbackList	C
XmNheight XmCHeight	0 Dimension	CSG
XmNmappedWhenManaged XmCMappedWhenManaged	True Boolean	CSG
XmNscreen XmCScreen	XtCopyScreen Pointer	CG
XmNsensitive XmCSensitive	True Boolean	CSG

Name Class	Default Type	Access
XmNtranslations XmCTranslations	NULL XtTranslations	CSG
XmNwidth XmCWidth	0 Dimension	CSG
XmNx XmCPosition	0 Position	CSG
XmNy XmCPosition	0 Position	CSG

Related Information

Composite(3X), **Core(3X)**, **Shell(3X)**, **TransientShell(3X)**, **WMShell(3X)**, **VendorShell(3X)**, and **XmCreateDialogShell(3X)**.

XmDrawingArea

Purpose

The DrawingArea widget class

Synopsis

#include <Xm/DrawingA.h>

Description

DrawingArea is an empty widget that is easily adaptable to a variety of purposes. It does no drawing and defines no behavior except for invoking callbacks. Callbacks notify the application when graphics need to be drawn (exposure events or widget resize) and when the widget receives input from the keyboard or mouse. Applications are responsible for defining appearance and behavior as needed in response to DrawingArea callbacks.

DrawingArea is also a composite widget and subclass of **XmManager** that supports minimal geometry management for multiple widget or gadget children.

Classes

DrawingArea inherits behavior and resources from the **Core**, **Composite**, **Constraint**, and **XmManager** classes.

The class pointer is **xmDrawingAreaWidgetClass**.

The class name is **XmDrawingArea**.

New Resources

The following table defines a set of widget resources used by the programmer to specify data. The programmer can also set the resource values for the inherited classes to set attributes for this widget. To reference a resource by name or by class in a .Xdefaults file, remove the **XmN** or **XmC** prefix and use the remaining letters. To specify one of the defined values for a resource in a .Xdefaults file, remove the **Xm** prefix and use the remaining letters (in either lowercase or uppercase, but include any underscores between words). The codes in the access column indicate if the given resource can be set at creation time (**C**), set by using **XtSetValues** (**S**), retrieved by using **XtGetValues** (**G**), or is not applicable (**N/A**).

XmDrawingArea Resource Set

Name Class	Default Type	Access
XmNexposeCallback XmCCallback	NULL XtCallbackList	C
XmNinputCallback XmCCallback	NULL XtCallbackList	C
XmNmarginHeight XmCMarginHeight	10 short	CSG
XmNmarginWidth XmCMarginWidth	10 short	CSG
XmNresizeCallback XmCCallback	NULL XtCallbackList	C

Name Class	Default Type	Access
XmNresizePolicy XmCResizePolicy	XmRESIZE_ANY unsigned char	CSG

XmNexposeCallback
Specifies the list of callbacks that is called when DrawingArea receives an exposure event. The callback reason is **XmCR_EXPOSE**. The callback structure also includes the exposure event.

XmNinputCallback
Specifies the list of callbacks that is called when the DrawingArea receives a keyboard or mouse event (key or button, up or down). The callback reason is **XmCR_INPUT**. The callback structure also includes the input event.

XmNmarginHeight
Specifies the minimum spacing in pixels between the top or bottom edge of DrawingArea and any child widget.

XmNmarginWidth
Specifies the minimum spacing in pixels between the left or right edge of DrawingArea and any child widget.

XmNresizeCallback
Specifies the list of callbacks that is called when the DrawingArea is resized. The callback reason is **XmCR_RESIZE**.

XmNresizePolicy
Controls the policy for resizing DrawingArea widgets. Possible values include **XmRESIZE_NONE** (fixed size), **XmRESIZE_ANY** (shrink or grow as needed), and **XmRESIZE_GROW** (grow only).

Inherited Resources

DrawingArea inherits behavior and resources from the following superclasses. For a complete description of each resource, refer to the man page for that superclass.

XmManager Resource Set

Name **Class**	**Default** **Type**	**Access**
XmNbottomShadowColor XmCForeground	dynamic Pixel	CSG
XmNbottomShadowPixmap XmCBottomShadowPixmap	XmUNSPECIFIED_PIXMAP Pixmap	CSG
XmNforeground XmCForeground	dynamic Pixel	CSG
XmNhelpCallback XmCCallback	NULL XtCallbackList	C
XmNhighlightColor XmCForeground	Black Pixel	CSG
XmNhighlightPixmap XmCHighlightPixmap	dynamic Pixmap	CSG
XmNshadowThickness XmCShadowThickness	0 short	CSG
XmNtopShadowColor XmCBackground	dynamic Pixel	CSG
XmNtopShadowPixmap XmCTopShadowPixmap	XmUNSPECIFIED_PIXMAP Pixmap	CSG
XmNunitType XmCUnitType	XmPIXELS unsigned char	CSG
XmNuserData XmCUserData	NULL caddr_t	CSG

Composite Resource Set		
Name **Class**	**Default** **Type**	**Access**
XmNinsertPosition XmCInsertPosition	NULL XmRFunction	CSG

Core Resource Set		
Name **Class**	**Default** **Type**	**Access**
XmNaccelerators XmCAccelerators	NULL XtTranslations	CSG
XmNancestorSensitive XmCSensitive	True Boolean	G
XmNbackground XmCBackground	dynamic Pixel	CSG
XmNbackgroundPixmap XmCPixmap	XmUNSPECIFIED_PIXMAP Pixmap	CSG
XmNborderColor XmCBorderColor	Black Pixel	CSG

Name Class	Default Type	Access
XmNborderPixmap XmCPixmap	XmUNSPECIFIED_PIXMAP Pixmap	CSG
XmNborderWidth XmCBorderWidth	0 Dimension	CSG
XmNcolormap XmCColormap	XtCopyFromParent Colormap	CG
XmNdepth XmCDepth	XtCopyFromParent int	CG
XmNdestroyCallback XmCCallback	NULL XtCallbackList	C
XmNheight XmCHeight	0 Dimension	CSG
XmNmappedWhenManaged XmCMappedWhenManaged	True Boolean	CSG
XmNscreen XmCScreen	XtCopyScreen Pointer	CG
XmNsensitive XmCSensitive	True Boolean	CSG
XmNtranslations XmCTranslations	NULL XtTranslations	CSG
XmNwidth XmCWidth	0 Dimension	CSG
XmNx XmCPosition	0 Position	CSG
XmNy XmCPosition	0 Position	CSG

Callback Information

The following structure is returned with each callback.

typedef struct
{
    int *reason*;
    XEvent * *event*;
    Window *window*;
} **XmDrawingAreaCallbackStruct**;

reason Indicates why the callback was invoked

event Points to the **XEvent** that triggered the callback

window Is set to the widget window

Behavior

DrawingArea behavior is summarized below.

<KeyDown>, **<KeyUp>**, **<BtnDown>**, **<BtnUp>**:
The callbacks for **XmNinputCallback** are called when a keyboard key or mouse button is pressed or released.

<Expose>: The callbacks for **XmNexposeCallback** are called when the widget receives an exposure event.

<Widget Resize>:
The callbacks for **XmNresizeCallback** are called when the widget is resized.

Default Translations

The following are DrawingArea's default translations:

<Btn1Down>: **Arm()**
<Btn1Up>: **Activate()**
<EnterWindow>: **Enter()**
<FocusIn>: **FocusIn()**

Keyboard Traversal

For information on keyboard traversal, see the man page for **XmManager(3X)** and its sections on behavior and default translations.

Related Information

Composite(3X), **Constraint(3X)**, **Core(3X)**, **XmCreateDrawingArea(3X)**, and **XmManager(3X)**.

XmDrawnButton

Purpose

The DrawnButton widget class

Synopsis

#include <Xm/DrawnB.h>

Description

The DrawnButton widget consists of an empty widget window surrounded by a shadow border. It provides the application developer with a graphics area that can have PushButton input semantics.

Callback types are defined for widget exposure and widget resize to allow the application to redraw or reposition its graphics. If the DrawnButton widget has a highlight and shadow thickness, the application should not draw in that area. To avoid drawing in the highlight and shadow area, create the graphics context with a clipping rectangle for drawing in the widget. The clipping rectangle should take into account the size of the widget's highlight thickness and shadow.

Classes

DrawnButton inherits behavior and resources from **Core**, **XmPrimitive**, and **XmLabel** Classes.

The class pointer is **xmDrawnButtonWidgetClass**.

The class name is **XmDrawnButton**.

New Resources

The following table defines a set of widget resources used by the programmer to specify data. The programmer can also set the resource values for the inherited classes to set attributes for this widget. To reference a resource by name or by class in a .Xdefaults file, remove the **XmN** or **XmC** prefix and use the remaining letters. To specify one of the defined values for a resource in a .Xdefaults file, remove the **Xm** prefix and use the remaining letters (in either lowercase or uppercase, but include any underscores between words). The codes in the access column indicate if the given resource can be set at creation time (**C**), set by using **XtSetValues** (**S**), retrieved by using **XtGetValues** (**G**), or is not applicable (**N/A**).

XmDrawnButton Resource Set		
Name **Class**	**Default** **Type**	**Access**
XmNactivateCallback XmCCallback	NULL XtCallbackList	C
XmNarmCallback XmCCallback	NULL XtCallbackList	C
XmNdisarmCallback XmCCallback	NULL XtCallbackList	C
XmNexposeCallback XmCCallback	NULL XtCallbackList	C
XmNpushButtonEnabled XmCPushButtonEnabled	False Boolean	CSG
XmNresizeCallback XmCCallback	NULL XtCallbackList	C
XmNshadowType XmCShadowType	XmSHADOW_ETCHED_IN unsigned char	CSG

XmNactivateCallback

Specifies the list of callbacks that is called when the widget becomes selected. The reason sent by the callback is **XmCR_ACTIVATE**.

XmNarmCallback

Specifies the list of callbacks that is called when the widget becomes armed. The reason sent by the callback is **XmCR_ARM**.

XmNdisarmCallback

Specifies the list of callbacks that is called when the widget becomes disarmed. The reason sent by the callback is **XmCR_DISARM**.

XmNexposeCallback

Specifies the list of callbacks that is called when the widget receives an exposure event. The reason sent by the callback is **XmCR_EXPOSE**.

XmNpushButtonEnabled

Enables or disables the three-dimensional shadow drawing as in PushButton.

XmNresizeCallback

Specifies the list of callbacks that is called when the widget receives a resize event. The reason sent by the callback is **XmCR_RESIZE**. The event returned for this callback is NULL.

XmNshadowType

Describes the drawing style for the DrawnButton. This resource can have the following values:

- **XmSHADOW_IN** — draws the DrawnButton so that the shadow appears inset. This means that the bottom shadow visuals and top shadow visuals are reversed.
- **XmSHADOW_OUT** — draws the DrawnButton so that the shadow appears outset.
- **XmSHADOW_ETCHED_IN** — draws the DrawnButton using a double line. This gives the effect of a line etched into the window. The thickness of the double line is equal to the value of **XmNshadowThickness**.
- **XmSHADOW_ETCHED_OUT** — draws the DrawnButton using a double line. This gives the effect of a line coming out of the window. The thickness of the double line is equal to the value of **XmNshadowThickness**.

Inherited Resources

DrawnButton inherits behavior and resources from the following superclasses. For a complete description of each resource, refer to the man page for that superclass.

XmLabel Resource Set		
Name **Class**	**Default** **Type**	**Access**
XmNaccelerator XmCAccelerator	NULL String	CSG
XmNacceleratorText XmCAcceleratorText	NULL XmString	CSG
XmNalignment XmCAlignment	XmALIGNMENT_CENTER unsigned char	CSG
XmNfontList XmCFontList	"Fixed" XmFontList	CSG
XmNlabelInsensitivePixmap XmCLabelInsensitivePixmap	XmUNSPECIFIED_PIXMAP Pixmap	CSG
XmNlabelPixmap XmCPixmap	XmUNSPECIFIED_PIXMAP Pixmap	CSG
XmNlabelString XmCXmString	'\0' XmString	CSG
XmNlabelType XmCLabelType	XmSTRING unsigned char	CSG
XmNmarginBottom XmCMarginBottom	0 short	CSG
XmNmarginHeight XmCMarginHeight	dynamic short	CSG
XmNmarginLeft XmCMarginLeft	0 short	CSG
XmNmarginRight XmCMarginRight	0 short	CSG
XmNmarginTop XmCMarginTop	0 short	CSG
XmNmarginWidth XmCMarginWidth	dynamic short	CSG

Name Class	Default Type	Access
XmNmnemonic XmCMnemonic	'\0' char	CSG
XmNrecomputeSize XmCRecomputeSize	True Boolean	CSG
XmNstringDirection XmCStringDirection	XmSTRING_DIRECTION_L_TO_R XmStringDirection	CSG

XmPrimitive Resource Set		
Name **Class**	**Default** **Type**	**Access**
XmNbottomShadowColor XmCForeground	dynamic Pixel	CSG
XmNbottomShadowPixmap XmCBottomShadowPixmap	XmUNSPECIFIED_PIXMAP Pixmap	CSG
XmNforeground XmCForeground	dynamic Pixel	CSG
XmNhelpCallback XmCCallback	NULL XtCallbackList	C
XmNhighlightColor XmCForeground	Black Pixel	CSG
XmNhighlightOnEnter XmCHighlightOnEnter	False Boolean	CSG
XmNhighlightPixmap XmCHighlightPixmap	dynamic Pixmap	CSG
XmNhighlightThickness XmCHighlightThickness	0 short	CSG
XmNshadowThickness XmCShadowThickness	2 short	CSG
XmNtopShadowColor XmCBackground	dynamic Pixel	CSG
XmNtopShadowPixmap XmCTopShadowPixmap	XmUNSPECIFIED_PIXMAP Pixmap	CSG
XmNtraversalOn XmCTraversalOn	False Boolean	CSG
XmNunitType XmCUnitType	XmPIXELS unsigned char	CSG
XmNuserData XmCUserData	NULL caddr_t	CSG

Core Resource Set		
Name **Class**	**Default** **Type**	**Access**
XmNaccelerators XmCAccelerators	NULL XtTranslations	CSG
XmNancestorSensitive XmCSensitive	True Boolean	G
XmNbackground XmCBackground	dynamic Pixel	CSG
XmNbackgroundPixmap XmCPixmap	XmUNSPECIFIED_PIXMAP Pixmap	CSG
XmNborderColor XmCBorderColor	Black Pixel	CSG
XmNborderPixmap XmCPixmap	XmUNSPECIFIED_PIXMAP Pixmap	CSG
XmNborderWidth XmCBorderWidth	0 Dimension	CSG
XmNcolormap XmCColormap	XtCopyFromParent Colormap	CG
XmNdepth XmCDepth	XtCopyFromParent int	CG
XmNdestroyCallback XmCCallback	NULL XtCallbackList	C
XmNheight XmCHeight	0 Dimension	CSG
XmNmappedWhenManaged XmCMappedWhenManaged	True Boolean	CSG
XmNscreen XmCScreen	XtCopyScreen Pointer	CG
XmNsensitive XmCSensitive	True Boolean	CSG

Name Class	Default Type	Access
XmNtranslations XmCTranslations	NULL XtTranslations	CSG
XmNwidth XmCWidth	0 Dimension	CSG
XmNx XmCPosition	0 Position	CSG
XmNy XmCPosition	0 Position	CSG

Callback Information

The following structure is returned with each callback:

typedef struct
{
  int *reason*;
  XEvent * *event*;
  Window *window*;
} **XmDrawnButtonCallbackStruct;**

reason Indicates why the callback was invoked.

event Points to the **XEvent** that triggered the callback. NULL is returned by the *event* for **XmNresizeCallback**. This event is NULL for the **XmNactivateCallback** if the callback was triggered when Primitive's resource **XmNtraversalOn** was True or if the callback was accessed through the **ArmAndActivate** action routine.

window Is set to the window ID in which the event occurred.

Behavior

<Btn1Down>:
A selection on the DrawnButton causes its shadow to be drawn in the selected state if the **XmNpushButtonEnabled** flag is set to **True**. The callbacks for **XmNarmCallback** are also called.

<Btn1Up>: If **<Btn1Up>** occurs when the pointer is within the DrawnButton, the shadows are redrawn in the unselected state if the **XmNpushButtonEnabled** flag is set to True. The callbacks for **XmNactivateCallback** are called, followed by callbacks for **XmdisarmCallback**.

If **<Btn1Up>** occurs when the pointer is outside the DrawnButton, the callbacks for **XmNdisarmCallback** are called.

<Leave Window>:
If the mouse button is pressed and the cursor leaves the DrawnButtons window, the shadow is redrawn to its unselected state if the **XmNpushButtonEnabled** flag is set to True.

<Enter Window>:
If the mouse button is pressed and the cursor reenters the DrawnButton window, the shadow is drawn in the same manner as when the button was first selected.

Default Translations

<Btn1Down>:	**Arm()**
<Btn1Up>:	**Activate()**
	Disarm()
<Key>Return:	**ArmAndActivate()**
<Key>space:	**ArmAndActivate()**
<EnterWindow>:	**Enter()**
<LeaveWindow>:	**Leave()**

Keyboard Traversal

For information on keyboard traversal, see the man page for **XmPrimitive(3X)** and its sections on behavior and default translations.

Related Information

Core(3X), **XmCreateDrawnButton**, **XmLabel(3X)**, **XmPrimitive(3X)**, **XmPushButton**, and **XmSeparator(3X)**.

XmFileSelectionBox

Purpose

The FileSelectionBox widget class

Synopsis

#include <Xm/FileSB.h>

Description

FileSelectionBox traverses through directories, views the files in them, and then selects a file.

A FileSelectionBox has four main areas:

- A directory mask that includes a filter label and a directory-mask input field used to specify the directory that is to be examined
- A scrollable list of filenames
- A text input field for directly typing in a filename
- A group of PushButtons, labeled **OK**, **Filter**, **Cancel**, and **Help**

One additional **WorkArea** child may be added to the FileSelectionBox after creation.

The user can select a file by scrolling through the list of filenames and selecting the desired file or by entering the filename directly into the text edit area. Selecting a file from the list causes that filename to appear in the file selection text edit area.

The user may select a new file as many times as desired. The application is not notified until the user selects the **OK** PushButton or presses the return key while the selection text edit area has the keyboard focus.

FileSelectionBox initiates a file search when any of the following occurs:

- The function **XtSetValues** is used to change the directory mask.
- The user activates the **Filter** PushButton.
- The application calls **XmFileSelectionDoSearch**.
- The user presses the return key while the directory mask input field has the keyboard focus.

This may be useful when an application creates a new file and wants to incorporate it into the file list.

Classes

FileSelectionBox inherits behavior and resources from **Core**, **Composite**, **Constraint**, **XmManager**, **XmBulletinBoard**, and **XmSelectionBox**.

The class pointer is **xmFileSelectionBoxWidgetClass**.

The class name is **XmFileSelectionBox**.

New Resources

The following table defines a set of widget resources used by the programmer to specify data. The programmer can also set the resource values for the inherited classes to set attributes for this widget. To reference a resource by name or by class in a .Xdefaults file, remove the **XmN** or **XmC** prefix and use the remaining letters. To specify one of the defined values for a resource in a .Xdefaults file, remove the **Xm** prefix and use the remaining letters (in either lowercase or uppercase, but include any underscores between words). The codes in the access column indicate if the given resource can be set at creation time (**C**), set by using **XtSetValues** (**S**), retrieved by using **XtGetValues** (**G**), or is not applicable (**N/A**).

XmFileSelectionBox Resource Set		
Name **Class**	**Default** **Type**	**Access**
XmNdirMask XmCDirMask	"*" XmString	CSG
XmNdirSpec XmCDirSpec	NULL XmString	CSG
XmNfileSearchProc XmCFileSearchProc	see below XtProc	CSG
XmNfilterLabelString XmCFilterLabelString	"File Filter" XmString	CSG
XmNlistUpdated XmCListUpdated	True Boolean	CSG

XmNdirMask

Specifies the directory mask used in determining the files to be displayed in the list box.

XmNdirSpec

Specifies the full file specification. This resource overrides the **XmNtextString** resource in SelectionBox.

XmNfileSearchProc

Specifies a directory search procedure to replace the default file-search procedure. FileSelectionBox's default file-search procedure fulfills the needs of most applications. Because it is impossible to cover the requirements of all applications, you can replace the default search procedure.

The file search procedure is called with two arguments: the FileSelectionBox widget and the **XmFileSelectionCallbackStruct** structure. The callback structure contains all required information to conduct a directory search, including the current file search mask. Once called, it is up to the search routine to generate a new list of files and update the file selection widget by using **XtSetValues**.

The following attributes must be set: **XmNitems**, **XmNitemsCount**, **XmNlistUpdated**, and **XmNdirSpec**. Set **XmNitems** to the new list of files. If there are no files, set this attribute to NULL. This sets the **XmNitems** attribute associated with SelectionBox.

If there are no files, set **XmNitemsCount** to zero. This sets the **XmNitemsCount** associated with SelectionBox. Always set **XmNlistUpdated** to True when you use a search procedure to update the file list, even if there are no files. Setting **XmNdirSpec** is optional, but recommended. Set this attribute to the full file specification of the directory searched. The directory specification is displayed above the list box.

XmNfilterLabelString

Specifies the string value for the label located above the **DIR_MASK** text entry field.

XmNlistUpdated

Specifies an attribute that is set only by the file search procedure. Set to True, if the file list has been updated.

Inherited Resources

FileSelectionBox inherits behavior and resources from the following superclasses. For a complete description of each resource, refer to the man page for that superclass.

XmSelectionBox Resource Set		
Name **Class**	**Default** **Type**	**Access**
XmNapplyCallback XmCCallback	NULL XtCallbackList	C
XmNapplyLabelString XmCApplyLabelString	"Filter" XmString	CSG
XmNcancelCallback XmCCallback	NULL XtCallbackList	C
XmNcancelLabelString XmCXmString	"Cancel" XmString	CSG
XmNdialogType XmCDialogType	XmDIALOG_FILE_SELECTION unsigned char	CG
XmNhelpLabelString XmCXmString	"Help" XmString	CSG
XmNlistItemCount XmCItemCount	0 int	CSG
XmNlistItems XmCItems	NULL XmStringList	CSG
XmNlistLabelString XmCXmString	"Files" XmString	CSG
XmNlistVisibleItemCount XmCVisibleItemCount	8 int	CSG
XmNminimizeButtons XmCMinimizeButtons	False Boolean	CSG
XmNmustMatch XmCMustMatch	False Boolean	CSG
XmNnoMatchCallback XmCCallback	NULL XtCallbackList	C
XmNokCallback XmCCallback	NULL XtCallbackList	C

Name Class	Default Type	Access
XmNokLabelString XmCXmString	"OK" XmString	CSG
XmNselectionLabelString XmCXmString	"Selection" XmString	CSG
XmNtextAccelerators XmCTextAccelerators	see description XtTranslations	C
XmNtextColumns XmCTextColumns	31 int	CSG
XmNtextString XmCTextString	NULL XmString	CSG

XmBulletinBoard Resource Set		
Name **Class**	**Default** **Type**	**Access**
XmNallowOverlap XmCAllowOverlap	True Boolean	CSG
XmNautoUnmanage XmCAutoUnmanage	False Boolean	CSG
XmNbuttonFontList XmCButtonFontList	NULL XmFontList	CSG
XmNcancelButton XmCWidget	Cancel button Widget	SG
XmNdefaultButton XmCWidget	OK button Widget	SG
XmNdefaultPosition XmCDefaultPosition	True Boolean	CSG
XmNdialogStyle XmCDialogStyle	dynamic unsigned char	CSG
XmNdialogTitle XmCXmString	NULL XmString	CSG
XmNfocusCallback XmCCallback	NULL XtCallbackList	C
XmNlabelFontList XmCLabelFontList	NULL XmFontList	CSG
XmNmapCallback XmCCallback	NULL XtCallbackList	C
XmNmarginHeight XmCMarginHeight	10 short	CSG
XmNmarginWidth XmCMarginWidth	10 short	CSG
XmNnoResize XmCNoResize	False Boolean	CSG

Name Class	Default Type	Access
XmNresizePolicy XmCResizePolicy	XmRESIZE_ANY unsigned char	CSG
XmNshadowType XmCShadowType	XmSHADOW_OUT unsigned char	CSG
XmNstringDirection XmCStringDirection	XmSTRING_DIRECTION_L_TO_R XmStringDirection	CSG
XmNtextFontList XmCTextFontList	NULL XmFontList	CSG
XmNtextTranslations XmCTranslations	NULL XtTranslations	C
XmNunmapCallback XmCCallback	NULL XtCallbackList	C

XmManager Resource Set		
Name **Class**	**Default** **Type**	**Access**
XmNbottomShadowColor XmCForeground	dynamic Pixel	CSG
XmNbottomShadowPixmap XmCBottomShadowPixmap	XmUNSPECIFIED_PIXMAP Pixmap	CSG
XmNforeground XmCForeground	dynamic Pixel	CSG
XmNhelpCallback XmCCallback	NULL XtCallbackList	C
XmNhighlightColor XmCForeground	Black Pixel	CSG
XmNhighlightPixmap XmCHighlightPixmap	dynamic Pixmap	CSG
XmNshadowThickness XmCShadowThickness	dynamic short	CSG
XmNtopShadowColor XmCBackground	dynamic Pixel	CSG
XmNtopShadowPixmap XmCTopShadowPixmap	XmUNSPECIFIED_PIXMAP Pixmap	CSG
XmNunitType XmCUnitType	XmPIXELS unsigned char	CSG
XmNuserData XmCUserData	NULL caddr_t	CSG

Composite Resource Set		
Name **Class**	**Default** **Type**	**Access**
XmNinsertPosition XmCInsertPosition	NULL XmRFunction	CSG

Core Resource Set		
Name **Class**	**Default** **Type**	**Access**
XmNaccelerators XmCAccelerators	NULL XtTranslations	CSG
XmNancestorSensitive XmCSensitive	True Boolean	G
XmNbackground XmCBackground	dynamic Pixel	CSG
XmNbackgroundPixmap XmCPixmap	XmUNSPECIFIED_PIXMAP Pixmap	CSG
XmNborderColor XmCBorderColor	Black Pixel	CSG

Name Class	Default Type	Access
XmNborderPixmap XmCPixmap	XmUNSPECIFIED_PIXMAP Pixmap	CSG
XmNborderWidth XmCBorderWidth	0 Dimension	CSG
XmNcolormap XmCColormap	XtCopyFromParent Colormap	CG
XmNdepth XmCDepth	XtCopyFromParent int	CG
XmNdestroyCallback XmCCallback	NULL XtCallbackList	C
XmNheight XmCHeight	0 Dimension	CSG
XmNmappedWhenManaged XmCMappedWhenManaged	True Boolean	CSG
XmNscreen XmCScreen	XtCopyScreen Pointer	CG
XmNsensitive XmCSensitive	True Boolean	CSG
XmNtranslations XmCTranslations	NULL XtTranslations	CSG
XmNwidth XmCWidth	0 Dimension	CSG
XmNx XmCPosition	0 Position	CSG
XmNy XmCPosition	0 Position	CSG

Callback Information

The following structure is returned with each callback:

typedef struct
{
int *reason*;
XEvent * *event*;
XmString *value*;
int *length*;
XmString *mask*;
int *mask_length*;
} **XmFileSelectionBoxCallbackStruct;**

reason Indicates why the callback was invoked

event Points to the **XEvent** that triggered the callback

value Specifies the value of the current **XmNdirSpec**

length Specifies the number of bytes of the structure pointed to by *value*

mask Specifies the current value of **XmNdirMask**

mask_length Specifies the number of bytes of the structure pointed to by *mask*

Behavior

FileSelectionBox inherits behavior from SelectionBox and BulletinBoard and also has the following behavior.

<Apply Button Activated>:
A new file search begins when the apply button is activated.

Default Translations

FileSelectionBox inherits SelectionBox's default translations. See the man page for **XmSelectionBox(3X)**.

Default Accelerators

The following are the default accelerator translations added to descendants of a BulletinBoard if the parent of the BulletinBoard is a DialogShell:

```
#override
<Key>F1:        Help()
<Key>Return:    Return()
<Key>KP_Enter:  Return()
```

Default Text Accelerators

The following are the default text accelerators inherited from SelectionBox:

```
#override
<Key>Up:        UpOrDown(0)
<Key>Down:      UpOrDown(1)
<Key>F1:        Help()
<Key>Return:    Return()
<Key>KP_Enter:  Return()
```

Keyboard Traversal

For information on keyboard traversal, see the man page for **XmManager(3X)** and its sections on behavior and default translations.

Related Information

Composite(3X), **Constraint(3X)**, **Core(3X)**, **XmBulletinBoard(3X)**, **XmCreateFileSelectionBox(3X)**, **XmCreateFileSelectionDialog(3X)**, **XmFileSelectionBoxGetChild(3X)**, **XmFileSelectionDoSearch(3X)**, **XmManager(3X)**, and **XmSelectionBox(3X)**,

XmFileSelectionBoxGetChild

Purpose

A FileSelectionBox function that is used to access a component.

Synopsis

#include <Xm/FileSB.h>

Widget XmFileSelectionBoxGetChild (*widget, child*)
    Widget *widget*;
    unsigned char*child*;

Description

XmFileSelectionBoxGetChild is used to access a component within a FileSelectionBox. The parameters given to the function are the FileSelectionBox widget and a value indicating which child to access.

widget Specifies the FileSelectionBox widget ID.

child Specifies a component within the FileSelectionBox. The following are legal values for this parameter:

- **XmDIALOG_APPLY_BUTTON**
- **XmDialog_CANCEL_BUTTON**
- **XmDIALOG_DEFAULT_BUTTON**
- **XmDIALOG_FILTER_LABEL**
- **XmDIALOG_FILTER_TEXT**
- **XmDIALOG_HELP_BUTTON**
- **XmDIALOG_LIST**
- **XmDIALOG_LIST_LABEL**
- **XmDIALOG_OK_BUTTON**
- **XmDIALOG_SELECTION_LABEL**
- **XmDIALOG_TEXT**

For a complete definition of FileSelectionBox and its associated resources, see **XmFileSelectionBox(3X)**.

Return Value

Returns the widget ID of the specified FileSelectionBox child.

Related Information

XmFileSelectionBox(3X).

XmFileSelectionDoSearch

Purpose

A FileSelectionBox function that initiates a directory search.

Synopsis

#include <Xm/FileSB.h>

void XmFileSelectionDoSearch (*widget, dirmask*)
    Widget *widget*;
    XmString *dirmask*;

Description

XmFileSelectionDoSearch initiates a directory search. If the *dirmask* parameter is not NULL, the directory mask is updated before the search is initiated.

widget Specifies the FileSelectionBox widget ID.

dirmask Specifies the directory mask used in determining the files displayed in the FileSelectionBox list. This sets the **XmNdirMask** attribute associated with **XmCreateFileSelectionBox**. This is an optional attribute. If you do not specify a directory mask, the current directory mask is used.

For a complete definition of FileSelectionBox and its associated resources, see **XmFileSelectionBox(3X)**.

Related Information

XmFileSelectionBox(3X).

XmFontListAdd

Purpose

A compound string function that creates a new font list

Synopsis

#include <Xm/Xm.h>

XmFontList XmFontListAdd (*oldlist, font, charset*)
    XmFontList *oldlist*;
    XFontStruct **font*;
    XmStringCharSet*charset*;

Description

XmFontListAdd creates a new font list consisting of the contents of the *oldlist* and the new font-list element being added. This function deallocates the *oldlist* after extracting the required information; therefore, do not reference *oldlist* thereafter.

oldlist Specifies a pointer to the font list to which an entry will be added.

font Specifies a pointer to a font structure for which the new font list is generated. This is the structure returned by the XLib **XLoadQueryFont** function.

charset Specifies the character set identifier for the font. This can be **XmSTRING_DEFAULT_CHARSET**.

Return Value

Returns a new font list.

Related Information

XmFontListCreate(3X).

XmFontListCreate

Purpose

A compound string function that creates a font list

Synopsis

```
#include <Xm/Xm.h>

XmFontList XmFontListCreate (font, charset)
        XFontStruct     *font;
        XmStringCharSetcharset;
```

Description

XmFontListCreate creates a new font list with a single element specified by the provided font and character set. It also allocates the space for the font list.

font Specifies a pointer to a font structure for which the new font list is generated. This is the structure returned by the XLib **XLoadQueryFont** function.

charset Specifies the character set identifier for the font. This can be **XmSTRING_DEFAULT_CHARSET**.

Return Value

Returns a new font list.

Related Information

XmFontListAdd(3X), **XmFontListFree(3X)**, **XmStringBaseline(3X)**, **XmStringByteCompare(3X)**, **XmStringCompare(3X)**, **XmStringConcat(3X)**, **XmStringCopy(3X)**, **XmStringCreate(3X)**, **XmStringCreateLtoR(3X)**, **XmStringDirectionCreate(3X)**, **XmStringDraw(3X)**, **XmStringDrawImage(3X)**, **XmStringDrawUnderline(3X)**, **XmStringEmpty(3X)**, **XmStringExtent(3X)**, **XmStringFree(3X)**, **XmStringFreeContext(3X)**, **XmStringGetLtoR(3X)**, **XmStringGetNextComponent(3X)**, **XmStringGetNextSegment(3X)**, **XmStringHeight(3X)**, **XmStringInitContext(3X)**, **XmStringLength(3X)**, **XmStringLineCount(3X)**, **XmStringNConcat(3X)**, **XmStringNCopy(3X)**, **XmStringPeekNextComponent(3X)**, **XmStringSegmentCreate(3X)**, **XmStringSeparatorCreate(3X)**, and **XmStringWidth(3X)**.

XmFontListFree

Purpose

A compound string function that recovers memory used by a font list.

Synopsis

#include <Xm/Xm.h>

void XmFontListFree (*list*)
    XmFontList *list*;

Description

XmFontListFree recovers memory used by a font list.

list Specifies the font list to be freed

Related Information

XmFontListCreate(3X).

XmForm

Purpose

The Form widget class

Synopsis

#include <Xm/Form.h>

Description

Form is a container widget with no input semantics of its own. Constraints are placed on children of the Form to define attachments for each of the child's four sides. These attachments can be to the Form, to another child widget or gadget, to a relative position within the Form, or to the initial position of the child. The attachments determine the layout behavior of the Form when resizing occurs.

Classes

Form inherits behavior and resources from **Core**, **Composite**, **Constraint**, **XmManager**, and **XmBulletinBoard** classes.

The class pointer is **xmFormWidgetClass**.

The class name is **XmForm**.

New Resources

The following table defines a set of widget resources used by the programmer to specify data. The programmer can also set the resource values for the inherited classes to set attributes for this widget. To reference a resource by name or by class in a .Xdefaults file, remove the **XmN** or **XmC** prefix and use the remaining letters. To specify one of the defined values for a resource in a .Xdefaults file, remove the **Xm** prefix and use the remaining letters (in either lowercase or uppercase, but include any underscores between words). The codes in the access column indicate if the given resource can be set at creation time (**C**), set by using **XtSetValues** (**S**), retrieved by using **XtGetValues** (**G**), or is not applicable (**N/A**).

XmForm Resource Set

Name Class	Default Type	Access
XmNfractionBase XmCMaxValue	100 int	CSG
XmNhorizontalSpacing XmCSpacing	0 int	CSG
XmNrubberPositioning XmCRubberPositioning	False Boolean	CSG
XmNverticalSpacing XmCSpacing	0 int	CSG

XmNfractionBase

Specifies the denominator used in calculating the relative position of a child widget using **XmATTACH_POSITION** constraints.

XmNhorizontalSpacing

Specifies the offset for right and left attachments.

XmNrubberPositioning

Indicates the default attachment for a child of the Form. If this Boolean resource is set to False, the left and top of the child defaults to being attached to the left and top side of the Form. If this resource is set to True, the child defaults to being attached to its initial position in the Form.

XmNverticalSpacing

Specifies the offset for top and bottom attachments.

XmForm Constraint Resource Set		
Name **Class**	**Default** **Type**	**Access**
XmNbottomAttachment XmCAttachment	XmATTACH_NONE unsigned char	CSG
XmNbottomOffset XmCOffset	0 int	CSG
XmNbottomPosition XmCAttachment	0 int	CSG
XmNbottomWidget XmCWidget	NULL Widget	CSG
XmNleftAttachment XmCAttachment	XmATTACH_NONE unsigned char	CSG
XmNleftOffset XmCOffset	0 int	CSG
XmNleftPosition XmCAttachment	0 int	CSG
XmNleftWidget XmCWidget	NULL Widget	CSG
XmNresizable XmCBoolean	True Boolean	CSG
XmNrightAttachment XmCAttachment	XmATTACH_NONE unsigned char	CSG
XmNrightOffset XmCOffset	0 int	CSG
XmNrightPosition XmCAttachment	0 int	CSG
XmNrightWidget XmCWidget	NULL Widget	CSG
XmNtopAttachment XmCAttachment	XmATTACH_NONE unsigned char	CSG

Name Class	Default Type	Access
XmNtopOffset XmCOffset	0 int	CSG
XmNtopPosition XmCAttachment	0 int	CSG
XmNtopWidget XmCWidget	NULL Widget	CSG

XmNbottomAttachment

Specifies attachment of the bottom side of the child. It can have the following data values:

- **XmATTACH_NONE** — do not attach this side
- **XmATTACH_FORM** — attach the bottom side of the child to the bottom side of the Form
- **XmATTACH_OPPOSITE_FORM** — attach the bottom side of the child to the top side of the Form
- **XmATTACH_WIDGET** — attach the bottom side of the child to the top side of the widget or gadget specified in the **XmNbottomWidget** resource
- **XmATTACH_OPPOSITE_WIDGET** — attach the bottom side of the child to the bottom side of the widget or gadget specified in the **XmNbottomWidget** resource
- **XmATTACH_POSITION** — attach the bottom side of the child to a relative position in the Form. This position is specified by the **XmNbottomPosition** resource.
- **XmATTACH_SELF** — attach the bottom of the child to its initial position in the Form

XmNbottomOffset
Specifies the constant offset between the bottom side of the child and the object to which it is attached. This resource is ignored if **XmNbottomAttachment** is set to **XmATTACH_POSITION**. The relationship established remains, regardless of any resizing operations that occur.

XmNbottomPosition
Determines the relative position of the bottom side of the child. The relative position is a fraction of the height of the Form. The fraction is equal to the value of this resource divided by the value of **XmNfractionBase**. This resource is used only if **XmNbottomAttachment** is set to **XmATTACH_POSITION**.

XmNbottomWidget
Specifies the widget or gadget to which the bottom side of the child is attached. This resource is used if **XmNbottomAttachment** is set to either **XmATTACH_WIDGET** or **XmATTACH_OPPOSITE_WIDGET**.

XmNleftAttachment
Specifies attachment of the left side of the child. It can have the following data values:

- **XmATTACH_NONE** — do not attach this side
- **XmATTACH_FORM** — attach the left side of the child to the left side of the Form

- **XmATTACH_OPPOSITE_FORM** — attach the left side of the child to the right side of the Form
- **XmATTACH_WIDGET** — attach the left side of the child to the right side of the widget or gadget specified in the **XmNleftWidget** resource
- **XmATTACH_OPPOSITE_WIDGET** — attach the left side of the child to the left side of the widget or gadget specified in the **XmNleftWidget** resource
- **XmATTACH_POSITION** — attach the left side of the child to a relative position in the Form. This position is specified by the **XmNleftPosition** resource
- **XmATTACH_SELF** — attach the left side of the child to its initial position in the Form

XmNleftOffset

Specifies the constant offset between the left side of the child and the object to which it is attached. This resource is ignored if **XmNleftAttachment** is set to **XmATTACH_POSITION**. The relationship established remains, regardless of any resizing operations that occur.

XmNleftPosition

Determines the relative position of the left side of the child. The relative position is a fraction of the width of the Form. The fraction is equal to the value of this resource divided by the value of **XmNfractionBase**. This resource is used only if **XmNleftAttachment** is set to **XmATTACH_POSITION**.

XmNleftWidget

Specifies the widget or gadget to which the left side of the child is attached. This resource is used if **XmNleftAttachment** is set to either **XmATTACH_WIDGET** or **XmATTACH_OPPOSITE_WIDGET**.

XmNresizable

Specifies whether a child widget can be resized by the Form. The default value is True.

XmNrightAttachment

Specifies attachment of the right side of the child. It can have the following data values:

- **XmATTACH_NONE** — do not attach this side
- **XmATTACH_FORM** — attach the right side of the child to the right side of the Form
- **XmATTACH_OPPOSITE_FORM** — attach the right side of the child to the left side of the Form
- **XmATTACH_WIDGET** — attach the right side of the child to the left side of the widget or gadget specified in the **XmNrightWidget** resource
- **XmATTACH_OPPOSITE_WIDGET** — attach the right side of the child to the right side of the widget or gadget specified in the **XmNrightWidget** resource
- **XmATTACH_POSITION** — attach the right side of the child to a relative position in the Form. This position is specified by the **XmNrightPosition** resource
- **XmATTACH_SELF** — attach the right side of the child to its initial position in the Form

XmNrightOffset

Specifies the constant offset between the right side of the child and the object to which it is attached. This resource is ignored if **XmNrightAttachment** is set to **XmATTACH_POSITION**. The relationship established remains, regardless of any resizing operations that occur.

XmNrightPosition

Determines the relative position of the right side of the child. The relative position is a fraction of the width of the Form.

The fraction is equal to the value of this resource divided by the value of **XmNfractionBase**. This resource is used only if **XmNrightAttachment** is set to **XmATTACH_POSITION**.

XmNrightWidget

Specifies the widget or gadget to which the right side of the child is attached. This resource is used if **XmNrightAttachment** is set to either **XmATTACH_WIDGET** or **XmATTACH_OPPOSITE_WIDGET**.

XmNtopAttachment

Specifies attachment of the top side of the child. It can have the following data values:

- **XmATTACH_NONE** — do not attach this side
- **XmATTACH_FORM** — attach the top side of the child to the top side of the Form
- **XmATTACH_OPPOSITE_FORM** — attach the top side of the child to the bottom side of the Form
- **XmATTACH_WIDGET** — attach the top side of the child to the bottom side of the widget or gadget specified in the **XmNtopWidget** resource
- **XmATTACH_OPPOSITE_WIDGET** — attach the top side of the child to the top side of the widget or gadget specified in the **XmNtopWidget** resource
- **XmATTACH_POSITION** — attach the top side of the child to a relative position in the Form. This position is specified by the **XmNtopPosition** resource
- **XmATTACH_SELF** — attach the top side of the child to its initial position in the Form

XmNtopOffset

Specifies the constant offset between the top side of the child and the object to which it is attached. This resource is ignored if **XmNtopAttachment** is set to **XmATTACH_POSITION**. The relationship established remains, regardless of any resizing operations that occur.

XmNtopPosition
Determines the relative position of the top side of the child. The relative position is a fraction of the height of the Form. The fraction is equal to the value of this resource divided by the value of **XmNfractionBase**. This resource is used only if **XmNtopAttachment** is set to **XmATTACH_POSITION**.

XmNtopWidget
Specifies the widget or gadget to which the top side of the child is attached. This resource is used if **XmNtopAttachment** is set to either **XmATTACH_WIDGET** or **XmATTACH_OPPOSITE_WIDGET**.

Inherited Resources

Form inherits behavior and resources from the following superclasses. For a complete description of each resource, refer to the man page for that superclass.

XmBulletinBoard Resource Set		
Name **Class**	**Default** **Type**	**Access**
XmNallowOverlap XmCAllowOverlap	True Boolean	N/A
XmNautoUnmanage XmCAutoUnmanage	True Boolean	N/A
XmNbuttonFontList XmCButtonFontList	NULL XmFontList	N/A
XmNcancelButton XmCWidget	NULL Widget	N/A
XmNdefaultButton XmCWidget	NULL Widget	N/A
XmNdefaultPosition XmCDefaultPosition	True Boolean	N/A
XmNdialogStyle XmCDialogStyle	dynamic unsigned char	N/A
XmNdialogTitle XmCXmString	NULL XmString	N/A
XmNfocusCallback XmCCallback	NULL XtCallbackList	C
XmNlabelFontList XmCLabelFontList	NULL XmFontList	N/A
XmNmapCallback XmCCallback	NULL XtCallbackList	C
XmNmarginHeight XmCMarginHeight	10 short	N/A
XmNmarginWidth XmCMarginWidth	10 short	N/A
XmNnoResize XmCNoResize	False Boolean	N/A

Name Class	Default Type	Access
XmNresizePolicy XmCResizePolicy	XmRESIZE_ANY unsigned char	CSG
XmNshadowType XmCShadowType	XmSHADOW_OUT unsigned char	N/A
XmNstringDirection XmCStringDirection	XmSTRING_DIRECTION_L_TO_R XmStringDirection	N/A
XmNtextFontList XmCTextFontList	NULL XmFontList	N/A
XmNtextTranslations XmCTranslations	NULL XtTranslations	N/A
XmNunmapCallback XmCCallback	NULL XtCallbackList	C

XmManager Resource Set		
Name **Class**	**Default** **Type**	**Access**
XmNbottomShadowColor XmCForeground	dynamic Pixel	CSG
XmNbottomShadowPixmap XmCBottomShadowPixmap	XmUNSPECIFIED_PIXMAP Pixmap	CSG
XmNforeground XmCForeground	dynamic Pixel	CSG
XmNhelpCallback XmCCallback	NULL XtCallbackList	C
XmNhighlightColor XmCForeground	Black Pixel	CSG
XmNhighlightPixmap XmCHighlightPixmap	dynamic Pixmap	CSG
XmNshadowThickness XmCShadowThickness	0 short	N/A
XmNtopShadowColor XmCBackground	dynamic Pixel	CSG
XmNtopShadowPixmap XmCTopShadowPixmap	XmUNSPECIFIED_PIXMAP Pixmap	CSG
XmNunitType XmCUnitType	XmPIXELS unsigned char	CSG
XmNuserData XmCUserData	NULL caddr_t	CSG

Composite Resource Set		
Name **Class**	**Default** **Type**	**Access**
XmNinsertPosition XmCInsertPosition	NULL XmRFunction	CSG

Core Resource Set		
Name **Class**	**Default** **Type**	**Access**
XmNaccelerators XmCAccelerators	NULL XtTranslations	CSG
XmNancestorSensitive XmCSensitive	True Boolean	G
XmNbackground XmCBackground	dynamic Pixel	CSG
XmNbackgroundPixmap XmCPixmap	XmUNSPECIFIED_PIXMAP Pixmap	CSG
XmNborderColor XmCBorderColor	Black Pixel	CSG

Name Class	Default Type	Access
XmNborderPixmap XmCPixmap	XmUNSPECIFIED_PIXMAP Pixmap	CSG
XmNborderWidth XmCBorderWidth	0 Dimension	CSG
XmNcolormap XmCColormap	XtCopyFromParent Colormap	CG
XmNdepth XmCDepth	XtCopyFromParent int	CG
XmNdestroyCallback XmCCallback	NULL XtCallbackList	C
XmNheight XmCHeight	0 Dimension	CSG
XmNmappedWhenManaged XmCMappedWhenManaged	True Boolean	CSG
XmNscreen XmCScreen	XtCopyScreen Pointer	CG
XmNsensitive XmCSensitive	True Boolean	CSG
XmNtranslations XmCTranslations	NULL XtTranslations	CSG
XmNwidth XmCWidth	0 Dimension	CSG
XmNx XmCPosition	0 Position	CSG
XmNy XmCPosition	0 Position	CSG

Behavior

Form inherits BulletinBoard's behavior.

Default Translations

Form inherits BulletinBoard's default translations.

Keyboard Traversal

For information on keyboard traversal, see the man page for **XmManager(3X)** and its sections on behavior and default translations.

Related Information

Composite(3X), **Constraint(3X)**, **Core(3X)**, **XmBulletinBoard(3X)**, **XmCreateForm**, **XmCreateFormDialog(3X)**, and **XmManager(3X)**.

XmFrame

Purpose

The Frame widget class

Synopsis

#include <Xm/Frame.h>

Description

Frame is a very simple manager used to enclose a single child in a border drawn by Frame. It uses the Manager class resources for border drawing and performs geometry management so that its size always matches its child's size plus the margins defined for it.

Frame is most often used to enclose other managers when the application developer desires the manager to have the same border appearance as the primitive widgets. Frame can also be used to enclose primitive widgets that do not support the same type of border drawing. This gives visual consistency when you develop applications using diverse widget sets.

If the Frame's parent is a Shell widget, **XmNshadowType** is set to **XmSHADOW_OUT** and Manager's resource **XmNshadowThickness** is set to one by default.

Classes

Frame inherits behavior and resources from the **Core**, **Composite**, **Constraint**, and **XmManager** classes.

The class pointer is **xmFrameWidgetClass**.

The class name is **XmFrame**.

New Resources

The following table defines a set of widget resources used by the programmer to specify data. The programmer can also set the resource values for the inherited classes to set attributes for this widget. To reference a resource by name or by class in a .Xdefaults file, remove the **XmN** or **XmC** prefix and use the remaining letters. To specify one of the defined values for a resource in a .Xdefaults file, remove the **Xm** prefix and use the remaining letters (in either lowercase or uppercase, but include any underscores between words). The codes in the access column indicate if the given resource can be set at creation time (**C**), set by using **XtSetValues** (**S**), retrieved by using **XtGetValues** (**G**), or is not applicable (**N/A**).

XmFrame Resource Set		
Name **Class**	**Default** **Type**	**Access**
XmNmarginWidth XmCMarginWidth	0 short	CSG
XmNmarginHeight XmCMarginHeight	0 short	CSG
XmNshadowType XmCShadowType	XmSHADOW_ETCHED_IN unsigned char	CSG

XmNmarginWidth

Specifies the padding space on the left and right sides between Frame's child and Frame's shadow drawing.

XmNmarginHeight

Specifies the padding space on the top and bottom sides between Frame's child and Frame's shadow drawing.

XmNshadowType

Describes the drawing style for Frame. This resource can have the following values:

- **XmSHADOW_IN** — draws Frame so that it appears inset. This means that the bottom shadow visuals and top shadow visuals are reversed.
- **XmSHADOW_OUT** — draws Frame so that it appears outset.
- **XmSHADOW_ETCHED_IN** — draws Frame using a double line giving the effect of a line etched into the window. The thickness of the double line is equal to the value of **XmNshadowThickness**. This is the default if Frame's parent is a Shell widget.
- **XmSHADOW_ETCHED_OUT** — draws Frame using a double line giving the effect of a line coming out of the window. The thickness of the double line is equal to the value of **XmNshadowThickness**. This is the default except when Frame's parent is a Shell widget.

Inherited Resources

Frame inherits behavior and resources from the following superclasses. For a complete description of each resource, refer to the man page for that superclass.

XmManager Resource Set		
Name **Class**	**Default** **Type**	**Access**
XmNbottomShadowColor XmCForeground	dynamic Pixel	CSG
XmNbottomShadowPixmap XmCBottomShadowPixmap	XmUNSPECIFIED_PIXMAP Pixmap	CSG
XmNforeground XmCForeground	dynamic Pixel	CSG
XmNhelpCallback XmCCallback	NULL XtCallbackList	C
XmNhighlightColor XmCForeground	Black Pixel	CSG
XmNhighlightPixmap XmCHighlightPixmap	dynamic Pixmap	CSG
XmNshadowThickness XmCShadowThickness	dynamic short	CSG
XmNtopShadowColor XmCBackground	dynamic Pixel	CSG
XmNtopShadowPixmap XmCTopShadowPixmap	XmUNSPECIFIED_PIXMAP Pixmap	CSG
XmNunitType XmCUnitType	XmPIXELS unsigned char	CSG
XmNuserData XmCUserData	NULL caddr_t	CSG

Composite Resource Set		
Name **Class**	**Default** **Type**	**Access**
XmNinsertPosition XmCInsertPosition	NULL XmRFunction	CSG

Core Resource Set		
Name **Class**	**Default** **Type**	**Access**
XmNaccelerators XmCAccelerators	NULL XtTranslations	CSG
XmNancestorSensitive XmCSensitive	True Boolean	G
XmNbackground XmCBackground	dynamic Pixel	CSG
XmNbackgroundPixmap XmCPixmap	XmUNSPECIFIED_PIXMAP Pixmap	CSG
XmNborderColor XmCBorderColor	Black Pixel	CSG

Name Class	Default Type	Access
XmNborderPixmap XmCPixmap	XmUNSPECIFIED_PIXMAP Pixmap	CSG
XmNborderWidth XmCBorderWidth	0 Dimension	CSG
XmNcolormap XmCColormap	XtCopyFromParent Colormap	CG
XmNdepth XmCDepth	XtCopyFromParent int	CG
XmNdestroyCallback XmCCallback	NULL XtCallbackList	C
XmNheight XmCHeight	0 Dimension	CSG
XmNmappedWhenManaged XmCMappedWhenManaged	True Boolean	CSG
XmNscreen XmCScreen	XtCopyScreen Pointer	CG
XmNsensitive XmCSensitive	True Boolean	CSG
XmNtranslations XmCTranslations	NULL XtTranslations	CSG
XmNwidth XmCWidth	0 Dimension	CSG
XmNx XmCPosition	0 Position	CSG
XmNy XmCPosition	0 Position	CSG

Default Translations

<EnterWindow>:	**Enter()**
<FocusIn>:	**FocusIn()**
<Btn1Down>:	**Arm()**
<Btn1Up>:	**Activate()**

Related Information

Composite(3X), **Constraint(3X)**, **Core(3X)**, **XmCreateFrame(3X)**, and **XmManager(3X)**.

XmGadget

Purpose

The Gadget widget class

Synopsis

#include <Xm/Xm.h>

Description

Gadget is a widget class used as a supporting superclass for other gadget classes. It handles shadow-border drawing and highlighting, traversal activation and deactivation, and various callback lists needed by gadgets.

The color and pixmap resources defined by XmManager are directly used by gadgets. If **XtSetValues** is used to change one of the resources for a manager widget, all of the gadget children within the manager also change.

Classes

Gadget inherits behavior and resources from **Object** and **RectObj** classes.

The class pointer is **xmGadgetClass**.

The class name is **XmGadget**.

New Resources

The following table defines a set of widget resources used by the programmer to specify data. The programmer can also set the resource values for the inherited classes to set attributes for this widget. To reference a resource by name or by class in a .Xdefaults file, remove the **XmN** or **XmC** prefix and use the remaining letters. To specify one of the defined values for a resource in a .Xdefaults file, remove the **Xm** prefix and use the remaining letters (in either lowercase or uppercase, but include any underscores between words). The codes in the access column indicate if the given resource can be set at creation time (**C**), set by using **XtSetValues** (**S**), retrieved by using **XtGetValues** (**G**), or is not applicable (**N/A**).

XmGadget Resource Set		
Name **Class**	**Default** **Type**	**Access**
XmNhelpCallback XmCCallback	NULL XtCallbackList	C
XmNhighlightOnEnter XmCHighlightOnEnter	False Boolean	CSG
XmNhighlightThickness XmCHighlightThickness	0 short	CSG
XmNshadowThickness XmCShadowThickness	2 short	CSG
XmNtraversalOn XmCTraversalOn	False Boolean	CSG
XmNunitType XmCUnitType	XmPIXELS unsigned char	CSG
XmNuserData XmCUserData	NULL caddr_t	CSG

XmNhelpCallback

Specifies the list of callbacks that is called when the help key sequence is pressed. The reason sent by the callback is **XmCR_HELP**.

XmNhighlightOnEnter
Specifies whether to draw border highlighting. This resource is ignored if **XmNtraversalOn** is True.

XmNhighlightThickness
Specifies the thickness of the highlighting rectangle.

XmNshadowThickness
Specifies the size of the drawn border shadow.

XmNtraversalOn
Specifies traversal activation for this gadget.

XmNunitType
Provides the basic support for resolution independence. It defines the type of units a widget uses with sizing and positioning resources. Unless the **XmNunitType** resource is explicitly set, it defaults to the unit type of the parent widget. If the parent has a unit type of **Xm100TH_POINTS**, any of its children whose **XmNunitType** resource is not set also have a unit type of **Xm100TH_POINTS**. This feature applies only to widgets whose parents are a subclass of **XmManager**. Widgets whose parents are not subclasses of **XmManager** have a unit type of **XmPIXELS**.

XmNunitType can have the following values:

- **XmPIXELS** — all values provided to the widget are treated as normal pixel values. This is the default for the resource.
- **Xm100TH_MILLIMETERS** — all values provided to the widget are treated as 1/100 millimeter.
- **Xm1000TH_INCHES** — all values provided to the widget are treated as 1/1000 inch.
- **Xm100TH_POINTS** — all values provided to the widget are treated as 1/100 point. A point is a unit typically used in text processing applications and is defined as 1/72 inch.
- **Xm100TH_FONT_UNITS** — all values provided to the widget are treated as 1/100-font unit. The value to be used for the font unit is determined in one of two ways. The resource **XmNfont** can be used in a defaults file or on the command line. The standard command-line options of **-fn** and **-font** can also be used. The font unit value is taken as the **QUAD_WIDTH** property of the font. The function **XmSetFontUnits** allows applications to specify the font unit values.

XmNuserData

Allows the application to attach any necessary specific data to the gadget. This is an internally unused resource.

Inherited Resources

Gadget inherits the following resources from the named superclass. For a complete description of each resource, refer to the man page for that superclass.

RectObj Resource Set		
Name **Class**	**Default** **Type**	**Access**
XmNancestorSensitive XmCSensitive	XtCopyFromParent Boolean	CSG
XmNborderWidth XmCBorderWidth	0 Dimension	CSG
XmNheight XmCHeight	0 Dimension	CSG
XmNsensitive XmCSensitive	True Boolean	CSG
XmNwidth XmCWidth	0 Dimension	CSG
XmNx XmCPosition	0 Position	CSG
XmNy XmCPosition	0 Position	CSG

Object Resource Set		
Name **Class**	**Default** **Type**	**Access**
XmNdestroyCallback XmCCallback	NULL XtCallbackList	C

Behavior

Gadgets cannot have translations associated with them. Because of this, a Gadget's behavior is determined by the Manager widget into which the Gadget is placed. The following types of events are caught by a Manager widget and forwarded to a Gadget:

- ButtonPress
- ButtonRelease
- EnterNotify
- LeaveNotify
- FocusIn
- FocusOut
- MotionNotify

Refer to **XmManager(3X)** for a discussion of the translations supported by all Manager widgets.

Related Information

Object(3X), **RectObj(3X)**, and **XmManager(3X)**.

XmGetAtomName

Purpose

A function that returns the string representation for an atom.

Synopsis

#include <Xm/Xm.h>
#include <X11/AtomMgr.h>

String XmGetAtomName (*display, atom*)
    Display * *display*;
    Atom * *atom*;

Description

XmGetAtomName returns the string representation for an atom. It mirrors the **Xlib** interfaces for atom management but provides client-side caching. When and where caching is provided in **Xlib**, the routines will become pseudonyms for the **Xlib** routines.

display Specifies the connection to the X server

atom Specifies the atom for the property name you want returned

Return Value

Returns a string.

XmGetMenuCursor

Purpose

A RowColumn function that returns the cursor ID for the current menu cursor.

Synopsis

Cursor XmGetMenuCursor (*display*)
  Display * *display*;

Description

XmGetMenuCursor queries the menu cursor currently being used by this client on the specified display and returns the cursor ID.

display Specifies the display whose menu cursor is to be queried

For a complete definition of the menu cursor resource, see **XmRowColumn(3X)**.

Return Value

Returns the cursor ID for the current menu cursor or the value None if a cursor is not yet defined. A cursor will not be defined if the application makes this call before the client has created any menus on the specified display.

Related Information

XmRowColumn(3X).

XmGetPixmap

Purpose

A pixmap caching function that generates a pixmap, stores it in a pixmap cache, and returns the pixmap.

Synopsis

#include <Xm/Xm.h>

Pixmap XmGetPixmap (*screen, image_name, foreground, background*)

Screen	* *screen*;
char	* *image_name*;
Pixel	*foreground*;
Pixel	*background*;

Description

XmGetPixmap uses the parameter data to perform a lookup in the pixmap cache to see if a pixmap has already been generated that matches the data. If one is found, a reference count is incremented and the pixmap is returned. Applications should use **XmDestroyPixmap** when the pixmap is no longer needed.

If a pixmap is not found, *image_name* is used to perform a lookup in the image cache. If an image is found, it is used to generate the pixmap, which is then cached and returned.

If an image is not found, the *image_name* is used as a filename, and a search is made for an **X10** or **X11** bitmap file. If it is found, the file is read, converted into an image, and cached in the image cache. The image is then used to generate a pixmap, which is cached and returned.

Several paths are searched to find the file. The user can specify an environment variable **XBMLANGPATH**, which is used to generate one set of paths. See **XtInitialize(3X)** for an explanation of using this environment variable. If **XBMLANGPATH** is not set, the following path names are searched:

> **/usr/lib/X11/%L/bitmaps/%N/%B**
> **/usr/lib/X11/%L/bitmaps/%B**
> **/usr/lib/X11/bitmaps/%B**
> **/usr/include/X11/bitmaps/%B**

Parameter descriptions are listed below:

screen Specifies the display screen on which the pixmap is to be drawn and is used to ensure that the pixmap matches the visual required for the screen

image_name Specifies the name of the image to be used to generate the pixmap

foreground Combines the image with the *foreground* color to create the pixmap if the image referenced is a bit-per-pixel image

background Combines the image with the *background* color to create the pixmap if the image referenced is a bit-per-pixel image

Return Value

Returns a pixmap when successful; returns **XmUNSPECIFIED_PIXMAP** if the image corresponding to the *image_name* cannot be found.

Related Information

XmDestroyPixmap(3X), **XmInstallImage(3X)**, and **XmUninstallImage(3X)**.

XmInstallImage

Purpose

A pixmap caching function that adds an image to the pixmap cache.

Synopsis

```
#include <Xm/Xm.h>

Boolean XmInstallImage (image, image_name)
        XImage        * image;
        char          * image_name;
```

Description

XmInstallImage stores an image in an image cache that can later be used to generate a pixmap. Part of the installation process is to extend the resource converter used to reference these images. The resource converter is given the image name so that the image can be referenced in a .Xdefaults file. Since an image can be referenced by a widget through its pixmap resources, it is up to the application to ensure that the image is installed before the widget is created.

image Points to the image structure to be installed. The installation process does not make a local copy of the image. Therefore, the application should not destroy the image until it is uninstalled from the caching functions.

image_name Specifies a string that the application uses to name the image. After installation, this name can be used in .Xdefaults for referencing the image. A local copy of the name is created by the image caching functions.

The image caching functions provide a set of eight preinstalled images. These names can be used within a **.Xdefaults** file for generating pixmaps for the resource for which they are provided.

Image Name	Description
background	A tile of solid background
25_foreground	A tile of 25% foreground, 75% background
50_foreground	A tile of 50% foreground, 50% background
75_foreground	A tile of 75% foreground, 25% background
horizontal	A tile of horizontal lines of the two colors
vertical	A tile of vertical lines of the two colors
slant_right	A tile of slanting lines of the two colors
slant_left	A tile of slanting lines of the two colors

Return Value

Returns True when successful; returns False if NULL *image*, NULL *image_name*, or duplicate *image_name* are used as parameter values.

Related Information

XmUninstallImage(3X), **XmGetPixmap(3X)**, and **XmDestroyPixmap(3X)**.

XmInternAtom

Purpose

A function that returns an atom for a given name

Synopsis

```
#include <Xm/Xm.h>
#include <X11/AtomMgr.h>

Atom XmInternAtom (display, name, only_if_exists)
        Display     * display;
        String      name;
        Boolean     only_if_exists;
```

Description

XmInternAtom returns an atom for a given name. It mirrors the **Xlib** interfaces for atom management, but provides client-side caching. When and where caching is provided in **Xlib**, the routines will become pseudonyms for the **Xlib** routines.

display Specifies the connection to the X server

name Specifies the name associated with the atom you want returned

only_if_exists
Specifies a Boolean value that indicates whether **XInternAtom** creates the atom

Return Value

Returns an atom.

XmIsMotifWMRunning

Purpose

A function that specifies if the window manager is running.

Synopsis

```
#include <X11/Shell.h>

Boolean XmIsMotifWMRunning (shell)
        Widget       shell;
```

Description

XmIsMotifWMRunning lets a user know if the Motif Window Manager is running on a screen that contains a specific widget hierarchy. This function first sees whether the **MOTIF_WM_INFO** property is present on the root window of the shell's screen. If it is, its window field is used to query for the presence of the specified window as a child of root.

shell Specifies the shell whose screen will be tested for MWM's presence.

Return Value

Returns True if MWM is running.

XmLabel

Purpose

The Label widget class

Synopsis

#include <Xm/Label.h>

Description

Label is an instantiable widget and is also used as a superclass for other button widgets, such as PushButton and ToggleButton. The Label widget does not accept any button or key input, and the help callback is the only callback defined. Label also receives enter and leave events.

Label can contain either text or a pixmap. Label text is a compound string. Refer to the *OSF/Motif Programmer's Guide* for more information on compound strings. The text can be multidirectional, multiline, and/or multifont. When a Label is insensitive, its text is stippled, or the user-supplied insensitive pixmap is displayed.

Label supports both accelerators and mnemonics primarily for use in Label subclass widgets that are contained in menus. Mnemonics are available in a menu system when the button is visible. Accelerators in a menu system are accessible even when the button is not visible. The Label widget displays the mnemonic by underlining the first matching character in the text string. The accelerator is displayed as a text string to the right of the label text or pixmap.

Label consists of many margin fields surrounding the text or pixmap. These margin fields are resources that may be set by the user, but Label subclasses also modify some of these fields. The subclasses tend to modify the **XmNmarginLeft**, **XmNmarginRight**, **XmNmarginTop**, and **XmNmarginBottom** resources and leave the **XmNmarginWidth** and **XmNmarginHeight** resources as set by the application.

Classes

Label inherits behavior and resources from **Core** and **XmPrimitive** Classes.

The class pointer is **xmLabelWidgetClass**.

The class name is **XmLabel**.

New Resources

The following table defines a set of widget resources used by the programmer to specify data. The programmer can also set the resource values for the inherited classes to set attributes for this widget. To reference a resource by name or by class in a .Xdefaults file, remove the **XmN** or **XmC** prefix and use the remaining letters. To specify one of the defined values for a resource in a .Xdefaults file, remove the **Xm** prefix and use the remaining letters (in either lowercase or uppercase, but include any underscores between words). The codes in the access column indicate if the given resource can be set at creation time (**C**), set by using **XtSetValues** (**S**), retrieved by using **XtGetValues** (**G**), or is not applicable (**N/A**).

XmLabel Resource Set		
Name **Class**	**Default** **Type**	**Access**
XmNaccelerator XmCAccelerator	NULL String	CSG
XmNacceleratorText XmCAcceleratorText	NULL XmString	CSG
XmNalignment XmCAlignment	XmALIGNMENT_CENTER unsigned char	CSG
XmNfontList XmCFontList	"Fixed" XmFontList	CSG
XmNlabelInsensitivePixmap XmCLabelInsensitivePixmap	XmUNSPECIFIED_PIXMAP Pixmap	CSG
XmNlabelPixmap XmCPixmap	XmUNSPECIFIED_PIXMAP Pixmap	CSG
XmNlabelString XmCXmString	NULL XmString	CSG
XmNlabelType XmCLabelType	XmSTRING unsigned char	CSG
XmNmarginBottom XmCMarginBottom	0 short	CSG
XmNmarginHeight XmCMarginHeight	2 short	CSG
XmNmarginLeft XmCMarginLeft	0 short	CSG
XmNmarginRight XmCMarginRight	0 short	CSG
XmNmarginTop XmCMarginTop	0 short	CSG
XmNmarginWidth XmCMarginWidth	2 short	CSG

Name Class	Default Type	Access
XmNmnemonic XmCMnemonic	'\0' char	CSG
XmNrecomputeSize XmCRecomputeSize	True Boolean	CSG
XmNstringDirection XmCStringDirection	XmSTRING_DIRECTION_L_TO_R XmStringDirection	CSG

XmNaccelerator

Sets the accelerator on a button widget in a menu, which activates a visible or invisible button from the keyboard. This resource is a string that describes a set of modifiers and the key that may be used to select the button. The format of this string is identical to that used by the translations manager, with the exception that only a single event may be specified and only **KeyPress** events are allowed.

Accelerators for buttons are supported only for certain buttons in certain menu widgets, namely for PushButton and ToggleButton in Pulldown and Popup MenuPanes.

XmNacceleratorText

Specifies the text displayed for the accelerator. The text is displayed to the right of the label string or pixmap. Accelerator text for buttons is displayed only for PushButtons and ToggleButtons in Pulldown and Popup Menus.

XmNalignment

Specifies the label alignment for text or pixmap.

- **XmALIGNMENT_CENTER** (center alignment) — causes the centers of the lines of text to be vertically aligned in the center of the widget window. For a pixmap, its center is vertically aligned with the center of the widget window.
- **XmALIGNMENT_END** (right alignment) — causes the right sides of the lines of text to be vertically aligned with the right edge of the widget window. For a pixmap, its right side is vertically aligned with the right edge of the widget window.
- **XmALIGNMENT_BEGINNING** (left alignment) — causes the left sides of the lines of text to be vertically aligned with the left edge of the widget window. For a pixmap, its left side is vertically aligned with the left edge of the widget window.

The above descriptions for text are correct when **XmNstringDirection** is **XmSTRING_DIRECTION_L_TO_R**. When that resource is **XmSTRING_DIRECTION_R_TO_L**, the descriptions for **XmALIGNMENT_BEGINNING** and **XmALIGNMENT_END** are switched.

XmNfontList
Specifies the font of the text used in the widget. Refer to **XmFontListCreate(3X)** for more information on the creation and structure of a font list.

XmNlabelInsensitivePixmap
Specifies a pixmap used as the button face if **XmNlabelType** is **XmPIXMAP** and the button is insensitive.

XmNlabelPixmap
Specifies the pixmap when **XmNlabelType** is **XmPIXMAP**.

XmNlabelString
Specifies the compound string when the **XmNlabelType** is **XmSTRING**. Refer to **XmStringCreate(3X)** or **XmStringCreateLtoR(3X)** for more information on the creation and structure of compound strings.

XmNlabelType

Specifies the label type.

- **XmSTRING** — text displays **XmNlabelString**.
- **XmPIXMAP** — icon data in pixmap displays **XmNlabelInsensitivePixmap**.

XmNmarginBottom

Specifies the amount of spacing that is to be left after the bottom margin (**XmNmarginHeight**) of the widget, before the label is drawn. This may be modified by Label's subclasses. For example, CascadeButton may increase this field to make room for the cascade pixmap.

XmNmarginHeight

Specifies the amount of blank space between the bottom edge of the top shadow and the label, and the top edge of the bottom shadow and the label.

XmNmarginLeft

Specifies the amount of spacing that is to be left after the left margin (**XmNmarginWidth**) of the widget, before the label is drawn. This may be modified by Label's subclasses. For example, ToggleButton may increase this field to make room for the toggle indicator and for spacing between the indicator and label.

XmNmarginRight

Specifies the amount of spacing that is to be left after the right margin (**XmNmarginWidth**) of the widget, before the label is drawn. This may be modified by Label's subclasses. For example, CascadeButton may increase this field to make room for the cascade pixmap.

XmNmarginTop

Specifies the amount of spacing that is to be left, after the top margin (**XmNmarginHeight**) of the widget, before the label is drawn. This may be modified by Label's subclasses. For example, CascadeButton may increase this field to make room for the cascade pixmap.

XmNmarginWidth

Specifies the amount of blank space between the right edge of the left shadow and the label, and the left edge of the right shadow and the label.

XmNmnemonic

Provides the user with alternate means of selecting a button. The buttons must be visible for mnemonics to work. Buttons, which are in a MenuBar, a Popup MenuPane, or a Pulldown MenuPane, can have a mnemonic.

This resource contains a single character. The first character in the label string that exactly matches the mnemonic is underlined when the button is displayed.

When a mnemonic is specified for a MenuBar button, the user activates the mnemonic by pressing the **meta** key and the specified mnemonic key simultaneously. All other mnemonics are activated by pressing the specified mnemonic. Mnemonics are case insensitive; the character underlined can be a modified key, but the key pressed should always be unmodified.

XmNrecomputeSize

Specifies a Boolean value that indicates whether the widget attempts to be big enough to contain the label. If True, an **XtSetValues** with a new label string or pixmap, accelerator text, margins, font, or label type causes the widget to shrink or expand to exactly fit the new label string or pixmap. If False, the widget never attempts to change size on its own.

XmNstringDirection

Specifies the direction in which the string is to be drawn. The following are the values:

- **XmSTRING_DIRECTION_L_TO_R** — left to right
- **XmSTRING_DIRECTION_R_TO_L** — right to left

Inherited Resources

Label inherits behavior and resources from the following superclasses. For a complete description of each resource, refer to the man page for that superclass.

XmPrimitive Resource Set		
Name **Class**	**Default** **Type**	**Access**
XmNbottomShadowColor XmCForeground	dynamic Pixel	CSG
XmNbottomShadowPixmap XmCBottomShadowPixmap	XmUNSPECIFIED_PIXMAP Pixmap	CSG
XmNforeground XmCForeground	dynamic Pixel	CSG
XmNhelpCallback XmCCallback	NULL XtCallbackList	C
XmNhighlightColor XmCForeground	Black Pixel	CSG
XmNhighlightOnEnter XmCHighlightOnEnter	False Boolean	CSG
XmNhighlightPixmap XmCHighlightPixmap	dynamic Pixmap	CSG
XmNhighlightThickness XmCHighlightThickness	0 short	CSG
XmNshadowThickness XmCShadowThickness	0 short	CSG
XmNtopShadowColor XmCBackground	dynamic Pixel	CSG
XmNtopShadowPixmap XmCTopShadowPixmap	XmUNSPECIFIED_PIXMAP Pixmap	CSG

Name Class	Default Type	Access
XmNtraversalOn XmCTraversalOn	False Boolean	CSG
XmNunitType XmCUnitType	XmPIXELS unsigned char	CSG
XmNuserData XmCUserData	NULL caddr_t	CSG

Core Resource Set		
Name **Class**	**Default** **Type**	**Access**
XmNaccelerators XmCAccelerators	NULL XtTranslations	CSG
XmNancestorSensitive XmCSensitive	True Boolean	G
XmNbackground XmCBackground	dynamic Pixel	CSG
XmNbackgroundPixmap XmCPixmap	XmUNSPECIFIED_PIXMAP Pixmap	CSG
XmNborderColor XmCBorderColor	Black Pixel	CSG
XmNborderPixmap XmCPixmap	XmUNSPECIFIED_PIXMAP Pixmap	CSG
XmNborderWidth XmCBorderWidth	0 Dimension	CSG
XmNcolormap XmCColormap	XtCopyFromParent Colormap	CG

Name Class	Default Type	Access
XmNdepth XmCDepth	XtCopyFromParent int	CG
XmNdestroyCallback XmCCallback	NULL XtCallbackList	C
XmNheight XmCHeight	0 Dimension	CSG
XmNmappedWhenManaged XmCMappedWhenManaged	True Boolean	CSG
XmNscreen XmCScreen	XtCopyScreen Pointer	CG
XmNsensitive XmCSensitive	True Boolean	CSG
XmNtranslations XmCTranslations	NULL XtTranslations	CSG
XmNwidth XmCWidth	0 Dimension	CSG
XmNx XmCPosition	0 Position	CSG
XmNy XmCPosition	0 Position	CSG

Callback Information

The following structure is returned with each callback:

typedef struct
{
    int *reason*;
    XEvent * *event*;
} **XmAnyCallbackStruct;**

reason Indicates why the callback was invoked. For this callback, *reason* is set to **XmCR_HELP**.

event Points to the **XEvent** that triggered the callback.

Behavior

Default Translations

<EnterWindow>: Enter()
<LeaveWindow>: Leave()

Keyboard Traversal

For information on keyboard traversal, see the man page for **XmPrimitive(3X)** and its sections on behavior and default translations.

Related Information

Core(3X), **XmCreateLabel(3X)**, **XmFontListCreate(3X)**, **XmPrimitive(3X)**, **XmStringCreate(3X)**, and **XmStringCreateLtoR(3X)**.

XmLabelGadget

Purpose

The LabelGadget widget class

Synopsis

#include <Xm/LabelG.h>

Description

LabelGadget is an instantiable widget and is also used as a superclass for other button gadgets, such as PushButtonGadget and ToggleButtonGadget. The LabelGadget widget does not accept any button or key input, and the help callback is the only callback defined. LabelGadget also receives enter and leave events.

LabelGadget can contain either text or a pixmap. LabelGadget text is a compound string. Refer to **XmString** for more information on compound strings. The text can be multidirectional, multiline, and/or multifont. When a LabelGadget is insensitive, its text is stippled, or the user supplied insensitive pixmap is displayed.

LabelGadget supports both accelerators and mnemonics primarily for use in LabelGadget subclass widgets that are contained in menus. Mnemonics are available in a menu system when the button is visible. Accelerators in a menu system are accessible even when the button is not visible. The LabelGadget displays the mnemonic by underlining the first matching character in the text string. The accelerator is displayed as a text string to the right of the label text or pixmap.

LabelGadget consists of many margin fields surrounding the text or pixmap. These margin fields are resources that may be set by the user, but LabelGadget subclasses also modify some of these fields. The subclasses tend to modify the **XmNmarginLeft**, **XmNmarginRight**, **XmNmarginTop**, and **XmNmarginBottom** resources and leave the **XmNmarginWidth** and **XmNmarginHeight** resources as set by the application.

Classes

LabelGadget inherits behavior and resources from **Object**, **RectObj** and **XmGadget** classes.

The class pointer is **xmLabelGadgetClass**.

The class name is **XmLabelGadget**.

New Resources

The following table defines a set of widget resources used by the programmer to specify data. The programmer can also set the resource values for the inherited classes to set attributes for this widget. To reference a resource by name or by class in a .Xdefaults file, remove the **XmN** or **XmC** prefix and use the remaining letters. To specify one of the defined values for a resource in a .Xdefaults file, remove the **Xm** prefix and use the remaining letters (in either lowercase or uppercase, but include any underscores between words). The codes in the access column indicate if the given resource can be set at creation time (**C**), set by using **XtSetValues** (**S**), retrieved by using **XtGetValues** (**G**), or is not applicable (**N/A**).

XmLabelGadget Resource Set		
Name **Class**	**Default** **Type**	**Access**
XmNaccelerator XmCAccelerator	NULL String	CSG
XmNacceleratorText XmCAcceleratorText	NULL XmString	CSG
XmNalignment XmCAlignment	XmALIGNMENT_CENTER unsigned char	CSG
XmNfontList XmCFontList	"Fixed" XmFontList	CSG
XmNlabelInsensitivePixmap XmCLabelInsensitivePixmap	XmUNSPECIFIED_PIXMAP Pixmap	CSG
XmNlabelPixmap XmCPixmap	XmUNSPECIFIED_PIXMAP Pixmap	CSG
XmNlabelString XmCXmString	NULL XmString	CSG
XmNlabelType XmCLabelType	XmSTRING unsigned char	CSG
XmNmarginBottom XmCMarginBottom	0 short	CSG
XmNmarginHeight XmCMarginHeight	2 short	CSG
XmNmarginLeft XmCMarginLeft	0 short	CSG
XmNmarginRight XmCMarginRight	0 short	CSG
XmNmarginTop XmCMarginTop	0 short	CSG
XmNmarginWidth XmCMarginWidth	2 short	CSG

Name Class	Default Type	Access
XmNmnemonic XmCMnemonic	'\0' char	CSG
XmNrecomputeSize XmCRecomputeSize	True Boolean	CSG
XmNstringDirection XmCStringDirection	XmSTRING_DIRECTION_L_TO_R XmStringDirection	CSG

XmNaccelerator

Sets the accelerator on a button widget in a menu, which activates a visible or invisible button from the keyboard. This resource is a string that describes a set of modifiers and the key that may be used to select the button. The format of this string is identical to that used by the translations manager, with the exception that only a single event may be specified and only **KeyPress** events are allowed.

Accelerators for buttons are supported only for certain buttons in certain menu gadgets, namely for PushButtonGadget and ToggleButtonGadget in Pulldown and Popup menus.

XmNacceleratorText

Specifies the text displayed for the accelerator. The text is displayed to the right of the label string or pixmap. Accelerator text for buttons is displayed only for PushButtonGadgets and ToggleButtonGadgets in Pulldown and Popup Menus.

XmNalignment

Specifies the label alignment for text or pixmap.

- **XmALIGNMENT_CENTER** (center alignment) — causes the centers of the lines of text to be vertically aligned in the center of the parent window. For a pixmap, its center is vertically aligned with the center of the widget window.

- **XmALIGNMENT_END** (right alignment) — causes the right sides of the lines of text to be vertically aligned with the right edge of the parent window. For a pixmap, its right side is vertically aligned with the right edge of the widget window.
- **XmALIGNMENT_BEGINNING** (left alignment) — causes the left sides of the lines of text to be vertically aligned with the left edge of the parent window. For a pixmap, its left side is vertically aligned with the left edge of the widget window.

The above descriptions for text are correct when **XmNstringDirection** is **XmSTRING_DIRECTION_L_TO_R**; the descriptions for **XmALIGNMENT_BEGINNING** and **XmALIGNMENT_END** are switched When the resource is **XmSTRING_DIRECTION_R_TO_L**.

XmNfontList

Specifies the font of the text used in the gadget. Refer to **XmFontListCreate(3X)** for more information on the creation and the structure of a font list.

XmNlabelInsensitivePixmap

Specifies a pixmap used as the button face if **XmNlabelType** is **XmPIXMAP** and the button is insensitive.

XmNlabelPixmap

Specifies the pixmap when **XmNlabelType** is **XmPIXMAP**.

XmNlabelString

Specifies the compound string when **XmNlabelType** is **XmSTRING**. Refer to **XmStringCreate(3X)** or **XmStringCreateLtoR(3X)** for more information on the creation and the structure of compound strings.

XmNlabelType

Specifies the label type.

- **XmSTRING** — text displays **XmNlabelString**
- **XmPIXMAP** — icon data in pixmap displays **XmNlabelPixmap** or **XmNlabelInsensitivePixmap**

XmNmarginBottom
Specifies the amount of spacing that is to be left after the bottom margin (**XmNmarginHeight**) of the gadget, before the label is drawn. This may be modified by LabelGadget's subclasses. For example, CascadeButtonGadget may increase this field to make room for the cascade pixmap.

XmNmarginHeight
Specifies the amount of blank space between the bottom edge of the top shadow and the label, and the top edge of the bottom shadow and the label.

XmNmarginLeft
Specifies the amount of spacing that is to be left after the left margin (**XmNmarginWidth**) of the gadget, before the label is drawn. This may be modified by LabelGadget's subclasses. For example, ToggleButtonGadget may increase this field to make room for the toggle indicator and for spacing between the indicator and label.

XmNmarginRight
Specifies the amount of spacing that is to be left after the right margin (**XmNmarginWidth**) of the gadget, before the label is drawn. This may be modified by LabelGadget's subclasses. For example, CascadeButtonGadget may increase this field to make room for the cascade pixmap.

XmNmarginTop
Specifies the amount of spacing that is to be left, after the top margin (**XmNmarginHeight**) of the gadget, before the label is drawn. This may be modified by LabelGadget's subclasses. For example, CascadeButtonGadget may increase this field to make room for the cascade pixmap.

XmNmarginWidth
Specifies the amount of blank space between the right edge of the left shadow and the label, and the left edge of the right shadow and the label.

XmNmnemonic

Provides the user with alternate means for selecting a button. The buttons must be visible for mnemonics to work. Buttons that are in either a Popup MenuPane, a Pulldown MenuPane, or an Option menu are allowed to have a mnemonic.

This resource contains a single character. The first character in the label string that exactly matches the mnemonic is underlined when the button is displayed.

Mnemonics are activated by pressing the specified mnemonic. Mnemonics are case insensitive; the character underlined can be a modified key, but the key pressed should always be unmodified.

XmNrecomputeSize

Specifies a Boolean value that indicates whether the gadget attempts to be big enough to contain the label. If True, an **XtSetValues** with a new label string or pixmap, accelerator text, margins, font, or label type causes the gadget to shrink or expand to exactly fit the new label string or pixmap. If False, the gadget never attempts to change size on its own.

XmNstringDirection

Specifies the direction in which the string is to be drawn. The following are the values:

- **XmSTRING_DIRECTION_L_TO_R** — left to right
- **XmSTRING_DIRECTION_R_TO_L** — right to left

Inherited Resources

LabelGadget inherits behavior and resources from the following superclasses. For a complete description of each resource, refer to the man page for that superclass.

XmGadget Resource Set		
Name **Class**	**Default** **Type**	**Access**
XmNhelpCallback XmCCallback	NULL XtCallbackList	C
XmNhighlightOnEnter XmCHighlightOnEnter	False Boolean	CSG
XmNhighlightThickness XmCHighlightThickness	0 short	CSG
XmNshadowThickness XmCShadowThickness	0 short	CSG
XmNtraversalOn XmCTraversalOn	False Boolean	CSG
XmNunitType XmCUnitType	XmPIXELS unsigned char	CSG
XmNuserData XmCUserData	NULL caddr_t	CSG

RectObj Resource Set		
Name **Class**	**Default** **Type**	**Access**
XmNancestorSensitive XmCSensitive	XtCopyFromParent Boolean	CSG
XmNborderWidth XmCBorderWidth	0 Dimension	CSG
XmNheight XmCHeight	0 Dimension	CSG
XmNsensitive XmCSensitive	True Boolean	CSG
XmNwidth XmCWidth	0 Dimension	CSG
XmNx XmCPosition	0 Position	CSG
XmNy XmCPosition	0 Position	CSG

Object Resource Set		
Name **Class**	**Default** **Type**	**Access**
XmNdestroyCallback XmCCallback	NULL XtCallbackList	C

Keyboard Traversal

For information on keyboard traversal, see the man page for **XmGadget(3X)** and its sections on behavior and default translations.

Related Information

Object(3X), **RectObj(3X)**, **XmCreateLabelGadget(3X)**, **XmFontListCreate(3X)**, **XmGadget(3X)**, **XmStringCreate(3X)**, and **XmStringCreateLtoR(3X)**.

XmList

Purpose

The OSF/Motif List widget class

Synopsis

#include <Xm/List.h>

Description

List allows a user to select one or more items from a group of choices. Items are selected from the list in a variety of ways, using both the pointer and the keyboard.

List operates on an array of strings that are defined by the application. Each string becomes an item in List, with the first string becoming the item in position 1, the second string becoming the item in position 2, and so on.

The size of List is set by specifying the number of items that are visible. If selection scrolling ability through a large set of choices is desired, use the **XmCreateScrolledList** convenience function.

To select items, move the pointer or cursor to the desired item and press the mouse button or the key defined as Select. There are several styles of selection behavior, and they all highlight the selected item or items by displaying them in inverse colors. An appropriate callback is invoked to notify the application of the user's choice. The application then takes whatever action is required for the specified selection.

Classes

List inherits behavior and resources from **Core** and **XmPrimitive** classes.

The class pointer is **xmListWidgetClass**.

The class name is **XmList**.

New Resources

The following table defines a set of widget resources used by the programmer to specify data. The programmer can also set the resource values for the inherited classes to set attributes for this widget. To reference a resource by name or by class in a .Xdefaults file, remove the **XmN** or **XmC** prefix and use the remaining letters. To specify one of the defined values for a resource in a .Xdefaults file, remove the **Xm** prefix and use the remaining letters (in either lowercase or uppercase, but include any underscores between words). The codes in the access column indicate if the given resource can be set at creation time (**C**), set by using **XtSetValues** (**S**), retrieved by using **XtGetValues** (**G**), or is not applicable (**N/A**).

XmList Resource Set		
Name **Class**	**Default** **Type**	**Access**
XmNautomaticSelection XmCAutomaticSelection	False Boolean	CSG
XmNbrowseSelectionCallback XmCCallback	NULL XtCallbackList	C
XmNdefaultActionCallback XmCCallback	NULL XtCallbackList	C
XmNdoubleClickInterval XmCDoubleClickInterval	250 int	CSG
XmNextendedSelectionCallback XmCCallback	NULL XtCallbackList	C
XmNfontList XmCFontList	"fixed" XmFontList	CSG
XmNitemCount XmCItemCount	0 int	CSG
XmNitems XmCItems	NULL XmStringTable	CSG
XmNlistMarginHeight XmCListMarginHeight	0 Dimension	CSG
XmNlistMarginWidth XmCListMarginWidth	0 Dimension	CSG
XmNlistSpacing XmCListSpacing	0 short	CSG
XmNmultipleSelectionCallback XmCCallback	NULL XtCallbackList	C
XmNselectedItemCount XmCSelectedItemCount	0 int	CSG
XmNselectedItems XmCSelectedItems	NULL XmStringTable	CSG

Name Class	Default Type	Access
XmNselectionPolicy XmCSelectionPolicy	XmBROWSE_SELECT unsigned char	CSG
XmNsingleSelectionCallback XmCCallback	NULL XtCallbackList	C
XmNstringDirection XmCStringDirection	XmSTRING_DIRECTION_L_TO_R XmStringDirection	CSG
XmNvisibleItemCount XmCVisibleItemCount	1 int	CSG

XmNautomaticSelection

Invokes **XmNsingleSelectionCallback** when the user moves into a new item if the value is True and the selection mode is either **XmBROWSE_SELECT** or **XmEXTENDED_SELECT**. If False, no selection callbacks are invoked until the user releases the mouse button. See the Behavior section for further details on the interaction of this resource with the selection modes.

XmNbrowseSelectionCallback

Specifies a list of callbacks that is called when an item is selected in the browse selection mode. The reason is **XmCR_BROWSE_SELECT**.

XmNdefaultActionCallback

Specifies a list of callbacks that is called when an item is double clicked. The reason is **XmCR_DEFAULT_ACTION**.

XmNdoubleClickInterval

Specifies, in milliseconds, the maximum interval between two consecutive clicks if they are to be considered a double-click action, rather than two single-click actions.

XmNextendedSelectionCallback

Specifies a list of callbacks that is called when items are selected using the extended selection mode. The reason is **XmCR_EXTENDED_SELECT**.

XmNfontList
Specifies the font list associated with the list items. This is used in conjunction with the **XmNvisibleItemsCount** resource to determine the height of the List widget. Refer to **XmString(3X)** for more information on a font list structure.

XmNitemCount
Specifies the total number of items. This number must match **XmNitems**. It is automatically updated by the list whenever an element is added to or deleted from the list.

XmNitems Points to an array of compound strings that are to be displayed as the list items. Refer to **XmString(3X)** for more information on the creation and structure of compound strings.

XmNlistMarginHeight
Specifies the height of the margin between the list border and the items.

XmNlistMarginWidth
Specifies the width of the margin between the list border and the items.

XmNlistSpacing
Specifies the spacing between list items. When keyboard traversal is enabled, this spacing increases by the value of the **XmNhighlightThickness** parameter in Primitive.

XmNmultipleSelectionCallback
Specifies a list of callbacks that is called when an item is selected in multiple selection mode. The reason is **XmCR_MULTIPLE_SELECT**.

XmNselectedItemCount
Specifies the number of strings in the selected items list.

XmNselectedItems
Points to an array of compound strings that represents the list items that are currently selected, either by the user or by the application.

XmNselectionPolicy
Defines the interpretation of the selection action. This can be one of the following:

- **XmSINGLE_SELECT** — allows only single selections
- **XmMULTIPLE_SELECT** — allows multiple selections
- **XmEXTENDED_SELECT** — allows extended selections
- **XmBROWSE_SELECT** — allows PM "drag and browse" functionality

XmNsingleSelectionCallback
Specifies a list of callbacks that is called when an item is selected in single selection mode. The reason is **XmCR_SINGLE_SELECT**.

XmNstringDirection
Specifies the initial direction to draw the string. The values are **XmSTRING_DIRECTION_L_TO_R** and **XmSTRING_DIRECTION_R_TO_L**.

XmNvisibleItemCount
Specifies the number of items that can fit in the visible space of the list work area. The List uses this value to determine its height.

XmScrolledList Resource Set		
Name **Class**	**Default** **Type**	**Access**
XmNhorizontalScrollBar XmCHorizontalScrollBar	NULL Widget	CSG
XmNlistSizePolicy XmCListSizePolicy	XmVARIABLE unsigned char	CG
XmNscrollBarDisplayPolicy XmCScrollBarDisplayPolicy	XmAS_NEEDED unsigned char	CSG
XmNscrollBarPlacement XmCScrollBarPlacement	XmBOTTOM_RIGHT unsigned char	CSG
XmNscrolledWindowMarginHeight XmCScrolledWindowMarginHeight	0 Dimension	CSG
XmNscrolledWindowMarginWidth XmCScrolledWindowMarginWidth	0 Dimension	CSG
XmNspacing XmCSpacing	4 Dimension	CSG
XmNverticalScrollBar XmCVerticalScrollBar	NULL Widget	CSG

XmNhorizontalScrollBar

Specifies the widget ID of the horizontal ScrollBar. This widget is created automatically by the **XmCreateScrolledList** convenience function.

XmNlistSizePolicy

Controls the reaction of the List when an item grows horizontally beyond the current size of the list work area. If the value is **XmCONSTANT**, the list viewing area does not grow, and a horizontal ScrollBar is added. If this resource is set to **XmVARIABLE**, List grows to match the size of the longest item, and no horizontal ScrollBar appears.

When the value of this resource is **XmRESIZE_IF_POSSIBLE**, the List attempts to grow or shrink to match the width of the widest item. If it cannot grow to match the widest size, a horizontal ScrollBar is added if the longest item is wider than the list viewing area.

The size policy must be set at the time the List widget is created. It cannot be changed at a later time through **XtSetValues**.

XmNscrollBarDisplayPolicy
Specifies the ScrollBar display policy. When this resource is set to **XmAS_NEEDED**, the vertical ScrollBar is displayed only when the number of items in the List exceeds the number of visible items. If **XmNlistSizePolicy** is **XmCONSTANT** or **XmRESIZE_IF_POSSIBLE**, the horizontal ScrollBar is displayed only if there is an item that is wider than the current width of the list. When this resource is set to **XmSTATIC**, the vertical ScrollBar is always displayed. The horizontal ScrollBar is always displayed if **XmNlistSizePolicy** is set to **XmCONSTANT** or **XmRESIZE_IF_POSSIBLE**.

XmNscrollBarPlacement
Specifies the positioning of the ScrollBars in relation to the visible items. The following are the values:

- **XmTOP_LEFT** — The horizontal ScrollBar is placed above the visible items and the vertical ScrollBar to the left of the visible items.
- **XmBOTTOM_LEFT** — The horizontal ScrollBar is placed below the visible items and the vertical ScrollBar to the left of the visible items.
- **XmTOP_RIGHT** — The horizontal ScrollBar is placed above the visible items and the vertical ScrollBar to the right of the visible items.
- **XmBOTTOM_RIGHT** — The horizontal ScrollBar is placed below the visible items and the vertical ScrollBar to the right of the visible items.

XmNscrolledWindowMarginHeight
Specifies the margin height on the top and bottom of the ScrolledWindow.

XmNscrolledWindowMarginWidth
Specifies the margin width on the right and left sides of the ScrolledWindow.

XmNspacing
Specifies the distance between the ScrollBars from the visible items.

XmNverticalScrollBar
Specifies the widget ID of the vertical ScrollBar. This widget is created automatically by the **XmCreateScrolledList** convenience function.

Inherited Resources

List inherits behavior and resources from the following superclasses. For a complete description of each resource, refer to the man page for that superclass.

XmPrimitive Resource Set		
Name **Class**	**Default** **Type**	**Access**
XmNbottomShadowColor XmCForeground	dynamic Pixel	CSG
XmNbottomShadowPixmap XmCBottomShadowPixmap	XmUNSPECIFIED_PIXMAP Pixmap	CSG
XmNforeground XmCForeground	dynamic Pixel	CSG
XmNhelpCallback XmCCallback	NULL XtCallbackList	C
XmNhighlightColor XmCForeground	Black Pixel	CSG
XmNhighlightOnEnter XmCHighlightOnEnter	False Boolean	CSG
XmNhighlightPixmap XmCHighlightPixmap	dynamic Pixmap	CSG
XmNhighlightThickness XmCHighlightThickness	0 short	CSG
XmNshadowThickness XmCShadowThickness	2 short	CSG
XmNtopShadowColor XmCBackground	dynamic Pixel	CSG
XmNtopShadowPixmap XmCTopShadowPixmap	XmUNSPECIFIED_PIXMAP Pixmap	CSG
XmNtraversalOn XmCTraversalOn	False Boolean	CSG
XmNunitType XmCUnitType	XmPIXELS unsigned char	CSG
XmNuserData XmCUserData	NULL caddr_t	CSG

Core Resource Set		
Name **Class**	**Default** **Type**	**Access**
XmNaccelerators XmCAccelerators	NULL XtTranslations	CSG
XmNancestorSensitive XmCSensitive	True Boolean	G
XmNbackground XmCBackground	dynamic Pixel	CSG
XmNbackgroundPixmap XmCPixmap	XmUNSPECIFIED_PIXMAP Pixmap	CSG
XmNborderColor XmCBorderColor	Black Pixel	CSG
XmNborderPixmap XmCPixmap	XmUNSPECIFIED_PIXMAP Pixmap	CSG
XmNborderWidth XmCBorderWidth	0 Dimension	CSG
XmNcolormap XmCColormap	XtCopyFromParent Colormap	CG
XmNdepth XmCDepth	XtCopyFromParent int	CG
XmNdestroyCallback XmCCallback	NULL XtCallbackList	C
XmNheight XmCHeight	0 Dimension	CSG
XmNmappedWhenManaged XmCMappedWhenManaged	True Boolean	CSG
XmNscreen XmCScreen	XtCopyScreen Pointer	CG
XmNsensitive XmCSensitive	True Boolean	CSG

Name Class	Default Type	Access
XmNtranslations XmCTranslations	NULL XtTranslations	CSG
XmNwidth XmCWidth	0 Dimension	CSG
XmNx XmCPosition	0 Position	CSG
XmNy XmCPosition	0 Position	CSG

Callback Information

List defines a new callback structure. The application must first look at the reason field and use only the structure members that are valid for that particular reason, because not all fields are relevant for every possible reason. The callback structure is defined as follows:

```
typedef struct
{
    int          reason;
    XEvent       * event;
    XmString     item;
    int          item_length;
    int          item_position;
    XmString     * selected_items;
    int          selected_item_count;
    int          selection_type;
} XmListCallbackStruct;
```

reason — Indicates why the callback was invoked.

event — Points to the **XEvent** that triggered the callback. It can be NULL.

item Is the item selected by this action. *selected_items* points to a temporary storage space that is reused after the callback is finished. Therefore, if an application needs to save the selected list, it should copy the list into its own data space.

item_length Is the length of the item when the selection action occurred.

item_position Is the position in the List of the selected item.

selected_items Points to the list of items selected at the time of the *event* that caused the callback. *selected_items* points to a temporary storage space that is reused after the callback is finished. Therefore, if an application needs to save the selected list, it should copy the list into its own data space.

selected_items_count
Is the number of items in the *selected_items* list.

selection_type Indicates that the most recent extended selection was the initial selection (**XmINITIAL**), a modification of an existing selection (**XmMODIFICATION**), or an additional noncontiguous selection (**XmADDITION**).

The following table describes the reasons for which the individual callback structure fields are valid:

Reason	Valid Fields
XmCR_SINGLE_SELECT	*reason, event, item, item_length, item_position*
XmCR_DEFAULT_ACTION	*reason, event, item, item_length, item_position*
XmCR_BROWSE_SELECT	*reason, event, item, item_length, item_position*
XmCR_MULTIPLE_SELECT	*reason, event, item, selected_items, selected_item_count*
XmCR_EXTENDED_SELECT	*reason, event, item, selected_items, selected_item_count, selection_type*

Behavior

List provides several methods for selecting its items. The general selection model is as follows:

The user moves the pointer to the item to be selected, either by using the mouse to move the pointer over the desired item, or, in keyboard traversal mode, moving the active highlight to the desired item with the up and down arrow keys. The item is selected by clicking the select button on the mouse (usually the left mouse button), or by pressing the select key on the keyboard (usually the Space key). Each of the selection modes provides some variation of the above behavior.

Note that the keyboard selection interface is active only when traversal is enabled for the List widget.

The selection mode is set by the **XmNselectionPolicy** resource and is modified by the **XmNautomaticSelection** resource. The behavior of the various modes are defined below:

XmSINGLE_SELECT (Single Selection):
Move the mouse pointer or keyboard highlight until it is over the desired item and press the select button or key. The item inverts its foreground and background colors to indicate that it is the selected object. Any previously selected items are unselected (returned to their normal visual state). When the button or key is released, **XmNsingleSelectionCallback** is invoked.

XmBROWSE_SELECT (Browse Selection):
When using the mouse, press the select button; the item under the pointer is highlighted. While the button is held down, drag the selection by moving the pointer. When the select button is released, the object under the pointer becomes the selected item and the **XmNbrowseSelectionCallback** is invoked.

If **XmNautomaticSelection** is True, the **XmNbrowseSelectionCallback** is invoked when the select button is pressed. For each subsequent item entered while the select button is held down, the callback is invoked when the pointer moves into the item. No selection callback is invoked when the button is released.

When selecting through the keyboard and **XmNautomaticSelection** is False, browse selection is no different from single-selection mode. However, when **XmNautomaticSelection** is True, the callback is invoked for each element that is selected. Both the keyboard highlight and the selection highlight move as the user moves through the list.

XmMULTIPLE_SELECT (Multiple Selection):
Move the mouse pointer or keyboard highlight until it is over the desired item and press the select button or key. The item inverts its foreground and background colors to indicate that it is a selected object. Any previously selected items are not affected by this action. When the button or key is released, the **XmNmultipleSelectionCallback** is invoked. To unselect an item in this mode, move to a selected item and press the select button or key. The **XmNmultipleSelectionCallback** is invoked with the updated selection list.

XmEXTENDED_SELECT (Extended Selection):
This mode selects a contiguous range of objects with one action. Press the select button on the first item of the range. This begins a new selection process, which deselects any previous selection in the list. That item's colors are inverted to show its inclusion in the selection. While pressing the button, drag the cursor through other items in the List. As the pointer moves through the list, all the colors of items between the initial item and the item currently under the pointer are inverted to show that they are included in the selection. When the button is released, the **XmNextendedSelectionCallback** is invoked and contains a list of all selected items. The *selection_type* field is set to **XmINITIAL**.

Modify a selection by pressing and holding the shift key, moving to the new endpoint, and pressing the select button. The items between the initial start point and the new end point are selected. The rest of the selection process proceeds as above. Any previous selections are not unselected. When the select button is released, the **XmNextendedSelectionCallback** is invoked and contains a list of all selected items, both new and previous. The *selection_type* field is to **XmMODIFICATION**.

Items can be added to or deleted from a selected range by using the CTRL key. To add an additional range to an existing selection, move to the first item of the new group, press and hold the CTRL key, and then press the select button. The color of the item under the pointer inverts; any previous selections are unaffected. This item becomes the initial item for the new selection range. If the pointer is dragged through additional items while the CTRL key and select button are held down, those items' colors invert as described above. When the select button is released, the **XmNextendedSelectionCallback** is invoked and contains a list of all selected items, both new and previous. The *selection_type* field is set to **XmADDITION**.

To delete an item or a range of items from an existing selection, move to the first item to be deselected, press and hold the CTRL key, and then press the select button. The item under the pointer returns to its normal visual state to indicate that it is no longer in the selection. This item becomes the initial item for the range to be deselected. If the pointer is dragged through additional selected items while the CTRL key and select button are held down, those items are deselected. Any other selections are unaffected. When the select button is released, the **XmNextendedSelectionCallback** is invoked and contains a list of remaining selected items, both new and previous. The *selection_type* field is set to **XmADDITION**.

A range of items can also be deselected by setting the initial item for the range as described above, then moving to the end of the range, and pressing the select button while holding the Shift key down. All items between the two endpoints are deselected. When the button is released, the **XmNextendedSelectionCallback** is issued as described above.

If the **XmNautomaticSelection** resource is set to True, the **XmNextendedSelectionCallback** is invoked when the select button is pressed. For each subsequent item the user selects or deselects, the callback is invoked when the pointer is moved into the item. The *selection_type* field is set to reflect the current action. No selection callback is invoked when the button is released.

Keyboard selection in extended selection mode is accomplished by moving the keyboard highlight to the start of the desired range and pressing the select key. The selection callback is invoked with a *selection_type* value of **XmINITIAL**. Then, using the arrow keys, move the keyboard highlight to the end of the range, hold down the Shift key, and press the select key. The **XmNextendedSelectionCallback** is invoked with a value of **XmMODIFICATION**. Select additional ranges by moving to the beginning of a range, pressing the select key while holding down the CTRL key, and then moving to the end of the range and pressing the select key while holding the Shift key. Erase previously selected elements by moving to them and pressing the select key while holding down the CTRL key. In all cases, callbacks are issued as described above.

When using the keyboard with the **XmNautomaticSelection** resource set to True, the **XmNextendedSelectionCallback** is invoked when the select button is pressed. For each subsequent item the user selects, the callback is invoked when the pointer is moved into the item if there are modifier keys in use. For example, start the selection by pressing the select key, and then extend it by using the arrow keys while holding down the Shift key. The *selection_type* field is set to reflect the current action. There is no selection callback invoked when the button is released.

XmDEFAULT-ACTION (Double Click)

If an object is clicked twice within the interval defined by the **XmNdoubleClickInterval** resource, the List interprets that as a double click and the **XmNdefaultActionCallback** is invoked. The item's colors invert to indicate that it is selected.

Default Translations

The following are the default Translations for XmList:

Button1<Motion>: ListButtonMotion()
Shift Ctrl ~Meta<Btn1Down>: ListShiftCtrlSelect()
Shift Ctrl ~Meta<Btn1Up>: ListShiftCtrlUnSelect()
Shift Ctrl ~Meta<KeyDown>space:ListKbdShiftCtrlSelect()
Shift Ctrl ~Meta<KeyUp>space:ListKbdShiftCtrlUnSelect()
Shift Ctrl ~Meta<KeyDown>Select:ListKbdShiftCtrlSelect()
Shift Ctrl ~Meta<KeyUp>Select:ListKbdShiftCtrlUnSelect()
Shift ~Ctrl ~Meta<Btn1Down>: ListShiftSelect()
Shift ~Ctrl ~Meta<Btn1Up>: ListShiftUnSelect()
Shift ~Ctrl ~Meta<KeyDown>space:ListKbdShiftSelect()
Shift ~Ctrl ~Meta<KeyUp>space:ListKbdShiftUnSelect()
Shift ~Ctrl ~Meta<KeyDown>Select:ListKbdShiftSelect()
Shift ~Ctrl ~Meta<KeyUp>Select:ListKbdShiftUnSelect()
Ctrl ~Shift ~Meta<Btn1Down>: ListCtrlSelect()
Ctrl ~Shift ~Meta<Btn1Up>: ListCtrlUnSelect()
Ctrl ~Shift ~Meta<KeyDown>space:ListKbdCtrlSelect()

```
Ctrl ~Shift ~Meta<KeyUp>space:ListKbdCtrlUnSelect()
Ctrl ~Shift ~Meta<KeyDown>Select:ListKbdCtrlSelect()
Ctrl ~Shift ~Meta<KeyUp>Select:ListKbdCtrlUnSelect()
~Shift ~Ctrl ~Meta<Btn1Down>: ListElementSelect()
~Shift ~Ctrl ~Meta<Btn1Up>:   ListElementUnSelect()
~Shift ~Ctrl ~Meta<KeyDown>space:ListKbdSelect()
~Shift ~Ctrl ~Meta<KeyUp>space:ListKbdUnSelect()
~Shift ~Ctrl ~Meta<KeyDown>Select:ListKbdSelect()
~Shift ~Ctrl ~Meta<KeyUp>Select:ListKbdUnSelect()
Shift Ctrl ~Meta<Key>Up:        ListShiftCtrlPrevElement()
Shift Ctrl ~Meta<Key>Down:      ListShiftCtrlNextElement()
Shift ~Ctrl ~Meta<Key>Up:       ListShiftPrevElement()
Shift ~Ctrl ~Meta<Key>Down:     ListShiftNextElement()
~Shift Ctrl ~Meta<Key>Up:       ListCtrlPrevElement()
~Shift Ctrl ~Meta<Key>Down:     ListCtrlNextElement()
~Shift ~Ctrl ~Meta<Key>Up:      ListPrevElement()
~Shift ~Ctrl ~Meta<Key>Down:    ListNextElement()
<Enter>:                        ListEnter()
<Leave>:                        ListLeave()
<FocusIn>:                      ListFocusIn()
<FocusOut>:                     ListFocusOut()
<Unmap>:                        PrimitiveUnmap()
Shift<Key>Tab:                  PrimitivePrevTabGroup()
<Key>Tab:                       PrimitiveNextTabGroup()
<Key>Home:                      PrimitiveTraverseHome()
```

Keyboard Traversal

For those actions not inherited from **XmPrimitive(3X)**, keyboard traversal is described in the behavior section of this man page.

Related Information

Core(3X), **XmCreateList(3X)**, **XmCreateScrolledList(3X)**, **XmFontListCreate(3X) XmListAddItem(3X)**, **XmListAddItemUnselected(3X)**, **XmListDeleteItem(3X)**, **XmListDeletePos(3X)**, **XmListDeselectItem(3X)**, **XmListDeselectAllItems(3X)**, **XmListSelectItem(3X)**, **XmListSetHorizPos(3X)**, **XmListSetItem(3X)**, **XmListSetPos(3X)**, **XmListSetBottomItem(3X)**, **XmListSetBottomPos(3X)**, **XmListSelectPos(3X)**, **XmListDeselectPos(3X)**, **and XmListItemExists(3X)**, **XmPrimitive(3X)**, **and XmStringCreate(3X).**

XmListAddItem

Purpose

A List function that adds an item to the list

Synopsis

#include <Xm/List.h>

void XmListAddItem (*widget, item, position*)
  Widget *widget*;
  XmString *item*;
  int *position*;

Description

XmListAddItem adds an item to the list at the given position. The position specifies the location of the new item in the list. Position 1 is the first element, position 2 is the second, and so on. If the position argument is zero, the item is added after the last item in the list. When the item is inserted into the list, it is compared with the current **XmNselectedItems** list. If the new item matches an item on the selected list, it appears selected.

widget Specifies the ID of the List from whose list an item is added.

item Specifies the item to be added to the list.

position Specifies the placement of the item within the list in terms of its cell position. It uses an insert mode/cell number scheme with a 1 specifying the top-entry position and a zero specifying the bottom entry for adding an item to the bottom of the list.

For a complete definition of List and its associated resources, see **XmList(3X)**.

Related Information

XmList(3X).

XmListAddItemUnselected

Purpose

A List function that adds an item to the list

Synopsis

```
#include <Xm/List.h>

void XmListAddItemUnselected (widget, item, position)
        Widget      widget;
        XmString    item;
        int         position;
```

Description

XmListAddItemUnselected adds an item to the list at the given position. The position specifies the location of the new item in the list. Position 1 is the first element, position 2 is the second, and so on. If the position argument is zero, the item is added after the last item in the list.

widget Specifies the ID of the List from whose list an item is added.

item Specifies the item to be added to the list.

position Specifies the placement of the item within the list in terms of its cell position. It uses an insert mode/cell number scheme with a 1 specifying the top-entry position and a zero specifying the bottom-entry position.

For a complete definition of List and its associated resources, see **XmList(3X)**.

Related Information

XmList(3X).

XmListDeleteItem

Purpose

A List function that deletes an item from the list

Synopsis

```
#include <Xm/List.h>

void XmListDeleteItem (widget, item)
        Widget      widget;
        XmString    item;
```

Description

XmListDeleteItem deletes a specified item from the list. A warning message appears if the item does not exist.

widget Specifies the ID of the List from whose list an item is deleted

item Specifies the text of the item to be deleted from the list

For a complete definition of List and its associated resources, see **XmList(3X)**.

Related Information

XmList(3X).

XmListDeletePos

Purpose

A List function that deletes an item from a list at a specified position.

Synopsis

#include <Xm/List.h>

void XmListDeletePos (*widget, position*)
    Widget *widget*;
    int *position*;

Description

XmListDeletePos deletes an item at a specified position. A position argument of zero deletes the last item in the list. A warning message appears if the position does not exist.

widget Specifies the ID of the List from whose list an item is deleted

position Identifies the position of the item to be deleted

For a complete definition of List and its associated resources, see **XmList(3X)**.

Related Information

XmList(3X).

XmListDeselectAllItems

Purpose

A List function that unhighlights and removes all items from the selected list.

Synopsis

#include <Xm/List.h>

void XmListDeselectAllItems (*widget, item*)
    Widget   *widget*;

Description

XmListDeselectAllItems unhighlights and removes all items from the selected list.

widget Specifies the ID of the List widget from whose list all selected items are deselected

For a complete definition of List and its associated resources, see **XmList(3X)**.

Related Information

XmList(3X).

XmListDeselectItem

Purpose

A List function that deselects the specified item from the selected list.

Synopsis

```
#include <Xm/List.h>

void XmListDeselectItem (widget, item)
        Widget      widget;
        XmString    item;
```

Description

XmListDeselectItem unhighlights and removes the specified item from the selected list.

widget Specifies the ID of the List from whose list an item is deselected

item Specifies the item to be deselected from the list

For a complete definition of List and its associated resources, see **XmList(3X)**.

Related Information

XmList(3X).

XmListDeselectPos

Purpose

A List function that deselects an item at a specified position in the list.

Synopsis

```
#include <Xm/List.h>

void XmListDeselectPos (widget, position)
        Widget      widget;
        int         position;
```

Description

XmListDeselectPos unhighlights the item at the specified position and deletes it from the selected list.

widget Specifies the ID of the List widget

position Identifies the position of the item to be deselected

For a complete definition of List and its associated resources, see **XmList(3X)**.

Related Information

XmList(3X).

XmListItemExists

Purpose

A List function that checks if a specified item is in the list.

Synopsis

#include <Xm/List.h>

Boolean XmListItemExists (*widget, item*)
  Widget *widget*;
  XmString *item*;

Description

XmListItemExists is a Boolean function that checks if a specified item is present in the list.

widget Specifies the ID of the List widget

item Specifies the item whose presence is checked

For a complete definition of List and its associated resources, see **XmList(3X)**.

Return Value

Returns True if the specified item is present in the list.

Related Information

XmList(3X).

XmListSelectItem

Purpose

A List function that selects an item in the list

Synopsis

```
#include <Xm/List.h>

void XmListSelectItem (widget, item, notify)
        Widget      widget;
        XmString    item;
        Boolean     notify;
```

Description

XmListSelectItem highlights and adds the specified item to the current selected list.

widget Specifies the ID of the List widget from whose list an item is selected

item Specifies the item to be added to the List widget

notify Specifies a Boolean value that when True invokes the selection callback for the current mode. From an application interface view, calling this function with *notify* True is indistinguishable from a user-initiated selection action.

For a complete definition of List and its associated resources, see **XmList(3X)**.

Related Information

XmList(3X).

XmListSelectPos

Purpose

A List function that selects an item at a specified position in the list.

Synopsis

#include <Xm/List.h>

void XmListSelectPos (*widget, position, notify*)
  Widget *widget*;
  int *position*;
  Boolean *notify*;

Description

XmListSelectPos highlights an item at the specified position and adds it to the current selected list. A position of zero specifies the last item in the list.

widget Specifies the ID of the List widget

position Identifies the position of the item to be added

notify Specifies a Boolean value that when True invokes the selection callback for the current mode. From an application interface view, calling this function with *notify* True is indistinguishable from a user-initiated selection action.

For a complete definition of List and its associated resources, see **XmList(3X)**.

Related Information

XmList(3X).

XmListSetBottomItem

Purpose

A List function that makes an existing item the last visible item in the list.

Synopsis

#include <Xm/List.h>

void XmListSetBottomItem (*widget, item*)
    Widget   *widget*;
    XmString   *item*;

Description

XmListSetBottomItem makes an existing item the last visible item in the list. The item can be any valid item in the list.

widget Specifies the ID of the List widget from whose list an item is made the last visible

item Specifies the item

For a complete definition of List and its associated resources, see **XmList(3X)**.

Related Information

XmList(3X).

XmListSetBottomPos

Purpose

A List function that makes a specified item the last visible position in the list.

Synopsis

#include <Xm/List.h>

void XmListSetBottomPos (*widget, position*)
    Widget *widget*;
    int *position*;

Description

XmListSetBottomPos makes a given item the last visible position in the list. The position can be any valid position in the list. A position of 0 specifies the last item in the list.

widget Specifies the ID of the List widget

position Identifies the specified position

For a complete definition of List and its associated resources, see **XmList(3X)**.

Related Information

XmList(3X).

XmListSetHorizPos

Purpose

A List function that moves a ScrollBar to the specified position in the list.

Synopsis

```
#include <Xm/List.h>

void XmListSetHorizPos (widget, position)
        Widget      widget;
        int         position;
```

Description

XmListSetHorizPos sets the **XmNvalue** resource of the ScrollBar to the specified position and updates the visible portion of the list with the new value if the List widget's **XmNlistSizePolicy** is set to **XmCONSTANT** or **XmRESIZE_IF_POSSIBLE** and the horizontal ScrollBar is currently visible. This is equivalent to moving the ScrollBar to the specified position.

widget Specifies the ID of the List widget

position Identifies the specified position

For a complete definition of List and its associated resources, see **XmList(3X)**.

Related Information

XmList(3X).

XmListSetItem

Purpose

A List function that makes an existing item the first visible item in the list.

Synopsis

```
#include <Xm/List.h>

void XmListSetItem (widget, item)
        Widget      widget;
        XmString    item;
```

Description

XmListSetItem makes an existing item the first visible item in the list. The item can be any valid item in the list.

widget Specifies the ID of the List widget from whose list an item is made the first visible

item Specifies the item

For a complete definition of List and its associated resources, see **XmList(3X)**.

Related Information

XmList(3X).

XmListSetPos

Purpose

A List function that makes the item at the given position the first visible position in the list.

Synopsis

```
#include <Xm/List.h>

void XmListSetPos (widget, position)
        Widget      widget;
        int         position;
```

Description

XmListSetPos makes the item at the given position the first visible position in the list. The position can be any valid position in the list.

widget Specifies the ID of the List widget

position Specifies the position

For a complete definition of List and its associated resources, see **XmList(3X)**.

Related Information

XmList(3X).

XmMainWindow

Purpose

The MainWindow widget class

Synopsis

#include <Xm/MainW.h>

Description

MainWindow provides a standard layout for the primary window of an application. This layout includes a MenuBar, a CommandWindow, a work region, and ScrollBars. Any or all of these areas are optional. The work region and ScrollBars in the MainWindow behave identically to the work region and ScrollBars in the ScrolledWindow widget. The user can think of the MainWindow as an extended ScrolledWindow with an optional MenuBar and optional CommandWindow.

In a fully-loaded MainWindow, the MenuBar spans the top of the window horizontally. The CommandWindow spans the MainWindow horizontally just below the MenuBar, and the work region lies below the CommandWindow. Any space remaining below the CommandWindow is managed in a manner identical to ScrolledWindow. The behavior of ScrolledWindow can be controlled by the ScrolledWindow resources. To create a MainWindow, first create the work region elements, a MenuBar, a CommandWindow, a horizontal ScrollBar, and a vertical ScrollBar widget, and then call **XmMainWindowSetAreas** with those widget IDs.

MainWindow can also create two Separator widgets that provide a visual separation of MainWindow's three components.

Classes

MainWindow inherits behavior and resources from **Core**, **Composite**, **Constraint**, **XmManager**, and **ScrolledWindow** classes.

The class pointer is **xmMainWindowWidgetClass.**

The class name is **XmMainWindow**.

New Resources

The following table defines a set of widget resources used by the programmer to specify data. The programmer can also set the resource values for the inherited classes to set attributes for this widget. To reference a resource by name or by class in a .Xdefaults file, remove the **XmN** or **XmC** prefix and use the remaining letters. To specify one of the defined values for a resource in a .Xdefaults file, remove the **Xm** prefix and use the remaining letters (in either lowercase or uppercase, but include any underscores between words). The codes in the access column indicate if the given resource can be set at creation time (**C**), set by using **XtSetValues** (**S**), retrieved by using **XtGetValues** (**G**), or is not applicable (**N/A**).

XmMainWindow Resource Set		
Name **Class**	**Default** **Type**	**Access**
XmNcommandWindow XmCCommandWindow	NULL Widget	CSG
XmNmainWindowMarginHeight XmCMainWindowMarginHeight	0 Dimension	CSG
XmNmainWindowMarginWidth XmCMainWindowMarginWidth	0 Dimension	CSG
XmNmenuBar XmCMenuBar	NULL Widget	CSG
XmNshowSeparator XmCShowSeparator	False Boolean	CSG

XmNcommandWindow

Specifies the widget to be laid out as the CommandWindow. This widget must have been previously created and managed as a child of MainWindow.

XmNmainWindowMarginHeight

Specifies the margin height on the top and bottom of MainWindow. This resource overrides any setting of the ScrolledWindow resource **XmNscrolledWindowMarginHeight**.

XmNmainWindowMarginWidth

Specifies the margin width on the right and left sides of MainWindow. This resource overrides any setting of the ScrolledWindow resource **XmNscrolledWindowMarginWidth**.

XmNmenuBar

Specifies the widget to be laid out as the MenuBar. This widget must have been previously created and managed as a child of MainWindow.

XmNshowSeparator

Displays separators between the components of the MainWindow when set to True. If set to False, no separators are displayed.

Inherited Resources

MainWindow inherits behavior and resources from the following superclasses. For a complete description of each resource, refer to the man page for that superclass.

XmScrolledWindow Resource Set		
Name **Class**	**Default** **Type**	**Access**
XmNclipWindow XmCClipWindow	NULL Widget	G
XmNhorizontalScrollBar XmCHorizontalScrollBar	NULL Widget	CSG
XmNscrollBarDisplayPolicy XmCScrollBarDisplayPolicy	XmSTATIC unsigned char	CG
XmNscrollBarPlacement XmCScrollBarPlacement	XmBOTTOM_RIGHT unsigned char	CSG
XmNscrolledWindowMarginHeight XmCScrolledWindowMarginHeight	0 Dimension	CSG
XmNscrolledWindowMarginWidth XmCScrolledWindowMarginWidth	0 Dimension	CSG
XmNscrollingPolicy XmCScrollingPolicy	XmAPPLICATION_DEFINED unsigned char	CG
XmNspacing XmCSpacing	4 int	CSG
XmNverticalScrollBar XmCVerticalScrollBar	NULL Widget	CSG
XmNvisualPolicy XmCVisualPolicy	XmVARIABLE unsigned char	CG
XmNworkWindow XmCWorkWindow	NULL Widget	CSG

XmManager Resource Set		
Name **Class**	**Default** **Type**	**Access**
XmNbottomShadowColor XmCForeground	dynamic Pixel	CSG
XmNbottomShadowPixmap XmCBottomShadowPixmap	XmUNSPECIFIED_PIXMAP Pixmap	CSG
XmNforeground XmCForeground	dynamic Pixel	CSG
XmNhelpCallback XmCCallback	NULL XtCallbackList	C
XmNhighlightColor XmCForeground	Black Pixel	CSG
XmNhighlightPixmap XmCHighlightPixmap	dynamic Pixmap	CSG
XmNshadowThickness XmCShadowThickness	0 short	CSG
XmNtopShadowColor XmCBackground	dynamic Pixel	CSG
XmNtopShadowPixmap XmCTopShadowPixmap	XmUNSPECIFIED_PIXMAP Pixmap	CSG
XmNunitType XmCUnitType	XmPIXELS unsigned char	CSG
XmNuserData XmCUserData	NULL caddr_t	CSG

Composite Resource Set		
Name **Class**	**Default** **Type**	**Access**
XmNinsertPosition XmCInsertPosition	NULL XmRFunction	CSG

Core Resource Set		
Name **Class**	**Default** **Type**	**Access**
XmNaccelerators XmCAccelerators	NULL XtTranslations	CSG
XmNancestorSensitive XmCSensitive	True Boolean	G
XmNbackground XmCBackground	dynamic Pixel	CSG
XmNbackgroundPixmap XmCPixmap	XmUNSPECIFIED_PIXMAP Pixmap	CSG
XmNborderColor XmCBorderColor	Black Pixel	CSG

Name Class	Default Type	Access
XmNborderPixmap XmCPixmap	XmUNSPECIFIED_PIXMAP Pixmap	CSG
XmNborderWidth XmCBorderWidth	0 Dimension	CSG
XmNcolormap XmCColormap	XtCopyFromParent Colormap	CG
XmNdepth XmCDepth	XtCopyFromParent int	CG
XmNdestroyCallback XmCCallback	NULL XtCallbackList	C
XmNheight XmCHeight	0 Dimension	CSG
XmNmappedWhenManaged XmCMappedWhenManaged	True Boolean	CSG
XmNscreen XmCScreen	XtCopyScreen Pointer	CG
XmNsensitive XmCSensitive	True Boolean	CSG
XmNtranslations XmCTranslations	NULL XtTranslations	CSG
XmNwidth XmCWidth	0 Dimension	CSG
XmNx XmCPosition	0 Position	CSG
XmNy XmCPosition	0 Position	CSG

Behavior

MainWindow inherits behavior from ScrolledWindow.

Keyboard Traversal

For information on keyboard traversal, see the man page for **XmManager(3X)** and its sections on behavior and default translations.

Related Information

Composite(3X), **Constraint(3X)**, **Core(3X)**, **XmCreateMainWindow(3X)**, **XmMainWindowSep1(3X)**, **XmMainWindowSep2(3X)**, **XmMainWindowSetAreas(3X)**, **XmManager(3X)**, and **XmScrolledWindow(3X)**,

XmMainWindowSep1

Purpose

A MainWindow function that returns the widget ID of the first Separator widget.

Synopsis

```
#include <Xm/MainW.h>

Widget XmMainWindowSep1 (widget)
      Widget       widget;
```

Description

XmMainWindowSep1 returns the widget ID of the first Separator widget in the MainWindow. The first Separator widget is located between the MenuBar and the Command widget. This Separator is visible only when **XmNshowSeparator** is True.

widget Specifies the MainWindow widget ID

For a complete definition of MainWindow and its associated resources, see **XmMainWindow(3X)**.

Return Value

Returns the widget ID of the first Separator.

Related Information

XmMainWindow(3X).

XmMainWindowSep2

Purpose

A MainWindow function that returns the widget ID of the second Separator widget.

Synopsis

#include <Xm/MainW.h>

Widget XmMainWindowSep2 (*widget*)
    Widget *widget*;

Description

XmMainWindowSep2 returns the widget ID of the second Separator widget in the MainWindow. The second Separator widget is located between the Command widget and the ScrolledWindow. This Separator is visible only when **XmNshowSeparator** is True.

widget
    Specifies the MainWindow widget ID

For a complete definition of MainWindow and its associated resources, see **XmMainWindow(3X)**.

Return Value

Returns the widget ID of the second Separator.

Related Information

XmMainWindow(3X).

XmMainWindowSetAreas

Purpose

A MainWindow function that identifies manageable children for each area.

Synopsis

#include <Xm/MainW.h>

void XmMainWindowSetAreas (*widget, menu_bar, command_window, horizontal_scrollbar,*
vertical_scrollbar, work_region)

Widget	*widget*;
Widget	*menu_bar*;
Widget	*command_window*;
Widget	*horizontal_scrollbar*;
Widget	*vertical_scrollbar*;
Widget	*work_region*;

Description

XmMainWindowSetAreas identifies which of the valid children for each area (such as the MenuBar and work region) are to be actively managed by MainWindow. This function also sets up or adds the MenuBar, work window, command window, and ScrollBar widgets to the application's main window widget.

Each area is optional; therefore, the user can pass NULL to one or more of the following arguments. The window manager provides the title bar.

widget Specifies the MainWindow widget ID.

menu_bar Specifies the widget ID for the MenuBar to be associated with the MainWindow widget. Set this ID only after creating an instance of the MainWindow widget. The attribute name associated with this argument is **XmNmenuBar**.

command_window
Specifies the widget ID for the command window to be associated with the MainWindow widget. Set this ID only after creating an instance of the MainWindow widget. The attribute name associated with this argument is **XmNcommandWindow**.

horizontal_scrollbar
Specifies the ScrollBar widget ID for the horizontal ScrollBar to be associated with the MainWindow widget. Set this ID only after creating an instance of the MainWindow widget. The attribute name associated with this argument is **XmNhorizontalScrollBar**.

vertical_scrollbar
Specifies the ScrollBar widget ID for the vertical ScrollBar to be associated with the MainWindow widget. Set this ID only after creating an instance of the MainWindow widget. The attribute name associated with this argument is **XmNverticalScrollBar**.

work_region Specifies the widget ID for the work window to be associated with the MainWindow widget. Set this ID only after creating an instance of the MainWindow widget. The attribute name associated with this argument is **XmNworkWindow**.

For a complete definition of MainWindow and its associated resources, see **XmMainWindow(3X)**.

Related Information

XmMainWindow(3X).

XmManager

Purpose

The Manager widget class

Synopsis

#include <Xm/Xm.h>

Description

Manager is a widget class used as a supporting superclass for other widget classes. It supports the visual resources, graphics contexts, and traversal resources necessary for the graphics and traversal mechanisms.

Classes

Manager inherits behavior and resources from **Core**, **Composite**, and **Constraint** classes.

The class pointer is **xmManagerWidgetClass**.

The class name is **XmManager**.

New Resources

The following table defines a set of widget resources used by the programmer to specify data. The programmer can also set the resource values for the inherited classes to set attributes for this widget. To reference a resource by name or by class in a .Xdefaults file, remove the **XmN** or **XmC** prefix and use the remaining letters. To specify one of the defined values for a resource in a .Xdefaults file, remove the **Xm** prefix and use the remaining letters (in either lowercase or uppercase, but include any underscores between words). The codes in the access column indicate if the given resource can be set at creation time (**C**), set by using **XtSetValues** (**S**), retrieved by using **XtGetValues** (**G**), or is not applicable (**N/A**).

XmManager Resource Set		
Name **Class**	**Default** **Type**	**Access**
XmNbottomShadowColor XmCForeground	dynamic Pixel	CSG
XmNbottomShadowPixmap XmCBottomShadowPixmap	XmUNSPECIFIED_PIXMAP Pixmap	CSG
XmNforeground XmCForeground	dynamic Pixel	CSG
XmNhelpCallback XmCCallback	NULL XtCallbackList	C
XmNhighlightColor XmCForeground	Black Pixel	CSG
XmNhighlightPixmap XmCHighlightPixmap	dynamic Pixmap	CSG
XmNshadowThickness XmCShadowThickness	0 short	CSG
XmNtopShadowColor XmCBackground	dynamic Pixel	CSG
XmNtopShadowPixmap XmCTopShadowPixmap	XmUNSPECIFIED_PIXMAP Pixmap	CSG
XmNunitType XmCUnitType	XmPIXELS unsigned char	CSG
XmNuserData XmCUserData	NULL caddr_t	CSG

XmNbottomShadowColor
Specifies the color to use to draw the bottom and right sides of the border shadow. This color is used if the **XmNbottomShadowPixmap** resource is NULL.

XmNbottomShadowPixmap
Specifies the pixmap to use to draw the bottom and right sides of the border shadow.

XmNforeground
Specifies the foreground drawing color used by manager widgets.

XmNhelpCallback
Specifies the list of callbacks that are called when the help key sequence is pressed. The reason sent by this callback is **XmCR_HELP**. No translation is bound to this resource. It is up to the application to install a translation for help.

XmNhighlightColor
Specifies the color of the highlighting rectangle. This color is used if the highlight pixmap resource is **XmUNSPECIFIED_PIXMAP**.

XmNhighlightPixmap
Specifies the pixmap used to draw the highlighting rectangle.

XmNshadowThickness
Specifies the thickness of the drawn border shadow.

XmNtopShadowColor
Specifies the color to use to draw the top and left sides of the border shadow. This color is used if the **XmNtopShadowPixmap** resource is NULL.

XmNtopShadowPixmap
Specifies the pixmap to use to draw the top and left sides of the border shadow.

XmNunitType
Provides the basic support for resolution independence. It defines the type of units a widget uses with sizing and positioning resources. Unless the **XmNunitType** resource is explicitly set, it defaults to the unit type of the parent widget. If the parent has a unit type of **Xm100TH_POINTS**, any of its children whose **XmNunitType** resource is not set also have a unit type of **Xm100TH_POINTS**. This feature applies only to widgets whose parents are a subclass of XmManager. Widgets whose parents are not subclasses of **XmManager** have a unit type of **XmPIXELS**.

XmNunitType can have the following values:

- **XmPIXELS** — all values provided to the widget are treated as normal pixel values. This is the default for the resource.
- **Xm100TH_MILLIMETERS** — all values provided to the widget are treated as 1/100 millimeter.
- **Xm1000TH_INCHES** — all values provided to the widget are treated as 1/1000 inch.
- **Xm100TH_POINTS** — all values provided to the widget are treated as 1/100 point. A point is a unit typically used in text processing applications and is defined as 1/72 inch.
- **Xm100TH_FONT_UNITS** — all values provided to the widget are treated as 1/100-font unit. The value to be used for the font unit is determined in one of two ways. The resource **XmNfont** can be used in a defaults file or on the command line. The standard command line options of **-fn** and **-font** can also be used. The font unit value is taken as the **QUAD_WIDTH** property of the font. The function **XmSetFontUnits** allows applications to specify the font unit values.

XmNuserData

Allows the application to attach any necessary specific data to the widget. This is an internally unused resource.

Dynamic Color Defaults

The foreground, background, top shadow, and bottom shadow resources are dynamically defaulted. If no color data is specified, the colors are automatically generated. On a monochrome system, a black and white color scheme is generated. On a color system, four colors are generated, which display the correct shading for the 3-D visuals.

If the background is the only color specified for a widget, the top shadow, bottom shadow, and foreground colors are generated to give the 3-D appearance. The color generation works best with non-saturated colors.

Using pure red, green, or blue yields poor results.

Colors are generated only at creation. Resetting the background through **XtSetValues** does not regenerate the other colors.

Inherited Resources

Manager inherits the following resources from the named superclasses. For a complete description of each resource, refer to the man page for that superclass.

Composite Resource Set		
Name **Class**	**Default** **Type**	**Access**
XmNinsertPosition XmCInsertPosition	NULL XmRFunction	CSG

Core Resource Set		
Name **Class**	**Default** **Type**	**Access**
XmNaccelerators XmCAccelerators	NULL XtTranslations	CSG
XmNancestorSensitive XmCSensitive	True Boolean	G
XmNbackground XmCBackground	dynamic Pixel	CSG
XmNbackgroundPixmap XmCPixmap	XmUNSPECIFIED_PIXMAP Pixmap	CSG
XmNborderColor XmCBorderColor	Black Pixel	CSG
XmNborderPixmap XmCPixmap	XmUNSPECIFIED_PIXMAP Pixmap	CSG
XmNborderWidth XmCBorderWidth	0 Dimension	CSG
XmNcolormap XmCColormap	XtCopyFromParent Colormap	CG
XmNdepth XmCDepth	XtCopyFromParent int	CG
XmNdestroyCallback XmCCallback	NULL XtCallbackList	C
XmNheight XmCHeight	0 Dimension	CSG
XmNmappedWhenManaged XmCMappedWhenManaged	True Boolean	CSG
XmNscreen XmCScreen	XtCopyScreen Pointer	CG
XmNsensitive XmCSensitive	True Boolean	CSG

Name Class	Default Type	Access
XmNtranslations XmCTranslations	NULL XtTranslations	CSG
XmNwidth XmCWidth	0 Dimension	CSG
XmNx XmCPosition	0 Position	CSG
XmNy XmCPosition	0 Position	CSG

Behavior

The following set of translations are used by Manager widgets that have Gadget children. Since Gadgets cannot have translations associated with them, it is the responsibility of the Manager widget to intercept the events of interest and pass them to the appropriate Gadget child.

Shift<Key>Tab:
Moves the focus to the first item contained within the previous tab group. If the beginning of the tab group list is reached, it wraps to the end of the tab group list.

<Key>Tab: Moves the focus to the first item contained within the next tab group. If the current tab group is the last entry in the tab group list, it wraps to the beginning of the tab group list.

<Key>Up or **<Key>Left**:
Moves the keyboard focus to the previous Manager widget or gadget within the current tab group. The previous widget or gadget is the previous entry in the tab group's list of children. Wrapping occurs, if necessary.

<Key>Down or **<Key>Right**:
Moves the Keyboard focus to the next Manager widget or gadget within the current tab group. The previous widget or gadget is the next entry in the tab group's list of children. Wrapping occurs, if necessary.

<Key>Home:
Moves the keyboard focus to the first Manager widget or gadget in the current tab group.

Default Translations

The following are translations used by all Manager widgets.

<EnterWindow>: ManagerEnter()
<FocusOut>: ManagerFocusOut()
<FocusIn>: ManagerFocusIn()

The following are the translations necessary to provide gadget event processing

<Key>space: ManagerGadgetSelect()
<Key>Return: ManagerGadgetSelect()
Shift<Key>Tab: ManagerGadgetPrevTabGroup()
<Key>Tab: ManagerGadgetNextTabGroup()
<Key>Up: ManagerGadgetTraversePrev()
<Key>Down: ManagerGadgetTraverseNext()
<Key>Left: ManagerGadgetTraversePrev()
<Key>Right: ManagerGadgetTraverseNext()
<Key>Home: ManagerGadgetTraverseHome()

Related Information

Composite(3X), **Constraint(3X)**, **Core(3X)**, and **XmGadget3X)**.

XmMenuPosition

Purpose

A RowColumn function that positions a Popup MenuPane

Synopsis

#include <Xm/RowColumn.h>

void XmMenuPosition (*menu, event*)
  Widget *menu*;
  XButtonPressedEvent* *event*;

Description

XmMenuPosition positions a Popup MenuPane using the information in the specified event. Unless an application is positioning the MenuPane itself, it must first invoke this function before managing the PopupMenu. The *x_root* and *y_root* values in the specified event are used to determine the menu position.

menu Specifies the PopupMenu to be positioned

event Specifies the event passed to the action procedure which manages the PopupMenu

For a complete definition of RowColumn and its associated resources, see **XmRowColumn(3X)**.

Related Information

XmRowColumn(3X).

XmMenuShell

Purpose

The MenuShell widget class

Synopsis

#include <Xm/MenuShell.h>

Description

The MenuShell widget is a custom OverrideShell widget. An OverrideShell widget bypasses MWM when displaying itself. It is designed specifically to contain Popup or Pulldown MenuPanes.

Most application writers never encounter this widget if they use the menu-system convenience functions, **XmCreatePopupMenu** or **XmCreatePulldown Menu**, to create a Popup or Pulldown MenuPane. The convenience functions automatically create a MenuShell widget as the parent of the MenuPane. However, if the convenience functions are not used, the application programmer must create the required MenuShell. In this case, it is important to note that the type of parent of the MenuShell depends on the type of menu system being built.

- If the MenuShell is for the top-level Popup MenuPane, the MenuShell must be created as a child of the widget from which the Popup MenuPane is popped up.
- If the MenuShell is for a MenuPane that is pulled down from a Popup or another Pulldown MenuPane, the MenuShell must be created as a child of the Popup or Pulldown MenuPane's parent MenuShell.
- If the MenuShell is for a MenuPane that is pulled down from a MenuBar, the MenuShell must be created as a child of the MenuBar.
- If the MenuShell is for a Pulldown MenuPane in an OptionMenu, the MenuShell must have the same parent as the OptionMenu.

Classes

MenuShell inherits behavior and resources from **Core**, **Composite**, **Shell**, and **OverrideShell** classes.

The class pointer is **xmMenuShellWidgetClass**.

The class name is **XmMenuShell**.

New Resources

MenuShell defines no new resources, but overrides the **XmNallowShellResize** resource in Shell.

Inherited Resources

MenuShell inherits behavior and resources from the following superclasses. For a complete description of each resource, refer to the man page for that superclass. The following tables define a set of widget resources used by the programmer to specify data. The programmer can set the resource values for these inherited classes to set attributes for this widget. To reference a resource by name or by class in a .Xdefaults file, remove the **XmN** or **XmC** prefix and use the remaining letters. To specify one of the defined values for a resource in a .Xdefaults file, remove the **Xm** prefix and use the remaining letters (in either lowercase or uppercase, but include any underscores between words). The codes in the access column indicate if the given resource can be set at creation time (**C**), set by using **XtSetValues** (**S**), retrieved by using **XtGetValues** (**G**), or is not applicable (**N/A**).

Shell Resource Set		
Name **Class**	**Default** **Type**	**Access**
XmNallowShellResize XmCAllowShellResize	True Boolean	G
XmNancestorSensitive XmCSensitive	ShellAncestorSensitive Boolean	G
XmNcreatePopupChildProc XmCCreatePopupChildProc	NULL XmCreatePopupChildProc	CSG
XmNdepth XmCDepth	ShellDepth int	CSG
XmNgeometry XmCGeometry	NULL caddr_t	CSG
XmNoverrideRedirect XmCOverrideRedirect	True Boolean	CSG
XmNpopdownCallback XmCCallback	NULL caddr_t	C
XmNpopupCallback XmCCallback	NULL caddr_t	C
XmNsaveUnder XmCSaveUnder	True Boolean	CSG

Composite Resource Set		
Name **Class**	**Default** **Type**	**Access**
XmNinsertPosition XmCInsertPosition	NULL XmRFunction	CSG

Core Resource Set		
Name **Class**	**Default** **Type**	**Access**
XmNaccelerators XmCAccelerators	NULL XtTranslations	CSG
XmNancestorSensitive XmCSensitive	ShellAncestorSensitive Boolean	CSG
XmNbackground XmCBackground	White Pixel	CSG
XmNbackgroundPixmap XmCPixmap	XmUNSPECIFIED_PIXMAP Pixmap	CSG
XmNborderColor XmCBorderColor	Black Pixel	CSG
XmNborderPixmap XmCPixmap	XmUNSPECIFIED_PIXMAP Pixmap	CSG
XmNborderWidth XmCBorderWidth	1 Dimension	CSG
XmNcolormap XmCColormap	ShellColormap Colormap	CG
XmNdepth XmCDepth	ShellDepth int	CG
XmNdestroyCallback XmCCallback	NULL XtCallbackList	C
XmNheight XmCHeight	0 Dimension	CSG
XmNmappedWhenManaged XmCMappedWhenManaged	True Boolean	CSG
XmNscreen XmCScreen	XtCopyScreen Pointer	CG
XmNsensitive XmCSensitive	True Boolean	CSG

Name Class	Default Type	Access
XmNtranslations XmCTranslations	NULL XtTranslations	CSG
XmNwidth XmCWidth	0 Dimension	CSG
XmNx XmCPosition	0 Position	CSG
XmNy XmCPosition	0 Position	CSG

Behavior

The mouse button that is used depends upon the resources **XmNrowColumnType** and **XmNwhichButton** in the menu's top level RowColumn widget.

Default PopupMenu System

<Btn3Down>:
If this event has not already been processed by another menu component, this action disables keyboard traversal for the menus and returns the user to drag mode.

<Btn3Up>: If this event has not already been processed by another menu component, all visible MenuPanes are unposted.

<Key>Escape:
If this event has not already been processed by another menu component, all visible MenuPanes are unposted.

Default PulldownMenu System or OptionMenu System

<Btn1Down>:
If this event has not already been processed by another menu component, this action disables keyboard traversal for the menus and returns the user to drag mode.

<Btn1Up>: If this event has not already been processed by another menu component, all visible MenuPanes are unposted.

<Key>Escape:
If this event has not already been processed by another menu component, all visible MenuPanes are unposted.

Default Translations

The default translations for MenuShell are:

<BtnDown>:	**ClearTraversal()**
<Key>Escape:	**MenuShellPopdownDone()**
<BtnUp>:	**MenuShellPopdownDone()**

Related Information

Composite(3X), **Core(3X)**, **OverrideShell(3X)**, **Shell(3X)**, **XmCreateMenuShell(3X)**, **XmCreatePopupMenu(3X)**, **XmCreatePulldown(3X)**, and **XmRowColumn(3X)**.

XmMessageBox

Purpose

The MessageBox widget class

Synopsis

#include <Xm/MessageB.h>

Description

MessageBox is a dialog class used for creating simple message dialogs. Convenience dialogs based on MessageBox are provided for several common interaction tasks, which include giving information, asking questions, and reporting errors.

A MessageBox dialog is typically transient in nature, displayed for the duration of a single interaction. MessageBox is a subclass of XmBulletinBoard and depends on it for much of its general dialog behavior.

A MessageBox can contain a message symbol, a message, and up to three standard default PushButtons: **OK, Cancel**, and **Help**. It is laid out with the symbol in the top left, the message in the top and center-to-right side, and the PushButtons on the bottom. The help button is positioned to the right of the other push buttons. You can localize the default symbols and button labels for MessageBox convenience dialogs.

Button label defaults are easily modified by including the new values in any of the app-defaults file locations supported by Xt Intrinsics. Changing the defaults for MessageBox symbols is more complicated, since the Xt Intrinsics do not support specification of pixmaps by name in resource files.

At initialization, MessageBox looks for the following bitmap files:

- xm_error
- xm_information
- xm_question
- xm_working
- xm_warning

See **XmGetPixmap(3X)** for a list of the paths that are searched for these files.

Classes

MessageBox inherits behavior and resources from **Core**, **Composite**, **Constraint**, **XmManager**, and **XmBulletinBoard**.

The class pointer is **xmMessageBoxWidgetClass**.

The class name is **XmMessageBox**.

New Resources

The following table defines a set of widget resources used by the programmer to specify data. The programmer can also set the resource values for the inherited classes to set attributes for this widget. To reference a resource by name or by class in a .Xdefaults file, remove the **XmN** or **XmC** prefix and use the remaining letters. To specify one of the defined values for a resource in a .Xdefaults file, remove the **Xm** prefix and use the remaining letters (in either lowercase or uppercase, but include any underscores between words). The codes in the access column indicate if the given resource can be set at creation time (**C**), set by using **XtSetValues** (**S**), retrieved by using **XtGetValues** (**G**), or is not applicable (**N/A**).

XmMessageBox Resource Set		
Name **Class**	**Default** **Type**	**Access**
XmNcancelCallback XtCallbackList	NULL XtCallbackList	C
XmNcancelLabelString XmCXmString	"Cancel" XmString	CSG
XmNdefaultButtonType XmCDefaultButtonType	XmDIALOG_OK_BUTTON unsigned char	CSG
XmNdialogType XmCDialogType	XmDIALOG_MESSAGE unsigned char	CSG
XmNhelpLabelString XmCXmString	"Help" XmString	CSG
XmNmessageAlignment XmCAlignment	XmALIGNMENT_BEGINNING unsigned char	CSG
XmNmessageString XmCXmString	NULL XmString	CSG
XmNminimizeButtons XmCMinimizeButtons	False Boolean	CSG
XmNokCallback XtCallbackList	NULL XtCallbackList	C
XmNokLabelString XmCXmString	"OK" XmString	CSG
XmNsymbolPixmap XmCPixmap	dynamic Pixmap	CSG

XmNcancelCallback

Specifies the list of callbacks that is called when the user clicks on the cancel button. The reason sent by the callback is **XmCR_CANCEL**.

XmNcancelLabelString
Specifies the string label for the cancel button.

XmNdefaultButtonType
Specifies the default PushButton. The following are valid types:

- **XmDIALOG_CANCEL_BUTTON**
- **XmDIALOG_OK_BUTTON**
- **XmDIALOG_HELP_BUTTON**

XmNdialogType
Specifies the type of MessageBox dialog, which determines the default message symbol. The following are the possible values for this resource:

- **XmDIALOG_ERROR** — indicates an ErrorDialog
- **XmDIALOG_INFORMATION** — indicates an InformationDialog
- **XmDIALOG_MESSAGE** — indicates a MessageDialog. This is the default MessageBox dialog type. The default message symbol is NULL.
- **XmDIALOG_QUESTION** — indicates a QuestionDialog
- **XmDIALOG_WARNING** — indicates a WarningDialog
- **XmDIALOG_WORKING** — indicates a WorkingDialog

If this resource is changed via **XtSetValues**, the symbol bitmap is modified to the new **XmdialogType** bitmap unless **XmNsymbolPixmap** is also being set in **XtSetValues**.

XmNhelpLabelString
Specifies the string label for the help button.

XmNmessageAlignment

Controls the alignment of the message Label. Possible values include the following:

- **XmALIGNMENT_BEGINNING** — the default
- **XmALIGNMENT_CENTER**
- **XmALIGNMENT_END**

XmNmessageString

Specifies the string to be used as the message.

XmNminimizeButtons

Sets the buttons to the width of the widest button and height of the tallest button if False. If True, button width and height are set to the preferred size of each button.

XmNokCallback

Specifies the list of callbacks that is called when the user clicks on the OK button. The reason sent by the callback is **XmCR_OK**.

XmNokLabelString

Specifies the string label for the OK button.

XmNsymbolPixmap

Specifies the pixmap label to be used as the message symbol.

Inherited Resources

MessageBox inherits behavior and resources from the following superclasses. For a complete description of each resource, refer to the man page for that superclass.

XmBulletinBoard Resource Set		
Name **Class**	**Default** **Type**	**Access**
XmNallowOverlap XmCAllowOverlap	True Boolean	N/A
XmNautoUnmanage XmCAutoUnmanage	True Boolean	CSG
XmNbuttonFontList XmCButtonFontList	NULL XmFontList	CSG
XmNcancelButton XmCWidget	Cancel button Widget	G
XmNdefaultButton XmCWidget	OK button Widget	G
XmNdefaultPosition XmCDefaultPosition	True Boolean	CSG
XmNdialogStyle XmCDialogStyle	dynamic unsigned char	CSG
XmNdialogTitle XmCXmString	NULL XmString	CSG
XmNfocusCallback XmCCallback	NULL XtCallbackList	C
XmNlabelFontList XmCLabelFontList	NULL XmFontList	CSG
XmNmapCallback XmCCallback	NULL XtCallbackList	C
XmNmarginHeight XmCMarginHeight	10 short	CSG
XmNmarginWidth XmCMarginWidth	10 short	CSG
XmNnoResize XmCNoResize	False Boolean	CSG

Name Class	Default Type	Access
XmNresizePolicy XmCResizePolicy	XmRESIZE_ANY unsigned char	CSG
XmNshadowType XmCShadowType	XmSHADOW_OUT unsigned char	CSG
XmNstringDirection XmCStringDirection	XmSTRING_DIRECTION_L_TO_R XmStringDirection	CSG
XmNtextFontList XmCTextFontList	NULL XmFontList	N/A
XmNtextTranslations XmCTranslations	NULL XtTranslations	N/A
XmNunmapCallback XmCCallback	NULL XtCallbackList	C

Composite Resource Set		
Name **Class**	**Default** **Type**	**Access**
XmNinsertPosition XmCInsertPosition	NULL XmRFunction	CSG

Core Resource Set		
Name Class	Default Type	Access
XmNaccelerators XmCAccelerators	NULL XtTranslations	CSG
XmNancestorSensitive XmCSensitive	True Boolean	G
XmNbackground XmCBackground	dynamic Pixel	CSG
XmNbackgroundPixmap XmCPixmap	XmUNSPECIFIED_PIXMAP Pixmap	CSG
XmNborderColor XmCBorderColor	Black Pixel	CSG
XmNborderPixmap XmCPixmap	XmUNSPECIFIED_PIXMAP Pixmap	CSG
XmNborderWidth XmCBorderWidth	0 Dimension	CSG
XmNcolormap XmCColormap	XtCopyFromParent Colormap	CG
XmNdepth XmCDepth	XtCopyFromParent int	CG
XmNdestroyCallback XmCCallback	NULL XtCallbackList	C
XmNheight XmCHeight	0 Dimension	CSG
XmNmappedWhenManaged XmCMappedWhenManaged	True Boolean	CSG
XmNscreen XmCScreen	XtCopyScreen Pointer	CG
XmNsensitive XmCSensitive	True Boolean	CSG

Name Class	Default Type	Access
XmNtranslations XmCTranslations	NULL XtTranslations	CSG
XmNwidth XmCWidth	0 Dimension	CSG
XmNx XmCPosition	0 Position	CSG
XmNy XmCPosition	0 Position	CSG

Callback Information

The following structure is returned with each callback:

```
typedef struct
{
    int             reason;
    XEvent          * event;
} XmAnyCallbackStruct;
```

reason Indicates why the callback was invoked

event Points to the **XEvent** that triggered the callback

Behavior

Following is a summary of the behavior of MessageBox.

<Ok Button Activated>:
When the ok PushButton is activated, the callbacks for **XmNokCallback** are called.

<Cancel Button Activated>:
When the cancel PushButton is activated, the callbacks for **XmNcancelCallback** are called.

<Help Button Activated> or **<Key>F1**:
When the help button or **Function key 1** is pressed, the callbacks for **XmNhelpCallback** are called.

<Default Button Activated>:
When the default button is pressed, the activate callbacks of the default PushButton are called.

<FocusIn>: When a **FocusIn** event is generated on the widget window, the callbacks for **XmNfocusCallback** are called.

<MapWindow>:
When a **MapWindow** event is generated on the widget window, the callbacks for **XmNmapCallback** are called.

<UnmapWindow>:
When a **UnmapWindow** event is generated on the widget window, the callbacks for **XmNunmapCallback** are called.

Default Accelerators

The default accelerator translations added to descendants of a BulletinBoard if the parent of the BulletinBoard is a DialogShell are:

```
#override
<Key>F1:        Help()
<Key>Return:    Return()
<Key>KP_Enter:  Return()
```

Keyboard Traversal

For information on keyboard traversal, see the man page for **XmManager(3X)** and its sections on behavior and default translations.

Related Information

Composite(3X), **Constraint(3X)**, **Core(3X)**, **XmBulletinBoard(3X)**, **XmCreateErrorDialog(3X)**, **XmCreateInformationDialog(3X)**, **XmCreateMessageBox(3X)**, **XmCreateMessageDialog(3X)**, **XmCreateQuestionDialog(3X)**, **XmCreateWarningDialog(3X)**, **XmCreateWorkingDialog(3X)**, **XmManager(3X)**, and **XmMessageBoxGetChild(3X)**.

XmMessageBoxGetChild

Purpose

A MessageBox function that is used to access a component.

Synopsis

#include <Xm/MessageB.h>

Widget XmMessageBoxGetChild (*widget, child*)
    Widget *widget*;
    unsigned char*child*;

Description

XmMessageBoxGetChild is used to access a component within a MessageBox. The parameters given to the function are the MessageBox widget and a value indicating which child to access.

widget Specifies the MessageBox widget ID

child Specifies a component within the MessageBox. The following are legal values for this parameter:

- **XmDIALOG_CANCEL_BUTTON**
- **XmDIALOG_DEFAULT_BUTTON**
- **XmDIALOG_HELP_BUTTON**
- **XmDIALOG_MESSAGE_LABEL**
- **XmDIALOG_OK_BUTTON**
- **XmDIALOG_SEPARATOR**
- **XmDIALOG_SYMBOL_LABEL**

For a complete definition of MessageBox and its associated resources, see **XmMessageBox(3X)**.

Return Value

Returns the widget ID of the specified MessageBox child.

Related Information

XmMessageBox(3X).

XmOptionButtonGadget

Purpose

A RowColumn function that obtains the widget ID for the CascadeButtonGadget in an OptionMenu.

Synopsis

#include <Xm/RowColumn.h>

Widget XmOptionButtonGadget (*option_menu*)
    Widget   *option_menu*;

Description

XmOptionButtonGadget provides the application with the means for obtaining the widget ID for the internally created CascadeButtonGadget. Once the application has obtained the widget ID, it can adjust the visuals for the CascadeButtonGadget, if desired.

When an application creates an instance of the OptionMenu widget, the widget creates two internal gadgets. One is a LabelGadget that is used to display RowColumn's **XmNlabelString** resource. The other is a CascadeButtonGadget that displays the current selection and provides the means for posting the OptionMenu's submenu.

option_menu Specifies the OptionMenu widget ID

For a complete definition of RowColumn and its associated resources, see **XmRowColumn(3X)**.

Return Value

Returns the widget ID for the internal button.

Related Information

XmCreateOptionMenu(3X), **XmCascadeButtonGadget(3X)**, **XmOptionLabelGadget(3X)**, and **XmRowColumn(3X)**.

XmOptionLabelGadget

Purpose

A RowColumn function that obtains the widget ID for the LabelGadget in an OptionMenu.

Synopsis

#include <Xm/RowColumn.h>

Widget XmOptionLabelGadget (*option_menu*)
    Widget *option_menu*;

Description

XmOptionLabelGadget provides the application with the means for obtaining the widget ID for the internally created LabelGadget. Once the application has obtained the widget ID, it can adjust the visuals for the LabelGadget, if desired.

When an application creates an instance of the OptionMenu widget, the widget creates two internal gadgets. One is a LabelGadget that is used to display RowColumn's **XmNlabelString** resource. The other is a CascadeButtonGadget that displays the current selection and provides the means for posting the OptionMenu's submenu.

option_menu Specifies the OptionMenu widget ID

For a complete definition of RowColumn and its associated resources, see **XmRowColumn(3X)**.

Return Value

Returns the widget ID for the internal label.

Related Information

XmCreateOptionMenu(3X), **XmLabelGadget(3X)**, **XmOptionButtonGadget(3X)**, and **XmRowColumn(3X)**.

XmPanedWindow

Purpose

The PanedWindow widget class

Synopsis

#include <Xm/PanedW.h>

Description

PanedWindow is a composite widget that lays out children in a vertically tiled format. Children appear in top to bottom fashion, with the first child inserted appearing at the top of the PanedWindow and the last child inserted appearing at the bottom. The PanedWindow grows to match the width of its widest child and all other children are forced to this width. The height of the PanedWindow is equal to the sum of the heights of all its children, the spacing between them, and the size of the top and bottom margins.

The user can also adjust the size of the panes. To facilitate this adjustment, a pane control sash is created for most children. The sash appears as a square box positioned on the bottom of the pane that it controls. The user can adjust the size of a pane by using the mouse.

The PanedWindow is also a constraint widget, which means that it creates and manages a set of constraints for each child. You can specify a minimum and maximum size for each pane. The PanedWindow does not allow a pane to be resized below its minimum size or beyond its maximum size. Also, when the minimum size of a pane is equal to its maximum size, no control sash is presented for that pane or for the lowest pane.

Classes

PanedWindow inherits behavior and resources from the **Core**, **Composite**, **Constraint**, and **XmManager** classes.

The class pointer is **xmPanedWindowWidgetClass**.

The class name is **XmPanedWindow**.

New Resources

The following table defines a set of widget resources used by the programmer to specify data. The programmer can also set the resource values for the inherited classes to set attributes for this widget. To reference a resource by name or by class in a .Xdefaults file, remove the **XmN** or **XmC** prefix and use the remaining letters. To specify one of the defined values for a resource in a .Xdefaults file, remove the **Xm** prefix and use the remaining letters (in either lowercase or uppercase, but include any underscores between words). The codes in the access column indicate if the given resource can be set at creation time (**C**), set by using **XtSetValues** (**S**), retrieved by using **XtGetValues** (**G**), or is not applicable (**N/A**).

XmPanedWindow Resource Set		
Name **Class**	**Default** **Type**	**Access**
XmNmarginHeight XmCMarginHeight	3 short	CSG
XmNmarginWidth XmCMarginWidth	3 short	CSG
XmNrefigureMode XmCBoolean	True Boolean	CSG
XmNsashHeight XmCSashHeight	10 Dimension	CSG
XmNsashIndent XmCSashIndent	-10 Position	CSG
XmNsashShadowThickness XmCShadowThickness	2 int	CSG
XmNsashWidth XmCSashWidth	10 Dimension	CSG
XmNseparatorOn XmCSeparatorOn	True Boolean	CSG
XmNspacing XmCSpacing	8 int	CSG

XmNmarginHeight
Specifies the distance between the top and bottom edges of the PanedWindow and its children.

XmNmarginWidth
Specifies the distance between the left and right edges of the PanedWindow and its children.

XmNrefigureMode
Determines whether the panes' positions is recomputed and repositioned when programmatic changes are being made to the PanedWindow. Setting this resource to True resets the children to their appropriate positions.

XmNsashHeight
Specifies the height of the sash.

XmNsashIndent
Specifies the horizontal placement of the sash along each pane. A positive value causes the sash to be offset from the left side of the PanedWindow, and a negative value causes the sash to be offset from the right side of the PanedWindow. If the offset is greater than the width of the PanedWindow minus the width of the sash, the sash is placed flush against the left-hand side of the PanedWindow.

XmNsashShadowThickness
Specifies the thickness of the shadows of the sashes.

XmNsashWidth
Specifies the width of the sash.

XmNseparatorOn
Determines whether a separator is created between each of the panes. Setting this resource to True creates a Separator at the midpoint between each of the panes.

XmNspacing
Specifies the distance between each child pane.

XmPanedWindow Constraint Resource Set		
Name Class	Default Type	Access
XmNallowResize XmCBoolean	False Boolean	CSG
XmNmaximum XmRInt	1000 int	CSG
XmNminimum XmCMin	1 int	CSG
XmNskipAdjust XmCBoolean	False Boolean	CSG

XmNallowResize
Allows an application to specify whether the PanedWindow should allow a pane to request to be resized. This flag has an effect only after the PanedWindow and its children have been realized. If this flag is set to True, the PanedWindow tries to honor requests to alter the height of the pane. If False, it always denies pane requests to resize.

XmNmaximum
Allows an application to specify the maximum size to which a pane may be resized. This value must be greater than the specified minimum.

XmNminimum
Allows an application to specify the minimum size to which a pane may be resized. This value must be greater than 0.

XmNskipAdjust
When set to True, this Boolean resource allows an application to specify that the PanedWindow should not automatically resize this pane.

Inherited Resources

PanedWindow inherits behavior and resources from the following superclasses. For a complete description of each resource, refer to the man page for that superclass.

XmManager Resource Set		
Name **Class**	**Default** **Type**	**Access**
XmNbottomShadowColor XmCForeground	dynamic Pixel	CSG
XmNbottomShadowPixmap XmCBottomShadowPixmap	XmUNSPECIFIED_PIXMAP Pixmap	CSG
XmNforeground XmCForeground	dynamic Pixel	CSG
XmNhelpCallback XmCCallback	NULL XtCallbackList	C
XmNhighlightColor XmCForeground	Black Pixel	CSG
XmNhighlightPixmap XmCHighlightPixmap	dynamic Pixmap	CSG
XmNshadowThickness XmCShadowThickness	0 short	N/A
XmNtopShadowColor XmCBackground	dynamic Pixel	CSG
XmNtopShadowPixmap XmCTopShadowPixmap	XmUNSPECIFIED_PIXMAP Pixmap	CSG
XmNunitType XmCUnitType	XmPIXELS unsigned char	CSG
XmNuserData XmCUserData	NULL caddr_t	CSG

Core Resource Set		
Name **Class**	**Default** **Type**	**Access**
XmNaccelerators XmCAccelerators	NULL XtTranslations	CSG
XmNancestorSensitive XmCSensitive	True Boolean	G
XmNbackground XmCBackground	dynamic Pixel	CSG
XmNbackgroundPixmap XmCPixmap	XmUNSPECIFIED_PIXMAP Pixmap	CSG
XmNborderColor XmCBorderColor	Black Pixel	CSG
XmNborderPixmap XmCPixmap	XmUNSPECIFIED_PIXMAP Pixmap	CSG
XmNborderWidth XmCBorderWidth	0 Dimension	CSG
XmNcolormap XmCColormap	XtCopyFromParent Colormap	CG
XmNdepth XmCDepth	XtCopyFromParent int	CG
XmNdestroyCallback XmCCallback	NULL XtCallbackList	C
XmNheight XmCHeight	0 Dimension	CSG
XmNmappedWhenManaged XmCMappedWhenManaged	True Boolean	CSG
XmNscreen XmCScreen	XtCopyScreen Pointer	CG
XmNsensitive XmCSensitive	True Boolean	CSG

Name Class	Default Type	Access
XmNtranslations XmCTranslations	NULL XtTranslations	CSG
XmNwidth XmCWidth	0 Dimension	CSG
XmNx XmCPosition	0 Position	CSG
XmNy XmCPosition	0 Position	CSG

Behavior

Shift<Btn1Down>:
: **(in sash)**: Activates the interactive placement of the pane's borders. It changes the pointer cursor from a crosshair to an upward pointing arrow to indicate that the upper pane is adjusted (usually the pane to which the sash is attached). All panes below the sash that can be adjusted are adjusted.

<Btn1Down>:
: **(in sash)**: Activates the interactive placement of the pane's borders. It changes the pointer cursor from a crosshair to a double headed arrow to indicate that the pane to be adjusted is the pane to which the sash is attached and the first pane below it that can be adjusted. Unlike pane adjustment using **Shift Btn1Down** or **CTRL Btn1Down**, only two panes are affected. If one of the panes reaches its minimum or maximum size, adjustment stops instead of finding the next adjustable pane.

CTRL <Btn1Down>:

(in sash): Activates the interactive placement of the pane's borders. It changes the pointer cursor from a crosshair to a downward pointing arrow to indicate that the lower pane is adjusted (usually the pane below the pane to which the sash is attached). All panes above the sash that can be adjusted are adjusted.

Shift Button1<PtrMoved>:

If the button press occurs within the sash, the motion events draw a series of track lines to illustrate the height of the panes if the Commit action were invoked. This action determines which pane below the upper pane can be adjusted and makes the appropriate adjustments.

Button1<PtrMoved>:

If the button press occurs within the sash, the motion events draw a series of track lines to illustrate the height of the panes if the Commit action were invoked. This action adjusts as needed (and possible) the upper and lower panes selected when the Btn1Down action is invoked.

CTRL Button1<PtrMoved>:

If the button press occurs within the sash, the motion events draw a series of track lines to illustrate he height of the panes if the Commit action were invoked. This action determines which pane above the lower pane can be adjusted and makes the appropriate adjustments.

Any<BtnUp>:

Commits to any action taken since the interactive placement was activated. The sashes and the pane boundaries are moved to the committed positions of the panes.

Default Translations

The following are default translations for PanedWindow:

Shift<Btn1Down>: SashAction(Start, UpperPane)
<Btn1Down>: SashAction(Start, ThisBorderOnly)
CTRL<Btn1Down>:SashAction(Start, LowerPane)
Shift<Btn1Motion>:SashAction(Move, Upper)
<Btn1Motion>: SashAction(Move, ThisBorder)
CTRL<Btn1Motion>:SashAction(Move, Lower)
Any<BtnUp>: SashAction(Commit)
<EnterWindow>: enter()
<LeaveWindow>: leave()

Keyboard Traversal

For information on keyboard traversal, see the man page for **XmManager(3X)** and its sections on behavior and default translations.

Related Information

Composite(3X), **Constraint(3X)**, **Core(3X)**, **XmCreatePanedWindow(3X)**, and **XmManager(3X)**.

XmPrimitive

Purpose

The Primitive widget class

Synopsis

#include <Xm/Xm.h>

Description

Primitive is a widget class used as a supporting superclass for other widget classes. It handles border drawing and highlighting, traversal activation and deactivation, and various callback lists needed by Primitive widgets.

Classes

Primitive inherits behavior and resources from **Core** class.

The class pointer is **xmPrimitiveWidgetClass**.

The class name is **XmPrimitive**.

New Resources

The following table defines a set of widget resources used by the programmer to specify data. The programmer can also set the resource values for the inherited classes to set attributes for this widget. To reference a resource by name or by class in a .Xdefaults file, remove the **XmN** or **XmC** prefix and use the remaining letters. To specify one of the defined values for a resource in a .Xdefaults file, remove the **Xm** prefix and use the remaining letters (in either lowercase or uppercase, but include any underscores between words). The codes in the access column indicate if the given resource can be set at creation time (**C**), set by using **XtSetValues** (**S**), retrieved by using **XtGetValues** (**G**), or is not applicable (**N/A**).

XmPrimitive Resource Set		
Name **Class**	**Default** **Type**	**Access**
XmNbottomShadowColor XmCForeground	dynamic Pixel	CSG
XmNbottomShadowPixmap XmCBottomShadowPixmap	XmUNSPECIFIED_PIXMAP Pixmap	CSG
XmNforeground XmCForeground	dynamic Pixel	CSG
XmNhelpCallback XmCCallback	NULL XtCallbackList	C
XmNhighlightColor XmCForeground	Black Pixel	CSG
XmNhighlightOnEnter XmCHighlightOnEnter	False Boolean	CSG
XmNhighlightPixmap XmCHighlightPixmap	dynamic Pixmap	CSG
XmNhighlightThickness XmCHighlightThickness	0 short	CSG
XmNshadowThickness XmCShadowThickness	2 short	CSG
XmNtopShadowColor XmCBackground	dynamic Pixel	CSG
XmNtopShadowPixmap XmCTopShadowPixmap	XmUNSPECIFIED_PIXMAP Pixmap	CSG
XmNtraversalOn XmCTraversalOn	False Boolean	CSG
XmNunitType XmCUnitType	XmPIXELS unsigned char	CSG
XmNuserData XmCUserData	NULL caddr_t	CSG

XmNbottomShadowColor
Specifies the pixmap to use to draw the top and left sides of the border shadow.

XmNbottomShadowPixmap
Specifies the pixmap to use to draw the bottom and right sides of the border shadow.

XmNforeground
Specifies the foreground drawing color used by Primitive widgets.

XmNhelpCallback
Specifies the list of callbacks that is called when the help key sequence is pressed. The reason sent by the callback is **XmCR_HELP**. No translation is bound to this resource. It is up to the application to install a translation for help.

XmNhighlightColor
Specifies the color of the highlighting rectangle. This color is used if the highlight pixmap resource is **XmUNSPECIFIED_PIXMAP**.

XmNhighlightOnEnter
Specifies if the highlighting rectangle is drawn when the cursor moves into the widget. If this resource is True and **XmNtraversalOn** is False, the rectangle highlights the window when the cursor is moved into it. This resource is ignored if the **XmNtraversalOn** resource is set to True.

XmNhighlightPixmap
Specifies the pixmap used to draw the highlighting rectangle.

XmNhighlightThickness
Specifies the thickness of the highlighting rectangle.

XmNshadowThickness
Specifies the size of the drawn border shadow.

XmNtopShadowColor
Specifies the pixmap to use to draw the top and left sides of the border shadow. This color is used if the **XmNtopShadowPixmap** resource is NULL.

XmNtopShadowPixmap
Specifies the pixmap to use to draw the top and left sides of the border shadow.

XmNtraversalOn
Specifies if traversal is activated for this widget.

XmNunitType
Provides the basic support for resolution independence. It defines the type of units a widget uses with sizing and positioning resources. Unless the **XmNunitType** resource is explicitly set, it defaults to the unit type of the parent widget. If the parent has a unit type of **Xm100TH_POINTS**, any of its children whose **XmNunitType** resource is not set also have a unit type of **Xm100TH_POINTS**. This feature applies only to widgets whose parents are a subclass of XmManager. Widgets whose parents are not subclasses of **XmManager** have a unit type of **XmPIXELS**. **XmNunitType** can have the following values:

- **XmPIXELS** — all values provided to the widget are treated as normal pixel values. This is the default for the resource.
- **Xm100TH_MILLIMETERS** — all values provided to the widget are treated as 1/100 millimeter.
- **Xm1000TH_INCHES** — all values provided to the widget are treated as 1/1000 inch.
- **Xm100TH_POINTS** — all values provided to the widget are treated as 1/100 point. A point is a unit typically used in text processing applications and is defined as 1/72 inch.

- **Xm100TH_FONT_UNITS** — all values provided to the widget are treated as 1/100-font unit. The value to be used for the font unit is determined in one of two ways. The resource **XmNfont** can be used in a defaults file or on the command line. The standard command line options of **-fn** and **-font** can also be used. The font unit value is taken as the **QUAD_WIDTH** property of the font. The function **XmSetFontUnits** allows applications to specify the font unit values.

XmNuserData
Allows the application to attach any necessary specific data to the widget. It is an internally unused resource.

Dynamic Color Defaults

The foreground, background, top shadow, and bottom shadow resources are dynamically defaulted. If no color data is specified, the colors are automatically generated. On a monochrome system, a black and white color scheme is generated. On a color system, four colors are generated, which display the correct shading for the 3-D visuals.

If the background is the only color specified for a widget, the top shadow, bottom shadow, and foreground colors are generated to give the 3-D appearance. The color generation works best with non-saturated colors. Using pure red, green, or blue yields poor results.

Colors are generated only at creation. Resetting the background through **XtSetValues** does not regenerate the other colors.

Inherited Resources

Primitive inherits behavior and resources from the following superclass. For a complete description of each resource, refer to the man page for that superclass.

Core Resource Set		
Name **Class**	**Default** **Type**	**Access**
XmNaccelerators XmCAccelerators	NULL XtTranslations	CSG
XmNancestorSensitive XmCSensitive	True Boolean	G
XmNbackground XmCBackground	dynamic Pixel	CSG
XmNbackgroundPixmap XmCPixmap	XmUNSPECIFIED_PIXMAP Pixmap	CSG
XmNborderColor XmCBorderColor	Black Pixel	CSG
XmNborderPixmap XmCPixmap	XmUNSPECIFIED_PIXMAP Pixmap	CSG
XmNborderWidth XmCBorderWidth	0 Dimension	CSG
XmNcolormap XmCColormap	XtCopyFromParent Colormap	CG
XmNdepth XmCDepth	XtCopyFromParent int	CG
XmNdestroyCallback XmCCallback	NULL XtCallbackList	C
XmNheight XmCHeight	0 Dimension	CSG
XmNmappedWhenManaged XmCMappedWhenManaged	True Boolean	CSG
XmNscreen XmCScreen	XtCopyScreen Pointer	CG
XmNsensitive XmCSensitive	True Boolean	CSG

Name Class	Default Type	Access
XmNtranslations XmCTranslations	NULL XtTranslations	CSG
XmNwidth XmCWidth	0 Dimension	CSG
XmNx XmCPosition	0 Position	CSG
XmNy XmCPosition	0 Position	CSG

Behavior

Shift<Key>Tab:
Moves the focus to the first item contained within the previous tab group. If the beginning of the tab group list is reached, it wraps to the end of the tab group list.

<Key>Tab: Moves the focus to the first item contained within the next tab group. If the current tab group is the last entry in the tab group list, it wraps to the beginning of the tab group list.

<Key>Up or **<Key>Left**:
Moves the keyboard focus to the previous Primitive widget or gadget within the current tab group. The previous widget or gadget is the previous entry in the tab group's list of children. Wrapping occurs, if necessary.

<Key>Down or **<Key>Right**:
Moves the Keyboard focus to the next Primitive widget or gadget within the current tab group. The previous widget or gadget is the next entry in the tab group's list of children. Wrapping occurs, if necessary.

<Key>Home:
Moves the keyboard focus to the first Primitive widget or gadget in the current tab group.

Default Translations

The following are the default translations for Primitive:

<FocusIn>:	**PrimitiveFocusIn()**
<FocusOut>:	**PrimitiveFocusOut()**
<Unmap>:	**PrimitiveUnmap()**
Shift<Key>Tab:	**PrimitivePrevTabGroup()**
<Key>Tab:	**PrimitiveNextTabGroup()**
<Key>Up:	**PrimitiveTraversePrev()**
<Key>Down:	**PrimitiveTraverseNext()**
<Key>Left:	**PrimitiveTraversePrev()**
<Key>Right:	**PrimitiveTraverseNext()**
<Key>Home:	**PrimitiveTraverseHome()**

Related Information

Core(3X).

XmPushButton

Purpose

The PushButton widget class

Synopsis

#include <Xm/PushB.h>

Description

PushButton issues commands within an application. It consists of a text label or pixmap surrounded by a border shadow. When PushButton is selected, the shadow moves to give the appearance that it has been pressed in. When PushButton is unselected, the shadow moves to give the appearance that it is out.

The behavior of PushButton differs, depending on the active mouse button. The active mouse button may be determined by the parent widget. Normally, mouse button 1 is used to arm and activate the PushButton. However, if the PushButton resides within a menu, the mouse button used is determined by the RowColumn resources **XmNrowColumnType** and **XmNwhichButton**.

Thickness for a second shadow may be specified by using the **XmNshowAsDefault** resource. If it has a non-zero value, the Label's resources **XmNmarginLeft**, **XmNmarginRight**, **XmNmarginTop**, and **XmNmarginBottom** may be modified to accommodate the second shadow.

Classes

PushButton inherits behavior and resources from **Core**, **XmPrimitive**, and **XmLabel** Classes.

The class pointer is **xmPushButtonWidgetClass**.

The class name is **XmPushButton**.

New Resources

The following table defines a set of widget resources used by the programmer to specify data. The programmer can also set the resource values for the inherited classes to set attributes for this widget. To reference a resource by name or by class in a .Xdefaults file, remove the **XmN** or **XmC** prefix and use the remaining letters. To specify one of the defined values for a resource in a .Xdefaults file, remove the **Xm** prefix and use the remaining letters (in either lowercase or uppercase, but include any underscores between words). The codes in the access column indicate if the given resource can be set at creation time (**C**), set by using **XtSetValues** (**S**), retrieved by using **XtGetValues** (**G**), or is not applicable (**N/A**).

XmPushButton Resource Set		
Name **Class**	**Default** **Type**	**Access**
XmNactivateCallback XmCCallback	NULL XtCallbackList	C
XmNarmCallback XmCCallback	NULL XtCallbackList	C
XmNarmColor XmCArmColor	dynamic Pixel	CSG
XmNarmPixmap XmCArmPixmap	XmUNSPECIFIED_PIXMAP Pixmap	CSG
XmNdisarmCallback XmCCallback	NULL XtCallbackList	C
XmNfillOnArm XmCFillOnArm	True Boolean	CSG
XmNshowAsDefault XmCShowAsDefault	0 short	CSG

XmNactivateCallback

Specifies the list of callbacks that is called when PushButton is activated. PushButton is activated when the user presses and releases the active mouse button while the pointer is inside that widget. Activating the PushButton also disarms it. For this callback the reason is **XmCR_ACTIVATE**.

XmNarmCallback

Specifies the list of callbacks that is called when PushButton is armed. PushButton is armed when the user presses the active mouse button while the pointer is inside that widget. For this callback the reason is **XmCR_ARM**.

XmNarmColor

Specifies the color with which to fill the armed button. **XmNfillOnArm** must be set to True for this resource to have an effect. The default for a color display is a color between the background and the bottom shadow color. For a monochrome display, the default is set to the foreground color, and any text in the label appears in the background color when the button is armed.

XmNarmPixmap

Specifies the pixmap to be used as the button face if **XmNlabeltype** is **XmPIXMAP** and PushButton is armed. This resource is disabled when the PushButton is in a menu.

XmNdisarmCallback

Specifies the list of callbacks that is called when PushButton is disarmed. PushButton is disarmed when the user presses and releases the active mouse button while the pointer is inside that widget. For this callback, the reason is **XmCR_DISARM**.

XmNfillOnArm

Forces the PushButton to fill the background of the button with the color specified by **XmNarmColor** when the button is armed and when this resource is set to True. If False, only the top and bottom shadow colors are switched. When the PushButton is in a menu, this resource is ignored and assumed to be False.

XmNshowAsDefault

Specifies a shadow thickness for a second shadow to be drawn around the PushButton to visually mark it as a default button. The space between the shadow and the default shadow is equal to the sum of both shadows. The default value is zero. When this value is not zero, the Label resources **XmNmarginLeft**, **XmNmarginRight**, **XmNmarginTop**, and **XmNmarginBottom** may be modified to accommodate the second shadow. This resource is disabled when the PushButton is in a menu.

Inherited Resources

PushButton inherits behavior and resources from the following superclasses. For a complete description of each resource, refer to the man page for that superclass.

XmLabel Resource Set		
Name **Class**	**Default** **Type**	**Access**
XmNaccelerator XmCAccelerator	NULL String	CSG
XmNacceleratorText XmCAcceleratorText	NULL XmString	CSG
XmNalignment XmCAlignment	XmALIGNMENT_CENTER unsigned char	CSG
XmNfontList XmCFontList	"Fixed" XmFontList	CSG
XmNlabelInsensitivePixmap XmCLabelInsensitivePixmap	XmUNSPECIFIED_PIXMAP Pixmap	CSG
XmNlabelPixmap XmCPixmap	XmUNSPECIFIED_PIXMAP Pixmap	CSG
XmNlabelString XmCXmString	NULL XmString	CSG
XmNlabelType XmCLabelType	XmSTRING unsigned char	CSG

Name Class	Default Type	Access
XmNmarginBottom XmCMarginBottom	dynamic short	CSG
XmNmarginHeight XmCMarginHeight	2 short	CSG
XmNmarginLeft XmCMarginLeft	dynamic short	CSG
XmNmarginRight XmCMarginRight	dynamic short	CSG
XmNmarginTop XmCMarginTop	dynamic short	CSG
XmNmarginWidth XmCMarginWidth	2 short	CSG
XmNmnemonic XmCMnemonic	'\0' char	CSG
XmNrecomputeSize XmCRecomputeSize	True Boolean	CSG
XmNstringDirection XmCStringDirection	XmSTRING_DIRECTION_L_TO_R XmStringDirection	CSG

XmPrimitive Resource Set		
Name **Class**	**Default** **Type**	**Access**
XmNbottomShadowColor XmCForeground	dynamic Pixel	CSG
XmNbottomShadowPixmap XmCBottomShadowPixmap	XmUNSPECIFIED_PIXMAP Pixmap	CSG
XmNforeground XmCForeground	dynamic Pixel	CSG
XmNhelpCallback XmCCallback	NULL XtCallbackList	C
XmNhighlightColor XmCForeground	Black Pixel	CSG
XmNhighlightOnEnter XmCHighlightOnEnter	False Boolean	CSG
XmNhighlightPixmap XmCHighlightPixmap	dynamic Pixmap	CSG
XmNhighlightThickness XmCHighlightThickness	0 short	CSG
XmNshadowThickness XmCShadowThickness	2 short	CSG
XmNtopShadowColor XmCBackground	dynamic Pixel	CSG
XmNtopShadowPixmap XmCTopShadowPixmap	XmUNSPECIFIED_PIXMAP Pixmap	CSG
XmNtraversalOn XmCTraversalOn	False Boolean	CSG
XmNunitType XmCUnitType	XmPIXELS unsigned char	CSG
XmNuserData XmCUserData	NULL caddr_t	CSG

Core Resource Set		
Name **Class**	**Default** **Type**	**Access**
XmNaccelerators XmCAccelerators	NULL XtTranslations	CSG
XmNancestorSensitive XmCSensitive	True Boolean	G
XmNbackground XmCBackground	dynamic Pixel	CSG
XmNbackgroundPixmap XmCPixmap	XmUNSPECIFIED_PIXMAP Pixmap	CSG
XmNborderColor XmCBorderColor	Black Pixel	CSG
XmNborderPixmap XmCPixmap	XmUNSPECIFIED_PIXMAP Pixmap	CSG
XmNborderWidth XmCBorderWidth	0 Dimension	CSG
XmNcolormap XmCColormap	XtCopyFromParent Colormap	CG
XmNdepth XmCDepth	XtCopyFromParent int	CG
XmNdestroyCallback XmCCallback	NULL XtCallbackList	C
XmNheight XmCHeight	0 Dimension	CSG
XmNmappedWhenManaged XmCMappedWhenManaged	True Boolean	CSG
XmNscreen XmCScreen	XtCopyScreen Pointer	CG
XmNsensitive XmCSensitive	True Boolean	CSG

Name Class	Default Type	Access
XmNtranslations XmCTranslations	NULL XtTranslations	CSG
XmNwidth XmCWidth	0 Dimension	CSG
XmNx XmCPosition	0 Position	CSG
XmNy XmCPosition	0 Position	CSG

Callback Information

The following structure is returned with each callback:

```
typedef struct
{
    int         reason;
    XEvent      * event;
} XmAnyCallbackStruct;
```

reason Indicates why the callback was invoked.

event Points to the **XEvent** that triggered the callback. This event is NULL for the **XmNactivateCallback** if the callback was triggered when Primitive's resource **XmNtraversalOn** was True or if the callback was accessed through the **ArmAndActivate** action routine.

Behavior

PushButton is associated with the default behavior unless it is part of a menu system. In a menu system, the RowColumn parent determines which mouse button is used.

Default Behavior

<Btn1Down>:
This action causes the PushButton to be armed. The shadow is drawn in the armed state, and the button is filled with the color specified by **XmNarmColor** if **XmNfillOnArm** is set to True. The callbacks for **XmNarmCallback** are also called.

<Btn1Up>: **(in button)**: This action redraws the shadow in the unarmed state. The background color reverts to the unarmed color if **XmNfillOnArm** is set to True. The callbacks for **XmNactivateCallback** are called, followed by callbacks for **XmNdisarmCallback**.

(outside of button): This action causes the callbacks for **XmNdisarmCallback** to be called.

<Leave Window>:
If the button is pressed and the cursor leaves the widget's window, the shadow is redrawn in its unarmed state, and the background color reverts to the unarmed color if **XmNfillOnArm** is set to True.

<Enter Window>:
If the button is pressed and the cursor leaves and reenters the widget's window, the shadow is drawn in the armed state, and the button is filled with the color specified by **XmNarmColor** if **XmNfillOnArm** is set to True.

Default PopupMenu System

<Btn3Down>:
This action disables keyboard traversal for the menu and returns the user to drag mode, which is the mode in which the menu is manipulated by using the mouse. The shadow is drawn in the armed state, and the callbacks for **XmNarmCallback** are called.

<Btn3Up>: This action causes the PushButton to be activated and the menu to be unposted. The callbacks for **XmNactivateCallback** are called, followed by callbacks for **XmNdisarmCallback**.

<Leave Window>:
If button 3 is pressed and the cursor leaves the widget's window, the PushButton is redrawn with no shadow. The callbacks for **XmNdisarmCallback** are called. If keyboard traversal is enabled in the menu, this event is ignored.

<Enter Window>:
If button 3 is pressed and the cursor enters the widget's window, the shadow is drawn in the armed state. The callbacks for **XmNarmCallback** are called. If keyboard traversal is enabled in the menu, this event is ignored.

<Key>Return:
If keyboard traversal is enabled in the menu, this event causes the PushButton to be activated and the menu to be unposted. The callbacks for **XmNactivateCallback** are called, followed by callbacks for **XmNdisarmCallback**.

Default PulldownMenu and OptionMenu System

<Btn1Down>:
This action disables keyboard traversal for the menu and returns the user to drag mode, which is the mode in which the menu is manipulated by using the mouse. The shadow is drawn in the armed state, and the callbacks for **XmNarmCallback** are called.

<Btn1Up>: This action causes the PushButton to be activated and the menu to be unposted. The callbacks for **XmNactivateCallback** are called, followed by callbacks for **XmNdisarmCallback**.

<Leave Window>:
If mouse button 1 is pressed and the cursor leaves the widget's window, the PushButton is redrawn with no shadow. The callbacks for **XmNdisarmCallback** are called. If keyboard traversal is enabled in the menu, this event is ignored.

<Enter Window>:
If mouse button 1 is pressed and the cursor enters the widget's window, the shadow is drawn in the armed state. The

callbacks for **XmNarmCallback** are called. If keyboard traversal is enabled in the menu, this event is ignored.

<Key>Return:
If keyboard traversal is enabled in the menu, this event causes the PushButton to be activated and the menu to be unposted. The callbacks for **XmNactivateCallback** are called, followed by callbacks for **XmNdisarmCallback**.

Default Translations

When in a menu system, the following are PushButton's default translations:

<Btn1Down>:	**Arm()**
<Btn1Up>:	**Activate()**
	Disarm()
<Key>Return:	**ArmAndActivate()**
<Key>space:	**ArmAndActivate()**
<EnterWindow>:	**Enter()**
<LeaveWindow>:	**Leave()**

When in a menu system, the following are PushButton's default translations:

<BtnDown>:	**BtnDown()**
<BtnUp>:	**BtnUp()**
<EnterWindow>:	**Enter()**
<LeaveWindow>:	**Leave()**
<Key>Return:	**KeySelect()**
<Key>Escape:	**MenuShellPopdownDone()**

Keyboard Traversal

For information on keyboard traversal outside a menu system, see the man page for **XmPrimitive(3X)** and its sections on behavior and default translations. n a menu system, the following keyboard traversal translations are defined:

<Unmap>:	**Unmap()**
<FocusOut>:	**FocusOut()**
<FocusIn>:	**FocusIn()**
<Key>space:	**Noop()**
<Key>Left:	**MenuTraverseLeft()**
<Key>Right:	**MenuTraverseRight()**
<Key>Up:	**MenuTraverseUp()**
<Key>Down:	**MenuTraverseDown()**
<Key>Home:	**Noop()**

Related Information

Core(3X), **XmCreatePushButton(3X)**, **XmLabel(3X)**, **XmPrimitive(3X)**, and **XmRowColumn(3X)**.

XmPushButtonGadget

Purpose

The PushButtonGadget widget class

Synopsis

#include <Xm/PushBG.h>

Description

PushButtonGadget issues commands within an application. It consists of a text label or icon surrounded by a border shadow. When PushButtonGadget is selected, the shadow moves to give the appearance that the PushButtonGadget has been pressed in. When PushButtonGadget is unselected, the shadow moves to give the appearance that the PushButtonGadget is out.

The behavior of PushButtonGadget differs, depending on the active mouse button. The active mouse button may be determined by the parent widget. Normally, mouse button 1 is used to arm and activate the PushButtonGadget. However, if the PushButtonGadget resides within a menu, the mouse button used is determined by the RowColumn resources **XmNrowColumnType** and **XmNwhichButton**.

Thickness for a second shadow may be specified by using the **XmNshowAsDefault** resource. If it has a non-zero value, the Label's resources **XmNmarginLeft**, **XmNmarginRight**, **XmNmarginTop**, and **XmNmarginBottom** may be modified to accommodate the second shadow.

Classes

PushButtonGadget inherits behavior and resources from **Object**, **RectObj**, **XmGadget** and **XmLabelGadget** classes.

The class pointer is **xmPushButtonGadgetClass**.

The class name is **XmPushButtonGadget**.

New Resources

The following table defines a set of widget resources used by the programmer to specify data. The programmer can also set the resource values for the inherited classes to set attributes for this widget. To reference a resource by name or by class in a .Xdefaults file, remove the **XmN** or **XmC** prefix and use the remaining letters. To specify one of the defined values for a resource in a .Xdefaults file, remove the **Xm** prefix and use the remaining letters (in either lowercase or uppercase, but include any underscores between words). The codes in the access column indicate if the given resource can be set at creation time (**C**), set by using **XtSetValues** (**S**), retrieved by using **XtGetValues** (**G**), or is not applicable (**N/A**).

XmPushButtonGadget		
Name **Class**	**Default** **Type**	**Access**
XmNactivateCallback XmCCallback	NULL XtCallbackList	C
XmNarmCallback XmCCallback	NULL caddr_t	C
XmNarmColor XmCArmColor	dynamic Pixel	CSG
XmNarmPixmap XmCArmPixmap	XmUNSPECIFIED_PIXMAP Pixmap	CSG
XmNdisarmCallback XmCCallback	NULL caddr_t	C
XmNfillOnArm XmCFillOnArm	True Boolean	CSG
XmNshowAsDefault XmCShowAsDefault	0 short	CSG

XmNactivateCallback

Specifics thc list of callbacks that is called when the PushButtonGadget is activated. It is activated when the user presses and releases the active mouse button while the pointer is inside the PushButtonGadget. Activating PushButtonGadget also disarms it. For this callback the reason is **XmCR_ACTIVATE**.

XmNarmCallback

Specifies the list of callbacks that is called when PushButtonGadget is armed. It is armed when the user presses the active mouse button while the pointer is inside the PushButtonGadget. For this callback the reason is **XmCR_ARM**.

XmNarmColor

Specifies the color with which to fill the armed button. **XmNfillOnArm** must be set to True for this resource to have an effect. The default for a color display is a color between the background and the bottom shadow color. For a monochrome display, the default is set to the foreground color, and any text in the label appears in the background color when the button is armed.

XmNarmPixmap

Specifies the pixmap to be used as the button face if **XmNlabeltype** is **XmPIXMAP** and PushButtonGadget is armed. This resource is disabled when the PushButtonGadget is in a menu.

XmNdisarmCallback

Specifies the list of callbacks that is called when the PushButtonGadget is disarmed. PushButtonGadget is disarmed when the user presses and releases the active mouse button while the pointer is inside that gadget. For this callback, the reason is **XmCR_DISARM**.

XmNfillOnArm

Forces the PushButtonGadget to fill the background of the button with the color specified by **XmNarmColor** when the button is armed and when this resource is set to True. If False, only the top and bottom shadow colors are switched. When the PushButtonGadget is in a menu, this resource is ignored and assumed to be False.

XmNshowAsDefault

Specifies a shadow thickness for a second shadow to be drawn around the PushButtonGadget to visually mark it as a default button. The space between the shadow and the default shadow is equal to the sum of both shadows. The default value is zero. When this value is not zero, the Label resources **XmNmarginLeft**, **XmNmarginRight**, **XmNmarginTop**, and **XmNmarginbottom** may be modified to accommodate the second shadow. This resource is disabled when the PushButtonGadget is in a menu.

Inherited Resources

PushButtonGadget inherits behavior and resources from the following superclasses. For a complete description of each resource, refer to the man page for that superclass.

XmLabelGadget Resource Set		
Name **Class**	**Default** **Type**	**Access**
XmNaccelerator XmCAccelerator	NULL String	CSG
XmNacceleratorText XmCAcceleratorText	NULL XmString	CSG
XmNalignment XmCAlignment	XmALIGNMENT_CENTER unsigned char	CSG
XmNfontList XmCFontList	"Fixed" XmFontList	CSG
XmNlabelInsensitivePixmap XmCLabelInsensitivePixmap	XmUNSPECIFIED_PIXMAP Pixmap	CSG
XmNlabelPixmap XmCPixmap	XmUNSPECIFIED_PIXMAP Pixmap	CSG
XmNlabelString XmCXmString	NULL XmString	CSG
XmNlabelType XmCLabelType	XmSTRING unsigned char	CSG
XmNmarginBottom XmCMarginBottom	0 short	CSG
XmNmarginHeight XmCMarginHeight	2 short	CSG
XmNmarginLeft XmCMarginLeft	0 short	CSG

Name Class	Default Type	Access
XmNmarginRight XmCMarginRight	0 short	CSG
XmNmarginTop XmCMarginTop	0 short	CSG
XmNmarginWidth XmCMarginWidth	2 short	CSG
XmNmnemonic XmCMnemonic	'\0' char	CSG
XmNrecomputeSize XmCRecomputeSize	True Boolean	CSG
XmNstringDirection XmCStringDirection	XmSTRING_DIRECTION_L_TO_R XmStringDirection	CSG

XmGadget Resource Set		
Name **Class**	**Default** **Type**	**Access**
XmNhelpCallback XmCCallback	NULL XtCallbackList	C
XmNhighlightOnEnter XmCHighlightOnEnter	False Boolean	CSG
XmNhighlightThickness XmCHighlightThickness	0 short	CSG
XmNshadowThickness XmCShadowThickness	2 short	CSG
XmNtraversalOn XmCTraversalOn	False Boolean	CSG
XmNunitType XmCUnitType	XmPIXELS unsigned char	CSG
XmNuserData XmCUserData	NULL caddr_t	CSG

RectObj Resource Set		
Name **Class**	**Default** **Type**	**Access**
XmNancestorSensitive XmCSensitive	XtCopyFromParent Boolean	CSG
XmNborderWidth XmCBorderWidth	1 Dimension	CSG
XmNheight XmCHeight	0 Dimension	CSG
XmNsensitive XmCSensitive	True Boolean	CSG
XmNwidth XmCWidth	0 Dimension	CSG
XmNx XmCPosition	0 Position	CSG
XmNy XmCPosition	0 Position	CSG

Object Resource Set		
Name **Class**	**Default** **Type**	**Access**
XmNdestroyCallback XmCCallback	NULL XtCallbackList	C

Callback Information

The following structure is returned with each callback:

```
typedef struct
{
    int         reason;
    XEvent      * event;
} XmAnyCallbackStruct;
```

reason Indicates why the callback was invoked.

event Points to the **XEvent** that triggered the callback. This event is NULL for the **XmNactivateCallback** if the callback was triggered when Primitive's resource **XmNtraversalOn** was True or if the callback was accessed through the **ArmAndActivate** action routine.

Behavior

PushButtonGadget is associated with the default behavior unless it is part of a menu system. In a menu system, the RowColumn parent determines which mouse button is used.

Default Behavior

<Btn1Down>:
This action causes the PushButtonGadget to be armed. The shadow is drawn in the armed state, and the button is filled with the color specified by **XmNarmColor** if **XmNfillOnArm** is set to True. The callbacks for **XmNarmCallback** are also called.

<Btn1Up>: **(in button)**: This action redraws the shadow in the unarmed state. The background color reverts to the unarmed color if **XmNfillOnArm** is set to True. The callbacks for **XmNactivateCallback** are called, followed by callbacks for **XmNdisarmCallback**.

(outside of button): This action causes the callbacks for **XmNdisarmCallback** to be called.

<Leave Window>:
If the button is pressed and the cursor leaves the gadget's window, the shadow is redrawn in its unarmed state, and the background color reverts to the unarmed color if **XmNfillOnArm** is set to True.

<Enter Window>:
If the button is pressed and the cursor leaves and re-enters the gadget's window, the shadow is drawn in the armed state, and the button is filled with the color specified by **XmNarmColor** if **XmNfillOnArm** is set to True.

Default PopupMenu System

<Btn3Down>:
This action disables keyboard traversal for the menu and returns the user to drag mode, which is the mode in which the menu is manipulated by using the mouse. The shadow is drawn in the armed state, and the callbacks for **XmNarmCallback** are called.

<Btn3Up>: This action causes the PushButtonGadget to be activated and the menu to be unposted. The callbacks for **XmNactivateCallback** are called, followed by callbacks for **XmNdisarmCallback**.

<Leave Window>:
If button 3 is pressed and the cursor leaves the widget's window, the PushButtonGadget is redrawn with no shadow. The callbacks for **XmNdisarmCallback** are called. If keyboard traversal is enabled in the menu, this event is ignored.

<Enter Window>:
If button 3 is pressed and the cursor enters the widget's window, the shadow is drawn in the armed state. The callbacks for **XmNarmCallback** are called. If keyboard traversal is enabled in the menu, this event is ignored.

<Key>Return:
If keyboard traversal is enabled in the menu, this event causes the PushButtonGadget to be activated and the menu to be unposted. The callbacks for **XmNactivateCallback** are called, followed by callbacks for **XmNdisarmCallback**.

Default PulldownMenu System and OptionMenu System

<Btn1Down>:
This action disables keyboard traversal for the menu and returns the user to drag mode, which is the mode in which the menu is manipulated by using the mouse. The shadow is drawn in the armed state, and the callbacks for **XmNarmCallback** are called.

<Btn1Up>: This action causes the PushButtonGadget to be activated and the menu to be unposted. The callbacks for **XmNactivateCallback** are called, followed by callbacks for **XmNdisarmCallback**.

<Leave Window>:
If mouse button 1 is pressed and the cursor leaves the widget's window, the PushButtonGadget is redrawn with no shadow. The callbacks for **XmNdisarmCallback** are called. If keyboard traversal is enabled in the menu, this event is ignored.

<Enter Window>:
If mouse button 1 is pressed and the cursor enters the widget's window, the shadow is drawn in the armed state. The callbacks for **XmNarmCallback** are called. If keyboard traversal is enabled in the menu, this event is ignored.

<Key>Return:
If keyboard traversal is enabled in the menu, this event causes the PushButtonGadget to be activated and the menu to be unposted. The callbacks for **XmNactivateCallback** are called, followed by callbacks for **XmNdisarmCallback**.

Keyboard Traversal

For information on keyboard traversal outside of menu systems, see the man page for **XmGadget(3X)** and its sections on behavior and default translations. For information on keyboard traversal inside of menu systems, see **XmRowColumn(3X)**.

Related Information

Object(3X), **RectObj(3X)**, **XmCreatePushButtonGadget(3X)**, **XmGadget(3X)**, **XmLabelGadget(3X)**, and **XmRowColumn(3X)**.

XmRemoveProtocolCallback

Purpose

A VendorShell function that removes a callback from the internal list.

Synopsis

```
#include <Xm/Xm.h>
#include <X11/Protocols.h>

void XmRemoveProtocolCallback (shell, property, protocol, callback, closure)
        Widget          shell;
        Atom            property;
        Atom            protocol;
        XtCallbackProc  callback;
        caddr_t         closure;

void XmRemoveWMProtocolCallback (shell, protocol, callback, closure)
        Widget          shell;
        Atom            protocol;
        XtCallbackProc  callback;
        caddr_t         closure;
```

Description

XmRemoveProtocolCallback removes a callback from the internal list.

XmRemoveWMProtocolCallback is a convenience interface. It calls **XmRemoveProtocolCallback** with the property value set to the atom returned by interning **WM_PROTOCOLS**.

shell Specifies the widget with which the protocol property is associated

property Specifies the protocol property

protocol Specifies the protocol atom (or an int cast to Atom)

callback Specifies the procedure to call when a protocol message is received

closure Specifies the client data to be passed to the callback when it is invoked

For a complete definition of VendorShell and its associated resources, see **VendorShell(3X)**.

Related Information

VendorShell(3X), **XmInternAtom(3X)**, and **XmRemoveWMProtocolCallback(3X)**.

XmRemoveProtocols

Purpose

A VendorShell function that removes the protocols from the protocol manager and deallocates the internal tables.

Synopsis

#include <Xm/Xm.h>
#include <X11/Protocols.h>

void XmRemoveProtocols (*shell, property, protocols, num_protocols*)
  Widget *shell*;
  Atom *property*;
  Atom * *protocols*;
  Cardinal *num_protocols*;

void XmRemoveWMProtocols (*shell, protocols, num_protocols*)
  Widget *shell*;
  Atom * *protocols*;
  Cardinal *num_protocols*;

Description

XmRemoveProtocols removes the protocols from the protocol manager and deallocates the internal tables. If any of the protocols are active, it will update the handlers and update the property if *shell* is realized.

XmRemoveWMProtocols is a convenience interface. It calls **XmRemoveProtocols** with the property value set to the atom returned by interning **WM_PROTOCOLS**.

shell Specifies the widget with which the protocol property is associated

property Specifies the protocol property

protocols Specifies the protocol atoms (or ints cast to Atom)

num_protocols Specifies the number of elements in protocols

For a complete definition of VendorShell and its associated resources, see **VendorShell(3X)**.

Related Information

VendorShell(3X), **XmInternAtom(3X)**, and **XmRemoveWMProtocols(3X)**.

XmRemoveTabGroup

Purpose

A function that removes a tab group

Synopsis

```
#include <Xm/Xm.h>

void XmRemoveTabGroup (tab_group)
        Widget        tab_group;
```

Description

XmRemoveTabGroup removes a Manager or Primitive widget from the list of tab groups associated with a particular widget hierarchy.

tab_group
Specifies the Manager or Primitive widget ID

Related Information

XmAddTabGroup(3X), **XmManager(3X)**, and **XmPrimitive(3X)**.

XmRemoveWMProtocolCallback

Purpose

A VendorShell convenience interface that removes a callback from the internal list.

Synopsis

```
#include <Xm/Xm.h>
#include <X11/Protocols.h>

void XmRemoveWMProtocolCallback (shell, protocol, callback, closure)
        Widget              shell;
        Atom                protocol;
        XtCallbackProc      callback;
        caddr_t             closure;
```

Description

XmRemoveWMProtocolCallback is a convenience interface. It calls **XmRemoveProtocolCallback** with the property value set to the atom returned by interning **WM_PROTOCOLS**.

shell Specifies the widget with which the protocol property is associated

protocol Specifies the protocol atom (or an int type cast to Atom) *callback* Specifies the procedure to call when a protocol message is received

closure Specifies the client data to be passed to the callback when it is invoked

For a complete definition of VendorShell and its associated resources, see **VendorShell(3X)**.

Related Information

VendorShell(3X), **XmInternAtom(3X)**, and **XmRemoveProtocolCallback(3X)**.

XmRemoveWMProtocols

Purpose

A VendorShell convenience interface that removes the protocols from the protocol manager and deallocates the internal tables.

Synopsis

```
#include <Xm/Xm.h>
#include <X11/Protocols.h>

void XmRemoveWMProtocols (shell, protocols, num_protocols)
        Widget      shell;
        Atom        * protocols;
        Cardinal    num_protocols;
```

Description

XmRemoveWMProtocols is a convenience interface. It calls **XmRemoveProtocols** with the property value set to the atom returned by interning **WM_PROTOCOLS**.

shell	Specifies the widget with which the protocol property is associated
protocols	Specifies the protocol atoms (or ints cast to Atom)
num_protocols	Specifies the number of elements in protocols

For a complete definition of VendorShell and its associated resources, see **VendorShell(3X)**.

Related Information

VendorShell(3X), **XmInternAtom(3X)**, and **XmRemoveProtocols(3X)**.

XmResolvePartOffsets

Purpose

A function that allows writing of upward-compatible applications and widgets.

Synopsis

#include <Xm/XmP.h>

void XmResolvePartOffsets (*widget_class, offset*)
  WidgetClass *widget_class*;
  XmOffsetPtr * *offset*;

Description

The use of offset records requires one extra global variable per widget class. The variable consists of a pointer to an array of offsets into the widget record for each part of the widget structure. The **XmResolvePartOffsets** function allocates the offset records needed by an application to guarantee upward-compatible applications and widgets. These offset records are used by the widget to access all of the widget's variables. A widget needs to take the following steps:

- Instead of creating a resource list, the widget creates an offset resource list. To help you accomplish this, use the **XmPartResource** structure and the **XmPartOffset** macro. The **XmPartResource** data structure looks just like a resource list, but instead of having one integer for its offset, it has two shorts. This is put into the class record as if it were a normal resource list. Instead of using **XtOffset** for the offset, the widget uses **XmPartOffset**.
- Instead of putting the widget size in the class record, the widget puts the widget part in the same field.
- Instead of putting **XtVersion** in the class record, the widget puts **XtVersionDontCheck** in the class record.
- The widget defines a variable to point to the offset record. This can be part of the widget's class record or a separate global variable.
- In class initialization, the widget calls **XmResolvePartOffsets**, passing it the offset address and the class record. This does several things:

  Adds the superclass (which, by definition, has already been initialized) size field to the part size field

  Allocates an array based upon the number of superclasses

  Fills in the offsets of all the widget parts with the appropriate values, determined by examining the size fields of all superclass records

  Uses the part offset array to modify the offset entries in the resource list to be real offsets, in place
- Instead of accessing fields directly, the widget must always go through the offset table. You can define macros for each field to make this easier. Assume an integer field ‘‘xyz’’:

  ```
  #define BarXyz(w) (*(int *)(((char *) w) +\
     offset[BarIndex] + XtOffset(BarPart,xyz)))
  ```

  The **XmField** macro helps you access these fields. Because the **XmPartOffset** and **XmField** macros concatenate things together, you must ensure that there is no space before or after the part argument. For example, the following macros do not work because of the space before or after the part (Label) argument:

XmField(w, offset, Label, text, char *)

XmPartOffset(Label, text).

Therefore, you must not have any spaces before or after the part (Label) argument, as illustrated here:

XmField(w, offset,Label, text, char *)

The parameters for **XmResolvePartOffsets** are defined below:

widget_class Specifies the widget class pointer for the created widget

offset Specifies the offset record

XmRowColumn

Purpose

The RowColumn widget class

Synopsis

#include <Xm/RowColumn.h>

Description

The RowColumn widget is a general purpose RowColumn manager capable of containing any widget type as a child. In general, it requires no special knowledge about how its children function and provides nothing beyond support for several different layout styles. However, it can be configured as a menu, in which case, it expects only certain children, and it configures to a particular layout. The menus supported are: MenuBar, Pulldown or Popup MenuPanes, and OptionMenu.

The type of layout performed is controlled by how the application has set the various layout resources. It can be configured to lay out its children in either rows or columns. In addition, the application can specify how the children are laid out, as follows:

- The children are packed tightly together (not into organized rows and columns).

- Each child is placed in an identically-sized box (producing a symmetrical look).
- A specific layout (the current *x* and *y* positions of the children control their location).

In addition, the application has control over both the spacing that occurs between each row and column and the margin spacing present between the edges of the RowColumn widget and any children that are placed against it.

In most cases, the RowColumn widget has no 3-D visuals associated with it; if an application wishes to have a 3-D shadow placed around this widget, it can create the RowColumn as a child of a Frame widget.

Classes

RowColumn inherits behavior and resources from **Core**, **Composite**, **Constraint**, and **XmManager** classes.

The class pointer is **xmRowColumnWidgetClass**.

The class name is **XmRowColumn**.

New Resources

The following table defines a set of widget resources used by the programmer to specify data. The programmer can also set the resource values for the inherited classes to set attributes for this widget. To reference a resource by name or by class in a .Xdefaults file, remove the **XmN** or **XmC** prefix and use the remaining letters. To specify one of the defined values for a resource in a .Xdefaults file, remove the **Xm** prefix and use the remaining letters (in either lowercase or uppercase, but include any underscores between words). The codes in the access column indicate if the given resource can be set at creation time (**C**), set by using **XtSetValues** (**S**), retrieved by using **XtGetValues** (**G**), or is not applicable (**N/A**).

XmRowColumn Resource Set		
Name **Class**	**Default** **Type**	**Access**
XmNadjustLast XmCAdjustLast	True Boolean	CSG
XmNadjustMargin XmCAdjustMargin	True Boolean	CSG
XmNentryAlignment XmCAlignment	dynamic unsigned char	CSG
XmNentryBorder XmCEntryBorder	dynamic short	CSG
XmNentryCallback XtCCallback	NULL XtCallbackList	C
XmNentryClass XmCEntryClass	dynamic WidgetClass	CSG
XmNisAligned XmCIsAligned	True Boolean	CSG
XmNisHomogeneous XmCIsHomogeneous	dynamic Boolean	CSG
XmNlabelString XtCString	NULL XmString	C
XmNmapCallback XtCCallback	NULL XtCallbackList	C
XmNmarginHeight XmCMarginHeight	dynamic Dimension	CSG
XmNmarginWidth XmCMarginWidth	3 Dimension	CSG
XmNmenuAccelerator XmCAccelerators	dynamic String	CSG

Name Class	Default Type	Access
XmNmenuHelpWidget XmCMenuWidget	NULL Widget	CSG
XmNmenuHistory XmCMenuWidget	NULL Widget	CSG
XmNmnemonic XmCMnemonic	dynamic char	CSG
XmNnumColumns XmCNumColumns	dynamic short	CSG
XmNorientation XmCOrientation	dynamic unsigned char	CSG
XmNpacking XmCPacking	dynamic unsigned char	CSG
XmNpopupEnabled XmCPopupEnabled	True Boolean	CSG
XmNradioAlwaysOne XmCRadioAlwaysOne	True Boolean	CSG
XmNradioBehavior XmCRadioBehavior	False Boolean	CSG
XmNresizeHeight XmCResizeHeight	True Boolean	CSG
XmNresizeWidth XmCResizeWidth	True Boolean	CSG
XmNrowColumnType XmCRowColumnType	XmWORK_AREA unsigned char	CG
XmNshadowThickness XmCShadowThickness	dynamic int	CSG
XmNspacing XmCSpacing	dynamic short	CSG

Name Class	Default Type	Access
XmNsubMenuId XmCMenuWidget	NULL Widget	CG
XmNunmapCallback XtCCallback	NULL XtCallbackList	C
XmNwhichButton XmCWhichButton	dynamic unsigned int	CSG

XmNadjustLast

Extends the last row of children to the bottom edge of RowColumn (when **XmOrientation** is **XmHORIZONTAL**) or extends the last column to the right edge of RowColumn (when **XmOrientation** is **XmVERTICAL**). This feature is disabled by setting **XmNadjustLast** to False.

XmNadjustMargin

Specifies whether the inner minor margins of all items contained within the RowColumn widget are forced to the same value. The inner minor margin corresponds to the **XmNmarginLeft**, **XmNmarginRight**, **XmNmarginTop** , and **XmNmarginBottom** resources supported by **XmLabel** and **XmLabelGadget**.

A horizontal orientation causes **XmNmarginTop** and **XmNmarginBottom** for all items in a particular row to be forced to the same value; the value is the largest margin specified for one of the Label items.

A vertical orientation causes **XmNmarginLeft** and **XmNmarginRight** for all items in a particular column to be forced to the same value; the value is the largest margin specified for one of the Label items.

This keeps all text within each row or column lined up with all other text in its row or column. If the **XmNrowColumnType** is either **XmMENU_POPUP** or **XmMENU_PULLDOWN** and this resource is True, only button children have their margins adjusted.

XmNentryAlignment

Specifies the alignment type for Label or LabelGadget children when **XmNisAligned** is enabled. The following are textual alignment types:

- **XmALIGNMENT_BEGINNING** — the default
- **XmALIGNMENT_CENTER**
- **XmALIGNMENT_END**

  See the description of **XmNalignment** in the **XmLabel(3X)** man page for an explanation of these actions.

XmNentryBorder

Imposes a uniform border width upon all RowColumn's children. The default value is 0, which disables the feature.

XmNentryCallback

Disables the activation callbacks for all ToggleButton, PushButton, and CascadeButton widgets and gadgets contained within the RowColumn widget. If the application supplies this resource, the activation callbacks are then revectored to this callback. This allows an application to supply a single callback routine for handling all items contained in a RowColumn widget. The application must supply this resource when this widget is created.

If the application does not supply this resource, the activation callbacks for each item in the RowColumn widget work as normal. The callback reason is **XmCR_ACTIVATE** and the default value is NULL. Changing this resource using the **XtSetValues** is not supported.

XmNentryClass

Specifies the only widget class that can be added to the RowColumn widget; this resource is meaningful only when the **XmNisHomogeneous** resource is set to True. When **XmNrowColumnType** is set to **XmWORK_AREA** and **XmNradioBehavior** is True, the default value for **XmNentryClass** is **xmToggleButtonGadgetClass**. When **XmNrowColumnType** is set to **XmMENU_BAR**, the value of **XmNentryClass** is forced to **xmCascadeButtonWidgetClass**.

XmNisAligned

Specifies text alignment for each item within the RowColumn widget; this applies only to items that are a subclass of **XmLabel** or **XmLabelGadget**. However, if the item is a Label widget or gadget and its parent is either a Popup MenuPane or a Pulldown MenuPane, alignment is not performed; the Label is treated as the title within the MenuPane, and the alignment set by the application is not overridden. **XmNentryAlignment** controls the type of textual alignment.

XmNisHomogeneous

Indicates if the RowColumn widget should enforce exact homogeneity among the items it contains; if True, only the widgets that are of the class indicated by **XmNentryClass** are allowed as children of the RowColumn widget. This is most often used when creating a MenuBar or a RadioBox widget.

Attempting to insert a child that is not a member of the specified class generates a warning message. The default value is False, except when creating a MenuBar or a RadioBox, when the default is True.

XmNlabelString

Points to a text string, which displays the label to the left of the selection area when **XmNrowColumnType** is set to **XmMENU_OPTION**. This resource is not meaningful for all other RowColumn types. If the application wishes to change the label after creation, it must get the LabelGadget ID (**XmOptionLabelGadget**) and call **XtSetValues** on the LabelGadget directly. The default value is no label.

XmNmapCallback

Specifies a widget-specific callback function that is invoked when the window associated with the RowColumn widget is about to be mapped. The callback reason is **XmCRMap**.

XmNmarginHeight

Specifies the amount of blank space between the top edge of the RowColumn widget and the first item in each column, and the bottom edge of the RowColumn widget and the last item in each column. The default value is three pixels.

XmNmarginWidth

Specifies the amount of blank space between the left edge of the RowColumn widget and the first item in each row, and the right edge of the RowColumn widget and the last item in each row. The default value is three pixels.

XmNmenuAccelerator

This resource is useful only when the RowColumn widget has been configured to operate as a Popup MenuPane or a MenuBar. The format of this resource is similar to the left side specification of a translation string, with the limitation that it must specify a key event. For a Popup MenuPane, when the accelerator is typed by the user, the Popup MenuPane is posted. For a MenuBar, when the accelerator is typed by the user, the first item in the MenuBar is highlighted, and traversal is enabled in the MenuBar. The default for a Popup MenuPane is **<Key>F4**. The default for a MenuBar is **<Key>F10**. The accelerator can be disabled by setting the **XmNpopupEnabled** resource to False.

XmNmenuHelpWidget

Specifies the widget ID for the CascadeButton, which is treated as the Help widget if **XmNrowColumnType** is set to **XmMENU_BAR**. The MenuBar always places the Help widget at the lower right corner. If the RowColumn widget is any type other than **XmMENU_BAR**, this resource is not meaningful.

XmNmenuHistory

Specifies the widget ID of the last menu entry to be activated. It is also useful for specifying the current selection for an OptionMenu. If **XmNrowColumnType** is set to **XmMENU_OPTION**, the specified menu item is positioned under the cursor when the menu is displayed.

If the RowColumn widget has the **XmNradioBehavior** resource set to True, the widget field associated with this resource contains the widget ID of the last ToggleButton or ToggleButtonGadget to change from unselected to selected. The default value is the widget ID of the first child in the widget.

XmNmnemonic

This resource is useful only when **XmNrowColumnType** is set to **XmMENU_OPTION**. Specifies a single character which, when typed by the user, posts the associated Pulldown MenuPane. The character is underlined if it appears in the OptionMenu label, giving the user a visual cue that the character has special functionality associated with it. The default is no mnemonic.

XmNnumColumns

Specifies the number of minor dimension extensions that are made to accommodate the entries; this attribute is meaningful only when **XmNpacking** is set to **XmPACK_COLUMN**.

For vertically-oriented RowColumn widgets, this attribute indicates how many columns are built; the number of entries per column is adjusted to maintain this number of columns, if possible.

For horizontally-oriented RowColumn widgets, this attribute indicates how many rows are built.

The default value is one.

XmNorientation

Determines whether RowColumn layouts are row-major or column-major. In a column-major layout, the children of the RowColumn are laid out in columns top to bottom within the widget. In a row-major layout the children of the RowColumn are laid out in rows. **XmVERTICAL** resource value selects a column-major layout. **XmHORIZONTAL** resource value selects a row-major layout.

The default value is **XmVERTICAL**, except when creating a MenuBar, when the default is **XmHORIZONTAL**.

XmNpacking

Specifies how to pack the items contained within a RowColumn widget. This can be set to **XmPACK_TIGHT, XmPACK_COLUMN** or **XmPACK_NONE**. When a RowColumn widget packs the items it contains, it determines its major dimension using the value of the **XmNorientation** resource.

XmPACK_TIGHT indicates that given the current major dimension (for example, vertical if **XmNorientation** is **XmVERTICAL**), entries are placed one after the other until the RowColumn widget must wrap. RowColumn wraps when there is no room left for a complete child in that dimension. Wrapping occurs by beginning a new row or column in the next available space. Wrapping continues, as often as necessary, until all of the children are laid out. In the vertical dimension (columns), boxes are set to the same width; in the horizontal dimension (rows), boxes are set to the same depth. Each entry's position in the major dimension is left unaltered (for example, **XmNy** is left unchanged when **XmNorientation** is **XmVERTICAL**); its position in the minor dimension is set to the same value as the greatest entry in that particular row or column. The position in the minor dimension of any particular row or column is independent of all other rows or columns.

XmPACK_COLUMN indicates that all entries are placed in identically sized boxes. The box is based on the largest height and width values of all the children widgets. The value of the **XmNnumColumns** resource determines how many boxes are placed in the major dimension, before extending in the minor dimension.

XmPACK_NONE indicates that no packing is performed. The x and y attributes of each entry are left alone, and the RowColumn widget attempts to become large enough to enclose all entries.

The default value is **XmPACK_TIGHT** except when building an OptionMenu or a RadioBox, when the default is **XmPACK_COLUMN**.

XmNpopupEnabled

Allows the menu system to enable keyboard input (accelerators and mnemonics) defined for the Popup MenuPane and any of its submenus. The Popup MenuPane needs to be informed whenever its accessibility to the user changes because posting of the Popup MenuPane is controlled by the application. The default value for this resource is True (keyboard input — accelerators and mnemonics — defined for the Popup MenuPane and any of its submenus is enabled).

XmNradioAlwaysOne

Forces the active ToggleButton or ToggleButtonGadget to be automatically selected after having been unselected (if no other toggle was activated), if True. If False, the active toggle may be unselected. The default value is True. This resource is important only when **XmNradioBehavior** is True.

The application can always add and subtract toggles from RowColumn regardless of the selected/unselected state of the toggle. The application can also manage and unmanage toggle children of RowColumn at any time regardless of state. Therefore, the application can sometimes create a RowColumn that has **XmNradioAlwaysOne** set to True and none of the toggle children selected.

XmNradioBehavior

Specifies a Boolean value that when True, indicates that the RowColumn widget should enforce a RadioBox-type behavior on all of its children that are ToggleButtons or ToggleButtonGadgets.

Two ToggleButton and ToggleButtonGadget resources are forced to specified values at creation time: **XmNindicator** is forced to **XmONE_OF_MANY** and **XmNvisibleWhenOff** is forced to True.

RadioBox behavior dictates that when one toggle is selected and the user selects another toggle, the first toggle is unselected automatically. The default value is False, except when creating a RadioBox, when the default is True.

XmNresizeHeight
Requests a new height if necessary, when set to True. When set to False, the widget does not request a new height regardless of any changes to the widget or its children.

XmNresizeWidth
Requests a new width if necessary, when set to True. When set to False, the widget does not request a new width regardless of any changes to the widget or its children.

XmNrowColumnType
Specifies the type of RowColumn widget to be created. It is a non-standard resource that cannot be changed after it is set. If an application uses any of the convenience routines, except **XmCreateRowColumn**, this resource is automatically forced to the appropriate value by the convenience routine. If an application uses the Xt Intrinsics API to create its RowColumn widgets, it must specify this resource itself. The set of possible settings for this resource are:

- **XmWORK_AREA** — the default
- **XmMENU_BAR**
- **XmMENU_PULLDOWN**
- **XmMENU_POPUP**
- **XmMENU_OPTION**

This resource cannot be changed after the RowColumn widget is created. Any changes attempted through **XtSetValues** are ignored.

XmNspacing
Specifies the horizontal and vertical spacing between items contained within the RowColumn widget. The default value is one pixel, except for a horizontal MenuBar, which defaults to 0 pixels.

XmNsubMenuId
Specifies the widget ID for the Pulldown MenuPane to be associated with an OptionMenu. This resource is useful only when **XmNrowColumnType** is set to **XmMENU_OPTION**. This resource must be specified at creation time for an OptionMenu to function properly; it is unused for all other RowColumn types. The default value is NULL.

XmNunmapCallback
Specifies a list of callbacks that is called after the window associated with the RowColumn widget has been unmapped. The callback reason is **XmCR_Unmap**. The default value is NULL.

XmNwhichButton
Specifies the mouse button to which a menu system is sensitive. The default for **XmMENU_POPUP** is button 3. The default for **XmMENU_OPTION** and **XmMENU_BAR** is button 1. This resource is not useful for RowColumn widgets of type **XmWORK_AREA** and **XmMENU_PULLDOWN**.

XmRowColumn Special Menu Resource		
Name **Class**	**Default** **Type**	**Access**
XmNmenuCursor XmCCursor	arrow String	C

XmNmenuCursor
Sets a variable that controls the cursor used whenever this application posts a menu. This resource can be specified only once at application startup time, either by placing it within a defaults file or by using the **-xrm** command line argument.

Example: myProg -xrm "*menuCursor: arrow"

The menu cursor can also be selected programmatically by using the function **XmSetMenuCursor**. The following is a list of acceptable cursor names. If the application does not specify a cursor or if an invalid name is supplied, the default cursor (an arrow pointing up and to the right) is used.

X_cursor	dotbox	man	sizing
arrow	double_arrow	middlebutton	spider
based_arrow_down	draft_large	mouse	spraycan
based_arrow_up	draft_small	pencil	star
boat	draped_box	pirate	target
bogosity	exchange	plus	tcross
bottom_left_corner	fleur	question_arrow	top_left_arrow
bottom_right_corner	gobbler	right_ptr	top_left_corner
bottom_side	gumby	right_side	top_right_corner
bottom_tee	hand1	right_tee	top_side
box_spiral	hand2	rightbutton	top_tee
center_ptr	heart	rtl_logo	trek
circle	icon	sailboat	ul_angle
clock	iron_cross	sb_down_arrow	umbrella
coffee_mug	left_ptr	sb_h_double_arrow	ur_angle
cross	left_side	sb_left_arrow	watch
cross_reverse	left_tee	sb_right_arrow	xterm
crosshair	leftbutton	sb_up_arrow	
diamond_cross	ll_angle	sb_v_double_arrow	
dot	lr_angle	shuttle	

Inherited Resources

RowColumn inherits behavior and resources from the following named superclasses. For a complete description of each resource, refer to the man page for that superclass.

XmManager Resource Set		
Name **Class**	**Default** **Type**	**Access**
XmNbottomShadowColor XmCForeground	dynamic Pixel	CSG
XmNbottomShadowPixmap XmCBottomShadowPixmap	XmUNSPECIFIED_PIXMAP Pixmap	CSG
XmNforeground XmCForeground	dynamic Pixel	CSG
XmNhelpCallback XmCCallback	NULL XtCallbackList	C
XmNhighlightColor XmCForeground	Black Pixel	CSG
XmNhighlightPixmap XmCHighlightPixmap	dynamic Pixmap	CSG
XmNshadowThickness XmCShadowThickness	0 short	CSG
XmNtopShadowColor XmCBackground	dynamic Pixel	CSG
XmNtopShadowPixmap XmCTopShadowPixmap	XmUNSPECIFIED_PIXMAP Pixmap	CSG
XmNunitType XmCUnitType	XmPIXELS unsigned char	CSG
XmNuserData XmCUserData	NULL caddr_t	CSG

Composite Resource Set		
Name **Class**	**Default** **Type**	**Access**
XmNinsertPosition XmCInsertPosition	NULL XmRFunction	CSG

Core Resource Set		
Name **Class**	**Default** **Type**	**Access**
XmNaccelerators XmCAccelerators	NULL XtTranslations	CSG
XmNancestorSensitive XmCSensitive	True Boolean	G
XmNbackground XmCBackground	dynamic Pixel	CSG
XmNbackgroundPixmap XmCPixmap	XmUNSPECIFIED_PIXMAP Pixmap	CSG
XmNborderColor XmCBorderColor	Black Pixel	CSG
XmNborderPixmap XmCPixmap	XmUNSPECIFIED_PIXMAP Pixmap	CSG
XmNborderWidth XmCBorderWidth	dynamic Dimension	CSG
XmNcolormap XmCColormap	XtCopyFromParent Colormap	CG
XmNdepth XmCDepth	XtCopyFromParent int	CG
XmNdestroyCallback XmCCallback	NULL XtCallbackList	C

Name Class	Default Type	Access
XmNheight XmCHeight	16 Dimension	CSG
XmNmappedWhenManaged XmCMappedWhenManaged	True Boolean	CSG
XmNscreen XmCScreen	XtCopyScreen Pointer	CG
XmNsensitive XmCSensitive	True Boolean	CSG
XmNtranslations XmCTranslations	NULL XtTranslations	CSG
XmNwidth XmCWidth	16 Dimension	CSG
XmNx XmCPosition	0 Position	CSG
XmNy XmCPosition	0 Position	CSG

Callback Information

The following structure is returned with each callback:

```
typedef struct
{
    int         reason;
    XEvent      * event;
    Widget      widget;
    char        * data;
    char        * callbackstruct;
} XmRowColumnCallbackStruct;
```

reason Indicates why the callback was invoked

event Points to the **XEvent** that triggered the callback

The following fields apply only when the callback reason is **XmCR_ACTIVATE**; for all other callback reasons, these fields are set to NULL. The **XmCR_ACTIVATE** callback reason is generated only when the application has supplied an entry callback, which overrides any activation callbacks registered with the individual RowColumn items.

widget Is set to the widget ID of the RowColumn item that has been activated

data Contains the client-data value supplied by the application when the RowColumn item's activation callback was registered

callbackstruct
Points to the callback structure generated by the RowColumn item's activation callback

Behavior

A RowColumn widget's behavior depends on its type (such as MenuBar or Popup MenuPane) and the type of menu system in which it resides (Pulldown, Popup, or Option). The specific mouse button depends on the **XmNwhichButton** resource.

Default MenuBar

<Btn1Down>:
If the button event occurs within one of the MenuBar buttons, the MenuBar is armed (if not already armed) and the submenu associated with the selected button is posted. The user can move the mouse to access the MenuPanes attached to the MenuBar.

If the button event does not occur within one of the MenuBar buttons and if the MenuBar is already armed, it is disarmed, and any visible MenuPanes are unposted; if the MenuBar is not already armed, nothing occurs.

<Btn1Up>: If the MenuBar is armed, this event unposts all visible MenuPanes and then disarms the menubar.

Default OptionMenu

<Btn1Down>:
When this event occurs within the selection area, the Pulldown MenuPane is posted. If this event occurs outside of the selection area and if the MenuPane is already posted, the Pulldown MenuPane is unposted.

<Btn1Up>: When this event occurs while the Pulldown MenuPane is posted, it is unposted.

<Return>: If this key is pressed while the focus is set to the selection area, the Pulldown MenuPane is posted.

Default Pulldown MenuPane from a Popup MenuPane

<Btn3Down>:
When this event occurs, the menu system disables traversal mode, and re-enters drag mode. Depending upon where the button-down event occurs, certain portions of the visible set of MenuPanes are unposted.

<Btn3Up>: When this event occurs within a gadget child of the MenuPane, the indicated child is activated. If the child is not a CascadeButton (widget or gadget), this also results in all visible MenuPanes being unposted. If the child is a CascadeButton (widget or gadget), this results in the associated submenu being posted and traversal being enabled. When this event occurs outside of a gadget child, all visible MenuPanes are unposted.

<Return>: If this key is pressed while the focus is set to a gadget child of the MenuPane, the indicated child is activated. If the child is not a CascadeButton (widget or gadget), this also results in all visible MenuPanes being unposted. If the child is a CascadeButton (widget or gadget), this results in the associated submenu being posted and traversal being enabled.

<Escape>: This event unposts all visible MenuPanes.

<Right>: If the current focus item is a CascadeButtonGadget, this posts the associated Pulldown MenuPane and highlights the first accessible item within the Pulldown MenuPane.

<Left>: If this occurs within a MenuPane that is a submenu of another MenuPane, this causes the last MenuPane to be unposted and the focus to move to the previous MenuPane.

<Up>: This moves the focus to the previous menu item; the previous menu item is defined as the widget that was created prior to the one that currently has the focus. Wrapping occurs, if necessary.

<Down>: This moves the focus to the next menu item; the next menu item is defined as the widget that was created after the one that currently has the focus. Wrapping occurs, if necessary.

Default Pulldown MenuPane from a MenuBar or from an OptionMenu

<Btn1Down>:

When this event occurs, the menu system disables traversal mode and re-enters drag mode. Depending upon where the button down event occurs, certain portions of the visible set of MenuPanes are unposted.

<Btn1Up>: When this event occurs within a gadget child of the MenuPane, the indicated child is activated. If the child is not a CascadeButton (widget or gadget), this also results in all visible MenuPanes being unposted. If the child is a CascadeButton (widget or gadget), this results in the associated submenu being posted and traversal being enabled. When this event occurs outside of a gadget child, all visible MenuPanes are unposted.

<Return>: If this key is pressed while the focus is set to a gadget child of the MenuPane, the indicated child is activated. If the child is not a CascadeButton (widget or gadget), this also results in all visible MenuPanes being unposted. If the child is a CascadeButton (widget or gadget), this results in the associated submenu being posted and traversal being enabled.

<Escape>: This event unposts all visible MenuPanes.

<Right>: If the current focus item is a CascadeButtonGadget, this posts the associated Pulldown MenuPane and highlights the first accessible item within the Pulldown MenuPane. If the current focus item is not a CascadeButton, the visible set of MenuPanes are unposted, and the top level Pulldown MenuPane associated with the next MenuBar item is posted.

<Left>: If this is occurs within a MenuPane that is a submenu of another MenuPane, this event causes the last MenuPane to be unposted and the focus to move to the previous MenuPane. If this is occurs within a MenuPane that is connected directly to the MenuBar, the visible set of MenuPanes are unposted, and the top level Pulldown MenuPane associated with the previous menubar item is posted.

<Up>: This moves the focus to the previous menu item; the previous menu item is defined as the widget that was created prior to the one that currently has the focus. Wrapping occurs, if necessary.

<Down>: This moves the focus to the next menu item; the next menu item is defined as the widget that was created after the one that currently has the focus. Wrapping occurs, if necessary.

WorkArea

<Btn1Down>

If the button press occurred in a gadget child, it is dispatched to it.

<Btn1Up> If the button press occurred in a gadget child, it is dispatched to it.

Default Translations

The following are the default translations for an OptionMenu:

<BtnDown>: PopupBtnDown()
<BtnUp>: PopupBtnUp()
<Key>Return: MenuGadgetReturn()

The following are the default translations for a Popup MenuPane:

<BtnDown>: PopupBtnDown()
<BtnUp>: PopupBtnUp()
<Key>Return: MenuGadgetReturn()
<Key>Escape: MenuGadgetEscape()
<Unmap>: MenuUnmap()
<FocusIn>: MenuFocusIn()
<FocusOut>: MenuFocusOut()
<EnterWindow>: MenuEnter()
<Key>Left: MenuGadgetTraverseLeft()
<Key>Right: MenuGadgetTraverseRight()
<Key>Up: MenuGadgetTraverseUp()
<Key>Down: MenuGadgetTraverseDown()

The following are the default translations are for a Pulldown MenuPane:

<BtnDown>: PulldownBtnDown()
<BtnUp>: PulldownBtnUp()
<Key>Return: MenuGadgetReturn()
<Key>Escape: MenuGadgetEscape()
<Unmap>: MenuUnmap()
<FocusIn>: MenuFocusIn()
<FocusOut>: MenuFocusOut()
<EnterWindow>: MenuEnter()
<Key>Left: MenuGadgetTraverseLeft()
<Key>Right: MenuGadgetTraverseRight()
<Key>Up: MenuGadgetTraverseUp()
<Key>Down: MenuGadgetTraverseDown()

The following are the default translations for a MenuBar:

<BtnDown>:	**MenuBarBtnDown()**
<BtnUp>:	**MenuBarBtnUp()**
<Unmap>:	**MenuUnmap()**
<FocusIn>:	**MenuFocusIn()**
<FocusOut>:	**MenuFocusOut()**
<EnterWindow>:	**MenuEnter()**

The following are the default translations for a WorkArea:

<Btn1Down>:	**WorkAreaBtnDown()**
<Btn1Up>:	**WorkAreaBtnUp()**

Keyboard Traversal

For information on keyboard traversal in a WorkArea, see the man page for **XmManager(3X)** and its sections on behavior and default translations.

Related Information

Composite(3X), **Constraint(3X)**, **Core(3X)**, **XmCreateRowColumn(3X)**, **XmCreateMenuBar(3X)**, **XmCreateOptionMenu(3X)**, **XmCreatePopupMenu(3X)**, **XmCreatePulldownMenu(3X)**, **XmCreateRadioBox(3X)**, **XmGetMenuCursor(3X)**, **XmLabel(3X)**, **XmManager(3X)**, **XmOptionButtonGadget(3X)**, **XmOptionLabelGadget(3X)**, **XmSetMenuCursor(3X)**, **XmMenuPosition(3X)**, and **XmUpdateDisplay(3X)**.

XmScale

Purpose

The Scale widget class

Synopsis

#include <Xm/Scale.h>

Description

Scale is used by an application to indicate a value from within a range of values, and it allows the user to input or modify a value from the same range.

A Scale has an elongated rectangular region similar to a ScrollBar. A slider inside this region indicates the current value along the Scale. The user can also modify the Scale's value by moving the slider within the rectangular region of the Scale. A Scale can also include a label set located outside the Scale region. These can indicate the relative value at various positions along the scale.

A Scale can be either input/output or output only. An input/output Scale's value can be set by the application and also modified by the user with the slider. An output-only Scale is used strictly as an indicator of the current value of something and cannot be modified interactively by the user. The **Core** resource **XmNsensitive** specifies whether the user can interactively modify the Scale's value.

Classes

Scale inherits behavior and resources from **Core**, **Composite**, **Constraint**, and **XmManager** classes.

The class pointer is **xmScaleWidgetClass**.

The class name is **XmScale**.

New Resources

The following table defines a set of widget resources used by the programmer to specify data. The programmer can also set the resource values for the inherited classes to set attributes for this widget. To reference a resource by name or by class in a .Xdefaults file, remove the **XmN** or **XmC** prefix and use the remaining letters. To specify one of the defined values for a resource in a .Xdefaults file, remove the **Xm** prefix and use the remaining letters (in either lowercase or uppercase, but include any underscores between words). The codes in the access column indicate if the given resource can be set at creation time (**C**), set by using **XtSetValues** (**S**), retrieved by using **XtGetValues** (**G**), or is not applicable (**N/A**).

XmScale Resource Set		
Name **Class**	**Default** **Type**	**Access**
XmNdecimalPoints XmCDecimalPoints	0 short	CSG
XmNdragCallback XmCCallback	NULL XtCallbackList	C
XmNfontList XmCFontList	"Fixed" XmFontList	CSG
XmNhighlightOnEnter XmCHighlightOnEnter	False Boolean	CSG
XmNhighlightThickness XmCHighlightThickness	0 short	CSG
XmNmaximum XmCMaximum	100 int	CSG
XmNminimum XmCMinimum	0 int	CSG
XmNorientation XmCOrientation	XmVERTICAL unsigned char	CSG
XmNprocessingDirection XmCProcessingDirection	XmMAX_ON_TOP unsigned char	CSG
XmNscaleHeight XmCScaleHeight	0 Dimension	CSG
XmNscaleWidth XmCScaleWidth	0 Dimension	CSG
XmNshowValue XmCShowValue	False Boolean	CSG
XmNtitleString XmCTitleString	NULL XmString	CSG
XmNtraversalOn XmCTraversalOn	False Boolean	CSG

Name Class	Default Type	Access
XmNvalue XmCValue	0 int	CSG
XmNvalueChangedCallback XmCCallback	NULL XtCallbackList	C

XmNdecimalPoints

Specifies the number of decimal points to shift the slider value when displaying it. For example, a slider value of 2,350 and an **XmdecimalPoints** value of 2 results in a display value of 23.50.

XmNdragCallback

Specifies the list of callbacks that is called when the slider position changes as the slider is being dragged. The reason sent by the callback is **XmCR_DRAG**.

XmNfontList

Specifies the font list to use for the title text string specified by **XmNtitleString**.

XmNhighlightOnEnter

Specifies whether to draw the slider's border highlight on enter-window events. This resource is ignored if the **XmNtraversalOn** resource is set to True.

XmNhighlightThickness

Specifies the size of the slider's border drawing rectangle used for enter window and traversal highlight drawing.

XmNmaximum

Specifies the slider's maximum value.

XmNminimum

Specifies the slider's minimum value.

XmNorientation

Displays Scale vertically or horizontally. This resource can have values of **XmVERTICAL and XmHORIZONTAL.**

XmNprocessingDirection
Specifies whether the value for **XmNmaximum** is on the right or left side of **XmNminimum** for horizontal Scales or above or below **XmNminimum** for vertical Scales. This resource can have values of **XmMAX_ON_TOP, XmMAX_ON_BOTTOM,** **XmMAX_ON_LEFT**, and **XmMAX_ON_RIGHT**.

XmNscaleHeight
Specifies the height of the slider area. The value should be in the specified unit type (the default is pixels).

XmNscaleWidth
Specifies the width of the slider area. The value should be in the specified unit type (the default is pixels).

XmNshowValue
Specifies if a label for the current slider value should be displayed next to the slider. If it is True, the current slider value is displayed.

XmNtitleString
Specifies the title text string to appear in the Scale widget window.

XmNtraversalOn
Specifies whether the Scale's slider is to have traversal on for it.

XmNvalue Specifies the slider's current position along the scale, between minimum and maximum.

XmNvalueChangedCallback
Specifies the list of callbacks that is called when the value of the slider has changed. The reason sent by the callback is **XmCR_VALUE_CHANGED**.

Inherited Resources

Scale inherits behavior and resources from the following superclasses. For a complete description of each resource, refer to the man page for that superclass.

XmManager Resource Set		
Name **Class**	**Default** **Type**	**Access**
XmNbottomShadowColor XmCForeground	dynamic Pixel	CSG
XmNbottomShadowPixmap XmCBottomShadowPixmap	XmUNSPECIFIED_PIXMAP Pixmap	CSG
XmNforeground XmCForeground	dynamic Pixel	CSG
XmNhelpCallback XmCCallback	NULL XtCallbackList	C
XmNhighlightColor XmCForeground	Black Pixel	CSG
XmNhighlightPixmap XmCHighlightPixmap	dynamic Pixmap	CSG
XmNshadowThickness XmCShadowThickness	0 short	N/A
XmNtopShadowColor XmCBackground	dynamic Pixel	CSG
XmNtopShadowPixmap XmCTopShadowPixmap	XmUNSPECIFIED_PIXMAP Pixmap	CSG
XmNunitType XmCUnitType	XmPIXELS unsigned char	CSG
XmNuserData XmCUserData	NULL caddr_t	CSG

Composite Resource Set		
Name **Class**	**Default** **Type**	**Access**
XmNinsertPosition XmCInsertPosition	NULL XmRFunction	CSG

Core Resource Set		
Name **Class**	**Default** **Type**	**Access**
XmNaccelerators XmCAccelerators	NULL XtTranslations	CSG
XmNancestorSensitive XmCSensitive	True Boolean	G
XmNbackground XmCBackground	dynamic Pixel	CSG
XmNbackgroundPixmap XmCPixmap	XmUNSPECIFIED_PIXMAP Pixmap	CSG
XmNborderColor XmCBorderColor	Black Pixel	CSG
XmNborderPixmap XmCPixmap	XmUNSPECIFIED_PIXMAP Pixmap	CSG
XmNborderWidth XmCBorderWidth	0 Dimension	CSG
XmNcolormap XmCColormap	XtCopyFromParent Colormap	CG
XmNdepth XmCDepth	XtCopyFromParent int	CG
XmNdestroyCallback XmCCallback	NULL XtCallbackList	C
XmNheight XmCHeight	0 Dimension	CSG
XmNmappedWhenManaged XmCMappedWhenManaged	True Boolean	CSG
XmNscreen XmCScreen	XtCopyScreen Pointer	CG
XmNsensitive XmCSensitive	True Boolean	CSG

Name Class	Default Type	Access
XmNtranslations XmCTranslations	NULL XtTranslations	CSG
XmNwidth XmCWidth	0 Dimension	CSG
XmNx XmCPosition	0 Position	CSG
XmNy XmCPosition	0 Position	CSG

Callback Information

The following structure is returned with each callback.

```
typedef struct
{
    int         reason;
    XEvent      * event;
    int         value;
} XmScaleCallbackStruct;
```

reason Indicates why the callback was invoked

event Points to the **XEvent** that triggered the callback

value Is the new slider location value

Behavior

<Btn1Down>:
Activates the interactive dragging of the slider if the button is pressed anywhere inside the scale rectangle, including the slider.

Button1<PtrMoved>:
Moves the slider to the new position and calls the callbacks for **XmNdragCallback** if the button press occurs within the slider.

<Btn1Up>: Calls the callbacks for **XmNvalueChangedCallback** if the button press occurs within the scale rectangle and if the slider position was changed.

Default Translations

The following are Scale's default translations:

<Btn1Down>:	**Arm()**
<Btn1Up>:	**Activate()**
<EnterWindow>:	**Enter()**
<FocusIn>:	**FocusIn()**

Keyboard Traversal

For information on keyboard traversal, see the man page for **XmManager(3X)** and its sections on behavior and default translations.

Related Information

Composite(3X), **Constraint(3X)**, **Core(3X)**, **XmCreateScale(3X)**, **XmManager(3X)**, **XmScaleGetValue(3X)**, and **XmScaleSetValue(3X)**.

XmScaleGetValue

Purpose

A Scale function that returns the current slider position.

Synopsis

#include <Xm/Scale.h>

void XmScaleGetValue (*widget, value_return*)
    Widget   *widget*;
    int   * *value_return*;

Description

XmScaleGetValue returns the current slider position value displayed in the scale.

widget Specifies the Scale widget ID.

value_return Returns the current slider position value

For a complete definition of Scale and its associated resources, see **XmScale(3X)**

Related Information

XmScale(3X).

XmScaleSetValue

Purpose

A Scale function that sets a slider value

Synopsis

```
#include <Xm/Scale.h>

void XmScaleSetValue (widget, value)
        Widget      widget;
        int         value;
```

Description

XmScaleSetValue sets the slider *value* within the Scale widget.

widget Specifies the Scale widget ID.

value Specifies the slider position along the scale. This sets the **XmNvalue** resource.

For a complete definition of Scale and its associated resources, see **XmScale(3X)**.

Related Information

XmScale(3X).

XmScrollBar

Purpose

The ScrollBar widget class

Synopsis

#include <Xm/ScrollBar.h>

Description

The ScrollBar widget allows the user to view data that is too large to be displayed all at once. ScrollBars are usually located beside or within the widget that contains the data to be viewed. When the user interacts with the ScrollBar, the data within the other widget scrolls.

A ScrollBar consists of two arrows placed at each end of a rectangle. The rectangle is called the scroll region. A smaller rectangle, called the slider, is placed within the scroll region. The data is scrolled by selecting either arrow, selecting the scroll region, or dragging the slider. When an arrow is selected, the slider within the scroll region is moved in the direction of the arrow by an amount supplied by the application. If the mouse button is held down, the slider continues to move at a constant rate.

The ratio of the slider size to the scroll region size corresponds to the relationship between the size of the visible data and the total size of the data. For example, if 10 percent of the data is visible, the slider occupies 10 percent of the scroll region. This provides the user with a visual clue to the size of the invisible data.

Classes

ScrollBar inherits behavior and resources from the **Core** and **XmPrimitive** classes.

The class pointer is **xmScrollBarWidgetClass**.

The class name is **XmScrollBar**.

New Resources

The following table defines a set of widget resources used by the programmer to specify data. The programmer can also set the resource values for the inherited classes to set attributes for this widget. To reference a resource by name or by class in a .Xdefaults file, remove the **XmN** or **XmC** prefix and use the remaining letters. To specify one of the defined values for a resource in a .Xdefaults file, remove the **Xm** prefix and use the remaining letters (in either lowercase or uppercase, but include any underscores between words). The codes in the access column indicate if the given resource can be set at creation time (**C**), set by using **XtSetValues** (**S**), retrieved by using **XtGetValues** (**G**), or is not applicable (**N/A**).

XmScrollBar Resource Set		
Name **Class**	**Default** **Type**	**Access**
XmNdecrementCallback XmCCallback	NULL XtCallbackList	C
XmNdragCallback XmCCallback	NULL XtCallbackList	C
XmNincrement XmCIncrement	1 int	CSG
XmNincrementCallback XmCCallback	NULL XtCallbackList	C
XmNinitialDelay XmCInitialDelay	250 int	CSG
XmNmaximum XmCMaximum	0 int	CSG
XmNminimum XmCMinimum	0 int	CSG
XmNorientation XmCOrientation	XmVERTICAL unsigned char	CSG
XmNpageDecrementCallback XmCCallback	NULL XtCallbackList	CSG
XmNpageIncrement XmCPageIncrement	10 int	C
XmNpageIncrementCallback XmCCallback	NULL XtCallbackList	C
XmNprocessingDirection XmCProcessingDirection	XmMAX_ON_BOTTOM unsigned char	CSG
XmNrepeatDelay XmCRepeatDelay	50 int	CSG
XmNshowArrows XmCShowArrows	True Boolean	CSG

Name Class	Default Type	Access
XmNsliderSize XmCSliderSize	10 int	CSG
XmNtoBottomCallback XmCCallback	NULL XtCallbackList	C
XmNtoTopCallback XmCCallback	NULL XtCallbackList	C
XmNvalue XmCValue	0 int	CSG
XmNvalueChangedCallback XmCCallback	NULL XtCallbackList	C

XmNdecrementCallback
Specifies the list of callbacks that is called when an arrow is selected that decreases the slider value by one increment. The reason sent by the callback is **XmCR_DECREMENT**.

XmNdragCallback
Specifies the list of callbacks that is called on each incremental change of position when the slider is being dragged. The reason sent by the callback is **XmCR_DRAG**.

XmNincrement
Specifies the amount to move the slider when the corresponding arrow is selected.

XmNincrementCallback
Specifies the list of callbacks that is called when an arrow that increases the slider value by one increment is selected. The reason sent by the callback is **XmCR_INCREMENT**.

XmNinitialDelay
Specifies the amount of time to wait (milliseconds) before starting continuous slider movement while an arrow or the scroll region is being pressed.

XmNmaximum
Specifies the slider's maximum value.

XmNminimum
Specifies the slider's minimum value.

XmNorientation
Specifies whether the ScrollBar is displayed vertically or horizontally. This resource can have values of **XmVERTICAL** and **XmHORIZONTAL**.

XmNpageDecrementCallback
Specifies the list of callbacks that is called when the slider area is selected and the slider value is decreased by one page increment. The reason sent by the callback is **XmCR_PAGE_DECREMENT**.

XmNpageIncrement
Specifies the amount to move the slider when selection occurs on the slide area.

XmNpageIncrementCallback
Specifies the list of callbacks that is called when the slider area is selected and the slider value is increased by one page increment. The reason sent by the callback is **XmCR_PAGE_INCREMENT**.

XmNprocessingDirection
Specifies whether the value for **XmNmaximum** should be on the right or left side of **XmNminimum** for horizontal ScrollBars or above or below **XmNminimum** for vertical ScrollBars. This resource can have values of **XmMAX_ON_TOP,** **XmMAX_ON_BOTTOM,** **XmMAX_ON_LEFT**, and **XmMAX_ON_RIGHT**.

XmNrepeatDelay
Specifies the amount of time to wait (milliseconds) between subsequent slider movements after the **XmNinitialDelay** has been processed.

XmNshowArrows
Specifies whether the arrows are displayed.

XmNsliderSize
Specifies the size of the slider between the values of 0 and maximum - minimum.

XmNtoBottomCallback
Specifies the list of callbacks that is called when the user selects <**Shift**> mouse button 1 down in the bottom arrow button. This callback sends as a value the maximum ScrollBar value minus the ScrollBar slider size. The slider location is not automatically repositioned. The reason sent by the callback is **XmCR_TO_BOTTOM**.

XmNtoTopCallback
Specifies the list of callbacks that is called when the user selects <**Shift**> mouse button 1 down in the top arrow button. This callback sends as a value the minimum ScrollBar slider value. The slider location is not automatically repositioned. The reason sent by the callback is **XmCR_TO_TOP**.

XmNvalue Specifies the slider's position between minimum and maximum.

XmNvalueChangedCallback
Specifies the list of callbacks that is called when the slider is released while being dragged; this is in place of **XmNincrementCallback**, **XmNdecrementCallback**, **XmNpageIncrementCallback** or **XmNpageDecrementCallback** when they do not have any callbacks attached. The reason sent by the callback is **XmCR_VALUE_CHANGED**.

Inherited Resources

ScrollBar inherits behavior and resources from the following superclasses. For a complete description of each resource, refer to the man page for that superclass.

XmPrimitive Resource Set		
Name **Class**	**Default** **Type**	**Access**
XmNbottomShadowColor XmCForeground	dynamic Pixel	CSG
XmNbottomShadowPixmap XmCBottomShadowPixmap	XmUNSPECIFIED_PIXMAP Pixmap	CSG
XmNforeground XmCForeground	dynamic Pixel	CSG
XmNhelpCallback XmCCallback	NULL XtCallbackList	C
XmNhighlightColor XmCForeground	Black Pixel	CSG
XmNhighlightOnEnter XmCHighlightOnEnter	False Boolean	CSG
XmNhighlightPixmap XmCHighlightPixmap	dynamic Pixmap	CSG
XmNhighlightThickness XmCHighlightThickness	0 short	CSG
XmNshadowThickness XmCShadowThickness	2 short	CSG
XmNtopShadowColor XmCBackground	dynamic Pixel	CSG
XmNtopShadowPixmap XmCTopShadowPixmap	XmUNSPECIFIED_PIXMAP Pixmap	CSG
XmNtraversalOn XmCTraversalOn	False Boolean	CSG
XmNunitType XmCUnitType	XmPIXELS unsigned char	CSG
XmNuserData XmCUserData	NULL caddr_t	CSG

Core Resource Set		
Name **Class**	**Default** **Type**	**Access**
XmNaccelerators XmCAccelerators	NULL XtTranslations	CSG
XmNancestorSensitive XmCSensitive	True Boolean	G
XmNbackground XmCBackground	dynamic Pixel	CSG
XmNbackgroundPixmap XmCPixmap	XmUNSPECIFIED_PIXMAP Pixmap	CSG
XmNborderColor XmCBorderColor	Black Pixel	CSG
XmNborderPixmap XmCPixmap	XmUNSPECIFIED_PIXMAP Pixmap	CSG
XmNborderWidth XmCBorderWidth	0 Dimension	CSG
XmNcolormap XmCColormap	XtCopyFromParent Colormap	CG
XmNdepth XmCDepth	XtCopyFromParent int	CG
XmNdestroyCallback XmCCallback	NULL XtCallbackList	C
XmNheight XmCHeight	0 Dimension	CSG
XmNmappedWhenManaged XmCMappedWhenManaged	True Boolean	CSG
XmNscreen XmCScreen	XtCopyScreen Pointer	CG
XmNsensitive XmCSensitive	True Boolean	CSG

Name **Class**	**Default** **Type**	**Access**
XmNtranslations XmCTranslations	NULL XtTranslations	CSG
XmNwidth XmCWidth	0 Dimension	CSG
XmNx XmCPosition	0 Position	CSG
XmNy XmCPosition	0 Position	CSG

Callback Information

The following structure is returned with each callback.

```
typedef struct
{
    int         reason;
    XEvent      * event;
    int         value;
    int         pixel;
} XmScrollBarCallbackStruct;
```

reason Indicates why the callback was invoked.

event Points to the **XEvent** that triggered the callback.

value Contains the new slider location value.

pixel Is used only for **XmNtoTopCallback** and **XmNtoBottomCallback**. For horizontal ScrollBars, it contains the *x* coordinate of where the mouse button selection occurred. For vertical ScrollBars, it contains the *y* coordinate.

Behavior

<Btn1Down>:

(in arrow): Moves the slider one increment or decrement in the direction of the arrow and calls the callbacks for **XmNincrementCallback** or **XmNdecrementCallback**. The **XmNvalueChangedCallbacks** is called if the **XmNincrementCallbacks** or **XmNdecrementCallbacks** are empty.

(in scroll region): Moves the slider one page increment or page decrement depending on which side of the slider is selected and calls the callbacks for **XmNpageIncrementCallback** or **XmNpageDecrementCallback**. The **XmNvalueChangedCallbacks** is called if the **XmNpageIncrementCallbacks** or **XmNpageDecrementCallbacks** are empty.

(in slider): Activates the interactive dragging of the slider. If the button is held down in either the arrows or the scroll region longer than the **XmNinitialDelay** resource, the slider is moved again by the same increment and the same callbacks are called. After the initial delay has been used, the time delay changes to the time defined by the resource **XmNrepeatDelay**.

Button1<PtrMoved>:

If the button press occurs within the slider, the subsequent motion events move the slider to the new position and the callbacks for **XmNdragCallback** are called.

<Btn1Up>: If the button press occurs within the slider and the slider position is changed, the callbacks for **XmNvalueChangedCallback** are called.

Shift<Btn1Down>:

This mouse-button press in the top arrow button causes the callbacks for **XmNtoTopCallback** to be called.

Shift<Btn1Down>:
: This mouse-button press in the bottom arrow button causes the callbacks for **XmNtoBottomCallback** to be called.

<Key>Up:
: For vertical ScrollBars, pressing the up-arrow cursor key decrements the slider one unit and calls **XmNdecrementCallback**. The **XmNvalueChangedCallbacks** is called if the **XmNdecrementCallbacks** are empty.

<Key>Down:
: For vertical ScrollBars, pressing the down-arrow cursor key increments the slider one unit and calls **XmNincrementCallback**. The **XmNvalueChangedCallbacks** is called if the **XmNincrementCallbacks** are empty.

<Key>Left:
: For horizontal ScrollBars, pressing the left-arrow cursor key decrements the slider one unit and calls **XmNdecrementCallback**. The **XmNvalueChangedCallbacks** is called if the **XmNdecrementCallbacks** are empty.

<Key>Right:
: For horizontal ScrollBars, pressing the right-arrow cursor key increments the slider one unit and calls **XmNincrementCallback**. The **XmNvalueChangedCallbacks** is called if the **XmNincrementCallbacks** are empty.

Default Translations

~Shift ~Ctrl ~Meta ~Alt <Btn1Down>: Select()
~Shift ~Ctrl ~Meta ~Alt <Btn1Up>: Release()
~Shift ~Ctrl ~Meta ~Alt Button1<PtrMoved>:Moved()
Shift ~Ctrl ~Meta ~Alt <Btn1Down>: GoToTop()
Shift ~Ctrl ~Meta ~Alt <Btn1Down>: GoToBottom()
~Shift ~Ctrl ~Meta ~Alt <Key>Up: UpOrLeft(0)
~Shift ~Ctrl ~Meta ~Alt <Key>Down: DownOrRight(0)
~Shift ~Ctrl ~Meta ~Alt <Key>Left: UpOrLeft(1)
~Shift ~Ctrl ~Meta ~Alt <Key>Right: DownOrRight(1)
<EnterWindow>: Enter()
<LeaveWindow>: Leave()

Keyboard Traversal

If the **XtNtraversalOn** resource is set to True either at create time or during a call to **XtSetValues**, the Manager superclass automatically augments the Manager widget's translations to support keyboard traversal. Refer to **XmManager(3X)** for a complete description of these translations.

Related Information

Core(3X), **XmCreateScrollBar(3X)**, **XmPrimitive(3X)**, **XmScrollBarGetValues(3X)**, and **XmScrollBarSetValues(3X)**.

XmScrollBarGetValues

Purpose

A ScrollBar function that returns the ScrollBar's increment values and changes the slider's size and position.

Synopsis

#include <Xm/ScrollBar.h>

void XmScrollBarGetValues (*widget, value_return, slider_size_return, increment_return,*
page_increment_return)

```
Widget    widget;
int       * value_return;
int       * slider_size_return;
int       * increment_return;
int       * page_increment_return;
```

Description

XmScrollBarGetValues returns the the ScrollBar's increment values and changes the slider's size and position. The scroll region is overlaid with a slider bar that is adjusted in size and position using the main ScrollBar or set slider function attributes.

widget	Specifies the ScrollBar widget ID.
value_return	Returns the ScrollBar's slider position between the **XmNminimum** and **XmNmaximum** resources to the ScrollBar widget.
slider_size_return	Returns the size of the slider as a value between zero and the absolute value of **XmNmaximum** minus **XmNminimum**. The size of the slider varies, depending on how much of the slider scroll area it represents.
increment_return	Returns the amount of button increment and decrement.
page_increment_return	Returns the amount of page increment and decrement.

For a complete definition of ScrollBar and its associated resources, see **XmScrollBar(3X)**.

Return Value

Returns the ScrollBar's increment values and changes the slider's size and position.

Related Information

XmScrollBar(3X).

XmScrollBarSetValues

Purpose

A ScrollBar function that changes ScrollBar's increment values and the slider's size and position.

Synopsis

#include <Xm/ScrollBar.h>

void XmScrollBarSetValues (*widget, value, slider_size, increment, page_increment, notify*)

```
Widget    widget;
int       value;
int       slider_size;
int       increment;
int       page_increment;
Boolean   notify;
```

Description

XmSetScrollBarValues changes the ScrollBar's increment values and the slider's size and position. The scroll region is overlaid with a slider bar that is adjusted in size and position using the main ScrollBar or set slider function attributes.

widget Specifies the ScrollBar widget ID.

value Specifies the ScrollBar's slider position between **XmNminimum** and **XmNmaximum**. The resource name associated with this argument is **XmNvalue**.

slider_size Specifies the size of the slider as a value between zero and the absolute value of **XmNmaximum** minus **XmNminimum**. The size of the slider varies, depending on how much of the slider scroll area it represents. This sets the **XmNsliderSize** resource associated with ScrollBar.

increment Specifies the amount of button increment and decrement. If this argument is not zero, the ScrollBar widget automatically adjusts the slider when an increment or decrement action occurs. This sets the **XmNincrement** resource associated with ScrollBar.

page_increment
Specifies the amount of page increment and decrement. If this argument is not zero, the ScrollBar widget automatically adjusts the slider when an increment or decrement action occurs. This sets the **XmNpageIncrement** resource associated with ScrollBar.

notify Specifies a Boolean value that when True, indicates a change in the ScrollBar value and also specifies that the ScrollBar widget automatically activates the **XmNvalueChangedCallback** with the recent change. If False, no change has occurred in the ScrollBar's value, and **XmNvalueChangedCallback** is not activated.

For a complete definition of ScrollBar and its associated resources, see **XmScrollBar(3X)**.

Related Information

XmScrollBar(3X).

XmScrolledWindow

Purpose

The ScrolledWindow widget class

Synopsis

#include <Xm/ScrolledW.h>

Description

The ScrolledWindow widget combines one or more ScrollBar widgets and a viewing area to implement a visible window onto some other (usually larger) data display. The visible part of the window can be scrolled through the larger display by the use of ScrollBars.

To use ScrolledWindow, an application first creates a ScrolledWindow widget, any needed ScrollBar widgets, and a widget capable of displaying any desired data as the work area of ScrolledWindow. ScrolledWindow positions the work area widget and display the ScrollBars if so requested. When the user performs some action on the ScrollBar, the application is notified through the normal ScrollBar callback interface.

ScrolledWindow can be configured to operate automatically so that it performs all scrolling and display actions with no need for application program involvement. It can also be configured to provide a minimal support framework in which the application is responsible for processing all user input and making all visual changes to the displayed data in response to that input.

When ScrolledWindow is performing automatic scrolling it creates a clipping window. Conceptually, this window becomes the viewport through which the user examines the larger underlying data area. The application simply creates the desired data, then makes that data the work area of the ScrolledWindow. When the user moves the slider to change the displayed data, the workspace is moved under the viewing area so that a new portion of the data becomes visible.

Sometimes it is impractical for an application to create a large data space and simply display it through a small clipping window. For example, in a text editor, creating a single data area that consisted of a large file would involve an undesirable amount of overhead. The application needs to use a ScrolledWindow (a small viewport onto some larger data), but needs to be notified when the user scrolled the viewport so it could bring in more data from storage and update the display area. For these cases the ScrolledWindow can be configured so that it provides only visual layout support. No clipping window is created, and the application must maintain the data displayed in the work area, as well as respond to user input on the ScrollBars.

Classes

ScrolledWindow inherits behavior and resources from **Core**, **Composite**, **Constraint**, and **XmManager** Classes.

The class pointer is **xmScrolledWindowWidgetClass**.

The class name is **XmScrolledWindow**.

New Resources

The following table defines a set of widget resources used by the programmer to specify data. The programmer can also set the resource values for the inherited classes to set attributes for this widget. To reference a resource by name or by class in a .Xdefaults file, remove the **XmN** or **XmC** prefix and use the remaining letters. To specify one of the defined values for a resource in a .Xdefaults file, remove the **Xm** prefix and use the remaining letters (in either lowercase or uppercase, but include any underscores between words). The codes in the access column indicate if the given resource can be set at creation time (**C**), set by using **XtSetValues** (**S**), retrieved by using **XtGetValues** (**G**), or is not applicable (**N/A**).

XmScrolledWindow Resource Set		
Name **Class**	**Default** **Type**	**Access**
XmNclipWindow XmCClipWindow	NULL Widget	G
XmNhorizontalScrollBar XmCHorizontalScrollBar	NULL Widget	CSG
XmNscrollBarDisplayPolicy XmCScrollBarDisplayPolicy	XmSTATIC unsigned char	CG
XmNscrollBarPlacement XmCScrollBarPlacement	XmBOTTOM_RIGHT unsigned char	CSG
XmNscrolledWindowMarginHeight XmCScrolledWindowMarginHeight	0 Dimension	CSG
XmNscrolledWindowMarginWidth XmCScrolledWindowMarginWidth	0 Dimension	CSG
XmNscrollingPolicy XmCScrollingPolicy	XmAPPLICATION_DEFINED unsigned char	CG
XmNspacing XmCSpacing	4 Dimension	CSG
XmNverticalScrollBar XmCVerticalScrollBar	NULL Widget	CSG
XmNvisualPolicy XmCVisualPolicy	XmVARIABLE unsigned char	CG
XmNworkWindow XmCWorkWindow	NULL Widget	CSG

XmNclipWindow

Specifies the widget ID of the clipping area. This is automatically created by ScrolledWindow when the **XmNvisualPolicy** resource is set to **XmCONSTANT** and can be read only by the application. Any attempt to set this resource to a new value causes a warning message to be printed by the scrolled window. If the **XmNvisualPolicy** resource is set to **XmVARIABLE**, this resource is set to NULL, and no clipping window is created.

XmNhorizontalScrollBar
Specifies the widget ID of the horizontal ScrollBar.

XmNscrollBarDisplayPolicy
Controls the automatic placement of the ScrollBars. If it is set to **XmAS_NEEDED** and if **XmNscrollingPolicy** is set to **XmAUTOMATIC**, ScrollBars is displayed only if the workspace exceeds the clip area in one or both dimensions. A resource value of **XmSTATIC** causes the ScrolledWindow to display the ScrollBars whenever they are managed, regardless of the relationship between the clip window and the work area. This resource must be **XmSTATIC** when **XmNscrollingPolicy** is **XmAPPLICATION_DEFINED**.

XmNscrollBarPlacement
Specifies the positioning of the ScrollBars in relation to the work window. The following are the values:

- **XmTOP_LEFT** — The horizontal ScrollBar is placed above the work window; the vertical ScrollBar to the left.
- **XmBOTTOM_LEFT** — The horizontal ScrollBar is placed below the work window; the vertical ScrollBar to the left.
- **XmTOP_RIGHT** — The horizontal ScrollBar is placed above the work window; the vertical ScrollBar to the right.
- **XmBOTTOM_RIGHT** — The horizontal ScrollBar is placed below the work window; the vertical ScrollBar to the right.

XmNscrolledWindowMarginHeight
Specifies the margin height on the top and bottom of the ScrolledWindow.

XmNscrolledWindowMarginWidth
Specifies the margin width on the right and left sides of the ScrolledWindow.

XmNscrollingPolicy

Performs automatic scrolling of the work area with no application interaction. If the value of this resource is **XmAUTOMATIC**, ScrolledWindow automatically creates the ScrollBars; attaches callbacks to the ScrollBars; sets the visual policy to **XmCONSTANT**; and automatically moves the work area through the clip window in response to any user interaction with the ScrollBars. An application can also add its own callbacks to the ScrollBars. This allows the application to be notified of a scroll event without having to perform any layout procedures.

NOTE: Since the ScrolledWindow adds callbacks to the ScrollBars, an application should not perform an **XtRemoveAllCallbacks** on any of the ScrollBar widgets.

When **XmNscrollingPolicy** is set to **XmAPPLICATION_DEFINED**, the application is responsible for all aspects of scrolling. The ScrollBars must be created by the application, and it is responsible for performing any visual changes in the work area in response to user input.

This resource must be set to the desired policy at the time the ScrolledWindow is created. It cannot be changed through **SetValues**.

XmNspacing

Specifies the distance that separates the ScrollBars from the work window.

XmNverticalScrollBar

Specifies the widget ID of the vertical ScrollBar.

XmNvisualPolicy

Grows the ScrolledWindow to match the size of the work area, or it can be used as a static viewport onto a larger data space. If the visual policy is **XmVARIABLE**, the ScrolledWindow forces the ScrollBar display policy to **XmSTATIC** and allow the work area to grow or shrink at any time and adjusts its layout to accommodate the new size. When the policy is **XmCONSTANT**, the work area grows or shrinks as requested, but a clipping window forces the size of the visible portion to remain constant. The only time the viewing area can grow is in response to a resize from the ScrolledWindow's parent.

NOTE: This resource must be set to the desired policy at the time the ScrolledWindow is created. It cannot be changed through **SetValues**.

XmNworkWindow

Specifies the widget ID of the viewing area.

Inherited Resources

ScrolledWindow inherits behavior and resources from the following superclasses. For a complete description of each resource, refer to the man page for that superclass.

XmManager Resource Set		
Name **Class**	**Default** **Type**	**Access**
XmNbottomShadowColor XmCForeground	dynamic Pixel	CSG
XmNbottomShadowPixmap XmCBottomShadowPixmap	XmUNSPECIFIED_PIXMAP Pixmap	CSG
XmNforeground XmCForeground	dynamic Pixel	CSG
XmNhelpCallback XmCCallback	NULL XtCallbackList	C
XmNhighlightColor XmCForeground	Black Pixel	CSG
XmNhighlightPixmap XmCHighlightPixmap	dynamic Pixmap	CSG
XmNshadowThickness XmCShadowThickness	0 short	CSG
XmNtopShadowColor XmCBackground	dynamic Pixel	CSG
XmNtopShadowPixmap XmCTopShadowPixmap	XmUNSPECIFIED_PIXMAP Pixmap	CSG
XmNunitType XmCUnitType	XmPIXELS unsigned char	CSG
XmNuserData XmCUserData	NULL caddr_t	CSG

Composite Resource Set		
Name **Class**	**Default** **Type**	**Access**
XmNinsertPosition XmCInsertPosition	NULL XmRFunction	CSG

Core Resource Set		
Name **Class**	**Default** **Type**	**Access**
XmNaccelerators XmCAccelerators	NULL XtTranslations	CSG
XmNancestorSensitive XmCSensitive	True Boolean	G
XmNbackground XmCBackground	dynamic Pixel	CSG
XmNbackgroundPixmap XmCPixmap	XmUNSPECIFIED_PIXMAP Pixmap	CSG
XmNborderColor XmCBorderColor	Black Pixel	CSG

Name Class	Default Type	Access
XmNborderPixmap XmCPixmap	XmUNSPECIFIED_PIXMAP Pixmap	CSG
XmNborderWidth XmCBorderWidth	0 Dimension	CSG
XmNcolormap XmCColormap	XtCopyFromParent Colormap	CG
XmNdepth XmCDepth	XtCopyFromParent int	CG
XmNdestroyCallback XmCCallback	NULL XtCallbackList	C
XmNheight XmCHeight	0 Dimension	CSG
XmNmappedWhenManaged XmCMappedWhenManaged	True Boolean	CSG
XmNscreen XmCScreen	XtCopyScreen Pointer	CG
XmNsensitive XmCSensitive	True Boolean	CSG
XmNtranslations XmCTranslations	NULL XtTranslations	CSG
XmNwidth XmCWidth	0 Dimension	CSG
XmNx XmCPosition	0 Position	CSG
XmNy XmCPosition	0 Position	CSG

Callback Information

ScrolledWindow defines no new callback structures. The application must use the ScrollBar callbacks to be notified of user input.

Behavior

ScrolledWindow makes extensive use of the **XtQueryGeometry** functionality to facilitate geometry communication between application levels. In the **XmAPPLICATION_DEFINED** scrolling policy, the WorkWindow's query procedure is called by the ScrolledWindow whenever the ScrolledWindow is going to change its size. The widget calculates the largest possible workspace area and passes this size to the WorkWindow widget's query procedure. The query procedure can then examine this new size and determine if any changes, such as managing or unmanaging a ScrollBar, are necessary. The query procedure performs whatever actions it needs and then returns to the ScrolledWindow. The ScrolledWindow then examines the ScrollBars to see which (if any) are managed, allocates a portion of the visible space for them, and resizes the WorkWindow to fit in the rest of the space.

When the scrolling policy is **XmCONSTANT**, the ScrolledWindow can be queried to return the optimal size for a given dimension. The optimal size is defined to be the size that just encloses the WorkWindow. By using this mechanism, an application can size the ScrolledWindow so that it needs to display a ScrollBar only for one dimension. When the ScrolledWindow's query procedure is called via **XtQueryGeometry**, the request is examined to see if the width or height has been specified. If so, the routine uses the given dimension as the basis for its calculations. It determines the minimum value for the other dimension that just encloses the WorkWindow, fills in the appropriate elements in the reply structure, and returns to the calling program. Occasionally, using the specified width or height and the other minimum dimension results in neither ScrollBar appearing. When this happens, the query procedure sets both the width and height fields, indicating that in this situation the ideal size causes a change in both dimensions. If the calling application sets both the width and height fields, the ScrolledWindow determines the minimum size for both dimensions and return those values in the reply structure.

Keyboard Traversal

For information on keyboard traversal, see the man page for **XmManager(3X)** and its sections on behavior and default translations.

Related Information

Composite(3X), **Constraint(3X)**, **Core(3X)**, **XmCreateScrolledWindow(3X)**, **XmManager(3X)**, and **XmScrolledWindowSetAreas(3X)**.

XmScrolledWindowSetAreas

Purpose

A ScrolledWindow function that adds or changes a window work region and a horizontal or vertical ScrollBar widget to the ScrolledWindow widget.

Synopsis

#include <Xm/ScrolledW.h>

void XmScrolledWindowSetAreas (*widget, horizontal_scrollbar, vertical_scrollbar, work_region*)
    Widget *widget*;
    Widget *horizontal_scrollbar*;
    Widget *vertical_scrollbar*;
    Widget *work_region*;

Description

XmScrolledWindowSetAreas adds or changes a window work region and a horizontal or vertical ScrollBar widget to the ScrolledWindow widget for the application. Each widget is optional and may be passed as NULL.

widget Specifies the ScrolledWindow widget ID.

horizontal_scrollbar
Specifies the ScrollBar widget ID for the horizontal ScrollBar to be associated with the ScrolledWindow widget. Set this ID only after creating an instance of the ScrolledWindow widget. The resource name associated with this argument is **XmNhorizontalScrollBar**.

vertical_scrollbar Specifies the ScrollBar widget ID for the vertical ScrollBar to be associated with the ScrolledWindow widget. Set this ID only after creating an instance of the ScrolledWindow widget. The resource name associated with this argument is **XmNverticalScrollBar**.

work_region Specifies the widget ID for the work window to be associated with the ScrolledWindow widget. Set this ID only after creating an instance of the ScrolledWindow widget. The attribute name associated with this argument is **XmNworkWindow**.

For a complete definition of ScrolledWindow and its associated resources, see **XmScrolledWindow(3X)**.

Related Information

XmScrolledWindow(3X).

XmSelectionBox

Purpose

The SelectionBox widget class

Synopsis

#include <Xm/SelectioB.h>

Description

SelectionBox is a general dialog widget that allows the user to select one item from a list. A SelectionBox includes the following:

- A scrolling list of alternatives
- An editable text field for the selected alternative
- Labels for the list and text field
- Three buttons.

The default button labels are **OK**, **Cancel**, and **Help**. An **Apply** button is created unmanaged and may be explicitly managed as needed. One additional **WorkArea** child may be added to the SelectionBox after creation.

The user can select an item in two ways: by scrolling through the list and selecting the desired item or by entering the item name directly into the text edit area. Selecting an item from the list causes that item name to appear in the selection text edit area.

The user may select a new item as many times as desired. The item is not actually selected until the user presses the **OK** PushButton.

Classes

SelectionBox inherits behavior and resources from **Core**, **Composite**, **Constraint**, **XmManager**, and **XmBulletinBoard** Classes.

The class pointer is **xmSelectionBoxWidgetClass**.

The class name is **XmSelectionBox**.

New Resources

The following table defines a set of widget resources used by the programmer to specify data. The programmer can also set the resource values for the inherited classes to set attributes for this widget. To reference a resource by name or by class in a .Xdefaults file, remove the **XmN** or **XmC** prefix and use the remaining letters. To specify one of the defined values for a resource in a .Xdefaults file, remove the **Xm** prefix and use the remaining letters (in either lowercase or uppercase, but include any underscores between words). The codes in the access column indicate if the given resource can be set at creation time (**C**), set by using **XtSetValues** (**S**), retrieved by using **XtGetValues** (**G**), or is not applicable (**N/A**).

XmSelectionBox Resource Set		
Name **Class**	**Default** **Type**	**Access**
XmNapplyCallback XmCCallback	NULL XtCallbackList	C
XmNapplyLabelString XmCApplyLabelString	"Apply" XmString	CSG
XmNcancelCallback XmCCallback	NULL XtCallbackList	CSG
XmNcancelLabelString XmCXmString	"Cancel" XmString	CSG
XmNdialogType XmCDialogType	dynamic unsigned char	CG
XmNhelpLabelString XmCXmString	"Help" XmString	CSG
XmNlistItemCount XmCItemCount	0 int	CSG
XmNlistItems XmCItems	NULL XmStringList	CSG
XmNlistLabelString XmCXmString	NULL XmString	CSG
XmNlistVisibleItemCount XmCVisibleItemCount	8 int	CSG
XmNminimizeButtons XmCMinimizeButtons	False Boolean	CSG
XmNmustMatch XmCMustMatch	False Boolean	CSG
XmNnoMatchCallback XmCCallback	NULL XtCallbackList	C
XmNokCallback XmCCallback	NULL XtCallbackList	C

Name Class	Default Type	Access
XmNokLabelString XmCXmString	"OK" XmString	CSG
XmNselectionLabelString XmCXmString	"Selection" XmString	CSG
XmNtextAccelerators XmCTextAccelerators	see below XtTranslations	C
XmNtextColumns XmCTextColumns	20 int	CSG
XmNtextString XmCTextString	NULL XmString	CSG

XmNapplyCallback
Specifies the list of callbacks called when the user clicks on the **Apply** button. The callback reason is **XmCR_APPLY**.

XmNapplyLabelString
Specifies the string label for the **Apply** button.

XmNcancelCallback
Specifies the list of callbacks called when the user clicks on the **Cancel** button. The callback reason is **XmCR_CANCEL**.

XmNcancelLabelString
Specifies the string label for the **Cancel** button.

XmNdialogType
Determines the set of SelectionBox children widgets that are created and managed at initialization. The following are possible values:

- **XmDIALOG_PROMPT** — the list and list label are not created, and the **Apply** button is unmanaged
- **XmDIALOG_SELECTION** — all standard children are created and managed except the **Apply** button
- **XmDIALOG_WORK_AREA** — all standard children are created and managed

If the parent of the SelectionBox is a DialogShell, the default is **XmDIALOG_SELECTION**; otherwise, the default is **XmDIALOG_WORK_AREA**. **XmCreatePromptDialog** and **XmCreateSelectionDialog** set and append this resource to the creation *arglist* supplied by the application. This resource cannot be modified after creation.

XmNhelpLabelString
Specifies the string label for the **Help** button.

XmNlistItems
Specifies the items in the SelectionBox list.

XmNlistItemCount
Specifies the number of items in the SelectionBox list.

XmNlistLabelString
Specifies the string label to appear above the SelectionBox list containing the selection items.

XmNlistVisibleItemCount
Specifies the number of items displayed in the SelectionBox list.

XmNminimizeButtons
Sets the buttons to the width of the widest button and height of the tallest button if False. If True, button width and height are not modified.

XmNmustMatch
Specifies whether the selection widget should check if the user's selection in the text edit field has an exact match in the SelectionBox list. If the selection does not have an exact match, and **XmNmustMatch** is True, the **XmNnoMatchCallback** is activated. If the selection does have an exact match, either **XmNapplyCallback** or **XmNokCallback** is activated.

XmNnoMatchCallback
Specifies the list of callbacks called when the user makes a selection from the text edit field that does not have an exact match with any of the items in the list box. The callback reason is **XmCR_NO_MATCH**. Callbacks in this list are called only if XmNmustMatch is true.

XmNokCallback
Specifies the list of callbacks called when the user clicks the **OK** button. The callback reason is **XmCR_OK**.

XmNokLabelString
Specifies the string label for the **OK** button.

XmNselectionLabelString
Specifies the string label for the selection text edit field.

XmNtextAccelerators
Specifies translations added to the Text widget child of the SelectionBox. The default includes bindings for the up and down keys for auto selection of list items; it also includes the normal accelerator translations defined by BulletinBoard for dialog components.

XmNtextColumns
Specifies the number of columns in the Text widget.

XmNtextString
Specifies the text in the text edit selection field.

Inherited Resources

SelectionBox inherits behavior and resources from the following superclasses. For a complete description of each resource, refer to the man page for that superclass.

XmBulletinBoard Resource Set		
Name **Class**	**Default** **Type**	**Access**
XmNallowOverlap XmCAllowOverlap	True Boolean	CSG
XmNautoUnmanage XmCAutoUnmanage	True Boolean	CSG
XmNbuttonFontList XmCButtonFontList	NULL XmFontList	CSG
XmNcancelButton XmCWidget	Cancel button Widget	SG
XmNdefaultButton XmCWidget	OK button Widget	SG
XmNdefaultPosition XmCDefaultPosition	True Boolean	CSG
XmNdialogStyle XmCDialogStyle	dynamic unsigned char	CSG
XmNdialogTitle XmCXmString	NULL XmString	CSG
XmNfocusCallback XmCCallback	NULL XtCallbackList	C
XmNlabelFontList XmCLabelFontList	NULL XmFontList	CSG
XmNmapCallback XmCCallback	NULL XtCallbackList	C
XmNmarginHeight XmCMarginHeight	10 short	CSG
XmNmarginWidth XmCMarginWidth	10 short	CSG
XmNnoResize XmCNoResize	False Boolean	CSG

Name Class	Default Type	Access
XmNresizePolicy XmCResizePolicy	XmRESIZE_ANY unsigned char	CSG
XmNshadowType XmCShadowType	XmSHADOW_OUT unsigned char	CSG
XmNstringDirection XmCStringDirection	XmSTRING_DIRECTION_L_TO_R XmStringDirection	CSG
XmNtextFontList XmCTextFontList	NULL XmFontList	CSG
XmNtextTranslations XmCTranslations	NULL XtTranslations	C
XmNunmapCallback XmCCallback	NULL XtCallbackList	C

XmManager Resource Set		
Name **Class**	**Default** **Type**	**Access**
XmNbottomShadowColor XmCForeground	dynamic Pixel	CSG
XmNbottomShadowPixmap XmCBottomShadowPixmap	XmUNSPECIFIED_PIXMAP Pixmap	CSG
XmNforeground XmCForeground	dynamic Pixel	CSG
XmNhelpCallback XmCCallback	NULL XtCallbackList	C
XmNhighlightColor XmCForeground	Black Pixel	CSG
XmNhighlightPixmap XmCHighlightPixmap	dynamic Pixmap	CSG
XmNshadowThickness XmCShadowThickness	dynamic short	CSG
XmNtopShadowColor XmCBackground	dynamic Pixel	CSG
XmNtopShadowPixmap XmCTopShadowPixmap	XmUNSPECIFIED_PIXMAP Pixmap	CSG
XmNunitType XmCUnitType	XmPIXELS unsigned char	CSG
XmNuserData XmCUserData	NULL caddr_t	CSG

Composite Resource Set		
Name **Class**	**Default** **Type**	**Access**
XmNinsertPosition XmCInsertPosition	NULL XmRFunction	CSG

Core Resource Set		
Name **Class**	**Default** **Type**	**Access**
XmNaccelerators XmCAccelerators	NULL XtTranslations	CSG
XmNancestorSensitive XmCSensitive	True Boolean	G
XmNbackground XmCBackground	dynamic Pixel	CSG
XmNbackgroundPixmap XmCPixmap	XmUNSPECIFIED_PIXMAP Pixmap	CSG
XmNborderColor XmCBorderColor	Black Pixel	CSG
XmNborderPixmap XmCPixmap	XmUNSPECIFIED_PIXMAP Pixmap	CSG

Name Class	Default Type	Access
XmNborderWidth XmCBorderWidth	0 Dimension	CSG
XmNcolormap XmCColormap	XtCopyFromParent Colormap	CG
XmNdepth XmCDepth	XtCopyFromParent int	CG
XmNdestroyCallback XmCCallback	NULL XtCallbackList	C
XmNheight XmCHeight	0 Dimension	CSG
XmNmappedWhenManaged XmCMappedWhenManaged	True Boolean	CSG
XmNscreen XmCScreen	XtCopyScreen Pointer	CG
XmNsensitive XmCSensitive	True Boolean	CSG
XmNtranslations XmCTranslations	NULL XtTranslations	CSG
XmNwidth XmCWidth	0 Dimension	CSG
XmNx XmCPosition	0 Position	CSG
XmNy XmCPosition	0 Position	CSG

Callback Information

The following structure is returned with each callback:

```
typedef struct
{
    int            reason;
    XEvent         * event;
    XmString       value;
    int            length;
} XmSelectionBoxCallbackStruct;
```

reason	Indicates why the callback was invoked
event	Points to the **XEvent** that triggered the callback
value	Indicates the **XmString** value selected by the user from the SelectionBox list or entered into the SelectionBox text field
length	Indicates the size in bytes of the **XmString** value

Behavior

The following is a summary of the behavior of SelectionBox.

<OK Button Activated>:

When the **OK** button is activated, the callback **XmNokCallback** is called. The reason is **XmCR_OK**. When an invalid selection is made and it does not match any items in the list, the callback for **XmNnoMatchCallback** is called if **XmNmustMatch** is also True. The callback reason is **XmCR_NO_MATCH.**

<Apply Button Activated>:
When the **Apply** button is activated, the callback **XmNapplyCallback** is called. The callback reason is **XmCR_APPLY**. When an invalid selection is made and it does not match any items in the list, the callback for **XmNnoMatchCallback** is called, if **XmNmustMatch** is also True. The callback reason is **XmCR_NO_MATCH.**

<Cancel Button Activated>:
When the **Cancel** button is activated, the callback **XmNcancelCallback** is called. The callback reason is **XmCR_CANCEL**.

<Help Button Activated> or **<Key>F1**:
When the Help button or **Function key 1** is pressed, the callbacks for **XmNhelpCallback** are called.

<Default Button Activated> or **<Key>Return**:
When the default button or return key is pressed, the corresponding callback is called (**XmNokCallback**, **XmNapplyCallback**, **XmNcancelCallback**, or **XmNhelpCallback**).

<Key>Up or **<Key>Down**:
When the up or down key is pressed within the Text subwidget of the SelectionBox, the text value is replaced with the previous or next item in the List subwidget.

<FocusIn>: When a **FocusIn** event is generated on the widget window, the callbacks for **XmNfocusCallback** are called.

<MapWindow>:
When a SelectionBox that is the child of a DialogShell is mapped, the callbacks for **XmNmapCallback** are invoked. When a SelectionBox that is not the child of a DialogShell is mapped, the callbacks are not invoked.

<UnmapWindow>:
When a SelectionBox that is the child of a DialogShell is unmapped, the callbacks for **XmNunmapCallback** are invoked. When a SelectionBox that is not the child of a DialogShell is unmapped, the callbacks are not invoked.

Default Translations

The following are the default translations defined for SelectionBox widgets:

```
<EnterWindow>:   Enter()
<FocusIn>:       FocusIn()
<Btn1Down>:      Arm()
<Btn1Up>:        Activate()
<Key>F1:         Help()
<Key>Return:     Return()
<Key>KP_Enter:   Return()
```

Default Accelerators

The following are the default accelerator translations added to the descendants of a SelectionBox:

#override	
<Key>F1:	**Help()**
<Key>Return:	**Return()**
<Key>KP_Enter:	**Return()**

Default Text Accelerators

The following are the default accelerators added to the Text child of the SelectionBox:

#override	
<Key>Up:	**UpOrDown(0)**
<Key>Down:	**UpOrDown(1)**
<Key>F1:	**Help()**
<Key>Return:	**Return()**
<Key>KP_Enter:	**Return()**

Keyboard Traversal

For information on keyboard traversal, see the man page for **XmManager(3X)** and its sections on behavior and default translations.

Related Information

Composite(3X), **Constraint(3X)**, **Core(3X)**, **XmBulletinBoard(3X)**, **XmCreateSelectionBox(3X)**, **XmCreateSelectionDialog(3X)**, **XmCreatePromptDialog(3X)**, **XmManager(3X)**, and **XmSelectionBoxGetChild(3X)**.

XmSelectionBoxGetChild

Purpose

A SelectionBox function that is used to access a component.

Synopsis

#include <Xm/SelectioB.h>

Widget XmSelectionBoxGetChild (*widget, child*)

Widget *widget*;
unsigned char*child*;

Description

XmSelectionBoxGetChild is used to access a component within a SelectionBox. The parameters given to the function are the SelectionBox widget and a value indicating which child to access.

widget Specifies the SelectionBox widget ID.

child Specifies a component within the SelectionBox. The following are legal values for this parameter:

- **XmDIALOG_APPLY_BUTTON**
- **XmDIALOG_CANCEL_BUTTON**
- **XmDIALOG_DEFAULT_BUTTON**
- **XmDIALOG_HELP_BUTTON**
- **XmDIALOG_LIST**
- **XmDIALOG_LIST_LABEL**
- **XmDIALOG_OK_BUTTON**
- **XmDIALOG_SELECTION_LABEL**
- **XmDIALOG_SEPARATOR**
- **XmDIALOG_TEXT**
- **XmDIALOG_WORK_AREA**

For a complete definition of SelectionBox and its associated resources, see **XmSelectionBox(3X)**.

Return Value

Returns the widget ID of the specified SelectionBox child.

Related Information

XmSelectionBox(3X).

XmSeparator

Purpose

The Separator widget class

Synopsis

#include <Xm/Separator.h>

Description

Separator is a primitive widget that separates items in a display. Several different line drawing styles are provided, as well as horizontal or vertical orientation.

The Separator line drawing is automatically centered within the height of the widget for a horizontal orientation and centered within the width of the widget for a vertical orientation. An **XtSetValues** with a new **XmNseparatorType** resizes the widget to its minimal height (for horizontal orientation) or its minimal width (for vertical orientation) unless height or width is explicitly set in the **XtSetValues** call.

Separator does not draw shadows. The Primitive resource **XmNshadowThickness** is used for the Separator's thickness when **XmNshadowType** is **XmSHADOW_ETCHED_IN** or **XmSHADOW_ETCHED_OUT**.

Separator does not highlight and allows no traversing. The primitive resource **XmNtraversalOn** is forced to False.

The **XmNseparatorType** of **XmNO_LINE** provides an escape to the application programmer who needs a different style of drawing. A pixmap the height of the widget can be created and used as the background pixmap by building an argument list using the **XmNbackgroundPixmap** argument type as defined by **Core**. Whenever the widget is redrawn, its background is displayed containing the desired separator drawing.

Classes

Separator inherits behavior and resources from **Core** and **XmPrimitive** Classes.

The class pointer is **xmSeparatorWidgetClass**.

The class name is **XmSeparator**.

New Resources

The following table defines a set of widget resources used by the programmer to specify data. The programmer can also set the resource values for the inherited classes to set attributes for this widget. To reference a resource by name or by class in a .Xdefaults file, remove the **XmN** or **XmC** prefix and use the remaining letters. To specify one of the defined values for a resource in a .Xdefaults file, remove the **Xm** prefix and use the remaining letters (in either lowercase or uppercase, but include any underscores between words). The codes in the access column indicate if the given resource can be set at creation time (**C**), set by using **XtSetValues** (**S**), retrieved by using **XtGetValues** (**G**), or is not applicable (**N/A**).

XmSeparator Resource Set		
Name **Class**	**Default** **Type**	**Access**
XmNmargin XmCMargin	0 short	CSG
XmNorientation XmCOrientation	XmHORIZONTAL unsigned char	CSG
XmNseparatorType XmCSeparatorType	XmSHADOW_ETCHED_IN unsigned char	CSG

XmNmargin
For horizontal orientation, specifies the space on the left and right sides between the border of the Separator and the line drawn. For vertical orientation, specifies the space on the top and bottom between the border of the Separator and the line drawn.

XmNorientation
Displays Separator vertically or horizontally. This resource can have values of **XmVERTICAL** and **XmHORIZONTAL**.

XmNseparatorType
Specifies the type of line drawing to be done in the Separator widget.

- **XmSINGLE_LINE** — single line.
- **XmDOUBLE_LINE** — double line.
- **XmSINGLE_DASHED_LINE** — single-dashed line.
- **XmDOUBLE_DASHED_LINE** — double-dashed line.
- **XmNO_LINE** — no line.
- **XmSHADOW_ETCHED_IN** — double line giving the effect of a line etched into the window. The thickness of the double line is equal to the value of **XmNshadowThickness**. For horizontal orientation, the top line is drawn in **XmNtopShadowColor** and the bottom line is drawn in **XmNbottomShadowColor**. For vertical

orientation, the left line is drawn in **XmNtopShadowColor** and the right line is drawn in **XmNbottomShadowColor**.

- **XmSHADOW_ETCHED_OUT** — double line giving the effect of an etched line coming out from the window. The thickness of the double line is equal to the value of **XmNshadowThickness**. For horizontal orientation, the top line is drawn in **XmNbottomShadowColor** and the bottom line is drawn in **XmNtopShadowColor**. For vertical orientation, the left line is drawn in **XmNbottomShadowColor** and the right line is drawn in **XmNtopShadowColor**.

Inherited Resources

Separator inherits behavior and resources from the following superclasses. For a complete description of each resource, refer to the man page for that superclass.

XmPrimitive Resource Set		
Name **Class**	**Default** **Type**	**Access**
XmNbottomShadowColor XmCForeground	dynamic Pixel	CSG
XmNbottomShadowPixmap XmCBottomShadowPixmap	XmUNSPECIFIED_PIXMAP Pixmap	CSG
XmNforeground XmCForeground	dynamic Pixel	CSG
XmNhelpCallback XmCCallback	NULL XtCallbackList	C
XmNhighlightColor XmCForeground	Black Pixel	CSG
XmNhighlightOnEnter XmCHighlightOnEnter	False Boolean	CSG
XmNhighlightPixmap XmCHighlightPixmap	dynamic Pixmap	CSG
XmNhighlightThickness XmCHighlightThickness	0 short	CSG
XmNshadowThickness XmCShadowThickness	2 short	CSG
XmNtopShadowColor XmCBackground	dynamic Pixel	CSG
XmNtopShadowPixmap XmCTopShadowPixmap	XmUNSPECIFIED_PIXMAP Pixmap	CSG
XmNtraversalOn XmCTraversalOn	False Boolean	CSG
XmNunitType XmCUnitType	XmPIXELS unsigned char	CSG
XmNuserData XmCUserData	NULL caddr_t	CSG

Core Resource Set		
Name **Class**	**Default** **Type**	**Access**
XmNaccelerators XmCAccelerators	NULL XtTranslations	CSG
XmNancestorSensitive XmCSensitive	True Boolean	G
XmNbackground XmCBackground	dynamic Pixel	CSG
XmNbackgroundPixmap XmCPixmap	XmUNSPECIFIED_PIXMAP Pixmap	CSG
XmNborderColor XmCBorderColor	Black Pixel	CSG
XmNborderPixmap XmCPixmap	XmUNSPECIFIED_PIXMAP Pixmap	CSG
XmNborderWidth XmCBorderWidth	0 Dimension	CSG
XmNcolormap XmCColormap	XtCopyFromParent Colormap	CG
XmNdepth XmCDepth	XtCopyFromParent int	CG
XmNdestroyCallback XmCCallback	NULL XtCallbackList	C
XmNheight XmCHeight	0 Dimension	CSG
XmNmappedWhenManaged XmCMappedWhenManaged	True Boolean	CSG
XmNscreen XmCScreen	XtCopyScreen Pointer	CG
XmNsensitive XmCSensitive	True Boolean	CSG

Name Class	Default Type	Access
XmNtranslations XmCTranslations	NULL XtTranslations	CSG
XmNwidth XmCWidth	0 Dimension	CSG
XmNx XmCPosition	0 Position	CSG
XmNy XmCPosition	0 Position	CSG

Keyboard Traversal

For information on keyboard traversal, see the man page for **XmPrimitive(3X)** and its sections on behavior and default translations.

Related Information

Core(3X), **XmCreateSeparator(3X)**, and **XmPrimitive(3X)**.

XmSeparatorGadget

Purpose

The SeparatorGadget widget class

Synopsis

#include <Xm/SeparatoG.h>

Description

SeparatorGadget separates items in a display. Several line drawing styles are provided, as well as horizontal or vertical orientation.

Lines drawn within the SeparatorGadget are automatically centered within the height of the gadget for a horizontal orientation and centered within the width of the gadget for a vertical orientation. An **XtSetValues** with a new **XmNseparatorType** resizes the widget to its minimal height (for horizontal orientation) or its minimal width (for vertical orientation) unless height or width is explicitly set in the **XtSetValues** call.

SeparatorGadget does not draw shadows. The Gadget resource **XmNshadowThickness** is used for the SeparatorGadget's thickness when **XmNshadowType** is **XmSHADOW_ETCHED_IN** or **XmSHADOW_ETCHED_OUT**.

SeparatorGadget does not highlight and allows no traversing. The Gadget resource **XmNtraversalOn** is forced to False.

Classes

SeparatorGadget inherits behavior and resources from **Object**, **RectObj**, and **XmGadget** Classes.

The class pointer is **xmSeparatorGadgetClass**.

The class name is **XmSeparatorGadget**.

New Resources

The following table defines a set of widget resources used by the programmer to specify data. The programmer can also set the resource values for the inherited classes to set attributes for this widget. To reference a resource by name or by class in a .Xdefaults file, remove the **XmN** or **XmC** prefix and use the remaining letters. To specify one of the defined values for a resource in a .Xdefaults file, remove the **Xm** prefix and use the remaining letters (in either lowercase or uppercase, but include any underscores between words). The codes in the access column indicate if the given resource can be set at creation time (**C**), set by using **XtSetValues** (**S**), retrieved by using **XtGetValues** (**G**), or is not applicable (**N/A**).

XmSeparatorGadget Resource Set		
Name **Class**	**Default** **Type**	**Access**
XmNmargin XmCMargin	0 short	CSG
XmNorientation XmCOrientation	XmHORIZONTAL unsigned char	CSG
XmNseparatorType XmCSeparatorType	XmSHADOW_ETCHED_IN unsigned char	CSG

XmNmargin

For horizontal orientation, specifies the space on the left and right sides between the border of SeparatorGadget and the line drawn. For vertical orientation, specifies the space on the top and bottom between the border of SeparatorGadget and the line drawn.

XmNorientation
Specifies whether SeparatorGadget is displayed vertically or horizontally. This resource can have values of **XmVERTICAL** and **XmHORIZONTAL**.

XmNseparatorType
Specifies the type of line drawing to be done in the Separator widget.

- **XmSINGLE_LINE** — single line.
- **XmDOUBLE_LINE** — double line.
- **XmSINGLE_DASHED_LINE** — single-dashed line.
- **XmDOUBLE_DASHED_LINE** — double-dashed line.
- **XmNO_LINE** — no line.
- **XmSHADOW_ETCHED_IN** — double line giving the effect of a line etched into the window. The thickness of the double line is equal to the value of **XmNshadowThickness**. For horizontal orientation, the top line is drawn in **XmNtopShadowColor** and the bottom line is drawn in **XmNbottomShadowColor**. For vertical orientation, the left line is drawn in **XmNtopShadowColor** and the right line is drawn in **XmNbottomShadowColor**.
- **XmSHADOW_ETCHED_OUT** — double line giving the effect of an etched line coming out from the window. The thickness of the double line is equal to the value of **XmNshadowThickness**. For horizontal orientation, the top line is drawn in **XmNbottomShadowColor** and the bottom line is drawn in **XmNtopShadowColor**. For vertical orientation, the left line is drawn in **XmNbottomShadowColor** and the right line is drawn in **XmNtopShadowColor**.

Inherited Resources

SeparatorGadget inherits behavior and resources from the following superclasses. For a complete description of each resource, refer to the man page for that superclass.

XmGadget Resource Set		
Name **Class**	**Default** **Type**	**Access**
XmNhelpCallback XmCCallback	NULL XtCallbackList	C
XmNhighlightOnEnter XmCHighlightOnEnter	False Boolean	CSG
XmNhighlightThickness XmCHighlightThickness	0 short	CSG
XmNshadowThickness XmCShadowThickness	2 short	CSG
XmNtraversalOn XmCTraversalOn	False Boolean	CSG
XmNunitType XmCUnitType	XmPIXELS unsigned char	CSG
XmNuserData XmCUserData	NULL caddr_t	CSG

RectObj Resource Set		
Name **Class**	**Default** **Type**	**Access**
XmNancestorSensitive XmCSensitive	XtCopyFromParent Boolean	CSG
XmNborderWidth XmCBorderWidth	1 Dimension	CSG
XmNheight XmCHeight	0 Dimension	CSG
XmNsensitive XmCSensitive	True Boolean	CSG
XmNwidth XmCWidth	0 Dimension	CSG
XmNx XmCPosition	0 Position	CSG
XmNy XmCPosition	0 Position	CSG

Object Resource Set		
Name **Class**	**Default** **Type**	**Access**
XmNdestroyCallback XmCCallback	NULL XtCallbackList	C

Keyboard Traversal

For information on keyboard traversal, see the man page for **XmGadget(3X)** and its sections on behavior and default translations.

Related Information

Object(3X), **RectObject(3X)**, **XmCreateSeparatorGadget(3X)**, and **XmGadget(3X)**.

XmSetFontUnit

Purpose

A function that sets the font unit value for a display.

Synopsis

#include <Xm/Xm.h>

void XmSetFontUnit (*display, font_unit_value*)
    Display   *display*;
    int   *font_unit_value*;

Description

XmSetFontUnit provides an external function to initialize font unit values. Applications may want to specify resolution-independent data based on a global font size. This function must be called before any widgets with resolution-independent data are created. See the **XmNunitType** resource description in the man pages for **XmGadget**, **XmManager**, and **XmPrimitive** for more information on resolution independence.

display Defines the display for which this font unit value is to be applied.

font_unit_value Specifies the value to be used in the conversion calculations. The font unit value is normally taken as the **QUAD_WIDTH** property of the font; however, the application can specify any integer value.

Related Information

XmConvertUnits(3X).

XmSetMenuCursor

Purpose

A RowColumn function that modifies the menu cursor for a client.

Synopsis

void XmSetMenuCursor (*display, cursorId*)
    Display * *display*;
    Cursor *cursorId*;

Description

XmSetMenuCursor programmatically modifies the menu cursor for a client; after the cursor has been created by the client, this function registers the cursor with the menu system. After calling this function, the specified cursor is displayed whenever this client displays a Motif menu on the indicated display. The client can then specify different cursors on different displays.

display Specifies the display to which the cursor is to be associated

cursorId Specifies the **X** cursor ID

For a complete definition of the menu cursor resource, see **XmRowColumn(3X)**.

Related Information

XmRowColumn(3X).

XmSetProtocolHooks

Purpose

A VendorShell function that allows pre and post actions to be executed when a protocol message is received from MWM.

Synopsis

#include <Xm/Xm.h>
#include <X11/Protocols.h>

void XmSetProtocolHooks (*shell, property, protocol, prehook, pre_closure, posthook, post_closure*)
Widget *shell*;
Atom *property*;
Atom *protocol*;
XtCallbackProc *prehook*;
caddr_t *pre_closure*;
XtCallbackProc *posthook*;
caddr_t *post_closure*;

void XmSetWMProtocolHooks (*shell, protocol, prehook, pre_closure, posthook, post_closure*)
Widget *shell*;
Atom *protocol*;
XtCallbackProc *prehook*;
caddr_t *pre_closure*;
XtCallbackProc *posthook*;
caddr_t *post_closure*;

Description

XmSetProtocolHooks is used by shells that want to have pre and post actions executed when a protocol message is received from MWM. Since there is no guaranteed ordering in execution of event handlers or callback lists, this allows the shell to control the flow while leaving the protocol manager structures opaque.

XmSetWMProtocolHooks is a convenience interface. It calls **XmSetProtocolHooks** with the property value set to the atom returned by interning **WM_PROTOCOLS**.

shell Specifies the widget with which the protocol property is associated

property Specifies the protocol property

protocol Specifies the protocol atom (or an int cast to Atom)

prehook Specifies the procedure to call before calling entries on the client callback-list

pre_closure Specifies the client data to be passed to the prehook when it is invoked

posthook Specifies the procedure to call after calling entries on the client callback-list

post_closure Specifies the client data to be passed to the posthook when it is invoked

For a complete definition of VendorShell and its associated resources, see **VendorShell(3X)**.

Related Information

VendorShell(3X), **XmInternAtom(3X)**, and **XmSetWMProtocolHooks(3X)**.

XmSetWMProtocolHooks

Purpose

A VendorShell convenience interface that allows pre and post actions to be executed when a protocol message is received from the window manager.

Synopsis

#include <Xm/Xm.h>
#include <X11/Protocols.h>

void XmSetWMProtocolHooks (*shell, protocol, prehook, pre_closure, posthook, post_closure*)
    Widget *shell*;
    Atom *protocol*;
    XtCallbackProc*prehook*;
    caddr_t *pre_closure*;
    XtCallbackProc*posthook*;
    caddr_t *post_closure*;

Description

XmSetWMProtocolHooks is a convenience interface. It calls **XmSetProtocolHooks** with the property value set to the atom returned by interning **WM_PROTOCOLS**.

shell	Specifies the widget with which the protocol property is associated
protocol	Specifies the protocol atom (or an int cast to Atom)
prehook	Specifies the procedure to call before calling entries on the client callback-list
pre_closure	Specifies the client data to be passed to the prehook when it is invoked
posthook	Specifies the procedure to call after calling entries on the client callback-list
post_closure	Specifies the client data to be passed to the posthook when it is invoked

For a complete definition of VendorShell and its associated resources, see **VendorShell(3X)**.

Related Information

VendorShell(3X), **XmInternAtom(3X)**, and **XmSetProtocolHooks(3X)**.

XmStringBaseline

Purpose

A compound string function that returns the number of pixels between the top of the character box and the baseline of the first line of text.

Synopsis

#include <Xm/Xm.h>

Dimension XmStringBaseline (*fontlist, string*)
    XmFontList *fontlist*;
    XmString *string*;

Description

XmStringBaseline returns the number of pixels between the top of the character box and the baseline of the first line of text in the provided compound string.

fontlist Specifies the font list

string Specifies the string

Return Value

Returns the number of pixels between the top of the character box and the baseline of the first line of text.

Related Information

XmStringCreate(3X).

XmStringByteCompare

Purpose

A compound string function that indicates the results of a byte-by-byte comparison.

Synopsis

#include <Xm/Xm.h>

Boolean XmStringByteCompare (*s1, s2*)
    XmString *s1*;
    XmString *s2*;

Description

XmStringByteCompare returns a Boolean indicating the results of a byte-by-byte comparison of two compound strings. In some cases, once a compound string is put into a widget, that string is converted into an internal form to allow faster processing. Part of the conversion process strips out unnecessary or redundant information. If an application then does an **XtGetValues** to retrieve a compound string from a widget (specifically, Label and all of its subclasses), it is not guaranteed that the compound string returned is byte-for-byte the same as the string given to the widget originally.

s1 Specifies a compound string to be compared with *s2*

s2 Specifies a compound string to be compared with *s1*

Return Value

Returns True if two compound strings are identical byte-by-byte.

Related Information

XmStringCreate(3X).

XmStringCompare

Purpose

A compound string function that compares two strings

Synopsis

#include <Xm/Xm.h>

Boolean XmStringCompare (*s1*, *s2*)
    XmString *s1*;
    XmString *s2*;

Description

XmStringCompare returns a Boolean value indicating the results of a semantically equivalent comparison of two compound strings.

Semantically equivalent means that the strings have the same text components, directions, and separators. If character sets are specified, they must be equal as well. If either string has a character set of **XmSTRING_DEFAULT_CHARSET**, its character set matches the other string's character set.

s1 Specifies a compound string to be compared with *s2*

s2 Specifies a compound string to be compared with *s1*

Return Value

Returns True if two compound strings are equivalent.

Related Information

XmStringCreate(3X).

XmStringConcat

Purpose

A compound string function that appends one string to another.

Synopsis

```
#include <Xm/Xm.h>

XmString XmStringConcat (s1, s2)
        XmString   s1;
        XmString   s2;
```

Description

XmStringConcat appends *s2* to the end of *s1* and returns the resulting compound string. The original strings are preserved. The space for the resulting compound string is allocated within the function. After using this function, free this space by calling **XmStringFree**.

s1 Specifies the compound string to which a copy of *s2* is appended

s2 Specifies the compound string that is appended to the end of *s1*

Return Value

Returns a new compound string.

Related Information

XmStringCreate(3X) and **XmStringFree(3X)**.

XmStringCopy

Purpose

A compound string function that makes a copy of a string.

Synopsis

```
#include <Xm/Xm.h>

XmString XmStringCopy (s1)
      XmString    s1;
```

Description

XmStringCopy makes a copy of a compound string. The space for the resulting compound string is allocated within the function. The application is responsible for managing the allocated space. The memory can be recovered by calling **XmStringFree**.

s1 Specifies the compound string to be copied

Return Value

Returns a new compound string.

Related Information

XmStringCreate(3X) and **XmStringFree(3X)**.

XmStringCreate

Purpose

A compound string function that creates a compound string.

Synopsis

#include <Xm/Xm.h>

XmString XmStringCreate (*text, charset*)
  char * *text*;
  XmStringCharSet*charset*;

Description

XmStringCreate creates a compound string with two components: text and a character set.

text Specifies a pointer to a null terminated string.

charset Specifies the character set identifier to be associated with the given text. This can be **XmSTRING_DEFAULT_CHARSET**.

Return Value

Returns a new compound string.

Related Information

XmFontListAdd(3X), **XmFontListCreate(3X)**, **XmFontListFree(3X)**, **XmStringBaseline(3X)**, **XmStringByteCompare(3X)**, **XmStringCompare(3X)**, **XmStringConcat(3X)**, **XmStringCopy(3X)**, **XmStringCreateLtoR(3X)**, **XmStringDirectionCreate(3X)**, **XmStringDraw(3X)**, **XmStringDrawImage(3X)**, **XmStringDrawUnderline(3X)**, **XmStringEmpty(3X)**, **XmStringExtent(3X)**, **XmStringFree(3X)**, **XmStringFreeContext(3X)**, **XmStringGetLtoR(3X)**, **XmStringGetNextComponent(3X)**, **XmStringGetNextSegment(3X)**, **XmStringHeight(3X)**, **XmStringInitContext(3X)**, **XmStringLength(3X)**, **XmStringLineCount(3X)**, **XmStringNConcat(3X)**, **XmStringNCopy(3X)**, **XmStringPeekNextComponent(3X)**, **XmStringSegmentCreate(3X)**, **XmStringSeparatorCreate(3X)**, and **XmStringWidth(3X)**.

XmStringCreateLtoR

Purpose

A compound string function that creates a compound string.

Synopsis

#include <Xm/Xm.h>

XmString XmStringCreateLtoR (*text, charset*)
    char * *text*;
    XmStringCharSet*charset*;

Description

XmStringCreateLtoR creates a compound string with two components: text and a character set. This function imposes the semantic of scanning for **\n** characters in the text. When one is found, the text up to that point is put into a segment followed by a separator component. No final separator component is appended to the end of the compound string. The direction defaults to left-to-right. This function assumes that the encoding is single octet rather than double octet per character of text.

text Specifies a pointer to a null terminated string.

charset Specifies the character set identifier to be associated with the given text. This can be **XmSTRING_DEFAULT_CHARSET**.

Return Value

Returns a new compound string.

Related Information

XmStringCreate(3X).

XmStringDirectionCreate

Purpose

A compound string function that creates a compound string.

Synopsis

#include <Xm/Xm.h>

XmString XmStringDirectionCreate (*direction*)
XmStringDirection*direction*;

Description

XmStringDirectionCreate creates a compound string with a single component, a direction with the given value.

direction Specifies the value of the directional component

Return Value

Returns a new compound string.

Related Information

XmStringCreate(3X).

XmStringDraw

Purpose

A compound string function that draws a compound string in an X window.

Synopsis

#include <Xm/Xm.h>

void XmStringDraw (*d, w, fontlist, string, gc, x, y, width, alignment, layout_direction, clip*)

Display	* *d*;
Window	*w*;
XmFontList	*fontlist*;
XmString	*string*;
GC	*gc*;
Position	*x*;
Position	*y*;
Dimension	*width*;
Byte	*alignment*;
Byte	*layout_direction*;
XRectangle	* *clip*;

Description

XmStringDraw draws a compound string in an X Window.

d Specifies the display.

w Specifies the window.

fontlist Specifies the font list.

string Specifies the string.

gc Specifies the graphics context to use.

x Specifies a coordinate of the rectangle that will contain the displayed compound string.

y Specifies a coordinate of the rectangle that will contain the displayed compound string.

width Specifies the width of the rectangle that will contain the displayed compound string.

alignment Specifies how the string will be aligned within the specified rectangle. It is either **XmALIGNMENT_BEGINNING**, **XmALIGNMENT_CENTER**, or **XmALIGNMENT_END**.

layout_direction
Controls the direction in which the segments of the compound string will be laid out. It also determines the meaning of the *alignment* parameter.

clip Allows the application to restrict the area into which the compound string will be drawn. If NULL, no clipping will be done.

Related Information

XmStringCreate(3X).

XmStringDrawImage

Purpose

A compound string function that draws a compound string in an X Window and creates an image.

Synopsis

#include <Xm/Xm.h>

void XmStringDrawImage (*d, w, fontlist, string, gc, x, y, width, alignment, layout_direction, clip*)

```
        Display      * d;
        Window       w;
        XmFontList   fontlist;
        XmString     string;
        GC           gc;
        Position     x;
        Position     y;
        Dimension    width;
        Byte         alignment;
        Byte         layout_direction;
        XRectangle   * clip;
```

Description

XmStringDrawImage draws a compound string in an X Window and paints both the foreground and background bits of each character.

d Specifies the display.

w Specifies the window.

fontlist Specifies the font list.

string Specifies the string.

gc Specifies the graphics context to use.

x Specifies a coordinate of the rectangle that will contain the displayed compound string.

y Specifies a coordinate of the rectangle that will contain the displayed compound string.

width Specifies the width of the rectangle that will contain the displayed compound string.

alignment Specifies how the string will be aligned within the specified rectangle. It is either **XmALIGNMENT_BEGINNING**, **XmALIGNMENT_CENTER**, or **XmALIGNMENT_END**.

layout_direction
Controls the direction in which the segments of the compound string will be laid out. It also determines the meaning of the *alignment* parameter.

clip Allows the application to restrict the area into which the compound string will be drawn. If NULL, no clipping will be done.

Related Information

XmStringCreate(3X).

XmStringDrawUnderline

Purpose

A compound string function that underlines a string drawn in an X Window.

Synopsis

#include <Xm/Xm.h>

void XmStringDrawUnderline (*d, w, fontlist, string, gc, x, y, width, alignment, layout_direction, clip, underline*)

Display	* *d*;
Window	*w*;
XmFontList	*fontlist*;
XmString	*string*;
GC	*gc*;
Position	*x*;
Position	*y*;
Dimension	*width*;
Byte	*alignment*;
Byte	*layout_direction*;
XRectangle	* *clip*;
XmString	*underline*;

Description

XmStringDrawUnderline draws a compound string in an X Window. If the substring identified by *underline* can be matched in *string*, the substring will be underlined. Once a match has occurred, no further matches or underlining will be done.

d Specifies the display.

w Specifies the window.

fontlist Specifies the font list.

string Specifies the string.

gc Specifies the graphics context to use.

x Specifies a coordinate of the rectangle that will contain the displayed compound string.

y Specifies a coordinate of the rectangle that will contain the displayed compound string.

width Specifies the width of the rectangle that will contain the displayed compound string.

alignment Specifies how the string will be aligned within the specified rectangle. It is one of **XmALIGNMENT_BEGINNING**, **XmALIGNMENT_CENTER**, or **XmALIGNMENT_END**.

layout_direction
Controls the direction in which the segments of the compound string will be laid out. It also determines the meaning of the *alignment* parameter.

clip Allows the application to restrict the area into which the compound string will be drawn. If NULL, no clipping will be done.

underline Specifies the substring to be underlined.

Related Information

XmStringCreate(3X).

XmStringEmpty

Purpose

A compound string function that provides information on the existence of non-zero length text components.

Synopsis

#include <Xm/Xm.h>

Boolean XmStringEmpty (*s1*)
  XmString *s1*;

Description

XmStringEmpty returns a Boolean value indicating whether any non-zero length text components exist in the provided compound string. It returns True if there are no text segments in the string. If this routine is passed NULL as the string, it returns True.

s1 Specifies the compound string

Return Value

Returns True if there are no text segments in the string. If this routine is passed NULL as the string, it returns True.

Related Information

XmStringCreate(3X).

XmStringExtent

Purpose

A compound string function that determines the size of the smallest rectangle that will enclose the compound string.

Synopsis

```
#include <Xm/Xm.h>

void XmStringExtent (fontlist, string, width, height)
        XmFontList fontlist;
        XmString   string;
        Dimension  width;
        Dimension  height;
```

Description

XmStringExtent determines the width and height, in pixels, of the smallest rectangle that will enclose the provided compound string.

fontlist Specifies the font list

string Specifies the string

width Specifies the width of the rectangle

height Specifies the height of the rectangle

Related Information

XmStringCreate(3X).

XmStringFree

Purpose

A compound string function that recovers memory

Synopsis

```
#include <Xm/Xm.h>

void XmStringFree (string)
        XmString    string;
```

Description

XmStringFree recovers memory used by a compound string.

string Specifies the compound string to be freed

Related Information

XmStringCreate(3X).

XmStringFreeContext

Purpose

A compound string function that instructs the toolkit that the context is no longer needed.

Synopsis

#include <Xm/Xm.h>

void XmStringFreeContext (*context*)
    XmStringContext* *context*;

Description

XmStringFreeContext instructs the toolkit that the context is no longer needed and will not be used without reinitialization.

context Specifies the string context structure that was allocated by the **XmStringInitContext** function

Related Information

XmStringCreate(3X) and **XmStringInitContext(3X)**.

XmStringGetLtoR

Purpose

A compound string function that searches for a text segment in the input compound string.

Synopsis

```
#include <Xm/Xm.h>

Boolean XmStringGetLtoR (string, charset, text)
      XmString            string;
      XmStringCharSet     charset;
      char                ** text;
```

Description

XmStringGetLtoR searches for a text segment in the input compound string that matches the given character set identifier.

string Specifies the compound string.

charset Specifies the character set identifier to be associated with the text. This can be **XmSTRING_DEFAULT_CHARSET**.

text Specifies a pointer to a null terminated string.

Return Value

Returns True if the matching text segment can be found. On return, *text* will have a null terminated octet sequence containing the matched segment.

Related Information

XmStringCreate(3X).

XmStringGetNextComponent

Purpose

A compound string function that returns the type and value of the next component in a compound string.

Synopsis

#include <Xm/Xm.h>

XmStringComponentType XmStringGetNextComponent (*context, text, charset, direction,*
unknown_tag, unknown_length, unknown_value)

```
XmStringContext        * context;
char                   ** text;
XmStringCharSet        * charset;
XmStringDirection      * direction;
XmStringComponentType* unknown_tag;
short                  * unknown_length;
char                   ** unknown_value;
```

Description

XmStringGetNextComponent returns the type and value of the next component in the compound string identified by *context*. It is a low-level component function. Components are returned one at a time. On return, only some output parameters will be valid; which ones can be determined by examining the return status. In the case of *text*, *charset* or *direction* components, only one output parameter is valid. If the return status indicates an unknown component was encountered, the tag, length, and value are returned. This function allocates the space necessary to hold returned values; freeing this space is the caller's responsibility.

context Specifies the string context structure which was allocated by the **XmStringInitContext** function.

text Specifies a pointer to a null terminated string.

charset Specifies the character set identifier to be associated with the text. This can be **XmSTRING_DEFAULT_CHARSET**.

direction Specifies the direction of the text.

unknown_tag Specifies the tag of an unknown component.

unknown_length Specifies the length of an unknown component.

unknown_value Specifies the value of an unknown component.

Return Value

Returns the type of component found.

Related Information

XmStringCreate(3X) and **XmStringInitContext(3X)**.

XmStringGetNextSegment

Purpose

A compound string function that fetches the octets in the next segment of a compound string.

Synopsis

#include <Xm/Xm.h>

Boolean XmStringGetNextSegment (*context, text, charset, direction, separator*)

```
    XmStringContext  * context;
    char             ** text;
    XmStringCharSet  * charset;
    XmStringDirection* direction;
    Boolean          * separator;
```

Description

XmStringGetNextSegment fetches the octets in the next segment; repeated calls fetch sequential segments. The *text*, *charset*, and *direction* of the fetched segment are returned each time. A Boolean status is returned to indicate whether a valid segment was successfully parsed.

context Specifies the string context structure which was allocated by the **XmStringInitContext** function.

text Specifies a pointer to a null terminated string.

charset Specifies the character set identifier to be associated with the text. This can be **XmSTRING_DEFAULT_CHARSET**.

direction Specifies the direction of the text.

separator Specifies if the next component of the compound string is a separator.

Return Value

Returns True if a valid segment is found.

Related Information

XmStringCreate(3X) and **XmStringInitContext(3X)**.

XmStringHeight

Purpose

A compound string function that returns the line height of the given compound string.

Synopsis

#include <Xm/Xm.h>

Dimension XmStringHeight (*fontlist, string*)
    XmFontList *fontlist*;
    XmString *string*;

Description

XmStringHeight returns the height, in pixels, of the sum of all the line heights of the given compound string. Separator components delimit lines.

fontlist Specifies the font list

string Specifies the string

Return Value

Returns the height of the specified string.

Related Information

XmStringCreate(3X).

XmStringInitContext

Purpose

A compound string function that allows applications to read out the content segment by segment.

Synopsis

#include <Xm/Xm.h>

Boolean XmStringInitContext (*context, string*)
    XmStringContext* *context*;
    XmString   *string*;

Description

XmStringInitContext maintains a context to allow applications to read out the contents of a compound string segment by segment. This function establishes the context for this read out. This context is used when reading subsequent segments out of the string. A Boolean status is returned to indicate if the input string could be parsed.

context Specifies a pointer to the allocated context

string Specifies the string.

Return Value

Returns True if the context was allocated

Related Information

XmStringCreate(3X).

XmStringLength

Purpose

A compound string function that obtains the length of a compound string.

Synopsis

```
#include <Xm/Xm.h>

int XmStringLength (s1)
      XmString    s1;
```

Description

XmStringLength obtains the length of a compound string. It returns the number of bytes in *s1* including all tags, direction indicators, and separators. If the compound string has an invalid structure, zero is returned.

s1 Specifies the compound string

Return Value

Returns the length of the compound string.

Related Information

XmStringCreate(3X).

XmStringLineCount

Purpose

A compound string function that returns the number of separators plus one in the provided compound string.

Synopsis

#include <Xm/Xm.h>

int XmStringLineCount (*string*)
    XmString   *string*;

Description

XmStringLineCount returns the number of separators plus one in the provided compound string. In effect, it counts the lines of text.

string   Specifies the string.

Return Value

Returns the number of lines in the compound string

Related Information

XmStringCreate(3X).

XmStringNConcat

Purpose

A compound string function that appends a specified number of bytes to a compound string.

Synopsis

```
#include <Xm/Xm.h>

XmString XmStringNConcat (s1, s2, num_bytes)
        XmString    s1;
        XmString    s2;
        int         num_bytes;
```

Description

XmStringNConcat appends a specified number of bytes from *s2* to the end of *s1*, including tags, directional indicators, and separators. It then returns the resulting compound string. The original strings are preserved. The space for the resulting compound string is allocated within the function. The application is responsible for managing the allocated space. The memory can be recovered by calling **XmStringFree**.

s1 Specifies the compound string to which a copy of *s2* is appended.

s2 Specifies the compound string that is appended to the end of *s1*.

num_bytes
Specifies the number of bytes of *s2* to append to *s1*. If this value is less than the length of *s2*, the resulting string will not be a valid compound string.

Return Value

Returns a new compound string.

Related Information

XmStringCreate(3X) and **XmStringFree(3X)**.

XmStringNCopy

Purpose

A compound string function that creates a copy of a compound string.

Synopsis

#include <Xm/Xm.h>

XmString XmStringNCopy (*s1*, *num_bytes*)
    XmString *s1*;
    int *num_bytes*;

Description

XmStringNCopy creates a copy of *s1* that contains a specified number of bytes, including tags, directional indicators, and separators. It then returns the resulting compound string. The original strings are preserved. The space for the resulting compound string is allocated within the function. The application is responsible for managing the allocated space. The memory can be recovered by calling **XmStringFree**.

s1 Specifies the compound string.

num_bytes
Specifies the number of bytes of *s1* to copy. If this value is less than the length of *s1*, the resulting string will not be a valid compound string.

Return Value

Returns a new compound string.

Related Information

XmStringCreate(3X) and **XmStringFree(3X)**.

XmStringPeekNextComponent

Purpose

A compound string function that returns the component type of the next component fetched.

Synopsis

#include <Xm/Xm.h>

XmStringComponentType XmStringPeekNextComponent (*context*)
    XmStringContext* *context*;

Description

XmStringPeekNextComponent examines the next component that would be fetched by **XmStringGetNextComponent** and returns the component type.

context Specifies the string context structure that was allocated by the **XmStringInitContext** function

Return Value

Returns the type of component found.

Related Information

XmStringCreate(3X) and **XmStringInitContext(3X)**.

XmStringSegmentCreate

Purpose

A compound string function that creates a compound string.

Synopsis

#include <Xm/Xm.h>

XmString XmStringSegmentCreate (*text, charset, direction, separator*)
    char * *text*;
    XmStringCharSet *charset*;
    XmStringDirection *direction*;
    Boolean *separator*;

Description

XmStringSegmentCreate is a high-level function that assembles a compound string consisting of a character set identifier, a direction component, a text component, and an optional separator component.

text Specifies a pointer to a null terminated string.

charset Specifies the character set identifier to be associated with the text. This can be **XmSTRING_DEFAULT_CHARSET**.

direction Specifies the direction of the text.

separator Specifies separator addition. If False, the compound string does not have a separator at the end. If True, a separator immediately follows the text component.

Return Value

Returns a new compound string.

Related Information

XmStringCreate(3X).

XmStringSeparatorCreate

Purpose

A compound string function that creates a compound string.

Synopsis

#include <Xm/Xm.h>

XmString XmStringSeparatorCreate ()

Description

XmStringSeparatorCreate creates a compound string with a single component, a separator.

Return Value

Returns a new compound string.

Related Information

XmStringCreate(3X).

XmStringWidth

Purpose

A compound string function that returns the width of the longest sequence of text components in a compound string.

Synopsis

#include <Xm/Xm.h>

Dimension XmStringWidth (*fontlist, string*)
    XmFontList *fontlist*;
    XmString   *string*;

Description

XmStringWidth returns the width, in pixels, of the longest sequence of text components in the provided compound string. Separator components are used to delimit sequences of text components.

fontlist Specifies the font list

string Specifies the string

Return Value

Returns the width of the compound string.

Related Information

XmStringCreate(3X).

XmText

Purpose

The Text widget class

Synopsis

#include <Xm/Text.h>

Description

Text provides a single-line and multiline text editor for customizing both user and programmatic interfaces. It can be used for single-line string entry, forms entry with verification procedures, and full-window editing. It provides an application with a consistent editing system for textual data. The screen's textual data adjusts to the application writer's needs.

Text provides separate callback lists to verify movement of the insert cursor, modification of the text, and changes in input focus. Each of these callbacks provides the verification function with the widget instance, the event that caused the callback, and a data structure specific to the verification type. From this information the function can verify if the application considers this to be a legitimate state change and can signal the widget whether to continue with the action.

The user interface tailors a new set of translations. The default translations provide key bindings for insert cursor movement, deletion, insertion, and selection of text.

Text allows the user to select regions of text. Selection is based on the Interclient Communication Conventions (lCCC) selection model. Text supports primary selection.

Primitive's resource **XmNtraversalOn** is always True in Text.

Classes

Text inherits behavior and resources from **Core** and **Primitive** classes.

The class pointer is **xmTextWidgetClass**.

The class name is **XmText**.

New Resources

The following table defines a set of widget resources used by the programmer to specify data. The programmer can also set the resource values for the inherited classes to set attributes for this widget. To reference a resource by name or by class in a .Xdefaults file, remove the **XmN** or **XmC** prefix and use the remaining letters. To specify one of the defined values for a resource in a .Xdefaults file, remove the **Xm** prefix and use the remaining letters (in either lowercase or uppercase, but include any undcrscores between words). The codes in the access column indicate if the given resource can be set at creation time (**C**), set by using **XtSetValues** (**S**), retrieved by using **XtGetValues** (**G**), or is not applicable (**N/A**).

XmText Resource Set		
Name **Class**	**Default** **Type**	**Access**
XmNactivateCallback XmCCallback	NULL XtCallbackList	C
XmNautoShowCursorPosition XmCAutoShowCursorPosition	True Boolean	CSG
XmNcursorPosition XmCCursorPosition	0 XmTextPosition	CSG
XmNeditable XmCEditable	True Boolean	CSG
XmNeditMode XmCEditMode	XmSINGLE_LINE_EDIT int	CSG
XmNfocusCallback XmCCallback	NULL XtCallbackList	C
XmNlosingFocusCallback XmCCallback	NULL XtCallbackList	C
XmNmarginHeight XmCMarginHeight	3 short	CSG
XmNmarginWidth XmCMarginWidth	3 short	CSG
XmNmaxLength XmCMaxLength	MAXINT int	CSG
XmNmodifyVerifyCallback XmCCallback	NULL XtCallbackList	C
XmNmotionVerifyCallback XmCCallback	NULL XtCallbackList	C
XmNtopPosition XmCTextPosition	0 XmTextPosition	CSG

Name Class	Default Type	Access
XmNvalue XmCValue	"" String	CSG
XmNvalueChangedCallback XmCCallback	NULL XtCallbackList	C

XmNactivateCallback

Specifies the list of callbacks that is called when the user invokes an event that calls the **Activate()** function. The structure returned by this callback is **XmAnyCallbackStruct**. The reason sent by the callback is **XmCR_ACTIVATE**.

XmNautoShowCursorPosition

Ensures that the visible text contains the insert cursor when set to True. If the insert cursor changes, the contents of Text may scroll in order to bring the insertion point into the window.

XmNcursorPosition

Indicates the position in the text where the current insert cursor is to be located. Position is determined by the number of characters from the beginning of the text.

XmNeditable

Indicates that the user can edit the text string when set to True. Prohibits the user from editing the text when set to False.

XmNeditMode

Specifies the set of keyboard bindings used in Text. The default keyboard bindings (**XmSINGLE_LINE_EDIT**) provides the set of key bindings to be used in editing single-line text. The multiline bindings (**XmMULTI_LINE_EDIT**) provides the set of key bindings to be used in editing multiline text.

XmNfocusCallback

Specifies the list of callbacks called before Text has accepted input focus. The structure returned by this callback is **XmAnyCallbackStruct**. The reason sent by the callback is **XmCR_FOCUS**.

XmNlosingFocusCallback
Specifies the list of callbacks called before Text loses input focus. The structure returned by this callback is **XmTextVerifyCallbackStruct**. The reason sent by the callback is **XmCR_LOSING_FOCUS**.

XmNmarginHeight
Specifies the distance between the top edge of the widget window and the text, and between the bottom edge of the widget window and the text. This resource is forced to True when the Text widget is placed in a ScrolledWindow with **XmNscrollingPolicy** set to **XmAUTOMATIC**.

XmNmarginWidth
Specifies the distance between the left edge of the widget window and the text, and between the right edge of the widget window and the text. This resource is forced to True when the Text widget is placed in a ScrolledWindow with **XmNscrollingPolicy** set to **XmAUTOMATIC**.

XmNmaxLength
Specifies the maximum length of the text string that can be entered into text from the keyboard. Strings that are entered using the **XmNvalue** resource or the **XmTextSetString** function ignore this resource.

XmNmodifyVerifyCallback
Specifies the list of callbacks called before text is deleted from or inserted into Text. The structure returned by this callback is **XmTextVerifyCallbackStruct**. The reason sent by the callback is **XmCR_MODIFYING_TEXT_VALUE**.

XmNmotionVerifyCallback
Specifies the list of callbacks called before the insert cursor is moved to a new position. The structure returned by this callback is **XmTextVerifyCallbackStruct**. The reason sent by the callback is **XmCR_MOVING_INSERT_CURSOR**.

XmNtopPosition
Displays the position of text at the top of the window. Position is determined by the number of characters from the beginning of the text.

XmNvalue Displays the string value. **XtGetValues** returns the value of the internal buffer and **XtSetValues** copies the string values into the internal buffer.

XmNvalueChangedCallback
Specifies the list of callbacks called after text is deleted from or inserted into Text. The structure returned by this callback is **XmAnyCallbackStruct**. The reason sent by the callback is **XmCR_VALUE_CHANGED**.

XmText Input Resource Set		
Name **Class**	**Default** **Type**	**Access**
XmNpendingDelete XmCPendingDelete	True Boolean	CSG
XmNselectionArray XmCSelectionArray	sarray Pointer	CSG
XmNselectThreshold XmCSelectThreshold	5 int	CSG

XmNpendingDelete
Indicates that pending delete mode is on when the Boolean value is True. Pending deletion is defined as deletion of the selected text when an insertion is made.

XmNselectionArray
Defines the actions for multiple mouse clicks. Each mouse click performed within a half of a second of the previous mouse click increments the index into this array and perform the defined action for that index. The possible actions are:

- **XmSELECT_POSITIONS** — resets the insert cursor position
- **XmSELECT_WORD** — selects a word
- **XmSELECT_LINE** — selects a line of text
- **XmSELECT_ALL** — selects all of the text

XmNselectThreshold

Specifies the number of pixels of motion that is required to select the next character when selection is performed using the click-drag mode of selection.

XmText Output Resource Set		
Name **Class**	**Default** **Type**	**Access**
XmNblinkRate XmCBlinkRate	500 int	CSG
XmNcolumns XmCColumns	20 short	CSG
XmNcursorPositionVisible XmCCursorPositionVisible	True Boolean	CSG
XmNfontList XmCFontList	fixed XmFontList	CSG
XmNresizeHeight XmCResizeHeight	False Boolean	CSG
XmNresizeWidth XmCResizeWidth	False Boolean	CSG
XmNrows XmCRows	1 short	CSG
XmNwordWrap XmCWordWrap	False Boolean	CSG

XmNblinkRate

Specifies the blink rate of the text cursor in milliseconds. The time indicated in the blink rate relates to the time the cursor is visible and the time the cursor is invisible (that is, the time it takes to blink the insertion cursor on and off is twice the blink rate). The cursor does not blink when the blink rate is set to zero.

XmNcolumns
Specifies the initial width of the text window measured in character spaces.

XmNfontList
Specifies the font list to be used for Text. See **XmFontListCreate(3X)** to create a font list.

XmNinsertionPointVisible
Indicates that the insert cursor position is marked by a blinking text cursor when the Boolean value is True.

XmNresizeHeight
Indicates that Text attempts to resize its height to accommodate all the text contained in the widget when the Boolean value is True. If the Boolean value is set to True, the text is always displayed starting from the first position in the source, even if instructed otherwise. This attribute is ignored when the application uses a ScrolledText widget and when **XmNscrollVertical** is True.

XmNresizeWidth
Indicates that Text attempts to resize its width to accommodate all the text contained in the widget when the Boolean value is True. This attribute is ignored if **XmNwordWrap** is True.

XmNrows
Specifies the initial height of the text window measured in character heights. This attribute is ignored if the text widget resource **XmNeditMode** is **XmSINGLE_LINE_EDIT**.

XmNwordWrap
Indicates that lines are to be broken at word breaks (that is, the text does not go off the right edge of the window) when the Boolean value is True. Words are defined as a sequence of characters separated by white space. White space is defined as a space, tab, or newline. This attribute is ignored if the text widget resource **XmNeditMode** is **XmSINGLE_LINE_EDIT**.

The following resources are used only when text is created in a ScrolledWindow. See the man page for **XmCreateScrolledText.**

XmText ScrolledText Resource Set		
Name **Class**	**Default** **Type**	**Access**
XmNscrollHorizontal XmCScroll	True Boolean	CG
XmNscrollLeftSide XmCScrollSide	False Boolean	CG
XmNscrollTopSide XmCScrollSide	False Boolean	CG
XmNscrollVertical XmCScroll	True Boolean	CG

XmNscrollHorizontal
Adds a ScrollBar that allows the user to scroll horizontally through text when the Boolean value is True. This attribute is ignored if the Text resource **XmNeditMode** is **XmSINGLE_LINE_EDIT**. This resource is forced to False when the Text widget is placed in a ScrolledWindow with **XmNscrollingPolicy** set to **XmAUTOMATIC**.

XmNscrollLeftSide
Indicates that the vertical ScrollBar should be placed on the left side of the scrolled text window when the Boolean value is True. This attribute is ignored if **XmNscrollVertical** is False or the Text resource **XmNeditMode** is **XmSINGLE_LINE_EDIT**.

XmNscrollTopSide
Indicates that the horizontal ScrollBar should be placed on the top side of the scrolled text window when the Boolean value is True.

XmNscrollVertical
Adds a ScrollBar that allows the user to scroll vertically through text when the Boolean value is True. This resource is forced to False when the Text widget is placed in a ScrolledWindow with **XmNscrollingPolicy** set to **XmAUTOMATIC**.

Inherited Resources

Text inherits behavior and resources from the following superclasses. For a complete description of each resource, refer to the man page for that superclass.

XmPrimitive Resource Set		
Name **Class**	**Default** **Type**	**Access**
XmNbottomShadowColor XmCForeground	dynamic Pixel	CSG
XmNbottomShadowPixmap XmCBottomShadowPixmap	XmUNSPECIFIED_PIXMAP Pixmap	CSG
XmNforeground XmCForeground	dynamic Pixel	CSG
XmNhelpCallback XmCCallback	NULL XtCallbackList	CSG
XmNhighlightColor XmCForeground	Black Pixel	CSG
XmNhighlightOnEnter XmCHighlightOnEnter	False Boolean	CSG
XmNhighlightPixmap XmCHighlightPixmap	dynamic Pixmap	CSG
XmNhighlightThickness XmCHighlightThickness	0 short	CSG
XmNshadowThickness XmCShadowThickness	2 short	CSG
XmNtopShadowColor XmCBackground	dynamic Pixel	CSG
XmNtopShadowPixmap XmCTopShadowPixmap	XmUNSPECIFIED_PIXMAP Pixmap	CSG

Name Class	Default Type	Access
XmNtraversalOn XmCTraversalOn	True Boolean	N/A
XmNunitType XmCUnitType	XmPIXELS unsigned char	CSG
XmNuserData XmCUserData	NULL caddr_t	CSG

Core Resource Set

Name Class	Default Type	Access
XmNaccelerators XmCAccelerators	NULL XtTranslations	CSG
XmNancestorSensitive XmCSensitive	True Boolean	G
XmNbackground XmCBackground	dynamic Pixel	CSG
XmNbackgroundPixmap XmCPixmap	XmUNSPECIFIED_PIXMAP Pixmap	CSG
XmNborderColor XmCBorderColor	Black Pixel	CSG
XmNborderPixmap XmCPixmap	XmUNSPECIFIED_PIXMAP Pixmap	CSG
XmNborderWidth XmCBorderWidth	0 Dimension	CSG
XmNcolormap XmCColormap	XtCopyFromParent Colormap	CG
XmNdepth XmCDepth	XtCopyFromParent int	CG

Name Class	Default Type	Access
XmNdestroyCallback XmCCallback	NULL XtCallbackList	C
XmNheight XmCHeight	0 Dimension	CSG
XmNmappedWhenManaged XmCMappedWhenManaged	True Boolean	CSG
XmNscreen XmCScreen	XtCopyScreen Pointer	CG
XmNsensitive XmCSensitive	True Boolean	CSG
XmNtranslations XmCTranslations	NULL XtTranslations	CSG
XmNwidth XmCWidth	0 Dimension	CSG
XmNx XmCPosition	0 Position	CSG
XmNy XmCPosition	0 Position	CSG

Callback Information

The following structure is returned with each callback.

```
typedef struct
{
    int         reason;
    XEvent      * event;
} XmAnyCallbackStruct;
```

reason Indicates why the callback was invoked

event Points to the **XEvent** that triggered the callback

The Text widget defines a new callback structure for use with verification callbacks. Note that not all fields are relevant for every callback reason. The application must first look at the reason field and use only the structure members that are valid for the particular reason. The following structure is returned with **XmNlosingFocusCallbacks**, **XmNmodifyVerifyCallbacks**, and **XmNmotionVerifyCallbacks**.

```
typedef struct
{
    int              reason;
    XEvent           * event;
    Boolean          doit;
    XmTextPosition   currInsert, newInsert;
    XmTextPosition   startPos, endPos;
    XmTextBlock      text;
} XmTextVerifyCallbackStruct, *XmTextVerifyPtr;
```

reason Indicates why the callback was invoked.

event Points to the **XEvent** that triggered the callback.

doit Indicates whether the action that invoked the callback is performed. Setting *doit* to False negates the action.

currInsert
Indicates the current position of the insert cursor.

newInsert
Indicates the position at which the user attempts to position the insert cursor.

startPos Indicates the starting position of the text to modify. If the callback is not a modify verification callback, this value is the same as *currInsert*.

endPos Indicates the ending position of the text to modify. If no text is replaced or deleted, the value is the same as *startPos*. If the callback is not a modify verification callback, this value is the same as *currInsert*.

text Points to a structure of type **XmTextBlockRec**. This structure holds the textual information to be inserted.

```
typedef struct
{
    char            * ptr;
    int             length;
    XmTextFormat    format;
} XmTextBlockRec, *XmTextBlock;
```

ptr Points to the text to be inserted

length Specifies the length of the text to be inserted

format Specifies the format of the text (for example, **FMT8BIT**)

The following table describes the reasons why the individual verification callback structure fields are valid:

Reason	Valid Fields
XmCR_LOSING_FOCUS	*reason, event, doit, currInsert, newInsert, startPos, endPos*
XmCR_MODIFYING_TEXT_VALUE	*reason, event, doit, currInsert, newInsert, startPos, endPos, text*
XmCR_MOVING_TEXT_CURSOR	*reason, event, doit, currInsert, newInsert*

Behavior

The behavior for the Text widget is determined by the **XmNeditMode** resource. Depending on how this resource is set, some of the key bindings perform different actions. The possible values for **XmNeditMode** are **XmSINGLE_LINE_EDIT** and **XmMULTI_LINE_EDIT**. The following describes the key bindings for these edit modes.

Default Behavior (Single-line Text Edit)

<Btn1Down>:
: This key binding performs the action defined in the selection array depending on the number of multiple mouse clicks. The default selection array ordering is one click to move the insertion cursor position, two clicks to select a word, and three clicks to select a line of text.

  It also begins text selection. Primary selected text that was previously selected becomes unselected.

Button1 <PtrMoved>:
: Text is selected in the direction of the pointer cursor movement. While the pointer cursor is moved along the text, the text is selected from the point the mouse button 1 was pressed to the present position of the pointer cursor. Moving the pointer cursor back over previously selected text while mouse button 1 is pressed deselects the text. Primary selected text is shown by inverted text.

<Btn1Up>: The selected text becomes the primary selection (that is, the selection is committed).

Shift <Btn1Down>:
: The end points of the selection move to the point where the pointer cursor is located when the shifted mouse button 1 is pressed. If the pointer cursor is located at a position where text is already selected, the text following this position becomes unselected.

<Btn2Up>: The text is copied from the primary selection to the insertion point located at the insert cursor. This is shown visibly by underlined text.

CTRL <Btn2Up>:
The text is copied and cut from the primary selection and is pasted to the insertion point located at the insert cursor.

<Key> Right:
The insert cursor moves one character to the right.

Shift <Key> Right:
The text character to the right of the insert cursor is selected and inverted (that is, primary selection). If text to the right of the insert cursor is already selected, this text becomes unselected one character at a time.

CTRL <Key> Right:
The insert cursor moves to the end of the line.

<Key> Left: The insert cursor moves one character to the left.

Shift <Key> Left:
The text character to the left of the insert cursor is selected and inverted. If the text to the left of the insert cursor is already selected, this text becomes unselected one character at a time.

CTRL <Key> Left:
The insert cursor moves to the beginning of the line.

<Key> Backspace:
The character of text immediately preceding the insert cursor is deleted.

<Key> Delete or **<Key>DeleteChar** (HP keyboard):
The character of text immediately following the insert cursor is deleted.

Any <Key>: This key binding inserts the character, associated with the key pressed, into the text of the Text widget.

<Key> Return:
Calls the callbacks for **XmNactivateCallback**.

Multiline Text Edit

Button1 <PtrMoved>:
Text is selected in the direction of the pointer cursor movement. While the pointer cursor is moved along the text, the text is selected from the point that mouse button 1 was pressed to the present position of the pointer cursor. Moving the cursor over several lines selects text to the end of each line the pointer cursor moves over and up its position on the current line. Moving the pointer cursor back over previously selected text while mouse button 1 is pressed deselects the text.

<Key> Up: The insert cursor moves to the line directly above the line where the insert cursor is currently residing.

<Key> Down:
The insert cursor moves to the line directly below the line where the insert cursor is currently residing.

<Key> Return:
Inserts a new line at the point where the insert cursor is positioned.

Default Translations

Default translations for Text are:

Shift<Key>Tab:	**prev-tab-group()**
<Key>Tab:	**next-tab-group()**
<Key>Up:	**traverse-prev()**
<Key>Down:	**traverse-next()**
<Key>Home:	**traverse-home()**
Ctrl<Key>Right:	**forward-word()**
Shift<Key>Right:	**key-select(right)**
<Key>Right:	**forward-character()**
Ctrl<Key>Left:	**backward-word()**
Shift<Key>Left:	**key-select(left)**
<Key>Left:	**backward-character()**
Shift<Key>BackSpace:	**delete-previous-word()**
<Key>BackSpace:	**delete-previous-character()**
<Key>Return:	**activate()**
<Key>:	**self-insert()**
Shift<Btn1Down>:	**extend-start()**
<Btn1Down>:	**grab-focus()**
Button1<PtrMoved>:	**extend-adjust()**
<Btn1Up>:	**extend-end()**
Ctrl<Btn3Up>:	**move-to()**
<Btn3Up>:	**copy-to()**
<LeaveWindow>:	**leave()**
<FocusIn>:	**focusIn()**
<FocusOut>:	**focusOut()**
<Unmap>:	**unmap()**

If using an HP keyboard, the following are the default translations:

Shift<Key>DeleteChar:delete-next-word()
<Key>DeleteChar: delete-next-character()

If using a DIGITAL keyboard, the following are the default translations:

Shift<Key>Delete:	**delete-previous-word()**
<Key>Delete:	**delete-previous-character()**
Shift<Key>Linefeed:	**delete-next-word()**
<Key>Linefeed:	**delete-next-character()**
Shift<Key>F13:	**delete-next-word()**
<Key>F13:	**delete-next-character()**

If using other than an HP or DIGITAL keyboard, the following are the default translations:

Shift<Key>Delete:	**delete-next-word()**
<Key>Delete:	**delete-next-character()**

The following default translations override the above default translations when using Multiline Text Edit:

<Key>Tab:	**self-insert()**
<Key>Up:	**previous-line()**
<Key>Down:	**next-line()**
<Key>Home:	**beginning-of-file()**
<Key>Return:	**newline()**

When changing from Multiline Text Edit to Single-line Text Edit, the following default translations override the Multiline Text Edit default translations.

<Key>Tab:	**next-tab-group()**
<Key>Up:	**traverse-prev()**
<Key>Down:	**traverse-next()**
<Key>Home:	**traverse-home()**
<Key>Return:	**activate()**

Keyboard Traversal

Multiline Text Edit differs from standard traversal in the following manner:

Up or Down Arrow — moves the insert cursor between lines

Tab — inserts a tab

Home — moves the insert cursor to the first position (top) of the file

Return — adds a new line

Both Single-line and Multiline Text Edit differs from standard traversal in the following manner:

Right or Left Arrows — moves the insert cursor to the right or to the left

For more information on keyboard traversal, see the man page for **XmPrimitive(3X)** and its sections on behavior and default translations.

Related Information

Core(3X), **XmCreateScrolledText(3X)**, **XmCreateText(3X)**, **XmFontListCreate(3X)**, **XmPrimitive(3X)**, **XmTextClearSelection(3X)**, **XmTextGetEditable(3X)**, **XmTextGetMaxLength(3X)**, **XmTextGetSelection(3X)**, **XmTextGetString(3X)**, **XmTextReplace(3X)**, **XmTextSetEditable(3X)**, **XmTextSetMaxLength(3X)**, **XmTextSetSelection(3X)**, and **XmTextSetString(3X)**.

XmTextClearSelection

Purpose

A Text function that clears the primary selection

Synopsis

#include <Xm/Text.h>

void XmTextClearSelection (*widget, time*)
    Widget   *widget*;
    Time   *time*;

Description

XmTextClearSelection clears the primary selection in the Text widget; it has no effect on the text that was previously selected.

widget Specifies the Text widget ID.

time Specifies the time at which the selection value is desired. This should be the time of the event which triggered this request.

For a complete definition of Text and its associated resources, see **XmText(3X)**.

Related Information

XmText(3X).

XmTextGetEditable

Purpose

A Text function that accesses the edit permission state.

Synopsis

#include <Xm/Text.h>

Boolean XmTextGetEditable (*widget*)
    Widget   *widget*;

Description

XmTextGetEditable accesses the edit permission state of the Text widget.

widget   Specifies the Text widget ID

For a complete definition of Text and its associated resources, see **XmText(3X)**.

Return Value

Returns a Boolean value that indicates the state of the **XmNeditable** resource.

Related Information

XmText(3X).

XmTextGetMaxLength

Purpose

A Text function that accesses the value of the current maximum allowable length of a text string entered from the keyboard.

Synopsis

#include <Xm/Text.h>

int XmTextGetMaxLength (*widget*)
    Widget   *widget*;

Description

XmTextGetMaxLength accesses the value of the current maximum allowable length of the text string in the Text widget entered from the keyboard. The maximum allowable length prevents the user from entering a text string larger than this limit.

widget Specifies the Text widget ID

For a complete definition of Text and its associated resources, see **XmText(3X)**.

Return Value

Returns the integer value that indicates the string's maximum allowable length that can be entered from the keyboard.

Related Information

XmText(3X).

XmTextGetSelection

Purpose

A Text function that retrieves the value of the primary selection.

Synopsis

#include <Xm/Text.h>

char * XmTextGetSelection (*widget*)
    Widget   *widget*;

Description

XmTextGetSelection retrieves the value of the primary selection. It returns a NULL pointer if no text is selected in the widget. The application is responsible for freeing the storage associated with the string by calling **XtFree**.

widget   Specifies the Text widget ID

For a complete definition of Text and its associated resources, see **XmText(3X)**.

Return Value

Returns a character pointer to the string that is associated with the primary selection.

Related Information

XmText(3X).

XmTextGetString

Purpose

A Text function that accesses the string value

Synopsis

#include <Xm/Text.h>

char * XmTextGetString (*widget*)
Widget *widget*;

Description

XmTextGetString accesses the string value of the Text widget. The application is responsible for freeing the storage associated with the string by calling **XtFree**.

widget Specifies the Text widget ID

For a complete definition of Text and its associated resources, see **XmText(3X)**.

Return Value

Returns a character pointer to the string value of the text widget.

Related Information

XmText(3X).

XmTextReplace

Purpose

A Text function that replaces part of a text string

Synopsis

#include <Xm/Text.h>

void XmTextReplace (*widget, from_pos, to_pos, value*)
  Widget *widget*;
  XmTextPosition *from_pos*;
  XmTextPosition *to_pos*;
  char * *value*;

Description

XmTextReplace replaces part of the text string in the Text widget. The character positions begin at zero and are numbered sequentially from the beginning of the text.

An example text replacement would be to replace the second and third characters in the text string. To accomplish this, the parameter *from_pos* must be 1 and *to_pos* must be 3. To insert a string after the fourth character, both parameters, *from_pos* and *to_pos*, must be 4.

widget Specifies the Text widget ID

from_pos Specifies the start position of the text to be replaced

to_pos Specifies the end position of the text to be replaced

value Specifies the character string value to be added to the text widget

For a complete definition of Text and its associated resources, see **XmText(3X)**.

Related Information

XmText(3X).

XmTextSetEditable

Purpose

A Text function that sets the edit permission

Synopsis

#include <Xm/Text.h>

void XmTextSetEditable (*widget, editable*)
    Widget *widget*;
    Boolean *editable*;

Description

XmTextSetEditable sets the edit permission state of the Text widget. When set to True, the text string can be edited.

widget Specifies the Text widget ID

editable Specifies a Boolean value that when True allows text string edits

For a complete definition of Text and its associated resources, see **XmText(3X)**.

Related Information

XmText(3X).

XmTextSetMaxLength

Purpose

A Text function that sets the value of the current maximum allowable length of a text string entered from the keyboard.

Synopsis

#include <Xm/Text.h>

void XmTextSetMaxLength (*widget, max_length*)
  Widget *widget*;
  int *max_length*;

Description

XmTextSetMaxLength sets the value of the current maximum allowable length of the text string in the Text widget. The maximum allowable length prevents the user from entering a text string from the keyboard that is larger than this limit. Strings that are entered using the **XmNvalue** resource or the **XmTextSetString** function ignore this resource.

widget Specifies the Text widget ID

max_length
  Specifies the maximum allowable length of the text string

For a complete definition of Text and its associated resources, see **XmText(3X)**.

Related Information

XmText(3X) and **XmTextSetString(3X)**.

XmTextSetSelection

Purpose

A Text function that sets the primary selection of the text.

Synopsis

```
#include <Xm/Text.h>

void XmTextSetSelection (widget, first, last, time)
        Widget          widget;
        XmTextPosition  first;
        XmTextPosition  last;
        Time            time;
```

Description

XmTextSetSelection sets the primary selection of the text in the widget.

widget Specifies the Text widget ID.

first Marks the first character position.

last Marks the last position of the text to be selected.

time Specifies the time at which the selection value is desired. This should be the same as the time of the event that triggered this request.

For a complete definition of Text and its associated resources, see **XmText(3X)**.

Related Information

XmText(3X).

XmTextSetString

Purpose

A Text function that sets the string value

Synopsis

#include <Xm/Text.h>

void XmTextSetString (*widget, value*)
    Widget *widget*;
    char * *value*;

Description

XmTextSetString sets the string value of the Text widget.

widget Specifies the Text widget ID

value Specifies the character pointer to the string value and places the string into the text edit window

For a complete definition of Text and its associated resources, see **XmText(3X)**.

Related Information

XmText(3X).

XmToggleButton

Purpose

The ToggleButton widget class

Synopsis

#include <Xm/ToggleB.h>

Description

ToggleButton sets nontransitory state data within an application. Usually this widget consists of an indicator (square or diamond) with either text or a pixmap to its right. However, it can also consist of just text or a pixmap without the indicator.

The toggle graphics display a **1-of-many** or **N-of-many** selection state. When a toggle indicator is displayed, a square indicator shows an **N-of-many** selection state and a diamond indicator shows a **1-of-many** selection state.

ToggleButton implies a selected or unselected state. In the case of a label and an indicator, an empty indicator (square or diamond shaped) indicates that ToggleButton is unselected, and a filled indicator shows that it is selected. In the case of a pixmap toggle, different pixmaps are used to display the selected/unselected states.

Normally, mouse button 1 is used to arm and activate the button. However, if the ToggleButton resides within a menu, the mouse button used is determined by the RowColumn resources **XmNrowColumnType** and **XmNwhichButton**.

To accommodate the toggle indicator when created, Label's resource **XmNmarginLeft** may be increased.

Classes

ToggleButton inherits behavior and resources from **Core**, **XmPrimitive**, and **XmLabel** Classes.

The class pointer is **xmToggleButtonWidgetClass**.

The class name is **XmToggleButton**.

New Resources

The following table defines a set of widget resources used by the programmer to specify data. The programmer can also set the resource values for the inherited classes to set attributes for this widget. To reference a resource by name or by class in a .Xdefaults file, remove the **XmN** or **XmC** prefix and use the remaining letters. To specify one of the defined values for a resource in a .Xdefaults file, remove the **Xm** prefix and use the remaining letters (in either lowercase or uppercase, but include any underscores between words). The codes in the access column indicate if the given resource can be set at creation time (**C**), set by using **XtSetValues** (**S**), retrieved by using **XtGetValues** (**G**), or is not applicable (**N/A**).

XmToggleButton Resource Set		
Name **Class**	**Default** **Type**	**Access**
XmNarmCallback XmCArmCallback	NULL XtCallbackList	C
XmNdisarmCallback XmCDisarmCallback	NULL XtCallbackList	C
XmNfillOnSelect XmCFillOnSelect	True Boolean	CSG
XmNindicatorOn XmCIndicatorOn	True Boolean	CSG
XmNindicatorType XmCIndicatorType	XmN_OF_MANY unsigned char	CSG
XmNselectColor XmCSelectColor	dynamic Pixel	CSG
XmNselectInsensitivePixmap XmCSelectInsensitivePixmap	XmUNSPECIFIED_PIXMAP Pixmap	CSG
XmNselectPixmap XmCSelectPixmap	XmUNSPECIFIED_PIXMAP Pixmap	CSG
XmNset XmCSet	False Boolean	CSG
XmNspacing XmCSpacing	4 short	CSG
XmNvalueChangedCallback XmCValueChangedCallback	NULL XtCallbackList	C
XmNvisibleWhenOff XmCVisibleWhenOff	True Boolean	CSG

XmNarmCallback

Specifies the list of callbacks called when the ToggleButton is armed. To arm this widget, press the active mouse button while the pointer is inside the ToggleButton. For this callback, the reason is **XmCR_ARM**.

XmNdisarmCallback
Specifies the list of callbacks called when ToggleButton is disarmed. To disarm this widget, press and release the active mouse button while the pointer is inside the ToggleButton. This widget is also disarmed when the user moves out of the widget and releases the mouse button when the pointer is outside the widget. For this callback, the reason is **XmCR_DISARM**.

XmNfillOnSelect
Fills the indicator with the color specified in **XmNselectColor** and switches the top and bottom shadow colors when set to True. Otherwise, it switches only the top and bottom shadow colors.

XmNindicatorOn
Specifies that a toggle indicator is drawn to the left of the toggle text or pixmap when set to True. When set to False, no space is allocated for the indicator, and it is not displayed. If **XmNindicatorOn** is True, the indicator shadows are switched when the button is selected or unselected, but, any shadows around the entire widget are not switched. However, if **XmNindicatorOn** is False, any shadows around the entire widget are switched when the toggle is selected or unselected.

XmNindicatorType
Specifies if the indicator is a **1-of** or **N-of** indicator. For the **1-of** indicator, the value is **XmONE_OF_MANY**. For the **N-of** indicator, the value is **XmN_OF_MANY**. The **N-of-many** indicator is square. The **1-of-many** indicator is diamond-shaped. This resource specifies only the visuals and does not enforce the behavior. When the ToggleButton is in a RadioBox, the parent forces this resource to **XmONE_OF_MANY**.

XmNselectColor
Allows the application to specify what color fills the center of the square or diamond-shaped indicator when it is set. If this color is the same as either the top or the bottom shadow color of the indicator, a one-pixel-wide margin is left between the

shadows and the fill; otherwise, it is filled completely. This resource's default for a color display is a color between the background and the bottom shadow color. For a monochrome display, the default is set to the foreground color.

XmNselectInsensitivePixmap
Specifies a pixmap used as the button face when the ToggleButton is selected and the button is insensitive if the Label resource **XmNlabelType** is set to **XmPIXMAP**. If the ToggleButton is unselected and the button is insensitive, the pixmap in **XmNlabelInsensitivePixmap** is used as the button face.

XmNselectPixmap
Specifies the pixmap to be used as the button face if **XmNlabelType** is **XmPIXMAP** and the ToggleButton is selected. When the ToggleButton is unselected, the pixmap specified in Label's **XmNlabelPixmap** is used.

XmNset Displays the button in its selected state if set to True. This shows some conditions as active when a set of buttons first appears.

XmNspacing
Specifies the amount of spacing between the toggle indicator and the toggle label (text or pixmap).

XmNvalueChangedCallback
Specifies the list of callbacks called when the ToggleButton value is changed. To change the value, press and release the active mouse button while the pointer is inside the ToggleButton. This action also causes this widget to be disarmed. For this callback, the reason is **XmCR_VALUE_CHANGED**.

XmNvisibleWhenOff
Indicates that the toggle indicator is visible in the unselected state when the Boolean value is True. When the ToggleButton is in a menu, the RowColumn parent forces this resource to False. When the ToggleButton is in a RadioBox, the parent forces this resource to True.

Inherited Resources

ToggleButton inherits behavior and resources from the following superclasses. For a complete description of each resource, refer to the man page for that superclass.

XmLabel Resource Set		
Name **Class**	**Default** **Type**	**Access**
XmNaccelerator XmCAccelerator	NULL String	CSG
XmNacceleratorText XmCAcceleratorText	NULL XmString	CSG
XmNalignment XmCAlignment	XmALIGNMENT_CENTER unsigned char	CSG
XmNfontList XmCFontList	"Fixed" XmFontList	CSG
XmNlabelInsensitivePixmap XmCLabelInsensitivePixmap	XmUNSPECIFIED_PIXMAP Pixmap	CSG
XmNlabelPixmap XmCPixmap	XmUNSPECIFIED_PIXMAP Pixmap	CSG
XmNlabelString XmCXmString	NULL XmString	CSG
XmNlabelType XmCLabelType	XmSTRING unsigned char	CSG

Name Class	Default Type	Access
XmNmarginBottom XmCMarginBottom	0 short	CSG
XmNmarginHeight XmCMarginHeight	2 short	CSG
XmNmarginLeft XmCMarginLeft	dynamic short	CSG
XmNmarginRight XmCMarginRight	0 short	CSG
XmNmarginTop XmCMarginTop	0 short	CSG
XmNmarginWidth XmCMarginWidth	2 short	CSG
XmNmnemonic XmCMnemonic	'\0' char	CSG
XmNrecomputeSize XmCRecomputeSize	True Boolean	CSG
XmNstringDirection XmCStringDirection	XmSTRING_DIRECTION_L_TO_R XmStringDirection	CSG

XmPrimitive Resource Set		
Name **Class**	**Default** **Type**	**Access**
XmNbottomShadowColor XmCForeground	dynamic Pixel	CSG
XmNbottomShadowPixmap XmCBottomShadowPixmap	XmUNSPECIFIED_PIXMAP Pixmap	CSG
XmNforeground XmCForeground	dynamic Pixel	CSG
XmNhelpCallback XmCCallback	NULL XtCallbackList	C
XmNhighlightColor XmCForeground	Black Pixel	CSG
XmNhighlightOnEnter XmCHighlightOnEnter	False Boolean	CSG
XmNhighlightPixmap XmCHighlightPixmap	dynamic Pixmap	CSG
XmNhighlightThickness XmCHighlightThickness	0 short	CSG
XmNshadowThickness XmCShadowThickness	0 short	CSG
XmNtopShadowColor XmCBackground	dynamic Pixel	CSG
XmNtopShadowPixmap XmCTopShadowPixmap	XmUNSPECIFIED_PIXMAP Pixmap	CSG
XmNtraversalOn XmCTraversalOn	False Boolean	CSG
XmNunitType XmCUnitType	XmPIXELS unsigned char	CSG
XmNuserData XmCUserData	NULL caddr_t	CSG

Core Resource Set		
Name Class	Default Type	Access
XmNaccelerators XmCAccelerators	NULL XtTranslations	CSG
XmNancestorSensitive XmCSensitive	True Boolean	G
XmNbackground XmCBackground	dynamic Pixel	CSG
XmNbackgroundPixmap XmCPixmap	XmUNSPECIFIED_PIXMAP Pixmap	CSG
XmNborderColor XmCBorderColor	Black Pixel	CSG
XmNborderPixmap XmCPixmap	XmUNSPECIFIED_PIXMAP Pixmap	CSG
XmNborderWidth XmCBorderWidth	0 Dimension	CSG
XmNcolormap XmCColormap	XtCopyFromParent Colormap	CG
XmNdepth XmCDepth	XtCopyFromParent int	CG
XmNdestroyCallback XmCCallback	NULL XtCallbackList	C
XmNheight XmCHeight	0 Dimension	CSG
XmNmappedWhenManaged XmCMappedWhenManaged	True Boolean	CSG
XmNscreen XmCScreen	XtCopyScreen Pointer	CG
XmNsensitive XmCSensitive	True Boolean	CSG

Name Class	Default Type	Access
XmNtranslations XmCTranslations	NULL XtTranslations	CSG
XmNwidth XmCWidth	0 Dimension	CSG
XmNx XmCPosition	0 Position	CSG
XmNy XmCPosition	0 Position	CSG

Callback Information

The following structure is returned with each callback:

```
typedef struct
{
    int             reason;
    XEvent          * event;
    Boolean         set;
} XmToggleButtonCallbackStruct;
```

reason Indicates why the callback was invoked

event Points to the **XEvent** that triggered the callback

set Reflects the ToggleButton's current state when the callback occurred, either True (selected) or False (unselected)

Behavior

ToggleButton is associated with the default behavior unless it is part of a menu system. In a menu system, the RowColumn parent determines which mouse button is used.

Default Behavior

<**Btn1Down**>:

(**if unset**): This action arms the ToggleButton widget. The indicator shadow is drawn so that the button looks pressed, and the indicator fills with the color specified in **XmNselectColor**. The callbacks for **XmNarmCallback** are also called.

(**if set**): This action arms the ToggleButton widget. The indicator shadow is drawn so that the button looks raised, and the indicator fills with the background color. The callbacks for **XmNarmCallback** are also called.

<**Btn1Up**>:

(**In Button**):

(**if unset**): This action selects the ToggleButton widget. Visually, it appears the same as when it is armed. The callbacks for **XmvalueChangedCallback** are called, followed by callbacks for **XmdisarmCallback**.

(**if set**): This action unselects the ToggleButton widget. Visually, it appears the same as when it is armed. The callbacks for **XmvalueChangedCallback** are called, followed by callbacks for **XmdisarmCallback**.

(**Outside Of Button**):

If the button release occurs outside the ToggleButton, the callbacks for **XmNdisarmCallback** are called.

<**Leave Window**>:

If the button is pressed and the cursor leaves the widget, it visually reverts to its previous unpressed state.

<Enter Window>:
If the button is pressed and the cursor leaves and re-enters the widget, it visually appears the same as when the button was first armed.

Default PopupMenu System

<Btn3Down>:
This action disables keyboard traversal for the menu and returns the user to drag mode, which is the mode in which the menu is manipulated by using the mouse. This action also causes the ToggleButton to be armed. A shadow is drawn around the ToggleButton. The callbacks for **XmNarmCallback** are also called.

<Btn3Up>: **(if unset)**: This action selects the ToggleButton widget. The indicator shadow is drawn so that it looks pressed, and the indicator fills with the color specified in **XmNselectColor**. The menu is then unposted and the callbacks for **XmvalueChangedCallback** are called, followed by callbacks for **XmdisarmCallback**.

(if set): This action unselects the ToggleButton widget. The indicator shadow is drawn so that it looks raised, and the indicator fills with the background color. The menu is then unposted and the callbacks for **XmvalueChangedCallback** are called, followed by callbacks for **XmdisarmCallback**.

<Leave Window>:
Pressing button 3 and moving the cursor out of the widget's window erases the shadow around the ToggleButton. This event is ignored if keyboard traversal is enabled in the menu.

<Enter Window>:
Pressing button 3 and moving the cursor into the widget's window draws a shadow around the ToggleButton. This event is ignored if keyboard traversal is enabled in the menu.

<Key>Return:
If keyboard traversal is enabled in the menu, this event sets or unsets the ToggleButton.

(if unset): Sets the ToggleButton. The indicator shadow is drawn so that looks pressed, and the indicator fills with the color specified in **XmNselectColor**.

(if set): Unsets the ToggleButton. The indicator shadow is drawn so that it looks raised, and the indicator fills with the background color.

For both set and unset cases, the menu is then unposted and the callbacks for **XmvalueChangedCallback** are called, followed by callbacks for **XmdisarmCallback**.

Default Pulldown Menu System and OptionMenu System

<Btn1Down>:
This action disables keyboard traversal for the menu and returns the user to drag mode (the mode in which the menu is manipulated using the mouse). This action also arms the ToggleButton. A shadow is drawn around the ToggleButton. The callbacks for **XmNarmCallback** are also called.

<Btn1Up>: **(if unset)**: This action selects the ToggleButton. The indicator shadow is drawn so that it looks pressed, and the indicator fills with the color specified in **XmNselectColor**. The menu then unposts, and the callbacks for **XmvalueChangedCallback** are called, followed by callbacks for **XmdisarmCallback**.

(if set): This action unselects the ToggleButton. The indicator shadow is drawn so that it looks raised, and the indicator fills with the background color. The menu then unposts, and the callbacks for **XmvalueChangedCallback** are called, followed by callbacks for **XmdisarmCallback**.

<Leave Window>:
Pressing button 1 and moving the cursor out of the widget's window erases the shadow around the ToggleButton. This event is ignored if keyboard traversal is enabled in the menu.

<Enter Window>:
Pressing button 1 and moving the cursor into the widget's window draws a shadow around the ToggleButton. This event is ignored if keyboard traversal is enabled in the menu.

<Key>Return:
This event sets or unsets the ToggleButton if keyboard traversal is enabled in the menu.

(if unset): Sets the ToggleButton. The indicator shadow is drawn so that it looks pressed, and the indicator fills with the color specified in **XmNselectColor**.

(if set): Unsets the ToggleButton. The indicator shadow is drawn so that it looks raised, and the indicator fills with the background color.

For both set and unset cases, the menu then unposts, and the callbacks for **XmvalueChangedCallback** are called, followed by callbacks for **XmdisarmCallback**.

Default Translations

When not in a menu system, the following are the default translations:

<Btn1Down>: **Arm()**
<Btn1Up>: **Select()**
Disarm()
<Key>Return: **ArmAndActivate()**
<Key>space: **ArmAndActivate()**
<EnterWindow>: **Enter()**
<LeaveWindow>: **Leave()**

When in a menu system, the following are the default translations:

<BtnDown>:	**BtnDown()**
<BtnUp>:	**BtnUp()**
<EnterWindow>:	**Enter()**
<LeaveWindow>:	**Leave()**
<Key>Return:	**KeySelect()**
<Key>Escape:	**MenuShellPopdownDone()**

Keyboard Traversal

When in a menu system, the following translations are added to ToggleButton.

<Unmap>:	**Unmap()**
<FocusOut>:	**FocusOut()**
<FocusIn>:	**FocusIn()**
<Key>space:	**Noop()**
<Key>Left:	**MenuTraverseLeft()**
<Key>Right:	**MenuTraverseRight()**
<Key>Up:	**MenuTraverseUp()**
<Key>Down:	**MenuTraverseDown()**
<Key>Home:	**Noop()**

For information on keyboard traversal when not in a menu, see the man page for **XmPrimitive(3X)** and its sections on behavior and default translations.

Related Information

Core(3X), **XmCreateToggleButton(3X)**, **XmLabel(3X)**, **XmPrimitive(3X)**, **XmRowColumn(3X)**, **XmToggleButtonGetState(3X)**, and **XmToggleButtonSetState(3X)**.

XmToggleButtonGadget

Purpose

The ToggleButtonGadget widget class

Synopsis

#include <Xm/ToggleBG.h>

Description

ToggleButtonGadget sets nontransitory state data within an application. Usually this gadget consists of an indicator (square or diamond-shaped) with either text or a pixmap to its right. However, it can also consist of just text or a pixmap without the indicator.

The toggle graphics display a **1-of-many** or **N-of-many** selection state. When a toggle indicator is displayed, a square indicator shows an **N-of-many** selection state and a diamond-shaped indicator shows a **1-of-many** selection state.

ToggleButtonGadget implies a selected or unselected state. In the case of a label and an indicator, an empty indicator (square or diamond-shaped) indicates that ToggleButtonGadget is unselected, and a filled indicator shows that it is selected. In the case of a pixmap toggle, different pixmaps are used to display the selected/unselected states.

Normally, mouse button 1 is used to arm and activate the button. However, if the ToggleButtonGadget resides within a menu, the mouse button used is determined by the RowColumn resources **XmNrowColumnType** and **XmNwhichButton**.

To accommodate the toggle indicator when created, Label's resource **XmNmarginLeft** may be increased.

Classes

ToggleButtonGadget inherits behavior and resources from **Object**, **RectObj**, **XmGadget** and **XmLabelGadget** classes.

The class pointer is **xmToggleButtonGadgetClass**.

The class name is **XmToggleButtonGadget**.

New Resources

The following table defines a set of widget resources used by the programmer to specify data. The programmer can also set the resource values for the inherited classes to set attributes for this widget. To reference a resource by name or by class in a .Xdefaults file, remove the **XmN** or **XmC** prefix and use the remaining letters. To specify one of the defined values for a resource in a .Xdefaults file, remove the **Xm** prefix and use the remaining letters (in either lowercase or uppercase, but include any underscores between words). The codes in the access column indicate if the given resource can be set at creation time (**C**), set by using **XtSetValues** (**S**), retrieved by using **XtGetValues** (**G**), or is not applicable (**N/A**).

XmToggleButtonGadget Resource Set		
Name **Class**	**Default** **Type**	**Access**
XmNarmCallback XmCArmCallback	NULL XtCallbackList	C
XmNdisarmCallback XmCDisarmCallback	NULL XtCallbackList	C
XmNfillOnSelect XmCFillOnSelect	True Boolean	CSG
XmNindicatorOn XmCIndicatorOn	True Boolean	CSG
XmNindicatorType XmCIndicatorType	XmN_OF_MANY unsigned char	CSG
XmNselectColor XmCSelectColor	dynamic Pixel	CSG
XmNselectInsensitivePixmap XmCSelectInsensitivePixmap	XmUNSPECIFIED_PIXMAP Pixmap	CSG
XmNselectPixmap XmCSelectPixmap	XmUNSPECIFIED_PIXMAP Pixmap	CSG
XmNset XmCSet	False Boolean	CSG
XmNspacing XmCSpacing	4 short	CSG
XmNvalueChangedCallback XmCValueChangedCallback	NULL XtCallbackList	C
XmNvisibleWhenOff XmCVisibleWhenOff	True Boolean	CSG

XmNarmCallback

Specifies a list of callbacks called when the ToggleButtonGadget is armed. To arm this gadget, press the active mouse button while the pointer is inside the ToggleButtonGadget. For this callback, the reason is **XmCR_ARM**.

XmNdisarmCallback
Specifies a list of callbacks called when ToggleButtonGadget is disarmed. To disarm this gadget, press and release the active mouse button while the pointer is inside the ToggleButtonGadget. The gadget is also disarmed when the user moves out of the gadget and releases the mouse button when the pointer is outside the gadget. For this callback, the reason is **XmCR_DISARM**.

XmNfillOnSelect
Fills the indicator with the color specified in **XmNselectColor** and switches the top and bottom shadow colors when set to True. Otherwise, it only switches the top and bottom shadow colors.

XmNindicatorOn
Specifies that a toggle indicator is drawn to the left of the toggle text or pixmap when set to True. When set to False, no space is allocated for the indicator, and it is not displayed. If **XmNindicatorOn** is True, the indicator shadows are switched when the button is selected or unselected, but any shadows around the entire gadget are not switched. However, if **XmNindicatorOn** is False, any shadows around the entire gadget are switched when the toggle is selected or unselected.

XmNindicatorType
Specifies if the indicator is a **1-of** or an **N-of** indicator. For the **1-of** indicator, the value is **XmONE_OF_MANY**. For the **N-of** indicator, the value is **XmN_OF_MANY**. The **N-of-many** indicator is square. The **1-of-many** indicator is diamond-shaped. This resource specifies only the visuals and does not enforce the behavior. When the ToggleButtonGadget is in a RadioBox, the parent forces this resource to **XmONE_OF_MANY**.

XmNselectColor
Allows the application to specify what color fills the center of the square or diamond-shaped indicator when it is set. If this color is the same as either the top or the bottom shadow color of the indicator, a one-pixel-wide margin is left between the

shadows and the fill; otherwise, it is filled completely. This resource's default for a color display is a color between the background and the bottom shadow color. For a monochrome display, the default is set to the foreground color.

XmNselectInsensitivePixmap
Specifies a pixmap used as the button face when the ToggleButtonGadget is selected and the button is insensitive if the LabelGadget resource **XmNlabelType** is **XmPIXMAP**. If the ToggleButtonGadget is unselected and the button is insensitive, the pixmap in **XmNlabelInsensitivePixmap** is used as the button face.

XmNselectPixmap
Specifies the pixmap to be used as the button face if **XmNlabelType** is **XmPIXMAP** and the ToggleButtonGadget is selected. When the ToggleButtonGadget is unselected, the pixmap specified in Label's **XmNlabelPixmap** is used.

XmNset Displays the button in its selected state if set to True. This shows some conditions as active when a set of buttons first appears.

XmNspacing
Specifies the amount of spacing between the toggle indicator and the toggle label (text or pixmap).

XmNvalueChangedCallback
Specifies a list of callbacks called when the ToggleButtonGadget value is changed. To change the value, press and release the active mouse button while the pointer is inside the ToggleButtonGadget. This action also causes the gadget to be disarmed. For this callback, the reason is **XmCR_VALUE_CHANGED**.

XmNvisibleWhenOff
Indicates that the toggle indicator is visible in the unselected state when the Boolean value is True. When the ToggleButtonGadget is in a menu, the RowColumn parent forces this resource to False. When the ToggleButtonGadget is in a RadioBox, the parent forces this resource to True.

Inherited Resources

ToggleButtonGadget inherits behavior and resources from the following superclasses. For a complete description of each resource, refer to the man page for that superclass.

XmLabelGadget Resource Set		
Name **Class**	**Default** **Type**	**Access**
XmNaccelerator XmCAccelerator	NULL String	CSG
XmNacceleratorText XmCAcceleratorText	NULL XmString	CSG
XmNalignment XmCAlignment	XmALIGNMENT_CENTER unsigned char	CSG
XmNfontList XmCFontList	"Fixed" XmFontList	CSG
XmNlabelInsensitivePixmap XmCLabelInsensitivePixmap	XmUNSPECIFIED_PIXMAP Pixmap	CSG
XmNlabelPixmap XmCPixmap	XmUNSPECIFIED_PIXMAP Pixmap	CSG
XmNlabelString XmCXmString	NULL XmString	CSG
XmNlabelType XmCLabelType	XmSTRING unsigned char	CSG

Name Class	Default Type	Access
XmNmarginBottom XmCMarginBottom	0 short	CSG
XmNmarginHeight XmCMarginHeight	2 short	CSG
XmNmarginLeft XmCMarginLeft	dynamic short	CSG
XmNmarginRight XmCMarginRight	0 short	CSG
XmNmarginTop XmCMarginTop	0 short	CSG
XmNmarginWidth XmCMarginWidth	2 short	CSG
XmNmnemonic XmCMnemonic	'\0' char	CSG
XmNrecomputeSize XmCRecomputeSize	True Boolean	CSG
XmNstringDirection XmCStringDirection	XmSTRING_DIRECTION_L_TO_R XmStringDirection	CSG

XmGadget Resource Set		
Name **Class**	**Default** **Type**	**Access**
XmNhelpCallback XmCCallback	NULL XtCallbackList	C
XmNhighlightOnEnter XmCHighlightOnEnter	False Boolean	CSG
XmNhighlightThickness XmCHighlightThickness	0 short	CSG
XmNshadowThickness XmCShadowThickness	0 short	CSG
XmNtraversalOn XmCTraversalOn	False Boolean	CSG
XmNunitType XmCUnitType	XmPIXELS unsigned char	CSG
XmNuserData XmCUserData	NULL caddr_t	CSG

RectObj Resource Set		
Name **Class**	**Default** **Type**	**Access**
XmNancestorSensitive XmCSensitive	XtCopyFromParent Boolean	CSG
XmNborderWidth XmCBorderWidth	0 Dimension	CSG
XmNheight XmCHeight	0 Dimension	CSG
XmNsensitive XmCSensitive	True Boolean	CSG
XmNwidth XmCWidth	0 Dimension	CSG
XmNx XmCPosition	0 Position	CSG
XmNy XmCPosition	0 Position	CSG

Callback Information

The following structure is returned with each callback:

```
typedef struct
{
    int          reason;
    XEvent       * event;
    Boolean      set;
} XmToggleButtonCallbackStruct;
```

reason Indicates why the callback was invoked

event Points to the **XEvent** that triggered the callback

set Reflects the ToggleButtonGadget's current state when the callback occurred, either True (selected) or False (unselected)

Behavior

ToggleButtonGadget is associated with the default behavior unless it is part of a menu system. In a menu system, the RowColumn parent determines which mouse button is used.

Default Behavior

<Btn1Down>:

(if unset): This action arms the ToggleButtonGadget. The indicator shadow is drawn so that the button looks pressed, and the indicator fills with the color specified in **XmNselectColor**. The callbacks for **XmNarmCallback** are also called.

(if set): This action arms the ToggleButtonGadget. The indicator shadow is drawn so that the button looks raised, and the indicator fills with the background color. The callbacks for **XmNarmCallback** are also called.

<Btn1Up>:

(In Button):

(if unset): This action selects the ToggleButtonGadget. Visually, it appears the same as when it is armed. The callbacks for **XmvalueChangedCallback** are called, followed by callbacks for **XmdisarmCallback**.

(if set): This action unselects the ToggleButtonGadget. Visually, it appears the same as when it is armed. The callbacks for **XmvalueChangedCallback** are called, followed by callbacks for **XmdisarmCallback**.

(Outside Of Button):

If the button release occurs outside the ToggleButtonGadget, the callbacks for **XmNdisarmCallback** are called.

<Leave Window>:

If the button is pressed and the cursor leaves the gadget, it visually reverts to its previous unpressed state.

<Enter Window>:
If the button is pressed and the cursor leaves and re-enters the gadget, it visually appears the same as when the button was first armed.

Default PopupMenu System

<Btn3Down>:
This action disables keyboard traversal for the menu and returns the user to drag mode, which is the mode in which the menu is manipulated by using the mouse. This action also causes the ToggleButtonGadget to be armed. A shadow is drawn around the ToggleButtonGadget. The callbacks for **XmNarmCallback** are also called.

<Btn3Up>: **(if unset)**: This action selects the ToggleButtonGadget. The indicator shadow is drawn so that it looks pressed, and the indicator fills with the color specified in **XmNselectColor**. The menu is then unposted and the callbacks for **XmvalueChangedCallback** are called, followed by callbacks for **XmdisarmCallback**.

(if set): This action unselects the ToggleButtonGadget. The indicator shadow is drawn so that it looks raised, and the indicator fills with the background color. The menu is then unposted and the callbacks for **XmvalueChangedCallback** are called, followed by callbacks for **XmdisarmCallback**.

<Leave Window>:
Pressing button 2 and moving the cursor out of the widget's window erases the shadow around the ToggleButtonGadget. This event is ignored if keyboard traversal is enabled in the menu.

<Enter Window>:
Pressing button 2 and moving the cursor into the widget's window draws a shadow around the ToggleButtonGadget. This event is ignored if keyboard traversal is enabled in the menu.

<Key>Return:

If keyboard traversal is enabled in the menu, this event sets or unsets the ToggleButtonGadget.

(if unset): Sets the ToggleButtonGadget. The indicator shadow is drawn so that looks pressed, and the indicator fills with the color specified in **XmNselectColor**.

(if set): Unsets the ToggleButtonGadget. The indicator shadow is drawn so that it looks raised, and the indicator fills with the background color.

For both set and unset cases, the menu is then unposted and the callbacks for **XmvalueChangedCallback** are called, followed by callbacks for **XmdisarmCallback**.

Default PulldownMenu System and OptionMenu System

<Btn1Down>:

This action disables keyboard traversal for the menu and returns the user to drag mode (the mode in which the menu is manipulated using the mouse). This action also arms the ToggleButtonGadget. A shadow is drawn around the ToggleButtonGadget. The callbacks for **XmNarmCallback** are also called.

<Btn1Up>: **(if unset)**: This action selects the ToggleButtonGadget. The indicator shadow is drawn so that it looks pressed, and the indicator fills with the color specified in **XmNselectColor**. The menu then unposts, and the callbacks for **XmvalueChangedCallback** are called, followed by callbacks for **XmdisarmCallback**.

(if set): This action unselects the ToggleButtonGadget. The indicator shadow is drawn so that it looks raised, and the indicator fills with the background color. The menu then unposts, and the callbacks for **XmvalueChangedCallback** are called, followed by callbacks for **XmdisarmCallback**.

<Leave Window>:
Pressing button 1 and moving the cursor out of the widget's window erases the shadow around the ToggleButtonGadget. This event is ignored if keyboard traversal is enabled in the menu.

<Enter Window>:
Pressing button 1 and moving the cursor into the widget's window draws a shadow around the ToggleButtonGadget. This event is ignored if keyboard traversal is enabled in the menu.

<Key>Return:
This event sets or unsets the ToggleButtonGadget if keyboard traversal is enabled in the menu.

(if unset): Sets the ToggleButtonGadget. The indicator shadow is drawn so that it looks pressed, and the indicator fills with the color specified in **XmNselectColor**.

(if set): Unsets the ToggleButtonGadget. The indicator shadow is drawn so that it looks raised, and the indicator fills with the background color.

For both set and unset cases, the menu then unposts, and the callbacks for **XmvalueChangedCallback** are called, followed by callbacks for **XmdisarmCallback**.

Keyboard Traversal

For information on keyboard traversal when not in a menu system, see the man page for **XmGadget(3X)** and its sections on behavior and default translations. When the ToggleButtonGadget is in a menu system, the keyboard traversal translations are defined by the RowColumn parent.

Related Information

Object(3X), **RectObj(3X)**, **XmCreateToggleButtonGadget(3X)**, **XmGadget(3X)**, **XmLabelGadget(3X)**, **XmRowColumn(3X)**, **XmToggleButtonGadgetGetState(3X)**, and **XmToggleButtonGadgetSetState(3X)**.

XmToggleButtonGadgetGetState

Purpose

A ToggleButtonGadget function that obtains the state of a ToggleButtonGadget.

Synopsis

#include <Xm/ToggleBG.h>

Boolean XmToggleButtonGadgetGetState (*widget***)**
    Widget *widget***;**

Description

XmToggleButtonGadgetGetState obtains the state of a ToggleButtonGadget.

widget Specifies the ToggleButtonGadget ID

For a complete definition of ToggleButtonGadget and its associated resources, see **XmToggleButtonGadget(3X)**.

Return Value

Returns True if the button is selected and False if the button is unselected.

Related Information

XmToggleButtonGadget(3X).

XmToggleButtonGadgetSetState

Purpose

A ToggleButtonGadget function that sets or changes the current state.

Synopsis

```
#include <Xm/ToggleBG.h>

void XmToggleButtonGadgetSetState (widget, state, notify)
        Widget      widget;
        Boolean     state;
        Boolean     notify;
```

Description

XmToggleButtonGadgetSetState sets or changes the ToggleButtonGadget's current state.

widget Specifies the ToggleButtonGadget widget ID.

state Specifies a Boolean value that indicates whether the ToggleButtonGadget state is selected or unselected. If True, the button state is selected; if False, the button state is unselected.

notify Indicates whether **XmNvalueChangedCallback** is called; it can be either True or False.

For a complete definition of ToggleButtonGadget and its associated resources, see **XmToggleButtonGadget(3X)**.

Related Information

XmToggleButtonGadget(3X).

XmToggleButtonGetState

Purpose

A ToggleButton function that obtains the state of a ToggleButton.

Synopsis

#include <Xm/ToggleB.h>

Boolean XmToggleButtonGetState (*widget*)
    Widget   *widget*;

Description

XmToggleButtonGetState obtains the state of a ToggleButton.

widget   Specifies the ToggleButton widget ID

For a complete definition of ToggleButton and its associated resources, see **XmToggleButton(3X)**.

Return Value

Returns True if the button is selected and False if the button is unselected.

Related Information

XmToggleButton(3X).

XmToggleButtonSetState

Purpose

A ToggleButton function that sets or changes the current state.

Synopsis

#include <Xm/ToggleB.h>

void XmToggleButtonSetState (*widget, state, notify*)
    Widget *widget*;
    Boolean *state*;
    Boolean *notify*;

Description

XmToggleButtonSetState sets or changes the ToggleButton's current state.

widget Specifies the ToggleButton widget ID.

state Specifies a Boolean value that indicates whether the ToggleButton state is selected or unselected. If True, the button state is selected; if False, the button state is unselected.

notify Indicates whether **XmNvalueChangedCallback** is called; it can be either True or False.

For a complete definition of ToggleButton and its associated resources, see **XmToggleButton(3X)**.

Related Information

XmToggleButton(3X).

XmUninstallImage

Purpose

A pixmap caching function that removes an image from the image cache.

Synopsis

```
#include <Xm/Xm.h>

Boolean XmUninstallImage (image)
        XImage      * image;
```

Description

XmUninstallImage removes an image from the image cache.

image Points to the image structure given to the **XmInstallImage()** routine

Return Value

Returns True when successful; returns False if the *image* is NULL, or if it cannot be found to be uninstalled.

Related Information

XmInstallImage(3X), **XmGetPixmap(3X)**, and **XmDestroyPixmap(3X)**.

XmUpdateDisplay

Purpose

A function that processes all pending exposure events immediately.

Synopsis

void XmUpdateDisplay (*widget*)
Widget *widget*;

Description

XmUpdateDisplay provides the application with a mechanism for forcing all pending exposure events to be removed from the input queue and processed immediately. When a user selects a button within a MenuPane, the MenuPanes are unposted and then any activation callbacks registered by the application are invoked. If one of the callbacks performs a time-consuming action, the portion of the application window that was covered by the MenuPanes will not have been redrawn; normal exposure processing does not occur until all of the callbacks have been invoked. If the application writer suspects that a callback will take a long time, then the callback may choose to invoke **XmUpdateDisplay** before starting its time-consuming operation. This function is also useful any time a transient window, such as a dialog box, is unposted; callbacks are invoked before normal exposure processing can occur.

widget Specifies any widget or gadget.

XtDisplayInitialize

Purpose

A function that initializes the toolkit's view of a display and adds it to an application context.

Synopsis

#include <Xm/Xm.h>

Widget XtDisplayInitialize (*app_context, display, application_name, application_class, options, num_options, argc, argv*)

```
XtAppContext        app_context;
Display             * display;
String              application_name;
String              application_class;
XrmOptionDescRec    options;
Cardinal            num_options;
Cardinal            * argc;
String              argv;
```

Description

XtDisplayInitialize parses the command line that invoked the application, and loads the resource database. **XtDisplayInitialize** is a back-end routine that is usually called by **XtInitialize**. It may be called directly if the application needs to open more than one display. **XtDiplayInitialize** is passed an open display. **XtOpenDisplay** can be used in the case where an open display has not yet been generated.

By passing the command line that invoked your application to **XtDisplayInitialize**, the function can parse the line to allow users to specify certain resources (such as fonts and colors) for your application at run time. **XtDisplayInitialize** scans the command line and removes those options. The rest of your application sees only the remaining options.

XtDisplayInitialize supports localization of defaults files based on the value of the LANG environment variable. The user can specify a language by using the **LANG** environment variable. Elements of this variable are then used to establish a path to the proper resource files. The following substitutions are used in building the path:

- %N is replaced by class_name of the application.
- %L is replaced by the value of **LANG** environment variable.
- %l is replaced by the language part of **LANG** environment variable.
- %t is replaced by the territory part of **LANG** environment variable.
- %c is replaced by the code set part of **LANG** environment variable.
- %% is replaced by %.

If the **LANG** environment variable is not defined, or if one of its parts is missing, then a % element that references it is replaced by NULL.

The paths contain a series of elements separated by colons. Each element denotes a filename, and the filenames are looked up left to right until one of them succeeds. Before doing the lookup, substitutions are performed.

NOTE: OSF/Motif uses the X/Open convention of collapsing multiple adjoining slashes in a filename into one slash.

The **XtInitalize** function loads the resource database by merging in resources from these sources:

- Application-speci fic *class* resource file on the local host
- Application-speci fic *user* resource file on the local host
- Resource property on the server or user preference resource file on the local host

- Per-host user environment resource file on the local host
- The application command line (**argv**)

To load the application-specific class resource file, **XtDisplayInitialize** performs the appropriate substitutions on this path:

- **/usr/lib/X11/%L/app-defaults/%N:/usr/lib/X11/app-defaults/%N**

If the **LANG** environment variable is not defined (or the first path lookup using **LANG** fails), then the lookup defaults to the current non-language specific location (/usr/lib/X11/app_defaults/%N).

To load the user's application resource file, **XtDisplayInitialize** performs the following steps:

- Use the **XAPPLRESLANGPATH** environment variable to look up the file. A possible value for **XAPPLRESLANGDIR** is:

  ./%N:**$HOME**/app-defaults/%L/%N:**$HOME**/app-defaults/%N:\
  $HOME**/%L/%N:**$HOME/%N

- If that fails, or if **XAPPLPRESLANGPATH** is not defined, and if **XAPPLRESDIR** is defined, use the following as the path:

  XAPPLRESDIR%L/%N:**XAPPLRESDIR**%N

- Otherwise, use:

  $HOME**/%L/%N:**$HOME/%N

Note that if the **XAPPLRESLANGPATH** lookup is not successful and LANG is not defined, the lookup is then equivalent to that used by the R3 specification of **XtInitialize** (actually described under **XtDisplayInitialize**).

The parameters for **XtDisplayInitialize** are defined below:

app_context Specifies the application context.

display Specifies the display. Note that a display can be in at most one application context.

application_name
Specifies the name of this application.

application_class
Specifies the class name of this application, which usually is the generic name for all instances of this application. By convention, the class name is formed by reversing the case of the application's first letter. The class name is used to locate the files used to initialize the resource database.

options Specifies how to parse the command line for any application-specific resources. The options argument is passed as a parameter to **XrmParseCommand**.

num_options Specifies the number of entries in the options list.

argc Specifies a pointer to the number of command line parameters.

argv Specifies the command line parameters.

Related Information

XtInitialize(3X).

XtGrabKey

Purpose

A function that establishes a passive grab on the specified keys.

Synopsis

#include <Xm/Xm.h>

void XtGrabKey (*widget, keycode, modifiers, owner_events, pointer_mode, keyboard_mode*)

Widget	*widget*;
Keycode	*keycode*;
unsigned int	*modifiers*;
Boolean	*owner_events*;
int	*pointer_mode*;
int	*keyboard_mode*;

Description

XtGrabKey establishes a passive grab on the specified keys, such that when the specified key/modifier combination is pressed, the keyboard is grabbed. It also allows the client to redirect the specified key event to the root widget of a hierarchy.

widget Specifies the root widget to the **XtGrabKeyboard** call. All key events that would have been dispatched to other subwindows are dispatched to it subject to *owner_events*.

keycode Specifies the Keycode. This maps to the specific key to be grabbed.

modifiers Specifies the set of keymasks. This mask is the bitwise inclusive OR of these keymask bits: **ShiftMask**, **LockMask**, **ControlMask**, **Mod1Mask**, **Mod2Mask**, **Mod3Mask**, **Mod4Mask**, **Mod5Mask**. You can also pass **AnyModifier**, which is equivalent to issuing the grab key request for all possible modifier combinations, including the combination of no modifiers.

owner_events Specifies if the pointer events are to be reported normally (pass True) or with respect to the grab window if selected by the event mask (pass False).

pointer_mode Specifies further processing of pointer events. You can pass **GrabModeSync** or **GrabModeAsync**.

keyboard_mode Specifies further processing of keyboard events. You can pass **GrabModeSync** or **GrabModeAsync**.

Related Information

XGrabKey(3X) and **XtUngrabKey(3X)**.

XtGrabKeyboard

Purpose

A function that actively grabs control of the main keyboard.

Synopsis

#include <X11/PassivGrab.h>

int XtGrabKeyboard (*widget, owner_events, pointer_mode, keyboard_mode, time*)

Widget	*widget*;
Boolean	*owner_events*;
int	*pointer_mode*;
int	*keyboard_mode*;
Time	*time*;

Description

XtGrabKeyboard actively grabs control of the main keyboard. If the grab is successful, it returns the constant **GrabSuccess**. Further key events are reported to the grab widget.

widget Specifies the root widget to the **XtGrabKeyboard** call. All key events that would have been dispatched to other subwindows are dispatched to it subject to *owner_events*.

owner_events Specifies if the pointer events are to be reported normally (pass True) or with respect to the grab window if selected by the event mask (pass False).

pointer_mode Specifies further processing of pointer events. You can pass **GrabModeSync** or **GrabModeAsync**.

keyboard_mode Specifies further processing of keyboard events. You can pass **GrabModeSync** or **GrabModeAsync**.

time Specifies the time. You can pass either a timestamp, expressed in milliseconds, or **CurrentTime**.

Return Value

Returns the constant **GrabSuccess**.

Related Information

XtUngrabKeyboard(3X).

XtInitialize

Purpose

A function that initializes the toolkit and returns a top-level shell.

Synopsis

#include <Xm/Xm.h>

Widget XtInitialize (*shell_name, application_class, options, num_options, argc, argv*)

```
String              shell_name;
String              application_class;
XrmOptionDescRecoptions;
Cardinal            num_options;
Cardinal            * argc;
String              argv;
```

Description

The Xt Intrinsics must be initialized before making any other calls to Xt Intrinsics functions. **XtInitialize** establishes the connection to the display server, parses the command line that invoked the application, loads the resource database, and creates a shell widget to serve as the parent of your application widgets.

By passing the command line that invoked your application to **XtInitialize**, the function can parse the line to allow users to specify certain resources (such as fonts and colors) for your application at run time. **XtInitialize** scans the command line and removes those options. The rest of your application sees only the remaining options.

There is an alternate set of functions that you can use to initialize the Xt Intrinsics that is not as convenient as **XtInitialize**; however, it is more flexible because it lets you decide the type of shell you want to use. The function **XtToolkitInitialize** just initializes the toolkit. It does not open the display or create an application shell. You must do this yourself using **XtOpenDisplay** and **XtAppCreateShell**.

XtInitialize supports localization of defaults files based on the value of the **LANG** environment variable. The user can specify a language by using the **LANG** environment variable. Elements of this variable are then used to establish a path to the proper resource files. The following substitutions are used in building the path:

- %N is replaced by class_name of the application.
- %L is replaced by the value of **LANG** environment variable.
- %l is replaced by the language part of **LANG** environment variable.
- %t is replaced by the territory part of **LANG** environment variable.
- %c is replaced by the code set part of **LANG** environment variable.
- %% is replaced by %.

If the **LANG** environment variable is not defined, or if one of its parts is missing, a % element that references it is replaced by NULL. The paths contain a series of elements separated by colons. Each element denotes a filename, and the filenames are looked up left to right till one of them succeeds. Before doing the lookup, substitutions are performed.

NOTE: We are using the X/Open convention of collapsing multiple adjoining slashes in a filename into one slash.

The **XtInitalize** function loads the resource database by merging in resources from these sources:

- Application-speci fic *class* resource file on the local host
- Application-speci fic *user* resource file on the local host
- Resource property on the server or user-preference resource file on the local host

- Per-host user-environment resource file on the local host
- The application command line (**argv**)

To load the application-speci fic class resource file, **XtInitialize** performs the appropriate substitutions on this path:

- **/usr/lib/X11/%L/app-defaults/%N:/usr/lib/X11/app-defaults/%N**

If the **LANG** environment variable is not defined (or the first path lookup using **LANG** fails), the lookup defaults to the current non-language specific location (/usr/lib/X11/app_defaults/%N).

To load the user's application resource file, **XtInitialize** performs the following steps:

- Use **XAPPLRESLANGPATH** environment variable to look up the file. A possible value for **XAPPLRESLANGDIR** is:

  ./%N:**$HOME**/app-defaults/%L/%N:**$HOME**/app-defaults/%N:**$HOME**/%L/%N:**$HOME**/%N

- If that fails, or if **XAPPLPRESLANGPATH** is not defined, and if **XAPPLRESDIR** is defined, use the following as the path:

  XAPPLRESDIR%L/%N:**XAPPLRESDIR**%N

- Otherwise, use:

  $HOME**/%L/%N:**$HOME/%N

Note that if the **XAPPLRESLANGPATH** lookup is not successful and LANG is not defined, the lookup is then equivalent to that used by the R3 specification of **XtInitialize** (actually described under **XtDisplayInitialize**).

The parameters for **XtInitialize** are defined below:

shell_name Specifies the name of the application shell widget instance, which is usually something generic like "main." This name is used by the Xt Intrinsics to search for resources that belong specifically to this shell widget. The application name is derived from the -name command line argument or if that is not present the trailing component of argv[0].

application_class
: Specifies the class name of this application, which usually is the generic name for all instances of this application. By convention, the class name is formed by reversing the case of the application's first letter. The class name is used to locate the files used to initialize the resource database.

options
: Specifies how to parse the command line for any application-specific resources. The options argument is passed as a parameter to **XrmParseCommand**.

num_options
: Specifies the number of entries in the options list.

argc
: Specifies a pointer to the number of command line parameters.

argv
: Specifies the command line parameters.

Return Value

Returns the widget ID of the top-level shell. The class of the shell is ApplicationShellWidgetClass.

Related Information

XtDisplayInitialize(3X).

XtUngrabKey

Purpose

A function that cancels a passive grab on a key combination.

Synopsis

```
#include <X11/PassivGrab.h>

void XtUngrabKey (widget, keycode, modifiers)
    Widget       widget;
    Keycode      keycode;
    unsigned int modifiers;
```

Description

XtUngrabKey cancels the passive grab on the key combination on the specified widget and allows the client to redirect the specified key event to the root widget of a hierarchy.

widget Specifies the root widget to the **XtUngrabKey** call.

keycode Specifies the Keycode. This maps to the specific key to be grabbed.

modifiers Specifies the set of keymasks. This mask is the bitwise inclusive OR of these keymask bits: **ShiftMask**, **LockMask**, **ControlMask**, **Mod1Mask**, **Mod2Mask**, **Mod3Mask**, **Mod4Mask**, **Mod5Mask**. You can also pass **AnyModifier**, which is equivalent to issuing the ungrab key request for all possible modifier combinations, including the combination of no modifiers.

Related Information

XtGrabKey(3X).

XtUngrabKeyboard

Purpose

A function releases an active grab on the keyboard

Synopsis

#include <X11/PassivGrab.h>

void XtUngrabKeyboard (*widget, time)*)
    Widget *widget*;
    Time *time*;

Description

XtUngrabKeyboard releases any active grab on the keyboard.

widget Specifies the root widget to the **XtUngrabKeyboard** call.

time Specifies the time. You can pass either a timestamp, expressed in milliseconds, or **CurrentTime**.

Related Information

XtGrabKeyboard(3X).

XtWidgetCallCallbacks

Purpose

A function that invokes the entries on a callback list.

Synopsis

```
#include <Xm/Xm.h>

void XtWidgetCallCallbacks (callbacks, call_data)
      XtCallbackList callbacks;
      Opaque       call_data;
```

Description

XtWidgetCallCallbacks calls the entries on a callback list. The widget knows the address of the callback list and avoids extra processing by using this function. The external version of this routine is **XtCallCallbacks**.

callbacks Specifies the callback list to execute

call_data Specifies a callback-list-speci fic data value to pass to each of the callback procedures in the list

Index

F

I

L

M

O

P

R

S

T

U

V

W

X

OPEN SOFTWARE FOUNDATION

INFORMATION REQUEST FORM

Please send me the following:

( ) OSF Membership Information

( ) OSF/Motif™ License Materials

( ) OSF/Motif™ Training Information

Contact Name ______________________________

Company Name ______________________________

Street Address ______________________________

Mail Stop ______________

City ____________ State ____________ Zip ____________

Phone ______________ FAX ______________

Electronic Mail ______________________________

MAIL TO:

Open Software Foundation
11 Cambridge Center
Cambridge, MA 02142

Attn: OSF/Motif™

For more information about OSF/Motif™, call 617-621-8755.